KV-513-596

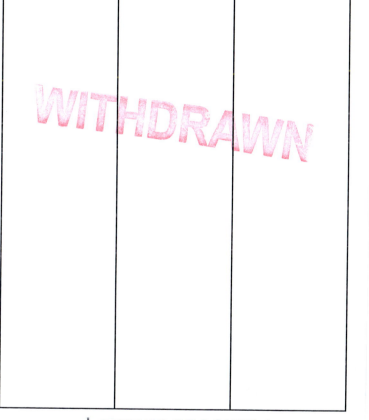

THE HISTORY OF CONTINENTAL PHILOSOPHY

General Editor: Alan D. Schrift

EMERGING TRENDS
IN CONTINENTAL PHILOSOPHY

Edited by Todd May

VOLUME 8
THE HISTORY OF CONTINENTAL PHILOSOPHY

General Editor: Alan D. Schrift

ACUMEN

First published in 2010 by Acumen
First published in paperback by Acumen in 2013

Acumen Publishing Limited
4 Saddler Street
Durham
DH1 3NP

www.acumenpublishing.com

ISBN: 978-1-84465-616-5 (paperback)
ISBN: 978-1-84465-668-4 (paperback 8-volume set)
ISBN: 978-1-84465-218-1 (hardcover)
ISBN: 978-1-84465-219-8 (hardcover 8-volume set)

British Library Cataloguing-in-Publication Data
A catalogue record for this book is available from the British Library.

Typeset in Minion Pro.
Printed and bound in the UK by CPI Group (UK) Ltd, Croydon, CR0 4YY.

CONTENTS

SERIES PREFACE

"Continental philosophy" is itself a contested concept. For some, it is understood to be any philosophy after 1780 originating on the European continent (Germany, France, Italy, etc.). Such an understanding would make Georg von Wright or Rudolf Carnap – respectively, a Finnish-born philosopher of language and a German-born logician who taught for many years in the US – a "continental philosopher," an interpretation neither they nor their followers would easily accept. For others, "continental philosophy" refers to a style of philosophizing, one more attentive to the world of experience and less focused on a rigorous analysis of concepts or linguistic usage. In this and the accompanying seven volumes in this series, "continental philosophy" will be understood *historically* as a tradition that has its roots in several different ways of approaching and responding to Immanuel Kant's critical philosophy, a tradition that takes its definitive form at the beginning of the twentieth century as the phenomenological tradition, with its modern roots in the work of Edmund Husserl. As such, continental philosophy emerges as a tradition distinct from the tradition that has identified itself as "analytic" or "Anglo-American," and that locates its own origins in the logical analyses and philosophy of language of Gottlob Frege. Whether or not there is in fact a sharp divergence between the work of Husserl and Frege is itself a contested question, but what cannot be contested is that two distinct historical traditions emerged early in the twentieth century from these traditions' respective interpretations of Husserl (and Heidegger) and Frege (and Russell). The aim of this history of continental philosophy is to trace the developments in one of these traditions from its roots in Kant and his contemporaries through to its most recent manifestations. Together, these volumes present a coherent and comprehensive account of the continental philosophical tradition that offers readers a unique resource for understanding this tradition's complex and interconnected history.

Because history does not unfold in a perfectly linear fashion, telling the history of continental philosophy cannot simply take the form of a chronologically organized series of "great thinker" essays. And because continental philosophy has not developed in a vacuum, telling its history must attend to the impact of figures and developments outside philosophy (in the sciences, social sciences, mathematics, art, politics, and culture more generally) as well as to the work of some philosophers not usually associated with continental philosophy. Such a series also must attend to significant philosophical movements and schools of thought and to the extended influence of certain philosophers within this history, either because their careers spanned a period during which they engaged with a range of different theorists and theoretical positions or because their work has been appropriated and reinterpreted by subsequent thinkers. For these reasons, the volumes have been organized with an eye toward chronological development but, in so far as the years covered in each volume overlap those covered in the subsequent volume, they have been organized as well with the aim of coordinating certain philosophical developments that intersect in a fashion that is not always strictly chronological.

Volume 1 begins with the origins of continental philosophy in Kant and the earliest responses to his critical philosophy, and presents an overview of German idealism, the major movement in philosophy from the late eighteenth to the middle of the nineteenth century. In addition to Kant, the period covered in the first volume was dominated by Fichte, Schelling, and Hegel, and together their work influenced not just philosophy, but also art, theology, and politics. This volume thus covers Kant's younger contemporary Herder, and his readers Schiller and Schlegel – who shaped much of the subsequent reception of Kant in art, literature, and aesthetics; the "Young Hegelians" – including Bruno Bauer, Ludwig Feuerbach, and David Friedrich Strauss – whose writings would influence Engels and Marx; and the tradition of French utopian thinking in such figures as Saint-Simon, Fourier, and Proudhon. In addition to Kant's early critics – Jacobi, Reinhold, and Maimon – significant attention is also paid to the later critic of German idealism Arthur Schopenhauer, whose appropriation and criticism of theories of cognition later had a decisive influence on Friedrich Nietzsche.

Volume 2 addresses the second half of the nineteenth century, in part as a response to the dominance of Hegelian philosophy. These years saw revolutionary developments in both European politics and philosophy, and five great critics dominated the European intellectual scene: Feuerbach, Marx, Søren Kierkegaard, Fyodor Dostoevsky, and Nietzsche. Responding in various ways to Hegelian philosophy and to the shifting political landscape of Europe and the United States, these thinkers brought to philosophy two guiding orientations – materialism and existentialism – that introduced themes that would continue to play out throughout the twentieth century. The second half of the nineteenth century also saw the emergence of new schools of thought and new disciplinary thinking, including the birth of sociology and the social sciences, the development of French spiritualism, the beginning of American pragmatism, radical developments in science and mathematics, and the development of hermeneutics beyond the domains of theology and philology into an approach to understanding all varieties of human endeavor.

Volume 3 covers the period between the 1890s and 1930s, a period that witnessed revolutions in the arts, science, and society that set the agenda for the twentieth century. In philosophy, these years saw the beginnings of what would grow into two distinct approaches to doing philosophy: analytic and continental. It also saw the emergence of phenomenology as a new rigorous science, the birth of Freudian psychoanalysis, and the maturing of the discipline of sociology. Volume 3 thus examines the most influential work of a remarkable series of thinkers who reviewed, evaluated, and transformed nineteenth-century thought, among them Henri Bergson, Émile Durkheim, Sigmund Freud, Martin Heidegger, Edmund Husserl, Karl Jaspers, Max Scheler, and Ludwig Wittgenstein. It also initiated an approach to philosophizing that saw philosophy move from the lecture hall or the private study into an active engagement with the world, an approach that would continue to mark continental philosophy's subsequent history.

The developments and responses to phenomenology after Husserl are the focus of the essays in Volume 4. An ambiguity inherent in phenomenology – between conscious experience and structural conditions – lent itself to a range of interpretations. While some existentialists focused on applying phenomenology to the concrete data of human experience, others developed phenomenology as conscious experience in order to analyze ethics and religion. Still other phenomenologists developed notions of structural conditions to explore questions of science, mathematics, and conceptualization. Volume 4 covers all the major innovators in phenomenology – notably Sartre, Merleau-Ponty, and the later Heidegger – as well as its extension into religion, ethics, aesthetics, hermeneutics, and science.

Volume 5 concentrates on philosophical developments in political theory and the social sciences between 1920 and 1968, as European thinkers responded to the difficult and world-transforming events of the time. While some of the significant figures and movements of this period drew on phenomenology, many went back further into the continental tradition, looking to Kant or Hegel, Marx or Nietzsche, for philosophical inspiration. Key figures and movements discussed in this volume include Adorno, Horkheimer, and the Frankfurt School,

Schmitt, Marcuse, Benjamin, Arendt, Bataille, black existentialism, French Marxism, Saussure, and structuralism. These individuals and schools of thought responded to the "crisis of modernity" in different ways, but largely focused on what they perceived to be liberal democracy's betrayal of its own rationalist ideals of freedom, equality, and fraternity. One other point about the period covered in this volume is worthy of note: it is during these years that we see the initial spread of continental philosophy beyond the European continent. This happens largely because of the emigration of European Jewish intellectuals to the US and UK in the 1930s and 1940s, be it the temporary emigration of figures such as Adorno, Horkheimer, Lévi-Strauss, and Jakobson or the permanent emigration of Marcuse, Arendt, and Gurwitsch. As the succeeding volumes will attest, this becomes a central feature of continental philosophy's subsequent history.

Volume 6 examines the major figures associated with poststructuralism and the second generation of critical theory, the two dominant movements that emerged in the 1960s, which together brought continental philosophy to the forefront of scholarship in a variety of humanities and social science disciplines and set the agenda for philosophical thought on the continent and elsewhere from the 1960s to the present. In addition to essays that discuss the work of such influential thinkers as Althusser, Foucault, Deleuze, Derrida, Lyotard, Irigaray, Habermas, Serres, Bourdieu, and Rorty, Volume 6 also includes thematic essays on issues including the Nietzschean legacy, the linguistic turn in continental thinking, the phenomenological inheritance of Gadamer and Ricoeur, the influence of psychoanalysis, the emergence of feminist thought and a philosophy of sexual difference, and the importation of continental philosophy into literary theory.

Before turning to Volume 7, a few words on the *institutional* history of continental philosophy in the United States are in order, in part because the developments addressed in Volumes 6–8 cannot be fully appreciated without recognizing some of the events that conditioned their North American and anglophone reception. As has been mentioned, phenomenologists such as Alfred Schutz and Aron Gurwitsch, and other European continental philosophers such as Herbert Marcuse and Hannah Arendt, began relocating to the United States in the 1930s and 1940s. Many of these philosophers began their work in the United States at the University in Exile, established in 1933 as a graduate division of the New School for Social Research for displaced European intellectuals. While some continental philosophy was taught elsewhere around the United States (at Harvard University, Yale University, the University at Buffalo, and elsewhere), and while the journal *Philosophy and Phenomenological Research* began publishing in 1939, continental philosophy first truly began to become an institutional presence in the United States in the 1960s. In 1961, John Wild (1902–72) left Harvard to become Chair of the Department of Philosophy at Northwestern University. With a commitment from the provost of the university and the Northwestern University Press to enable him to launch the Northwestern Series in Phenomenology and Existential Philosophy, Wild joined William Earle and James Edie, thus making Northwestern a center for the study of continental philosophy. Wild set up an organizational committee including himself, Earle, Edie, George Schrader of Yale, and Calvin Schrag (a former student of Wild's at Harvard, who was teaching at Northwestern and had recently accepted an appointment at Purdue University), to establish a professional society devoted to the examination of recent continental philosophy. That organization, the Society for Phenomenology and Existential Philosophy (SPEP), held its first meeting at Northwestern in 1962, with Wild and Gurwitsch as the dominant figures arguing for an existential phenomenology or a more strictly Husserlian phenomenology, respectively. Others attending the small meeting included Erwin Straus, as well as Northwestern graduate students Edward Casey and Robert Scharff, and today SPEP has grown into the second largest society of philosophers in the United States. Since those early days, many smaller societies (Heidegger Circle, Husserl Circle, Nietzsche Society, etc.) have formed and many journals and graduate programs devoted to continental philosophy have appeared. In addition, many of the important continental philosophers who first became known in the 1960s – including Gadamer, Ricoeur, Foucault, Derrida, Lyotard, and Habermas – came to hold continuing appointments at major American universities (although, it must be mentioned, not always housed in departments of philosophy) and, since the 1960s, much of the transmission of continental philosophy has come directly through teaching as well as through publications.

The transatlantic migration of continental philosophy plays a central role in Volume 7, which looks at developments in continental philosophy between 1980 and 1995, a time of great upheaval and profound social change that saw the fruits of the continental works of the 1960s beginning to shift the center of gravity of continental philosophizing from the European continent to the anglophone philosophical world and, in particular, to North America. During these years, the pace of translation into English of French and German philosophical works from the early twentieth century as well as the very recent past increased tremendously, and it was not uncommon to find essays or lectures from significant European philosophers appearing first in English and then subsequently being published in French or German. In addition, the period covered in this volume also saw the spread of continental philosophy beyond the confines of philosophy departments, as students and faculty in centers of humanities and departments of comparative literature, communication studies, rhetoric, and other interdisciplinary fields increasingly drew on the work of recent continental philosophers. Volume 7 ranges across several developments during these years – the birth of postmodernism, the differing philosophical traditions of France, Germany, and Italy, the third generation of critical theory, and the so-called "ethical turn" – while also examining the extension of philosophy into questions of radical democracy, postcolonial theory, feminism, religion, and the rise of performativity and post-analytic philosophy. Fueled by an intense ethical and political desire to reflect changing social and political conditions, the philosophical work of this period reveals how continental thinkers responded to the changing world and to the key issues of the time, notably globalization, technology, and ethnicity.

The eighth and final volume in this series attempts to chart the most recent trends in continental philosophy, which has now developed into an approach to thinking that is present throughout the world and engaged with classical philosophical problems as well as current concerns. The essays in this volume focus more on thematic developments than individual figures as they explore how contemporary philosophers are drawing on the resources of the traditions surveyed in the preceding seven volumes to address issues relating to gender, race, politics, art, the environment, science, citizenship, and globalization. While by no means claiming to have the last word, this volume makes clear the dynamic and engaged quality of continental philosophy as it confronts some of the most pressing issues of the contemporary world.

As a designation, "continental philosophy" can be traced back at least as far as John Stuart Mill's *On Bentham and Coleridge* (1840), where he uses it to distinguish the British empiricism of Bentham from a tradition on the continent in which he sees the influence of Kant. Since that time, and especially since the early twentieth century, the term has been used to designate philosophies from a particular geographical region, or with a particular style (poetic or dialectical, rather than logical or scientistic). For some, it has been appropriated as an honorific, while for others it has been used more pejoratively or dismissively. Rather than enter into these polemics, what the volumes in this series have sought to do is make clear that one way to understand "continental philosophy" is as an approach to philosophy that is deeply engaged in reflecting on its own history, and that, as a consequence, it is important to understand the *history* of continental philosophy.

While each of the volumes in this series was organized by its respective editor as a volume that could stand alone, the eight volumes have been coordinated in order to highlight various points of contact, influence, or debate across the historical period that they collectively survey. To facilitate these connections across the eight volumes, cross-referencing footnotes have been added to many of the essays by the General Editor. To distinguish these footnotes from those of the authors, they are indicated by an asterisk (*).

Alan D. Schrift, General Editor

CONTRIBUTORS

Bruno Bosteels is Associate Professor in Romance Studies at Cornell University. He is the author of *Badiou and Politics* (2009) and *Marx and Freud in Latin America* (forthcoming). He also serves as general editor of *Diacritics*.

Rosi Braidotti is Distinguished University Professor at Utrecht University in the Netherlands and founding Director of the Centre for the Humanities at Utrecht University. She was the founding Chair and Professor of Women's Studies in the Arts Faculty of Utrecht University (1988–2005), Scientific Director of the Netherlands Research School of Women's Studies (1995–2005), set up the Network of Interdisciplinary Women's Studies in Europe (NOI♀SE) within the Erasmus Programme in 1989, and has been elected to the Australian Academy of the Humanities. She has published extensively in feminist philosophy, epistemology, poststructuralism, and psychoanalysis, and is the author of several books, including *Patterns of Dissonance* (1991), *Nomadic Subjects: Embodiment and Sexual Difference in Contemporary Feminist Theory* (1994, 2011 [2nd ed.]), *Metamorphoses: Towards a Materialist Theory of Becoming* (2002), and *Transpositions: On Nomadic Ethics* (2006), and *Nomadic Theory: The Portable Rosi Braidotti* (2011).

John Fennell is Associate Professor of Philosophy at Grinnell College. His work, which focuses principally on naturalist and antinaturalist approaches to meaning and mind, has appeared in *European Journal of Philosophy* and *International Journal of Philosophical Studies*.

Ian James is a Fellow in Modern Languages at Downing College and a lecturer in the Department of French at the University of Cambridge. He is the author of *Pierre Klossowski: The Persistance of a Name* (2000), *The Fragmentary Demand: An Introduction to the Philosophy of Jean-Luc Nancy* (2006), *Paul Virilio* (2007), and *The New French Philosophy* (2012).

Jonathan Maskit is Assistant Professor of Philosophy at Denison University. He has published numerous articles and book chapters on continental environmental philosophy and environmental aesthetics. His work has appeared in *Philosophy & Geography*; *Ethics, Place, & Environment*; *Research in Philosophy and Technology*; *The European Journal of Geography*; and *Aesthetic Pathways*. He is working on a book about conceptions of nature in philosophy and art.

Todd May is Class of 1941 Memorial Professor of the Humanities at Clemson University. He is the author of eleven books of philosophy, most recently *The Political Philosophy of Jacques Rancière: Creating Equality* (2008), *Death* (2009), *Contemporary Movements and the Thought of Jacques Rancière* (2010), and *Friendship in an Age of Economics* (2012).

Eduardo Mendieta is Professor of Philosophy at Stony Brook University and is the author of *Global Fragments: Globalizations, Latinamericanisms and Critical Theory* (2007). He has translated and edited several volumes by and on Enrique Dussel.

Dorothea Olkowski is Professor of Philosophy, former Chair of Philosophy and former Director of Women's Studies at the University of Colorado at Colorado Springs. She is the author of *The Universal (In the Realm of the Sensible)* (2007), and *Gilles Deleuze and the Ruin of Representation* (1999), editor of *Resistance, Flight, Creation: Feminist Enactments of French Philosophy* (2000), and coeditor of books that include *Gilles Deleuze and the Theater of Philosophy* (with Constantin V. Boundas; 1994), *Feminist Interpretations of Maurice Merleau-Ponty* (with Gail Weiss; 2006), and *The Other: Feminist Reflections in Ethics* (with Helen Fielding, Gabrielle Hiltman, and Anne Reichold; 2007). She has recently completed the manuscript for a book called *Nature, Ethics, Love*.

Gabriel Rockhill is Assistant Professor of Philosophy at Villanova University and the Director of the Atelier de Théorie Critique at the Centre Parisien d'Études Critiques and the Collège International de Philosophie. He is the author of *Pour un historicisme radical: Entre art et politique avec Jacques Rancière* (forthcoming), the coeditor of *Politics of Culture and the Spirit of Critique: Dialogues* (with A.

Gomez-Muller; 2010), and the editor and translator of Jacques Rancière's *The Politics of Aesthetics* (2004).

Gayle Salamon is Assistant Professor of English at Princeton University. She works on phenomenology, feminist philosophy, and queer theory, and is the author of a manuscript on embodiment and transgender subjectivity, *Assuming a Body* (2010).

Emily Zakin is Professor of Philosophy at Miami University. She is coeditor of *Derrida and Feminism: Recasting the Question of Woman* (with Ellen K. Feder and Mary C. Rawlinson; 1997) and *Bound by the City: Greek Tragedy, Sexual Difference, and the Formation of the Polis* (with Denise Eileen McCoskey; 2009), and has published articles on psychoanalysis, French feminism, and political philosophy. She is also coeditor of the journal *philoSOPHIA* (SUNY). She is currently writing a book called *Tragic Fantasies: The Birth of the Polis and the Limits of Democracy.*

INTRODUCTION

Todd May

There is a nostalgia in recent French philosophy for the glory years surrounding May '68 and its aftermath. The early writings of Jacques Derrida, the genealogical works of Michel Foucault, Gilles Deleuze's *Difference and Repetition* and his subsequent work with Félix Guattari, much of the most influential work of French feminists such as Luce Irigaray and Julia Kristeva: these writings are rooted in that turbulent period. Of course, the turbulence was not restricted to France. The Prague Spring, the anti-Vietnam War demonstrations, and the Six-Day War and the beginnings of the Israeli occupation were all expressions of a time in which nothing seemed stable and everything appeared to be up for grabs.

It seems that turbulent times often produce great culture. This is the lesson of the Renaissance, and seems to have been repeated in the late 1960s. Moreover, for continental philosophy there is another period that exemplifies this lesson, one that has its own nostalgia. This is the existentialist period of the 1940s, when Jean-Paul Sartre and Maurice Merleau-Ponty led a movement that responded to the Second World War and postwar period with a body of work that remains powerful to this day. (One might also cite the emergence of the Frankfurt School in Germany in the 1930s.)

If the rise of important philosophical thought is associated with times of change and instability, however, this nostalgia may be misplaced. The period covered by this volume, roughly the 1990s to the present day, is perhaps as great a period of upheaval as that of either the 1940s or the 1960s. In order to verify this, let us canvass a few of the changes during our recent history.

First, and most obviously, one might point to the fall of the Berlin Wall in 1989 and the subsequent collapse of the Soviet Union. This collapse marked the definitive end of traditional Marxism as a theory of resistance to capitalism. Of course, Soviet Marxism had long been discredited in continental philosophy. The turning point for this change could indeed be marked with the date of May 1968. However, until the demise of the Soviet Union, the world in which philosophy took place remained a bipolar one. At the macropolitical level, if not the micropolitical one, the alternatives that presented themselves were American capitalism and Soviet (or Chinese) Marxism. With the demise of this bipolar world (or at least, in the Chinese case, its Marxist aspect), a global structure that had remained intact for the entirety of the post-Second World War period disappeared. No longer could American policy be justified by and strategized around countering communism, and no longer could opposition to the US look for support to a relatively stable bloc of communist states. Developing countries (or, in some cases, their corrupt leaders) could no longer hope to develop or enrich themselves by playing off one side against the other. What the first President George Bush called the New World Order is not necessarily an order at all.

The end of Soviet communism is said by some to have resulted in a unipolar world. But this does not capture the complexity of the times. Consider a second change: the rise of the virtual electronic world. Of course, during the twentieth century electronic communications and media developed by leaps and bounds. Radio, television, the telephone: all these changed the way people interact with one another. But no form of media communication has raised the questions of how we do and should interact with one another as urgently as the rise of the internet, and with it email communication and its subsequent forms of texting, and so on. The 1990s was the decade in which virtual communication became a primary, if not *the* primary, mode of business and social communication. Proximity in space and time was eclipsed by forms of interaction that allowed people to communicate across times, and especially places, that had previously been inaccessible. Moreover, this communication could be far richer (or, depending on one's viewpoint, far more impoverished) than was previously possible. These changes raised the questions of what it is to be human and what human interaction could – and should – consist in.

These two changes have been inseparable from a third one: economic globalization. The fall of the Soviet Union removed any barriers from the spread of global capital, and the rise of electronic communication has facilitated that movement as well as the coordination of diverse activities by transnational corporations. Economic globalization has integrated national economies and fostered a neoliberal approach to economic production. This approach, which has in many ways replaced the previous welfarist approach to economics, emphasizes deregulation, privatization, and the removal of trade barriers. The dominance of neoliberalism can be explained by the rise of economic globalization. Capital likes deregulated markets and the ability to flow easily from one market to another, and so will tend to drift toward those markets that foster deregulation and trade, while capital will be disinvested from other markets. With the rise of electronic communication, the movement of capital away from welfarist states and toward neoliberal ones becomes much easier. And thus welfarist states all tend to drift toward neoliberalism in order to keep capital from fleeing their countries.

Neoliberal economic globalization is related to another change, one that has largely affected developing countries. It is a particular kind of postcolonialism, one that has not only political but economic roots. Postcolonialism is not a new phenomenon. One might say that postcolonialism has been around since the end of colonialism, which began its major decline in the early 1960s. The postcolonial period has been a difficult one. Corrupt totalitarian states in Africa, failed Marxist projects in Latin America and Asia, and the intervention of the US and the former Soviet Union, as well as the devastating legacy of colonialism, have left many developing countries bereft. However, the rise of economic globalization has presented a new set of challenges to postcolonial states. Rather than political colonialism, they face an economic imperialism that is distinct in nature but not perhaps in effect from the previous colonial projects. The current postcolonial period is one of economic integration as well as exploitation. This period presents new obstacles to those who seek to understand and to change the developing world. These obstacles can be seen in sharp relief, particularly when we understand the contemporary urbanization of much of the developing world. More people now live in cities than in the countryside (although, ironically, in the US a plurality of people now inhabit the suburbs). This urbanization, or mega-urbanization, intersects with economic exploitation in explosive ways.

Related to but distinct from postcolonialism is a fifth change: the emergence, particularly in the 1990s, of identity politics. Feminist politics, black politics, and gay and lesbian politics all staked their claim to recognition during this period. One might date the birth of identity politics as early as the late 1960s and early 1970s. During that period, Marxist thought, which had previously held sway on the Left, began to give way to more decentered ways of conceiving oppression. Rather than reducing all oppression to class exploitation, thinkers and activists began to conceive of various oppressions as having their own character and history. To be sure, it was recognized that there were relationships among these oppressions. But they resisted reduction to a single type of oppression or domination that would ground or explain them. Since the 1970s, universities have begun to offer courses, and then minors, and finally majors in areas such as black studies and women's studies. By the 1990s, such thought became perhaps the dominant mode of conceiving progressive politics. Although identity politics has come under increased scrutiny and faced much skepticism in the past five to ten years, it remains an important element in the current intellectual and political context.

The sixth change, one that intersects with most of the others, is the change in the biosphere, especially global warming and the increasing demand for fossil fuels. Awareness of environmental degradation and the limits of natural resources has been with us for some time. The first Earth Day took place nearly forty years ago, in 1970. However, for many people environmental concerns have been, until recently, removed from everyday life. This is no longer the case. From the devastations of Hurricane Katrina and the tsunami of 2004 to the leaps in food and gasoline prices, the role played by the biosphere in limiting and determining our lives is very much in evidence. Moreover, there is a complex interaction between neoliberal economic globalization and environmental concerns. It is difficult, for instance, to reconcile a free and unregulated market with the preservation of energy sources or with the reduction of greenhouse gases. Of course, neoliberal theorists have offered market solutions to these issues, but the failure of those solutions is blindingly obvious.

These changes – the collapse of the Soviet Union, the pervasion of electronic media, economic globalization, the emergence of postcolonialism, the rise of identity politics, and the urgency of the environment – have combined to create a world that is very different from the world of twenty or twenty-five years ago. If upsurges in cultural creativity are fostered by turbulent times, we certainly live in a time that is propitious for such creativity. Rather than engaging in nostalgia for earlier thought, it would perhaps be better to ask ourselves whether there are types of thought that are equal to our times. Although there remains much to be learned from the thinkers canvassed in the previous volumes in this series, we should not remain content to look back wistfully at selected periods at the expense of seeking to understand and utilize our own historical situation for further thought and reflection.

As the essays in this volume demonstrate, there is much current creative work that seeks to grapple in one way or another with our time. Cut loose from the moorings of traditional Marxism, liberalism, linguistic thought, transcendental ethics, or other constraints that seem anachronistic in this period of upheaval, current continental thought is focused on giving voice to our time and the possibilities it offers. It does not reject longstanding philosophical questions of who we are, what we know, and how we should live. But it asks those questions with an eye to our current context. There is, for many who write continental philosophy, an urgency that stems from a recognition of the importance of what is happening today. The essays here cover a variety of perspectives within current continental philosophy that do not shirk the task of thinking ourselves and our tasks within the context of our situation.

Because of this orientation, contemporary continental philosophy is marked by normative concerns, that is, concerns about how we are called to take up our context or how that context calls on us. This normativity might be overlooked, since there is no single thinker devoted to ethics in the way, for instance, that Emmanuel Levinas was. However, this is not because there are no ethical concerns at play in the work of the thinkers considered here. To the contrary, many of the philosophers whose names appear in the following pages assume the significance of ethics specifically and normativity generally in their writing. They see normative concerns so woven into the fabric of our lives and our situation that they find no need to offer a distinct and isolated *ethical* position. Whether it is a question of feminism and the concerns of patriarchy, the environment, art and aesthetics, the politics of postmodernism, or even science studies, the normative impact and consequences of one's thought and one's views are inseparable aspects of many of the philosophers whose work is canvassed throughout this volume.

In the opening essay of the volume, "Rethinking Gender," Gayle Salamon traces the recent history of feminist thought, particularly as it appears in the work of Judith Butler. Butler's has been one of the most influential voices in recent years, particularly in feminist and queer theory. Her identity politics, however, is not essentialist in character. In fact, it is precisely the opposite. As Salamon points out, "Butler rethinks gender by casting it as a performative, a doing rather than a being." Rather than being the products of an inescapable essence, our gender identities are largely constructed by our social and historical circumstances. This type of thought cuts against both more conservative views that seek to justify a woman's subordinate role by reference to her sexual identity and, at the same time, essentialist feminisms, such as that of Irigaray, that seek to ground resistance to patriarchy in the nature of being woman.

If gender is a performative, then resistance can take the form of alternative performances, performances that are outside the recognized gender roles. Both Butler and Monique Wittig call for such alternative performances, although they differ on the role of language in these performances. Can the traditional language used to describe sex and gender be shaped to new use, as Butler often seems to believe, or must we, with Wittig, abandon sexual categories altogether?

Gabriel Rockhill takes up the question of the place of aesthetics in recent continental thought, particularly as it appears in the writings of Alain Badiou and Jacques Rancière. He argues that Badiou and Rancière offer us novel ways of conceiving aesthetics. For Badiou, art is one of the four procedures of truth he outlines in his major philosophical works, works that are discussed in Bruno Bosteels's essay in this volume, "Thinking the Event." In keeping with the tradition of high modernism, Badiou offers art a privileged place in human activity. Badiou's notion of truth, however, is a unique one. A truth brings an event that had previously been foreclosed by a situation into the situation. So truths, including artistic truths, do not just reveal or discover; they also resist the situation in which they take place.

Rancière, in contrast to Badiou, refuses to recognize art as a more or less transhistorical category. There is no art in general; rather, there are regimes of artistic practices. These different regimes have different themes associated with them. Modern artistic practices, in contrast to those characteristic of artistic regimes up until the early to mid-1800s, are characterized by a particular egalitarianism. They are not egalitarian in the sense that they promote political equality. Rather, they reject the idea of higher and lower themes and plots, and treat all aspects of life as equally worthy of artistic treatment.

The political side of Rancière's egalitarianism, as well as that of several other thinkers coming from the Marxist tradition, is taken up in Emily Zakin's essay "Rethinking Marxism." She shows there that although many contemporary political theorists reject any form of orthodox Marxism, they nevertheless remain influenced by it, and in particular by the structuralist Marxism of Louis Althusser. Rancière was a student of Althusser's, as was Badiou. Rancière broke with Althusser, however, in the wake of the events of May '68, in order to think a more egalitarian political view than was characteristic of his teacher.

Rancière and Badiou are not the only thinkers whose work engages the Marxist tradition. The Slovenian thinker Slavoj Žižek has combined a Lacanian view of psychoanalysis, a Hegelian view of the movement of history, and a Marxist sensitivity into a combination that seeks to understand the self-undermining way people carry out their political projects. For their part, Ernesto Laclau and Chantal Mouffe see the gaps that Žižek cites in political projects to be the very stuff of politics. A democratic politics is always centered on the antagonisms inherent in any social order. Where Žižek finds the futile project of restoring a seamless order, Laclau and Mouffe find the place in which the hierarchy of a given social order is contested. Finally, for his part, Giorgio Agamben concerns himself with the rise of a particular biopolitical order, one in which the state claims for itself unlimited power in the "state of exception," and people are treated as nothing other than sheer life, to be disposed of as befits state interests.

Bruno Bosteels's essay focuses on the work of Badiou as a whole. Badiou's thought has, in keeping with much of recent French philosophy, focused on the event. The concept of the event is an important one in recent French thought, particularly in the philosophy of Deleuze. In general, invoking the concept of the event marks a change in or break with a particular situation or configuration. It announces, or is, something novel, something that cannot be captured in the terms of the situation or configuration within which it arises. As such, the event has a positive valence. It is a moment of creativity. Badiou gives the idea of the event his own inflection, drawing from mathematics and particularly from set theory. For Badiou, set theory reveals a positive ontology, since it allows us to think pure multiplicity. Within that pure multiplicity, an event is that which inheres in the multiplicity but has not been represented in the situation. For

Badiou, Bosteels writes, "The event is this something, which is almost nothing, but which suffices to trigger a radical transformation of the situation as a whole." Events, in short, are revealings of truth in the sense that Rockhill captures in his discussion of Badiou and art. As such, Badiou's sense of events is distinct from that of Deleuze, for whom truth is not the issue in events. For Badiou, truth and the event are coextensive, while for Deleuze the idea of truth is on the hither side of the event: events do not reveal truth, but instead, as Nietzsche would also have it, they are indifferent to truth.

Badiou's recent thought has departed somewhat from the path that characterizes his earlier work. He introduces the concept of appearing, which seeks to keep the materialism of his dialectical materialism intact. In both his earlier and later thought, however, Badiou sees himself as renewing the Platonist tradition. Philosophy is a matter not of creation or of relativism, but of truth. And while philosophy does not create truths – only the "truth procedures" of politics, science, art, and love can do that – philosophy seeks to think the character of truth and of the compossibility of the truths of the distinct truth procedures.

John Fennell's "Rethinking Anglo-American Philosophy" reminds us that Anglo-American philosophy, particularly in recent years, is much richer than many continentalists recognize. Among continental philosophers, there is a tendency to think of Anglo-American philosophy as encompassing a narrowly analytic focus. The work of Donald Davidson, John McDowell, and Robert Brandom belies this view. They offer more encompassing accounts of who we are that provide important points of intersection with recent continental thought.

Drawing from the work of Ludwig Wittgenstein, Wilfrid Sellars, and W. V. Quine, the three Anglo-American figures who form the focus of Fennell's essay resist the easy reductionism of earlier analytic models of thought. Each of them finds a rich normative dimension to human thought and language, a dimension that cannot be explained in purely physical terms. Whether it is Davidson's appeal to interpretation, Brandom's inferentialism, or McDowell's concept of second nature, the antireductionism of these thinkers allows their thought to intersect with the wider social concerns of many continental philosophers. In particular, as Fennell notes, these thinkers can be seen as "continuing the breakthrough to hermeneutics and phenomenology (already begun by Wittgenstein and Sellars) within Anglo-American philosophy."

If Anglo-American philosophy is widening its scope to include concerns traditionally associated with continental thought, so too continental thought is increasingly embracing the concern with science often associated with analytic work. Dorothea Olkowski's "Rethinking Science as Science Studies" shows how science, considered as a human practice, is something other than a calculative and alienating project of the kind criticized by Martin Heidegger and those who follow him. Instead, it is a type of engagement with the world that has complex relationships with both its own theories and methods and the society in which it takes place.

Science often provides idealized models of reality. However, those models are themselves intertwined with conceptual frameworks that are present in the surrounding society. Therefore, rather than thinking of science as an insular and ahistorical project, thinkers like Bruno Latour, Isabelle Stengers, and Ilya Prigogine are returning an understanding of science to the social conditions with which it interacts. In addition, Stengers and Prigogine re-engage science with the complexity of the world, showing that the world is far more complex than earlier, simpler models would have us believe. This, in turn, intertwines science with notions of chaos and complexity that are also current in the surrounding social context.

That surrounding social context, particularly in its European mode, is the topic of Rosi Braidotti's "European Citizenship." Braidotti notes that the Eurocentric orientation of much European political history has come under fire and has recently been abandoned by many of the thinkers who seek to understand Europe's current standing and role. The current European scene is both postcolonial and posthomogenous. It can no longer hold itself up as a model of human development and thus intervene (and exploit) other cultures; and the internal character of each of its countries is no longer monolithic. Immigration and globalization raise questions for Europe that cannot be answered by appeal to older nationalist models.

These questions are occurring across a variety of registers. Some, such as Jürgen Habermas, argue for a new cosmopolitanism that sees members of Europe as world rather than national citizens. Others, such as Étienne Balibar, seek to turn reflection on Europe toward its own history and struggles, with an eye both on seeing its failures and on recognizing the process of struggles against those failures that can be seen as part of a trajectory of liberatory thought. Still others, for example Derrida, urge Europe to take up an engagement with its Others, an engagement that will bring its own concepts into permanent instability and self-critique.

Eduardo Mendieta's "Postcolonialism, Postorientalism, Postoccidentalism" stays on the political register, but shifts the focus from Europe to the developing world. He considers the rise of postcolonial thought, particularly in the wake of Edward Said's seminal book *Orientalism*. In that work, Said argues that the West has projected onto the East the notion of the Other, an Other against which it then identifies itself. This idea of self and other and the play of identification has been taken up by more recent thinkers who are grappling with the effects of colonization and the attempt to form identities in the wake of its decline.

Gayatri Spivak takes up the critique of the West's representation of non-Western populations. She shows how the West, by representing itself as universal, assumes an ahistorical, paternalistic, and often racist orientation toward non-Western countries and cultures. Homi Bhabha, by contrast, sees a more fluid process at work, one in which identification takes place, in a Lacanian fashion, by seeking to assume a position that is barred to one. As Mendieta writes, "Bhabha's work combines productively Lacanian psychoanalysis with Foucaultian genealogy, in order to make more nuanced Said's and Spivak's analyses of the discourses of imperialism and colonialism." For their part, Enrique Dussel, Fernando Coronil, and Walter Mignolo expand Said's view in different directions, particularly in light of the experience of colonization and postcolonization in Latin America.

In recent years, environmental concern has generated environmental thought and reflection in both the Anglo-American and continental traditions. Jonathan Maskit's "Continental Philosophy and the Environment" takes up recent continental thought as it grapples with issues that have arisen over the course of the past several decades. Rooted in the ontological considerations of Heidegger and the critiques of capitalism tracing back to the work of Theodor Adorno and Max Horkheimer, recent environmental thinking seeks to intertwine both an ontology of the relationships of humans with nature and the politics of capitalism that has destroyed those relationships.

Maskit notes that in Germany, where environmental issues have played an important role in public politics – Germany has long had a strong Green Party – theoretical reflection has, unexpectedly, been less developed than in the US or France. In France in particular, the work of Michel Serres, Latour, and especially Félix Guattari has undercut the opposition between humanity and nature. Drawing on both Heidegger's reflections on the relation of human to Being and Deleuze's antihumanist ontology, French theorists have engaged in a rethinking of social, environmental, and intra-subjective relationships.

My own contribution turns to the ways in which thinkers have directly confronted globalization, and to a lesser extent US hegemony. Taking up a number of thinkers whose work has already been canvassed, it divides the responses to globalization into four categories: critiques of media and the spectacle; proposals for a renewed vision of democracy; a conception of the rise of the multitude; and a renewal of the anarchist tradition. These categories are not exhaustive, nor do they necessary conflict with one another. However, they provide a framework within which to consider how recent continental thought has reflected on the time in which we live. Are we dominated by the media we have created to the point where we have become its creatures? How should we think democracy under new, more globalized conditions? Can we conceive of the globalized world as being sustained by a multitude whose energies can also liberate it from its oppressive aspects? Does the decline of the Marxist tradition open the way for a more egalitarian, anarchist-oriented conception of politics?

These are the questions that drive many of the thinkers who want to understand – and to change – a world whose geographical borders seem increasingly irrelevant.

Finally, Ian James's essay confronts current shifts in French thought. In particular, he sees a critique of the linguistic orientation of much of recent philosophy in favor of a more materialist approach. This materialism should not be understood simply as a denial of Berkeleyan idealism in favor of materialist monism. The conception of materiality in play in recent French philosophy is more wide ranging and variegated. It appears in the idea of a primordial givenness articulated in the thought of Jean-Luc Marion, in the concept of sense developed by Jean-Luc Nancy, in Badiou's turn to mathematics and in particular set theory in order to account for Being as multiplicity, in Rancière's insistence on the centrality of the partition and distribution of the sensible, in Laruelle's rejection of philosophy in favor of the real, as well as in the plasticity discussed by Catherine Malabou and the technology emphasized by Bernard Stiegler. What all these divergent approaches have in common is their attempt to move beyond what they see as reductions to a linguistic paradigm in order to capture a layer of existence that resists conceptual articulation.

All of the essays in this volume confront, in one way or another, the turbulent times in which we live. They take up one or more of the six themes I alluded to earlier. They are driven, although from different angles, by concerns about what is happening to us and what can be done about it. In that sense, the authors of these essays demonstrate that continental philosophy need not be nostalgic. It has risen to the task of thinking the present, and probably in ways that will yield thinkers to be read long into the future. Who, among the current crop, will be our next Heidegger, our next Merleau-Ponty, our next Foucault? Or will it be that, in the complexity of our time, none will assume a dominant position, but instead reflection will become a more collective effort? Maybe there will be no superstars, but rather a constellation that makes sense when seen as a pattern.

These considerations bring us to the question of the future of continental philosophy. Is there anything we can say about where continental thought will head, given its current situation? Prediction, of course, is a hazardous business. Nevertheless, even with limited predictive ability one can read a few current trends that might have a future. Among these, one of the most salient is interdisciplinarity. Contemporary continental philosophy is not only engaged with its time; it is also, and partly because of this, engaged with other areas of study and research. We can see this in the essays for this volume. The philosophical positions discussed here are in conversation with science, art, political science, the media, literature, and environmental studies. This, I believe, stems both from philosophy's engagement with the world and from an internal development of philosophy – both continental and Anglo-American – over the course of the twentieth century. The latter has to do with the demise of philosophical foundationalism, perhaps last seen in a full-blown way in the thought of Edmund Husserl.

The story behind this demise is a longer one than can be told here. It concerns the end, or perhaps exhaustion, of philosophy's attempt to be a foundation for all knowledge. The upshot of this end or exhaustion is that philosophy takes itself to stand no longer behind or beneath other areas of study, but rather alongside them. This, in turn, opens the door to conversation with other areas of study. When philosophy's task is no longer to stand outside other disciplines, it can borrow from them without a loss of its own integrity. We have seen this happening over the course of the latter part of the twentieth century, and it will likely continue.

Just as the boundaries between philosophy and other disciplines are beginning to break down, so is the internal boundary between Anglo-American and continental philosophy. For several decades, continental philosophers have referred to Anglo-American ones: Wittgenstein, John Austin, Saul Kripke, and more recently Brandom have found their way into continental thought. Conversely, Anglo-American philosophers have taken an interest particularly in the thought of Heidegger, Habermas, Merleau-Ponty, and Foucault. We can expect these borrowings to continue, especially since Anglo-American philosophy has in some quarters become more synoptic in its vision. Rather than being content with addressing small, specialized problems, many Anglo-American philosophers, chief among them those discussed in Fennell's essay, are attempting to build larger philosophical visions.

Alongside internal and external interdisciplinarity, one might expect that continental philosophy will seek to speak to a larger audience. There are several reasons for this. First, interdisciplinarity requires that those from other traditions can understand what one is saying. Interdisciplinary conversation, by its nature, cannot remain specialized. Second, in seeking to address the world in which we live, continental philosophy will have to find a way to address that world in terms people can understand. The turbulence of our times needs reflective understanding. Only by reaching out to a larger audience can philosophy provide that understanding. Finally, philosophy, like many of the liberal arts, is struggling against its marginalization by the corporatist mentality that has become dominant in many universities. As universities, partly driven by financial constraints, throw their resources into money-making ventures like the applied sciences, the humanities often find themselves under academic siege. The resort to arcane language and self-absorption will only reinforce the image of the humanities as irrelevant to students' concerns. Alternatively, when philosophy uses its resources in the service of reflection on people's lives and their situation, it struggles against the forces of marginalization. That struggle may, in fact, be threatening to the powers that be. After all, philosophy has always been a form of critical reflection. However, if critical reflection remains a part of university life, it is the task of philosophy as much as any discipline to contribute to it.

These are only a few of the directions continental philosophy may take. I would not want to hazard anything more fine-grained than that. However, as the volumes previous to this one have shown, the twentieth century was a rich one for continental philosophy. And as this volume demonstrates, recent continental thought retains a strength and vitality that allows it to keep asking important questions in the context of the time in which those questions are asked. Who we are, where we are, and what we might be remain its concerns; in a world fraught with uncertainty, there can be no greater intellectual task than to reflect rigorously on them.

1

RETHINKING GENDER:
JUDITH BUTLER AND FEMINIST PHILOSOPHY

Gayle Salamon

The historically fraught relationship between gender and philosophy has sometimes served to obscure the mutual necessity that has bound them together. Gender is that without which philosophy could not proceed, and yet it has historically evaded notice as a philosophically significant concept. Luce Irigaray[1] has demonstrated the extent to which the feminine has haunted philosophy all along, unincorporated and unacknowledged but central to its projects. If philosophy has been silently marked by gender, it is equally true that gender is in some sense marked for philosophy. Monique Wittig describes the relation between gender and philosophy as a question of ownership, and has framed their connection thus: "As an ontological concept that deals with the nature of Being, along with a whole nebula of other primitive concepts belonging to the same line of thought, gender seems to belong primarily to philosophy."[2] Wittig makes this assertion about gender in something of a disparaging mode, chastising philosophy for its unthought and reflexive conflation of gender with the natural order of things while also consigning gender to philosophy as a way of dispensing with it as yet another "primitive concept" relegated to irrelevance. The problem with gender in philosophy, according to Wittig, is that its putative self-evidence has rendered it invisible, and philosophy has become the end point at which gender transforms from a speculative question into an unnoticed fact.

---

*1. For a discussion of Irigaray, see the essay by Mary Beth Mader in *The History of Continental Philosophy: Volume 6*.

2. Monique Wittig, "The Mark of Gender," in *The Straight Mind and Other Essays* (Boston, MA: Beacon Press, 1992), 76–7.

Despite this lack of sustained attention – or perhaps because of it – gender persists as a question in and for philosophy. Even outside the domain of philosophy proper, some of the most influential feminist discourses have been those that take gender seriously as a philosophical problem, from the robust critique of ontology and neat Cartesian inversion offered by the "Am I?" of Denise Riley's *Am I That Name?* to the epistemological critique incited by Joan Scott's reading of the power of gender as a category of historical analysis. Both the concept of gender and feminist discourse as a whole have been given an explicitly philosophical genesis by at least one author: Donna Haraway has argued that "all the modern feminist meanings of gender have roots in Simone de Beauvoir's claim that 'one is not born a woman.'"[3] This genealogy understands gender, in any conceptual deployment, to already be engaged in a mode of critique, and offers gender as a way of questioning and challenging the naturalization of the social and identity formations that accrue around sex. This critical and interrogative relationship need not go by the name of "gender" at all, and indeed does not in Beauvoir's case. Locating the birth of gender with Beauvoir's philosophical critique asserts a kind of deontologization of gender from the start, since the essence of gender is then located in the relationship between "sex" and a critique meant to unseat presumptions of its naturalness or givenness.

Gayle Rubin's essay "The Traffic in Women" (1975) is often cited as the moment when the distinction between "sex" and "gender" became codified in feminist thinking, primarily because of her introduction of the phrase "sex/gender system," which she defines as "the set of arrangements by which a society transforms biological sexuality into products of human activity, and in which these transformed sexual needs are satisfied."[4] Rubin holds that sex, sexuality, and gender are unthinkable apart from the culture that gives them meaning, and elsewhere describes the relationship between biology and sexuality, paraphrasing Claude Lévi-Strauss, as "Kantianism without a transcendental libido."[5] Rubin's phrase soon began to circulate to support the idea that sex and gender were two different kinds of things that worked in concert as a system, and "The Traffic in Women" is often cited as the origin of the theorization of sex as biological raw material overlaid with a something nonmaterial called gender. However, this is a misreading: although Rubin's piece was indeed the first in this area to use the term "gender" to refer to identity and behaviors that are culturally tied to sexual dimorphism, it was clearly not her intent to formulate sex as biological

---

3. Donna Haraway, "Gender for a Marxist Dictionary," in *Simians, Cyborgs and Women: Feminism and the Reinvention of Nature* (New York: Routledge, 1991), 131.

4. Gayle Rubin, "The Traffic in Women: Notes on the 'Political Economy' of Sex," in *Toward an Anthropology of Women*, Rayna Reiter (ed.) (New York: Monthly Review Press, 1975), 159.

5. Gayle Rubin, "Thinking Sex," in *The Lesbian and Gay Studies Reader*, Henry Abelove *et al.* (eds) (New York: Routledge, 1993), 10.

and gender as cultural, since she is clear in her assertion that "sex as we know it – gender identity, sexual desire and fantasy, concepts of childhood – is itself a social product."[6] Rubin does not always distinguish between sex and gender; indeed, there are moments when the slash between sex and gender in the sex/gender system functions as a sign of collapse or dissolution rather than a marker of disjunction. Nor does she parse gender and sex and sexuality, although she will argue for their conceptual and methodological separateness a decade later in "Thinking Sex" (1984).

The work of Judith Butler (1956–) has a singular place in this genealogy. Butler completed her PhD in philosophy at Yale University in 1984, where she worked with phenomenologist Maurice Natanson, and has spent most of her career to date in the Departments of Rhetoric and Comparative Literature at the University of California at Berkeley. All of Butler's work might be described as an exploration of the conditions of possibility of the subject, where the condition that has received Butler's most sustained attention is gender. Butler rethinks gender by casting it as a performative, a doing rather than a being, and her theory of gender performativity can be read as a continuation of a tradition in twentieth-century French philosophy that finds its point of germination in Beauvoir's *The Second Sex*, although Beauvoir serves as an explicit interlocutor only in Butler's earliest work. In tracing the genealogy of Butler's reconceptualization of gender within and beyond its philosophical context, we will not ask what Butler's concept of gender does, less still what it *is*. We will ask instead after the conditions of gender's emergence and the possibilities of its subversion, psychically and socially, and suggest that a tension between legibility and possibility, between the structuring force of that which is given and the yet unseen horizon of the possible, motivates Butler's engagement with the philosophical tradition in her articulation of gender performativity.[7]

True to Haraway's assessment, Beauvoir's dictum also functions as a point of departure for Butler, particularly in the kinds of speculation it invites about choice and situatedness in relation to gender. Beauvoir is also a temporal starting-point for Butler's work, in that Butler quickly leaves the existential and phenomenological paradigm in which Beauvoir writes in favor of more psychoanalytic terrain, although some have asserted that the importance of her earlier phenomenological and, in particular, existential engagements has been overlooked.[8] Butler reads Beauvoir's assertion as an invitation to use insights about the formation and acquisition of gender as a kind of critique, with the aim of social transformation

---

6. Rubin, "The Traffic in Women," 166.
*7. Butler's account of performativity is discussed in some detail in the essay by José Medina in *The History of Continental Philosophy: Volume 7*.
8. See in particular Alan D. Schrift, "Judith Butler: Une Nouvelle Existentialiste?" *Philosophy Today* 45(1) (Spring 2001).

and change. In her earlier work, Butler's emphasis on gender as a doing rather than a being is a critique of ontology similar to Beauvoir's: a counterargument against fixed, essential, or materialist understandings of sex and gender. Butler offers this critique of gender determinism as given alongside a critique of gender as a free choice, and this dual critical impulse – the desire to deny gender and sex as essential or inevitable while at the same time rejecting a conception of gender (or sex) as a project freely chosen by a willful subject – is a persistent refrain in Butler's work and present in her earliest writings on the subject. These critical impulses are mobilized through her engagement with different philosophical figures, where Jean-Paul Sartre comes to stand in for the willful agent who would choose gender ("a 'project' in Sartrean terms"[9]) and Beauvoir's "become" is read sometimes as echoing that Sartrean project and sometimes as challenging it. Butler's conception of gender is a challenge to certain ideas that have long preoccupied philosophy: the possibility of universalizability; the metaphysics of substance; the relation between spirit and flesh. If the challenge that she poses to traditional conceptions of sex proceeds by arguing against a metaphysics of substance in thinking sex and gender, this challenge does not proceed through rejecting the language of philosophy or leaving its domain, but rather by reassembling its terms elsewhere. Butler offers Beauvoir as the progenitor of an "act" theory of gender, reading her formulation of woman's becoming as establishing gender as a "stylized repetition of acts," and the language of "acts" as Butler deploys it borrows from both speech act theory and phenomenology.[10] Butler has recently defined gender as "a practice of improvisation within a scene of constraint," and for Butler the question of gender involves two different kinds of inquiry.[11] The first is a description of the limits of intelligibility that constitute the borders of gender, and attention to how that constitution designates some subjects as livable and marks others as abject. Butler emphasizes the mutually constituting nature of these different positions, where that which is unassimilable to the domain of proper gender must still persist as a necessary and structuring ideal, giving coherence and boundedness to the category that excludes it. Her discussions of gender melancholia, most fully explicated in *The Psychic Life of Power*, describe just this structure, whereby those homosexual attachments that must be repudiated in order for the subject to achieve normative sexuality (and also gender) remain alive and stubbornly held at the heart of heterosexuality. The proximity and persistence of these repudiated

---

9. See Judith Butler, "Variations on Sex and Gender," in *Feminism as Critique: Essays on the Politics of Gender in Late Capitalist Societies*, Seyla Benhabib and Drucilla Cornell (eds) (Cambridge: Polity, 1987), 128.

10. Judith Butler, "Performative Acts and Gender Constitution: An Essay in Phenomenology and Feminist Theory," in *Writing on the Body: Female Embodiment and Feminist Theory*, Katie Conboy *et al.* (eds) (New York: Columbia University Press, 1997), 402.

11. Judith Butler, *Undoing Gender* (New York: Routledge, 2004), 1.

identifications or objects do not persist despite the subject; they are rather what form the subject:

> My sense is that it is always the case that the subject is produced through certain kinds of foreclosure – certain things become impossible for it; certain things become irrecoverable – and that this makes for the possibility of a temporarily coherent subject who can act. But I also want to say that its action can very often take up the foreclosure itself; it can renew the meaning and the effect of foreclosure. For instance, many people are inaugurated as subjects through the foreclosure of homosexuality; when homosexuality returns as a possibility, it returns precisely as the possibility of the unraveling of the subject itself: "I would not be I if I were a homosexual. I don't know who I would be. I would be undone by that possibility. Therefore, I cannot come in close proximity to that which threatens to undo me fundamentally." Miscegenation is another moment …
>
> Now I think it's possible sometimes to undergo an undoing, to submit to an undoing by virtue of what spectially threatens the subject, in order to reinstate the subject on a new and different ground. What have I done? Well, I've taken the psychoanalytic notion of foreclosure, and I've made it specifically social. Also, instead of seeing that notion as a founding act, I see it as a temporally renewable structure, and as temporally renewable, subject to a logic of iteration, which produces the possibility of its alteration.[12]

This then is the first kind of inquiry that Butler follows regarding the nature and operation of the psychic and social norms that constitute us as sexed and gendered subjects. Butler is committed to keeping a number of tensions in play with this formulation, most significantly the tension between the seemingly fixed norms of sex and gender, which always come to us from elsewhere, and the ability to style one's life in opposition to or to the side of those norms. This tension is inherent in her definition of gender, with its unresolvable pull between "improvisation" and "constraint." That conceptual balance requires a methodological tension as well, a pairing of the psychic with the social, so that the weight of the symbolic determinism of the socially enforced norm might be met with the possibility of choosing otherwise that iterability affords. The result is an undoing at the level of the subject as well as the symbolic; it is not only the

---

12. Judith Butler, with Gary A. Olson and Lynn Worsham, "Changing the Subject: Judith Butler's Politics of Radical Resignification," in *The Judith Butler Reader*, Judith Butler and Sarah Salih (eds) (Oxford: Blackwell, 2004), 333.

subject that is undone in this instance, but also some of the rigidity of the structure of the Lacanian symbolic.[13]

The notion of the "otherwise" occupies the second kind of inquiry Butler pursues: an interrogation of that "we" who are constituted as sexed and gendered subjects and an asking after the conditions of life on the sexual margins. Butler is interested in expanding the domains of legibility for those who violate the norms of gender and sexuality, and doing so without appeal to a shared sense of identity. That expansion cannot be achieved by simply enumerating a list of gender configurations that might supplement male and female, since such a list would quickly become proscriptive or positivist. Butler wants to secure gender as an open site of as yet unarticulated possibility in order to resist the kind of foundationalism or ontological thralldom that would restrict the realm of the possible to its normative iterations. The task of recognizing gender as it is lived outside norms necessarily entails a holding open or a suspension of the position, thus supplanting a description of norms with what might be considered a speculative project in a Hegelian sense. Describing gender becomes a matter of describing the way that it is done and the way that it is undone, and if gender is a doing, that doing is accomplished in several different modes at once.

There have been attempts to divide Butler's early work on gender from her later work in various ways: psychic versus political, normative versus ethical.[14] It could be suggested that the first decade of her work has been concerned with doing, and the second with undoing, evidenced by her recent works *Undoing Gender* and *Giving an Account of Oneself*, in which she poses the question: what does it mean to become undone by another? One of the limitations of such pairings is that they reinstall just the sorts of binaries that Butler's work seeks to undo. She uses Michel Foucault, for example, not only oppositionally to a Sartrean view of the relation between subject and world, but augmented with feminist theory at the same time as it is used in conjunction with more psychoanalytic or intrapsychic models. Butler asks that we attend to the constrictions and the violence wrought in the service of gender norms and the unequal distribution of that violence onto bodies depending on their markers of race, class, ethnicity, and ability, while at the same time insisting that we not misrecognize genders lived on the margins as necessarily marked by fatality. This paradox is central to Butler's theory of gender: to recognize the power of norms, to understand that there is no way to live outside the grasp of that power, and yet to affirm

---

*13. For a more detailed discussion of the symbolic, see the essay by Charles Shepherdson in *The History of Continental Philosophy: Volume 5*.

14. See for instance Moya Lloyd, *Judith Butler: From Norms to Politics* (Cambridge: Polity, 2006), and the "Critical Exchange" in *differences* 18(2) (2007): Catherine Mills, "Normative Violence, Vulnerability, and Responsibility"; Fiona Jenkins, "Toward a Nonviolent Ethics: Response to Catherine Mills"; and Judith Butler, "Reply from Judith Butler to Mills and Jenkins."

that such power can never be fully constituting, and that the future iterations of gender possibility cannot be mapped or predicted. We must both expand the bounds of what is recognized as a livable life, as fully human, yet must not understand legibility to be the sole precondition for a livable life. It is to this end that Butler has focused on undoing, in her most recent work on gender, using the term not in the sense of relinquishing or dismantling gender, but rather as a way to describe a more reflexive movement, a moment of vulnerability or openness that comes about in the face of my encounter with the other. If she is not quite calling for gender to be dismantled when she speaks of undoing, she is writing in favor of a partial dismantling of the conditions of its legibility, a disruption of its taken-for-granted signifying practices.

There are other paradoxes in the relation between sex and gender as Butler outlines them. Through an explanation of the ways in which girls are socialized into women, and her attention to the efforts and labors of becoming a woman, Beauvoir's reconception of sex as a series of acts provides the ground for what is for Butler a still more trenchant question: how can an understanding of gender as a stylized repetition of acts, where those acts come to materialize as something called sex, help us resignify gender itself as something that might have a slant on or critical relationship with the norms of both sex and sexuality? Although she is often described as a theorist of gender rather than of sex, Butler has been consistently committed to frustrating the distinction between those two terms, from before *Gender Trouble* to her most recent work. In her 1987 essay "Variations on Sex and Gender," she asks if Beauvoir's insights about sex as chosen rather than given ought to make us conclude that "the very distinction between sex and gender is anachronistic."[15] That distinction between sex and gender had been parsed in various ways within the tradition of feminist philosophy. It at first seems that what Beauvoir calls "sex" maps rather neatly onto the meaning that "gender" will have a few decades later, particularly her description of sex as a "project." Butler reads Beauvoir as eventually making the distinction between sex and gender in her description of the body as a "situation," which effectively circumvents the possibility of understanding sex as either essential or a simple bodily attribute.

Butler has said that her decision to use the term gender rather than sex or sexual difference was influenced by Gayle Rubin's use of the term in "The Traffic in Women."[16] Butler makes clear that gender is more than simply the contemporaneous name for sex, arguing that such a conflation has the effect

---

15. Butler, "Variations on Sex and Gender," 129.
16. Judith Butler and Gayle Rubin, "Sexual Traffic: Interview," in *Feminism Meets Queer Theory*, Elizabeth Weed and Naomi Schor (eds) (Bloomington, IN: Indiana University Press, 1997), 73–4.

of denying decades of feminist scholarship challenging the presumptions of sex and the unequal relations of power that rely on those presumptions. That feminist scholarship has insisted that while differences of sex have historically masqueraded as natural, an understanding of gender difference necessitates attention to relations of power and the unequal distribution of its material effects. The use of "gender" as a deliberate replacement for sex has a political and historical importance that becomes erased if gender is understood merely as a stand-in for sex. In figuring gender as a form of address, Butler is making gender do something specific that sex had not. The feminist distinction between the two made a point similar to Beauvoir's by insisting that women are such by virtue of social processes and cultural norms rather than a natural unfolding of a biological process that determines sex. In this frame, gender does its work by exposing both the conditions of possibility and the material effects of sex. Insisting on their conceptual distinctness secures the critical edge of gender, and helps denaturalize the binary of sex, whose "constitutive ambiguity" can be covered over or lost by a distinction that would understand gender as cultural and sex as natural, or gender as a behavioral role and sex as a material fact.[17]

However, that critical edge can also be dissipated to the extent that gender retains its conceptual distinctness, particularly its difference from sexuality. Butler has advanced both of these positions in "Against Proper Objects," claiming that if we are to understand "gender" to mean something other than simply "sex" and avail ourselves of its potential to disrupt binary notions of sexual difference that are commonly understood to be inevitable – and inevitably dimorphic – then we must allow the category itself to become corrupted. The imbrication Butler asks us to attend to there is not an ambiguity between sex and gender, but rather the ambiguity between gender and sexuality, with the denotative slipperiness of the category of "sex" shuttling between them. This is a disciplinary as well as conceptual problem; studies of sexuality that struggle to emphasize the difference between the domains of gender and sexuality can end up advocating a lesbian and gay studies that cannot attend to the kind of gender diversity represented by, for example, transsexuality. Gender then loses its critical edge to the extent that it remains a "proper object" acting as a heteronym for sex. Importantly, though, this distinction between sex and gender is conceptual rather than material. It points to a political and discursive history rather than a bodily fact. In other areas of her work, Butler makes clear that sex and gender cannot be separated, even if they are not entirely reducible to one another. Indeed, her challenge to traditional ways of thinking gender lies precisely in her insistence that their distinctness at the level of the body is a

---

17. Judith Butler, "Against Proper Objects," *Differences: A Journal of Feminist Cultural Studies* 6(2–3) (Summer–Fall 1994), 6.

myth, that parsing gender as behavioral (social and immaterial) and sex as bodily (biological and material) is to misconstrue them both. Butler sees sex as only retroactively installed as the purportedly material cause of the effect of gender, and asks "whether sex was not gender all along."[18] At the level of the body, there is no significant distinction between sex and gender.

Butler's theory of gender is also deeply engaged with other philosophical sources whose own legacies are not primarily concerned with gender, and the philosophical influences on her articulation of gender performativity are many. Although she occasionally engages analytic philosophy – her use of J. L. Austin's concept of performativity is one example – most of her interlocutors are from the continental tradition, from the engagement with Hegel that characterizes all of her work to the theories of deconstruction and iteration popularized by Jacques Derrida. She also works with less canonically philosophical figures, making much use of the reconfiguration of the relation between inside and outside, the psychic and the social offered by Sigmund Freud, Jacques Lacan, and Jean Laplanche, and the question of power and its effects on bodies and subjects as articulated by Foucault. Butler often theorizes by using works that do not themselves address the question of gender as a philosophical problem. Foucault's analyses of bodies and power, for instance, emphasize sexuality and have little to say about gender; Butler's reworking of his insights about the productive capacities of power are used in the service of gender. And the theory of the materialization of sex offered in *Bodies that Matter*'s "The Lesbian Phallus and the Morphological Imaginary" uses Freud to articulate a queer morphological imaginary, but it is the Freud of *The Ego and the Id* discussing pain and narcissism to which she turns, rather than the Freud of sexual difference. The project of rethinking gender as articulated in Butler's work is thus both deeply rooted in philosophical antecedents and heterodox in its approach to the question of gender.

These antecedents are clear in Butler's use of language, since gender, as she demonstrates, is always a matter of language. This does not mean that gender is disembodied or nonmaterial, since the effects of discourses of gender are inevitably and emphatically embodied. Gender performativity takes part of its logic from Austin's notion of the performative utterance, in which language has a creative rather than a descriptive function. For Austin, a performative utterance is one in which the speaker enacts that which he or she describes through that speaking. Butler enlarges the scope of the concept of performativity beyond the exclusively linguistic framing of Austin's examples and also the explicitly contractual force of performative utterances, replacing Austin's

---

18. Judith Butler, "Sex and Gender in Simone de Beauvoir's *Second Sex*," in *Yale French Studies* 72, *Simone de Beauvoir: Witness to a Century* (1986), 46.

contractual emphasis with a less defined and more expansive capacity: what she has referred to, using a phrase of Pierre Bourdieu's, as the "social magic" of performativity.[19] One does not *vow* gender, or ever articulate it fully or finally; this would be to misunderstand performativity as merely performance, the willed and staged acts of a choosing subject. Rather, gender is an embodied kind of belief. We speak and are spoken by gender at once, able to exert some control over its manifestation even as we are unable to choose the ways our acts signify, or who might receive them, or the conditions under which that performance is legible. Austin makes the distinction between felicitous and infelicitous conditions for a performative utterance, noting that certain conditions must be met in order for a performative to "succeed" and enact itself. So too for the performance of gender, in which the subject is constrained by categories that exceed her even as she may struggle to remake them in the shape of her own life. Butler suggests that gender is a constant navigation between these straits: one's ability to choose, on the one hand, and the constriction of that from which one is able to choose on the other.

Butler's challenge to binary categories, her disinclination toward intentionality, the careful attention to ambiguity in language that marks her close readings, and her adamance that there is no outside to the text, or the textual, would seem to mark her methods as deconstructionist. In one account, Butler offers Derrida's reading of Franz Kafka's "Before the Law" as the impetus for her theorization of gender performativity:

> I originally took my clue on how to read the performativity of gender from Jacques Derrida's reading of Kafka's "Before the Law." There the one who waits for the law, sits before the door of the law, attributes a certain force to the law for which one waits. The anticipation of an authoritative disclosure of meaning is the means by which that authority is attributed and installed: the anticipation conjures its object. I wondered whether we do not labor under a similar expectation concerning gender, that it operates as an interior essence that might be disclosed, an expectation that ends up producing the very phenomenon that it anticipates. In this first instance, the performativity of gender revolves around this metalepsis, the way in which the anticipation of a gendered essence produces that which it posits as outside itself. Secondly, performativity is not a singular act, but a repetition and a ritual which achieves its effects through its natural-

---

19. Judith Butler, "Performativity's Social Magic," in *Bourdieu: A Critical Reader*, Richard Shusterman (ed.) (Oxford: Blackwell, 1999).

ization in the context of a body, understood in part as a culturally sustained temporal duration.[20]

We can note the traversal of disciplinary boundaries at the very origin of Butler's theory of gender, so that Butler's rhetorical reading of a philosophical reading of a literary text gives rise to a theory of gender. Both philosophically grounded and disciplinarily itinerant, Butler moves between the literary, the philosophical and the rhetorical, less to establish multiple origins for her theory of gender than to unmoor all of them.[21] Her account of performativity replaces a proper and singular origin with an iterative chain where each iteration is different from the last, and none of those iterations ought to be taken for a cause. Gender and language are both representational practices that work through self-referential citation; language, according to poststructuralist accounts, achieves its effects through its references to other language, rather than reference to the material world of nonlinguistic things that it purports to represent. Gender, too, achieves its effects through its approximation of certain impossible ideal-izations of dress, comportment, desire, and behavior, and its performances are citations of these idealized norms rather than the precipitate of a material origin called sex. Also marked here are the ways in which both gender and language are bound to, even driven by, a kind of inevitable failure: the impossibility of a full or final performance that would finally settle the question of gender, thus requiring the performance to be endlessly repeated.

In Kafka's tale as retold by Derrida, the supplicant waiting before the law attri-butes an authority to the law, but the law's authority does not precede the attri-bution. Butler suggests that gender, too, works by this same logic: gendered acts, behaviors, and even a felt sense of gender are mistakenly assumed to emanate from an internal essence called sex, but that essence is in fact produced retro-actively, posited as the necessary cause for the acts that come before it. She has applied the same argument to sexuality as well, noting that heterosexuality, when it is understood to be the origin against which homosexuality mimeti-cally fashions itself, is only retroactively installed as a response to the challenge of the putative copy, thus reversing the terms that would understand the origin as necessarily prior to the copy.[22]

At stake is the question of language and its relation to gender: the way language both describes and enacts gender. If Beauvoir offers a conception of

---

20. From the preface to the 1999 edition of Judith Butler, *Gender Trouble* (New York: Routledge, 1993), xiv–xv.

*21. For an extended discussion of philosophy and disciplinary itinerancy, see the essay by Judith Butler and Rosi Braidotti in *The History of Continental Philosophy: Volume 7*.

22. Judith Butler, "Imitation and Gender Insubordination," in *The Lesbian and Gay Studies Reader*, Abelove *et al.* (eds), 307–20.

sex unmoored from the biological ground of the body and the necessity of determinism, Wittig offers a framework for understanding the discursive means by which this becoming occurs. For Wittig, as for Butler, sex happens through gender: Wittig understands that one becomes a woman through being captured by the linguistic sex that is gender. Language is thus the site and the mechanism for the reproduction and dissemination of sex. Butler's and Wittig's positions have many similarities on the question of the power of language, although they eventually part ways on the question of whether norms can be resisted, or only resignified. Can we offer resistance through language, or only by refraining from it? Is resignification possible? Butler does seem to suggest that Wittig has keenly understood something about the way that gender becomes materialized into sex: "if gender itself is naturalized through grammatical norms, as Monique Wittig has argued, then the alteration of gender at the most fundamental epistemic level will be conducted, in part, through contesting the grammar in which gender is given."[23] Butler's position on Wittig is not singular; in her later thought, she takes some distance from Wittig's stance on the bodily and conceptual violence engendered by language and naming. Wittig's response to the power and coercive violence of naming (a response that itself changes over the course of her own writing) is to refuse to name, to insist that a disidentification with the terms "man" or "woman," and a resistance to the terms "boy" or "girl," necessitates a refusal to use those terms either as markers of identity or even as tools of description. For, according to Wittig, these terms are always enactors rather than just descriptors.[24] If the lesbian is not a woman, nor for Wittig can she exactly be *masculine*: she is that which is and must remain oppositional to both of those categories. For Wittig, the lesbian is "beyond the categories of sex" because woman is a concept that draws its meaning exclusively from its relation to man, whether "economically, or politically, or ideologically." That relation is servitude, and to the extent that the lesbian embodies and lives a refusal of men, she exists outside this servitude and therefore outside the system of gender altogether. Wittig's fierce oppositionality is articulated systemically at the level of class, in that the lesbian is described as an "escapee" from women as a class, and the goal of this escape is nothing less than the destruction of heterosexuality as a governing system.[25]

The Butler of *Gender Trouble* has much in common with Wittig (or at least the early Wittig) on the question of naming, and Butler considers Wittig distinctive among the French feminists for her trenchant critiques of heterosexism and its linguistic dissemination. But in her later work Butler is reluctant to affirm the

23. Butler, *Gender Trouble*, xix.
24. Butler, with Olson and Worsham, "Changing the Subject," 337.
25. Wittig, *The Straight Mind and Other Essays*, 20.

possibility of a safer space outside of the violent power of language that Wittig appears to demand. In recasting the terms of language and in her project of focusing on the iterability of gender rather than the grammar of gender, Butler is in effect refusing to refuse to name. In describing her position on questioning presuppositions through careful deployment of language and the limits of what that deployment can achieve, Butler describes the change in her ideas on language and intentionality. She writes:

> The qualification I would like to add now, seven years later [after the publication of *Bodies That Matter*], is that although one can very often take a term like "masculine" and dislodge it from its metaphysical moorings – one can say, for example, that "masculine" does not necessarily apply exclusively to ostensibly anatomically male bodies and that it can function in another way, like, let's say, in the way that Judith Halberstam talks about "female masculinities" – it is important to question what of the prior context is brought forward as a kind of residue or trace. It is also important to question what new ontological effects the term can achieve, because to liberate it from its prior moorings in an established ontology is not to say that it will not acquire a new one.
>
> Spivak understood this when she reneged on her notion of "strategic essentialism." She at first thought she'd be able to use a term like "Third-World woman" and just have it be strategic rather than metaphysically grounded. It didn't have to describe her (or anyone else) fully or exhaustively; it could be relieved of its descriptive function. But, of course, it does begin to describe, because the author who strategically intends it as "X, Y, or Z" has also to recognize that the semantic life of the term will exceed the intention of the strategist and that as it travels through discourse, it can take on new ontological meanings and become established in ways that one never intended. So, I guess I would be a little less optimistic about the possibility of a radical unmooring than I was in 1993.[26]

Butler's conception of gender shares much with Wittig's, perhaps surprisingly, on the question of materiality. She has been taken to task for failing to attend to materiality, perhaps because what finally interests her most are the ways in which our bodies come to be through discourse, where that discourse is not always easy to disentangle from the body that it engenders. Gender and gesture become indistinguishable. For Butler and Wittig alike, there is an immensely

---

26. Butler, "Changing the Subject," 331.

generative power in language, a power that, in true performative fashion, brings about that which it names. But Wittig understands both gender and sex – as concepts, as categories, as linguistic practices – to be damaging for women, so to utilize the terms is to perpetuate the hierarchical division with inevitably dangerous consequences. Indeed, the theory behind Wittig's refusal to name can be understood as a kind of performativity, where the term "woman" works like a sovereign performative, materializing itself into reality through its incantation, its enaction in language.

For Wittig, sex and gender are distinct and distinguishable. Gender happens in language and sex is bodily. Yet they can each produce the other, and gender is complicit in the dissemination and perpetuation of distinct sex. But this does not mean that sex is simply bodily and gender is discursive and by contrast immaterial. Wittig describes gender as the enforcement of the law of sex through language, where the effects of that enforcement are bodily effects, and not merely linguistic ones. She writes, in a phrase that Butler cites: "Language casts sheaves of reality around the social body, stamping it and violently shaping it." This is not merely an alignment of culture against nature, flesh against the word. This body is not blank and unsignifying before submitting to the violent shaping of language; it is a "social body" from the start. When describing the origins of this phrase, Wittig explains that she had acting specifically in mind, once again making the act – an event that is bodily, that is temporal, but gestural rather than material – central to the relation of thinking gender.[27]

Wittig insists on a certain kind of categorical purity, rejecting the term "woman" for its ideological complicity with heterosexism. Refusing the conventional way that language is given, she uses the powers of neologism and refusal to recraft the categories of sex through deployment or withdrawal of grammatical gender. This same chiasmic relation to the categorical and attention to the conditions both of its constitution and its contamination can be seen in Butler's articulation of gender. For Wittig, the solution to heterosexism lies in creating new language, as in the experimental grammatical and pronominal structures of her novels *L'Opoponax* and *Les Guérillères*, or utterly refusing the common parlances through which gender is given, as she does when she calls for abandoning, and ultimately destroying, the term "woman." Gender as a grammatical problem gains its solution through abdication. Butler proceeds by different means, taking her distance from Wittig on the issue of conceptual purity within gender, and the question of contamination within language. For Butler, as for Derrida, there is no outside position from which we might utterly refuse the terms of language. She has described *Gender Trouble* as a text whose genealogy is philosophical, feminist, and political, and whose aim is the subversion of the

---

27. Wittig, "The Mark of Gender," 78.

category of sex precisely through use of the term, rather than through its refusal. Critical subversion for Butler necessitates the use of the contested term or structure in order to change it, rather than a radical or revolutionary break with that term or structure.

It is in dealing with subversion and otherness that Butler's Hegelian legacy is most profoundly manifest, both conceptually and rhetorically. Hegel appears in Butler's work as a way to reckon with radical alterity and subjectivity. It has been suggested that Hegel's greatest importance for Butler's theorization of gender is seen in her reading of Hegel's Antigone in *Antigone's Claim*, because the figure of Antigone is, for Butler as well as for other feminists, "the crucial point of encounter between feminists and Hegel."[28] Useful as the protofeminist Antigone is for Butler's discussions of gender, kinship, and the state, other aspects of Hegel's philosophy are still more influential for her thought. Hegel's influence can explicitly be found in her discussions of his account of the relation between the lord and the bondsman of *Phenomenology of Spirit*,[29] but his legacy is also apparent in the ways Butler understands recognition and desire to constitute subjects, or her insistence that the subject is never self-identical, and this in social, psychic, and relational terms. A less attended to but perhaps still more pervasive Hegelian influence is rhetorical. Butler has this to say on the issue of linguistic difficulty and the work of speculative grammar in Hegel:

> For instance, when Hegel talks about the "speculative sentence," he is trying to work against the propositional form as it's been received. When he says, "The subject is spirit," the first inclination, the one that received grammar in some sense prepares us for, is to establish the subject as the subject of the sentence, and then "spirit" becomes one way of determining or qualifying that subject. But, of course, what he wants us to be able to do is to reverse that sentence, to recognize something about how the "is" functions: it doesn't just point linearly in one direction; rather it points in both directions at once. He wants us to be able to experience the simultaneity of that sentence as it functions in its double directionality. Now that's a very hard thing to do given how profoundly inclined we are by what Nietzsche called the "seductions of grammar" to read in a linear way.[30]

---

28. Kimberly Hutchings, *Hegel and Feminist Philosophy* (Cambridge: Polity, 2003), 4; see also 91–5.

*29. See, in this regard, the essay by Terry Pinkard in *The History of Continental Philosophy: Volume 1*.

30. Butler, with Olson and Worsham, "Changing the Subject," 327. See also her section "Desire Rhetoric and Recognition in Hegel," in her *Subjects of Desire: Hegelian Reflections in Twentieth-Century France* (New York: Columbia University Press, 1987), 49.

Butler's reading bears some similarity to her reading of Nietzsche's assertion that there is no "doer behind the deed"[31] when explaining that there is no pregendered subject who performs individual acts of gender and thus collects the attribute of gender to add to an already established personhood, but rather the subject becomes a subject only through those acts. Hegel enacts this unexpected reversal at the level of the sentence, so that the very grammar is made to enact its concept, a different iteration of performative language. The relation between subject and object, cause and effect, becomes, in Butler's terms, doubly directional. The task she enjoins us to when thinking about gender is to become keen readers of what kinds of gendered possibilities language prepares us for, the normative constraints on what is possible that are wrought by our habitual practices of language. She also demonstrates how we might learn to read in excess of this preparation.

For Butler, language in this speculative mode, with all of its difficulty, can be a way of helping us think otherwise. The speculative mode, a kind of conceptual unfolding enacted through a confounding of the propositional form, is what Butler invites us to enter when thinking about gender. Thinking gender otherwise means attending to transsexuality, transgender, intersexuality, and as-yet-unarticulated others: what Butler calls the "otherwise gendered."[32] It is vital to note that this expansion of possibility is not quite the same as radical invention, and thinking about gender in a speculative mode does not mean musing about gender in an entirely fictive or futural way, or dreaming up wholly new genders, although this might have its own pleasures. It is rather about making those lives currently lived on the perimeters of gender and sexual legibility more recognizable and thus more livable. Expanding the horizon of possibility of gender is the task that Butler enjoins us to in both *Gender Trouble* and *Undoing Gender*. The last paragraph of *Gender Trouble* concludes: "The task here is not to celebrate each and every new possibility *qua* possibility, but to redescribe those possibilities that *already* exist, but which exist within cultural domains designated as culturally unintelligible and impossible."[33] The linguistic work of redescription is undertaken in order that we might apprehend the world more clearly as it is, an effort that sounds unmistakably phenomenological in its method. The task is undertaken, though, not just so the world might be seen with greater clarity, but also so that it might be changed. The seemingly esoteric mode of speculative grammar thus marries with the ethical imperative to articulate a future of open possibility, in order to increase the livability of those "otherwise gendered" subjects whose lives are most precarious:

---

31. See, for example, Nietzsche, *On the Genealogy of Morals*, Essay I, §13.
32. Butler, *Undoing Gender*, 28.
33. *Ibid.*, 148–9.

How do drag, butch, femme, transgender, transsexual persons enter into the political field? They make us not only question what is real, and what "must" be, but they also show us how the norms that govern contemporary notions of reality can be questioned and how new modes of reality can become instituted. … Some people have asked me what is the use of increasing possibilities for gender. I tend to answer: Possibility is not a luxury; it is as crucial as bread. I think we should not underestimate what the thought of the possible does for those for whom the very issue of survival is most urgent.[34]

---

34. *Ibid.*, 29.

2

RECENT DEVELOPMENTS IN AESTHETICS: BADIOU, RANCIÈRE, AND THEIR INTERLOCUTORS

Gabriel Rockhill

The following examination of the most recent developments in French aesthetics requires two preliminary remarks. First, the framework of analysis will be largely philosophic in nature, meaning that it will focus on the work of two major thinkers who have provided novel accounts of aesthetics: Alain Badiou and Jacques Rancière.[1] Unfortunately, this means leaving aside extremely significant developments in the work of lesser-known thinkers such as Yves Michaud and Christian Ruby, art historians such as Georges Didi-Huberman, sociologists of the likes of Nathalie Heinich and Eric Macé, literary critics such as Antoine Compagnon, and film theorists such as Raymond Bellour. Second, it is important to note that what is sometimes perceived by the English-speaking world as a significant generational gap between "recent developments" in the French intellectual avant-garde (the work of Badiou and Rancière) and the writings of their predecessors is partially an effect of parallax in transatlantic visibility. Indeed, it is true that Badiou (1937–) and Rancière (1940–) were the junior faculty members at the University of Paris VIII–Vincennes-St. Denis and were largely in the shadow of the founder of the philosophy department, Michel Foucault (1926–84), and prestigious faculty members such as Jean-François

---

1. Jacques Rancière (1940– ; born in Algiers) was a student at the École Normale Supérieure in the early 1960s. He began teaching at the University of Paris VIII–Vincennes-St. Denis in 1969, and occupied the Chair of Aesthetics and Politics from 1990 until his retirement in 2000. He was an active participant in the journal *Révoltes logiques* from 1975 to 1986, and he was a Director of Programs at the Collège International de Philosophie from 1986 to 1992. For biographical information on Alain Badiou, see the essay by Bruno Bosteels in this volume.

31

Lyotard (1924–98) and Gilles Deleuze (1925–95).[2] However, they are not far in age from Jacques Derrida (1930–2004) and are of the same generation as Jean-Luc Nancy (1940–), Philippe Lacoue-Labarthe (1940–2007), and Etienne Balibar (1942–). The massive importation of "poststructuralist theory" into the anglophone world, often at the expense of other intellectual developments, has created the unfortunate illusion that nothing else of great importance has been going on in France since the 1960s.

I. ALAIN BADIOU

Unlike many of his French compatriots, Badiou is a self-proclaimed systematic thinker. Although his position on aesthetics has developed since his early writings, I will focus on the more detailed description and systematized account of art he has provided since *Being and Event* (1988) and particularly *Manifesto for Philosophy* (1989).[3] In these works, art, and more precisely "the poem," is identified as one of the four truth procedures that – along with science, politics, and love – constitute the conditions of philosophy. Truth procedures are *not*, according to Badiou, founded on the encyclopedic accumulation of knowledge. Properly speaking, knowledge (*le savoir*) exists when correct statements are made about a given state of affairs, and nothing occurs that is not in conformity with the rules that regulate this state of affairs. Knowledge can therefore allow us to make veridical (*véridique*) statements through a process of discernment and classification, but it cannot attain truth (*la vérité*), which means that knowledge is fundamentally about "situations." Truth for Badiou is a "post-evental" process dependent on a pure event that supplements the situation, an event that can neither be named nor represented by the resources available in the situation. As a process or procedure, truth introduces an immanent break by tracking the effects of the supplementary event within the situation itself.

Badiou's examples of events include the following: the various instances of what he calls "modern poetry," Galileo's scientific revolution, the French Revolution, and Plato's theorization of love in the *Symposium*. For each of these events, the same basic process occurs: an undecidable event arises at the edge of the situation; a subject proclaims its existence and decides to relate to the situation from the point of view of the supplemental event; the truth procedure undertaken by the subject attempts to reconfigure the situation in relation to the

---

2. On the history of the philosophy department at the University of Paris VIII, see Charles Soulié's article "Le Destin d'une institution d'avant-garde: Histoire du département de philosophie de Paris VIII," *Histoire de l'éducation* 77 (January 1998), 47–69.

3. For reasons of space, the current analysis focuses on Badiou's theoretical, as opposed to literary, writings.

truth of the event, which requires resisting the *doxa* or "knowledge of the situation" in the name of the evental truth of the Idea.[4] This means that, at least at one level, Badiou has an interventionist, process-oriented conception of truth: "There is only authentic truth under the condition that we can choose truth."[5]

If truth is an evental hole in our situational knowledge produced via poetry, science, politics, or love, what, then, is philosophy? First of all, Badiou rejects what he takes great pleasure in castigating as modern sophism and historicist philosophizing. Against the modern sophists, which include the vast majority of his French predecessors, he maintains that there is indeed a definition of philosophy that is a historical invariant (since its inception in ancient Greece). "Philosophy," he writes, "is a construction of thought in which it is proclaimed, *against the art of the sophists*, that there are truths."[6] It is important to add, however, that philosophy is not itself a truth procedure, which means that it does *not* produce truths. The role of philosophy is to track down and stake out truth procedures in order to group them together in a unified conceptual space. It provides a systematic framework – a "shelter" – for the protection of artistic, scientific, political, and amorous truths. There is, moreover, always the danger of suturing philosophy to one of these truths and putting at risk its role as the neutral guardian of truth procedures. According to Badiou, this has been the case in recent history: philosophy was sutured to science under the reign of positivism; it was sutured to politics in Marxism; and it has been sutured to poetry since the time of Nietzsche.[7] For the philosophic renaissance advocated by Badiou to be successful, philosophy has to be de-sutured from the four truth procedures.

In relation to his immediate predecessors in France, Badiou's most notable difference is his stalwart emphasis on Platonism. In the realm of aesthetics, this

---

4. For the sake of concision, I am primarily drawing on Badiou's more schematic account of events in books such as *Manifesto for Philosophy* and *Ethics*. For a more detailed account, which introduces the important distinction between the "situation" and the "state of the situation" (as well as between presentation and representation, count-as-one and the count of the count, structure and metastructure, etc.), see *Being and Event*, Oliver Feltham (trans.) (London: Continuum, 2005).

5. Alain Badiou, *Petit manuel d'inesthétique* (Paris: Éditions du Seuil, 1998), 86; all translations of French works are my own. See also *Handbook of Inaesthetics*, Alberto Toscano (trans.) (Stanford, CA: Stanford University Press, 2004), 54. Badiou rejects, however, what he calls "speculative leftism," which imagines that interventions are founded solely on their own iconoclastic desire for new beginnings instead of being temporally inscribed in the circulation of events that have already been decided on. Strictly speaking, it is the event that founds the possibility of an intervention even though it is only through an intervention that an event "exists" by circulating in the situation.

6. Alain Badiou, *Conditions* (Paris: Éditions du Seuil, 1992), 65; see also 79–82.

7. See Alain Badiou, *Manifeste pour la philosophie* (Paris: Éditions du Seuil, 1989), 59; *Manifesto for Philosophy*, Norman Madarasz (ed. and trans.) (Albany, NY: SUNY Press, 1999), 79.

means that art for him does indeed have an essence that is a historical invariant: it is a *singular thought process of Ideas that traces the ephemeral event in the real*.[8] This is illustrated by the art form that Badiou openly identifies, in rather Heideggerian fashion, with the very essence of art: the poem. At its core, a poem is an act of naming, for all time, an undecidable evental presence at the limit of the situation.[9] Moreover, as an act of naming the disappearance of that which is presented, "every poem is an interruption of language, conceived as a simple tool of communication."[10] In short, a poem is a nominal trace of the event in the sensible that displaces the parameters of the given aesthetic situation.[11] This is precisely what distinguishes true art from false art: the former introduces an immanent break by bringing Ideas into the situation, while the latter simply capitalizes on possibilities already inventoried within the situation. Art is only true art, and truly acts on an event, if it is an event of thought.[12]

---

8. It is, of course, open to debate whether this is Plato's own view of art or, more precisely, *poiēsis*.
9. The influence of Heidegger is readily visible in Badiou's work on aesthetics. However, it would be a mistake to hastily identify their positions without being attentive to the points on which they diverge. Although a detailed comparison of their work goes well beyond the framework of the current analysis, it is nonetheless possible to highlight a series of similarities and differences. Regarding the points of convergence, both Heidegger and Badiou agree that: (i) art has an essence; (ii) the essence of art is the becoming or occurrence of truth; (iii) art can be distinguished from non-art based on its relation – or lack thereof – to truth; (iv) great art, which is the only true art, is clearly distinguishable from entertainment and other forms of non-art; and (v) poetry constitutes the very essence of art. Among their points of divergence, the following list can serve as a starting-point: (i) art is only one truth procedure among four according to Badiou, whereas it becomes one of the central, privileged avenues for truth in Heidegger; (ii) truth is defined as an evental hole in the situation for Badiou, while it is understood as *alētheia* or unconcealedness by Heidegger; and (iii) Badiou explicitly rejects Heidegger as a romantic and accuses him of suturing philosophy to poetry. At a more general level, one of the clear dividing lines between Badiou and Heidegger is their interpretation and evaluation of Platonism. Badiou repudiates what he labels Heidegger's "poetic ontology" and the latter's critique of the Platonic retreat from poetic *alētheia* due to his interpretation of Being as *idea*. Against Heidegger's conception of the history of metaphysics, Badiou valorizes Platonism as an essential part of the originary moment of philosophy insofar as it participates in the birth of "mathematical ontology."
10. Badiou, *Petit manuel d'inesthétique*, 124; *Handbook of Inaesthetics*, 80.
11. Badiou spurns the "Christly [*christique*]" vision of truth inherent in the idea that the work of art is *both* a truth *and* an event (Badiou, *Petit manuel d'inesthétique*, 24; *Handbook of Inaesthetics*, 11). However, he nonetheless states: "Since the poem is an operation, it is also an event" (*Petit manuel d'inesthétique*, 51; *Handbook of Inaesthetics*, 29).
12. Badiou appears to be remarkably close to Deleuze on this point and, in particular, to the position outlined in his two-volume analysis of film. Among his numerous objectives, Deleuze wanted to demonstrate that the great film directors had thought with images in much the same way as great thinkers (see *Cinéma I: L'Image-mouvement* [Paris: Éditions de Minuit, 1983], 7; *Cinema I: The Movement-Image*, Hugh Tomlinson and Barbara Habberjam [trans.] [Minneapolis, MN: University of Minnesota Press, 1986], xiv). This explains, moreover, the centrality of Henri Bergson in his analysis, whose philosophical thinking on movement and

RECENT DEVELOPMENTS IN AESTHETICS

It is important to highlight in this regard that Badiou rigorously maintains the "principle of genericity,"[13] which he inherited in part from Sartre's *What Is Literature?*, and ultimately from Aristotle's *Poetics*. The opening sentence of the latter work clearly announces the first two axioms of this principle. Aristotle proposes to discuss: "both poetic art in itself and its forms [*peri poiētikēs autēs te kai tōn eidōn autēs*]." This means that: (i) art – more specifically *poiētikē* – exists as a distinct entity in and of itself; and (ii) art or *poiētikē* is naturally divided into a set of distinct forms or genres. A third axiom is added later that, in the case of Badiou, has been only partially systematized: (iii) the forms or genres of art are arranged according to a natural hierarchy. As we have seen, the essence of art in general is defined by Badiou as "a thought whose works are the real."[14] He believes, moreover, in the universality of great works of art, which in striving toward the infinite bear eternal witness to the existence of events.[15] Regarding the delimitation of the arts, Badiou states that "there is in reality no way to move from one art to another. The arts are closed. No painting will ever change into music, no dance into a poem."[16] We have already seen, concerning the hierarchical organization of the arts, that the poem is the acme of art because it names the undecidable event in a language that extracts itself from the standard situation of language. Dance, to take an example from the opposite end of the spectrum, is not even properly speaking an art. Since it lacks words, and therefore the possibility of naming the event, it is only "the sign of the possibility of art, such as it is inscribed in the body."[17] Theater, while not occupying the imperial place

---

time is strictly coextensive with the thinking of movement and time within the history of filmic images (this is made extremely explicit in the recordings of Deleuze's seminar entitled *Gilles Deleuze: Cinéma* [Paris: Gallimard, 2006]). However, this proximity between Badiou and Deleuze is only partial. As we will see, for Badiou film is the impure art *par excellence*, which constantly runs the risk of slipping into simple entertainment or dissolving the strict limits that structure the relationship between the arts.

13. Although I am borrowing this expression from Rancière, I am not using it in the exact same sense that he does in *La Parole muette*.

14. Badiou, *Petit manuel d'inesthétique*, 21; *Handbook of Inaesthetics*, 9. See also: "an artistic truth is a happening of *l'Idée* in the sensible itself" ("Fifteen Theses on Contemporary Art," *Lacanian Ink* 23 [2004], 106).

15. See Badiou, *Petit manuel d'inesthétique*, 75; *Handbook of Inaesthetics*, 46. A similar idea is developed in "Fifteen Theses on Contemporary Art": "Art is not the sublime descent of the infinite into the finite abjection of the body and sexuality. It is the production of an infinite subjective series through the finite means of a material subtraction" (103–4).

16. Badiou, *Petit manuel d'inesthétique*, 127; *Handbook of Inaesthetics*, 82.

17. Badiou, *Petit manuel d'inesthétique*, 109 (see also 97, 107); *Handbook of Inaesthetics*, 69 (see also 61, 67–8). Seven years later, in *Le Siècle* (Paris: Éditions du Seuil, 2005), Badiou writes that dance is, since the Russian ballets of Isadora Duncan, "a major art [*un art capital*]" (224; *The Century*, Alberto Toscano [trans.] [Cambridge: Polity, 2007], 159). As with the example in note 11 of the relationship between Badiou's stance on truth and his critical comment regarding the Christly vision of truth, it is unclear whether this is an oversight on his part, a

of the poem, is nonetheless the positive obverse of dance: it is the arrangement of a near physical presentation of an Idea, which *does* have recourse to words. To return to the lower end of the spectrum, film is classified as the lowest art form because it is "an impure art."[18] Whereas painting is the art of donation that provides an integral presentation of the Idea, and music invents the pure time of the Idea by exploring the configurations of the movement of the thinkable, film combines allusions to the more mimetic arts and can only serve, at best, as an art of visitation where Ideas pass by but are never fully embodied.[19] For film to properly act as an art, it therefore appears to have only one path open to it: it has to show that it is *only* film and that "its images only bear witness to the real insofar as they are *manifestly* images."[20] The principle regulating the hierarchy of the arts is the Platonic principle of the proximity to the Idea. The poem is closest to the Idea and therefore comes first, followed apparently by theater (Badiou has yet to systematize these relations). Painting and music seem to be the median arts, whereas film is clearly the lowest and dance is excluded (the precise position of some of the other arts remains unclear). The delimitation of the arts is not strictly speaking based on their media or empirical characteristics but on the very being of each individual art. This is why Badiou delimits his claims regarding the principles of dance in the following way (a delimitation that could be generalized to all art forms): "Not [the principles] of dance thought out of itself, its technique and its history, but dance such as philosophy receives and protects it."[21] Ultimately, just as the distinction between art and non-art is founded on the existence or nonexistence of *thought*, the arts are themselves delimited philosophically according to an aesthetic ontology, and they are placed in a hierarchy based on their proximity to the Idea.[22]

---

contradiction in his work, an element easily clarified within his system or, in this particular case, the sign of an evolution in his thinking.

18. Badiou, *Petit manuel d'inesthétique*, 128; *Handbook of Inaesthetics*, 83.

19. Badiou, *Petit manuel d'inesthétique*, 134, 126–7; *Handbook of Inaesthetics*, 87, 82.

20. Alain Badiou, "Dialectiques de la fable," in Alain Badiou *et al.*, *Matrix: Machine philosophique* (Paris: Ellipses, 2003), 120. While it is true that all art forms, according to Badiou, have their own limit where they alienate themselves from "true art," it is clear that film is the lowest of the arts because it runs the greatest risks, especially when compared, for instance, to the risks of literature: "Film, that great impurifier, always runs the risk of pleasing too much, of being a figure of debasement. True literature, which is rigorous purification, runs the risk of getting lost in a proximity to the concept in which the effect of art is exhausted itself and prose (or poetry) is sutured to philosophy" (*Petit manuel d'inesthétique*, 135; *Handbook of Inaesthetics*, 88).

21. Badiou, *Petit manuel d'inesthétique*, 99; *Handbook of Inaesthetics*, 62–3. In another statement that could be generalized for all of the arts, Badiou asserts, regarding film, that formal elements must be invoked only to the extent that they contribute to the passing of the Idea (*Petit manuel d'inesthétique*, 131; *Handbook of Inaesthetics*, 85).

22. Strictly speaking, Badiou claims that his delimitation of the arts is not based on genres but on "configurations." A configuration is an identifiable sequence that produces a truth for a

In the opening essay of his major work on aesthetics to date, *Handbook of Inaesthetics* (1998), Badiou provides an account of the relationship between his own project and what he sees as the three preexisting schemas for thinking the connection between art and philosophy. According to the *didactic schema*, to begin with, "art is incapable of truth, … all truth is exterior to it."[23] As "the charm of a semblance of truth," art must, therefore, either be condemned or used in a purely instrumental fashion.[24] The *romantic schema* takes the opposite approach by asserting that art *alone* is capable of truth. Finally, the *classical schema* follows the didacticians in maintaining that art is incapable of truth, but it redefines the essence of art as mimetic. Art's distance from truth is thereby no longer worrisome precisely because its destination is *not* truth. On the contrary, art *qua* mimetic semblance has a therapeutic function, and the rules of art are to be deduced from this function. When Badiou inquires into recent developments in the arts and art theory, he concludes that the twentieth century has not introduced any new schemas. Identifying the three major dispositions of twentieth-century thought as Marxism, psychoanalysis, and hermeneutics, he asserts that: "Marxism is didactic, psychoanalysis is classical, and Heideggerian hermeneutics is romantic."[25] The avant-garde movements (from Dadaism to the Situationists) only added a mediating schema, the *didactico-romantic schema*. It is against the backdrop of this account that Badiou proposes a new, fourth, schema for thinking the relationship between art and philosophy. What is lacking in all prior work, according to him, is a way of thinking art's relation to truth as being both immanent *and* singular: truth is immanent in art and art is a singular form of truth irreducible to other such forms. It is this very simultaneity that Badiou wants to defend in claiming that art is in and of itself a singular truth procedure. He baptizes this new schema "inaesthetics."

Badiou has developed his account of contemporary art in *The Century* (2005).[26] Throughout this book, artwork from the twentieth century is marshaled to bear witness to the subjective nature of the century, which Badiou defines as the "passion for the real [*passion du réel*]."[27] The works cited are not used,

---

particular art, and it is philosophy's role to outline such configurations. As examples, Badiou cites "Greek tragedy," "classical music," and "the novel" (*Petit manuel d'inesthétique*, 26–7; *Handbook of Inaesthetics*, 13). His rejection of the term "genre" for these art forms is an additional indication that the delimitation of the arts is of a deeply philosophic nature.

23. Badiou, *Petit manuel d'inesthétique*, 10; *Handbook of Inaesthetics*, 2.
24. Badiou, *Petit manuel d'inesthétique*, 11; *Handbook of Inaesthetics*, 2.
25. Badiou, *Petit manuel d'inesthétique*, 15; *Handbook of Inaesthetics*, 5.
26. "Fifteen Theses on Contemporary Art" is an equally good example that focuses on art in the era of "globalization."
27. In addition to the criticisms of Badiou's work that will be highlighted in the conclusion, it is worth noting that his personification of "the century" is rife with historiographical problems, including those poignantly described by Henri Focillon: "We have trouble not conceiving a

properly speaking, as historical documents, but rather as forms of testimony (*témoignage*) that attest to the subjective commitments of the century. Badiou thus remains faithful to the idea that art *thinks* in and of itself, and he is primarily interested in how the century has thought itself through art and the three other truth procedures. His central claim is that all four truth procedures became impassioned with the real in the twentieth century. They attempted to bring the Idea – *qua real* – into reality by radical acts of foundation aimed at new beginnings, which were disjunctively synthesized with acts of destruction. The entire century, he argues, was structured by nondialectical battles, which manifested themselves in the art world through the constant avant-garde struggles to overcome preexistent, classical forms in the name of an Idea. At the very end of the book, Badiou gives "less esoteric" names to the war of the century, which the reader will easily recognize as a battle between Badiou's major philosophic concepts: the Idea and reality; the event and the situational state of affairs; truth and opinions; and so on.[28]

It is therefore not difficult to reconcile Badiou's references to historical developments with his more systematic, ahistorical work on aesthetics: even though circumstances might change with time, the very essence of art nevertheless remains the same.[29] This central idea is perhaps best illustrated in the preface to *Logiques des mondes* (2006), where Badiou claims that in spite of all of the circumstantial differences separating Picasso from the creators of the cave paintings at Chauvet-Pont-d'Arc, their respective renderings of horses nonetheless attest to the same fundamental truth: the eternal Idea of a horse. The multiplicity of worlds does not preclude, according to Badiou, the existence of universal truths.

II. JACQUES RANCIÈRE

While it is true that Rancière's early work on politics and history shows signs of a longstanding interest in aesthetics, it is primarily since the 1990s that he has

---

century like a living being, refusing it a resemblance with man himself. Each century shows itself to us with its color, its physiognomy, and projects the shadow of a certain silhouette" (*Vie des formes* [Paris: Presses Universitaires de France, 1943], 84–5).

28. Badiou, *Le Siècle*, 231; *The Century*, 164.

29. One way of understanding Badiou's references to history is in relation to his appropriation of the Hegelian notion of "concrete universality" (see "The Adventure of French Philosophy," *New Left Review* 35 [September–October 2005]) and his definition of "historical ages" as "epochal situations of philosophy" (see Alain Badiou, "L'Age des poètes," in *La Politique des poètes*, Jacques Rancière [ed.] [Paris: Albin Michel, 1992]).

presented what has become a general account of the arts.[30] Unlike Badiou, who has written relatively few books dedicated exclusively to art, Rancière's publication record over the past twenty years constitutes a veritable *tour de force* in the field of aesthetics. It might be said that whereas Badiou is more interested in establishing a totalizing philosophic system in which aesthetics plays a significant role, Rancière has dedicated his intellectual energies to making a singular intervention in the field of aesthetics, in much the same way as he has done in the fields of history and politics. He obviously does not share Badiou's penchant for grand theories, and his philosophic strategies owe more to guerrilla warfare than to epic frontal offensives *à la* Badiou.

This difference in scope and strategy is at least one of the reasons that the Badiou–Rancière debate has largely been a *dialogue de sourds*, that is to say, an exchange in which they talk past one another. In spite of running in the same intellectual circles, they have had little or no public debate on the two common areas of interest that seem to provide natural points of discussion: aesthetics and politics. On the one hand, Badiou's major essays on Rancière all deal with the question of politics (with only a few passing comments on aesthetics), and the latter has not provided a developed response to Badiou's account of their fundamental dissensus in this area.[31] On the other hand, Rancière's articles on Badiou are all dedicated to the question of aesthetics, and his former colleague has yet to reply to Rancière's detailed criticisms of his faulty methods and interpretations.[32]

In one of the rare passages where Badiou explicitly engages with Rancière's aesthetics, he tries to situate him within what he calls the "subjectivity of the century" by suggesting that some of his work is a "sophisticated echo" of what he sees as the *Tel Quel* thesis, that is, that the formal mutations of art are more political than politics itself.[33] Whether or not one agrees with the orientation Rancière has taken in his recent writings, it is important to avoid restricting

---

30. For an instructive account of Rancière's early work in light of his most recent interest in aesthetics, see his "The Method of Equality," in *Jacques Rancière: History, Politics, Aesthetics*, Gabriel Rockhill and Phil Watts (eds) (Durham, NC: Duke University Press, 2009).

31. See Badiou's two chapters on Rancière in *Abrégé de métapolitique* ("Rancière and the Community of Equals" and "Rancière and Apolitics", in *Metapolitics*, Jason Barker [trans.] [London: Verso, 2005]) and his article "Les leçons de Jacques Rancière, savoir et pouvoir après la tempête", in *La Philosophie déplacée: Autour de Jacques Rancière*, Laurence Cornu and Patrice Vermeren (eds) (Paris: Horlieu Éditions, 2006) ("The Lessons of Jacques Rancière: Knowledge and Power After the Storm", in *Jacques Rancière*, Rockhill and Watts [eds]).

32. See Rancière's "Esthétique, inesthétique, anti-esthétique," in *Alain Badiou: Penser le multiple*, C. Ramond (ed.) (Paris: L'Harmattan, 2002), published in English as "Aesthetics, Inaesthetics, Anti-Aesthetics," Ray Brassier (trans.), in *Think Again: Alain Badiou and the Future of Philosophy*, Peter Hallward (ed.) (London: Continuum, 2004), and his *Politique de la littérature* (Paris: Éditions Galilée, 2007).

33. Badiou, *Le Siècle*, 210; *The Century*, 148.

his work – as Badiou appears to be doing in this passage – to the opposition in postwar France between content-based commitment and formal commitment. Successful or unsuccessful, Rancière clearly wants to take a decisive step in aesthetics by breaking with *both* the Sartrean notion of prosaic commitment *and* the *Tel Quel* claims regarding the political potential of aesthetic form. To take but two representative publications, it might be said that what Rancière wants to reject is the simplistic choice between following Sartre's work in *What Is Literature?* (1948) and Barthes's formalist reworking of Sartre's thesis in *Writing Degree Zero* (1953). Rather than looking for the political dimension of art in the content of prose or in the third dimension of form (what Barthes calls *l'écriture*, distinct from both *la langue* and *le style*), Rancière wants to shift the conceptual tectonic plates on which this opposition is based. The very notion of "politicized art" presupposes that art and politics are distinct entities that can be joined, either by prosaic content (Sartre) or through writing as a social function (Barthes). However, it is precisely this presupposition that Rancière wants to reject. Art and politics, he claims, are in fact consanguineous insofar as they are both *distributions of the sensible* (*partages du sensible*), that is, ways of organizing the field of sensory experience by determining what is visible and audible, as well as what can be said, thought, made, or done. As a distribution of the sensible, art is inherently political precisely insofar as it presents a common world of experience (replete with a set of shared objects and recognized subjects), which distinguishes what is possible from what is impossible.

Rather than the *Tel Quel* group, the most obvious predecessor to Rancière's work is Foucault. Although Foucault was occasionally close to the *Tel Quel* group, his understanding of literature in his early writings goes beyond the framework of formal commitment. Literature was seen as a unique discourse born with the emergence of the modern *epistēmē* and the appearance of the human sciences around the end of the eighteenth century. In negating the existence of man and resisting the instrumentalization of language, it was properly speaking a "counter-discourse" aimed at bringing language back to its brute being, which had been buried since the Renaissance. The historical appearance of literature is thus structurally equivalent to the return of the repressed at the end of the classical age: the brute being of nonrepresentational language in its open relationship with madness (and after the "death of God"). All said and done, literature "compensates" European culture for its repression of madness by abandoning the strict Cartesian delimitation between reason and unreason, thereby allowing language to escape from the imperial mastery of the rational human subject.[34]

---

34. Literature also acts as the rabbit hole that allows Foucault to go through the looking glass of the modern *epistēmē*, as is evident most notably in the role played by Borges in the preface to *The Order of Things*.

Although Rancière does not share Foucault's preoccupation with madness and collective repression, the latter's historical approach to literature is essential to Rancière's project: "The genealogy of the concept of literature that I have attempted in *La Parole muette* [Silent speech], or in my current work on the systems of art, could be expressed in terms close to Foucault's concept of episteme."[35] Like Foucault, Rancière takes art to be a historically constituted practice that is always situated within a framework of possibility. This framework, which Rancière calls a *regime* instead of an *epistēmē*, has undergone significant transformations through the course of history. These changes vaguely follow the historical delimitation outlined by Foucault in his early work between the classical age and the modern age. However, Rancière's regimes differ from Foucault's *epistēmēs* in a few important ways. First, regimes are not mutually exclusive chronological blocks. Unlike *epistēmēs*, the chronology of regimes conforms to Augustine's description of the temporality of human souls in *The City of God*: although they are created in time, they will never perish in time. The ethical regime of images, which was born in ancient Greece, and the representative regime of arts, which dominated the classical age, both persist in the modern age, that is to say, the age that has been marked by the emergence of the third major regime: the aesthetic regime of art. Rancière thereby rejects the idea that structural blocks hegemonically dominate a given epoch until being cataclysmically replaced, through a discontinuous event, by another structural block. Although Foucault's position was more nuanced than this since he did allow for the possibility of a "counter-discourse" such as literature, it is nonetheless clear that, for Rancière, the "modern" era is characterized by conflicting regimes and that there are no tragic events separating historical epochs. To borrow from one of André Robinet's criticisms of Foucault, which perfectly applies to Rancière's reworking of Foucaultian *epistēmēs*, the conflict is not *between* time periods but *within* them.[36]

These differences in historical methodology lead to a divergence in hermeneutic practice. At least in his early work, Foucault tended to interpret individual works of art as signs of their times that reveal structural conditions of

35. Jacques Rancière, "Literature, Politics, Aesthetics," *SubStance* 29(2) (2000), 13.

36. See A. Robinet, *Le Langage à l'âge classique* (Paris: Éditions Klincksieck, 1978). An excellent example of Rancière's rejection of discontinuist historiography can be found in his criticisms of Deleuze's work on film, most notably in *La Fable cinématographique* [Film fables] (Paris: Éditions du Seuil, 2001) and "Les Ecarts du cinéma," *Trafic* 50 (Summer 2004). Unfortunately, Rancière has not sufficiently taken into account Deleuze's conception of becoming and its effects on his historical methodology (compare Rancière, "Les Ecarts du cinéma," 165, and Gilles Deleuze, *Cinéma II: L'Image-temps* [Paris: Éditions de Minuit, 1985], 59; *Cinema II: The Time-Image*, Hugh Tomlinson and Robert Galeta [eds] [Minneapolis, MN: University of Minnesota Press, 1989], 41).

possibility. Rancière is more interested in showing how individual works of art make choices within and between conflicting regimes by actualizing certain potentialities and ignoring others. Works of art can still be held up as indices of their historical conjuncture, but Rancière tends to focus on the ways in which each individual work carves out a unique space between the axioms of various regimes. He wants to avoid monolithic accounts of art-historical epochs in favor of a more detailed analysis of the specificity of individual works. In methodological terms, this amounts to saying that Rancière resists one of the working assumptions of what is called "structuralism," namely that there is a single set of determinants behind the totality of phenomena. At the same time, he is generally allergic to the "poststructuralist" reflex that consists in claiming that *every* structure is fissured and de-centered.[37] In short, Rancière rejects the simplistic choice between a totalizing structure and a de-centered structure by postulating that competing frameworks and axioms are at work within the same time period.

This being said, the backdrop to all of Rancière's recent studies in aesthetics is never difficult to discern: the three regimes of art, which are so many "distributions of the sensible." The *ethical regime of images*, to begin with, is best exemplified in the work of Plato. Within this regime, images are arranged and distributed according to their origin and their *telos*, based on how they can best educate the citizenry and contribute to the *ethos* of the community. The *representative regime of arts*, rooted in Aristotle's critique of Plato, liberated "the arts" from the communal *ethos* by redefining them as fictional imitations of action. This amounted to isolating an autonomous domain of fiction founded on a series of axioms of representation: the hierarchy of subject matter and genres, the principle of appropriateness by which modes of expression and action are to conform to the subject matter and genre, and the privileging of speech over action. The *aesthetic regime of art* abolishes the autonomous domain of fiction by blurring the lines between art and life. It also dismantles the axioms of representation by dissolving the hierarchy of subject matter and genres, promoting the indifference of style with regard to content, and privileging writing over the present truth of speech.

Since Rancière's work concentrates primarily on the contradiction between – and within – the representative and aesthetic regimes of art, it will be helpful to elucidate one extended example of this conflict. In the representative regime, which dominated the classical age, there was a strict hierarchical distinction between subject matter worthy of representation and subject matter that was best left outside of the artistic frame. Since around the end of the eighteenth

---

37. I use the categories "structuralism" and "poststructuralism" as purely heuristic tools. Since this is not the place to assess their explanatory power, let it suffice to say that I think they should be used with the utmost caution in discussing developments in postwar French thought.

century, this hierarchy has been widely contested in the name of the egalitarian principle that anything can become the subject matter of art. Rancière cites the example of Flaubert's decision to write an entire novel on the adulterous affairs of a promiscuous, bourgeois woman prone to novelistic fantasy: *Madame Bovary*. However, he traces this "aesthetic revolution" back to the later Kant and German Romanticism, where he finds an attempt to overcome the representative hierarchy between intelligent form and sensible matter (which is perhaps most visible in Schiller's concept of *Spiel*[38]).

It is precisely this egalitarian principle of the aesthetic regime that would later allow for the emergence of the mechanical arts of photography and film. Rancière argues, against Walter Benjamin, that in order for these to be recognized as arts, it was first necessary that it be recognized that *anything* could become the subject matter of art, including the recording of brute reality devoid – in principle – of all aesthetic hierarchies. In other words, photography and film became possible only after the artistic revolution that introduced the aesthetic regime of art. The technological revolution, for Rancière, came *after* the artistic revolution.[39] He makes a very similar argument concerning the historical emergence of psychoanalysis, which only became possible after the breakdown of the representative hierarchy between consciousness and the unconscious, *logos* and *pathos*.

Rancière refers to art within the aesthetic regime in much the same way as his American counterpart, Arthur Danto: the art of the commonplace (*l'art du quelconque*). Since there is no longer any hierarchy of subject matter in the aesthetic regime, anything – any commonplace object or occurrence – can in principle become art. This is, of course, what Danto has argued in his more recent analyses of the art world since Andy Warhol's 1964 *Brillo Box* project.[40] In producing objects that were visually identical to industrially produced Brillo boxes and lacked the artist's signature, Warhol definitively dissolved the borderlines between art and commonplace objects. Although the Danto–Rancière debate has yet to occur, it is nonetheless easy enough to underscore one inevitable point of contention. For Rancière, unlike for Danto, the postmodern era is not a separate historical sequence; it is only the unfolding of possibilities inherent in the aesthetic regime of art since approximately the late eighteenth century. In other words, Warhol's *Brillo Box* project is nothing more than a

---

*38. Schiller is discussed in the essay on aesthetics by Daniel Dahlstrom in *The History of Continental Philosophy. Volume 1*.

39. For a critical evaluation of the positions taken by Rancière and Benjamin, see my "Le Cinéma n'est jamais né," in *Le Milieu des appareil*, J.-L. Déotte (ed.) (Paris: L'Harmattan, forthcoming).

40. See Arthur C. Danto, *Beyond the Brillo Box: The Visual Arts in Post-Historical Perspective* (New York: Farrar, Straus & Giroux, 1992), and *After the End of Art: Contemporary Art and the Pale of History* (Princeton, NJ: Princeton University Press).

GABRIEL ROCKHILL

contemporary variation on a theme going back to Flaubert, Schiller, and other
artists of the aesthetic regime. As with Foucault's discontinuous events, Rancière
rejects the idea of a "postmodern break."

In spite of this difference in historical analysis and in historiographical
method, Rancière and Danto both at least partially agree on the fundamental
contradiction of the art of the commonplace. We can take as an example here
Joseph Beuys's *7000 Eichen* project, which he began in 1982 for Documenta 7 by
planting oak trees in Kassel, Germany, and which he hoped would be extended
throughout the world as a global mission to effect social and environmental
change. In Rancière's terms, the contradiction of such art of the commonplace
can be expressed in two ways: (i) "Art of the *commonplace*" is only *commonplace*
by losing its status as art (in the case of Beuys, the artist is confounded with the
urban planner or forester); (ii) "*Art* of the commonplace" must not be entirely
commonplace in order to remain *art* (the *artistic* gesture of planting trees is
maintained only by its link to Beuys's name as an artist, implicitly manifest in
the columnar basalt markers accompanying the trees). Danto privileges the first
formulation of this contradiction by arguing that the distinction between art and
non-art is no longer guaranteed by a systematic historical narrative: "today there
is no longer any pale of history. Everything is permitted."[41] In the contradictory
era of the "end of art," it is up to the philosopher to distinguish between what
is properly art and what is not. Rancière emphasizes both formulations of this
contradiction and maintains that there is no way of resolving it. In fact, he views
it as a "productive contradiction" insofar as the search for solutions has been the
driving force behind two centuries of artistic production.

III. CONCLUDING QUESTIONS

Although there is much more that could be said about Badiou and Rancière, it
should at least be clear to what extent their positions on aesthetics differ. First
of all, Rancière rejects Badiou's Platonic essentialism in favor of a historical
approach to artistic regimes. It is not surprising, therefore, to see him castigate
Badiou for talking about Plato's theory of art, reminding him that for Plato and
the ethical regime of images, "art" in the singular did not exist, but only images
properly distributed for the good of the *ethos*. According to Rancière, there is
no art in general: there are only aesthetic practices and theories within historical
regimes. In conformity with his *explanatory and synthetic polemics*, by which his
criticisms of authors simultaneously serve to situate these exact same authors
within his own theory, Rancière perceives behind Badiou's anti-aestheticism an

---

41. Danto, *After the End of Art*, 12.

44

odd mixture between the ethical regime of images and the aesthetic regime of art. On the one hand, Badiou aligns himself with the modernism born out of the aesthetic regime, that is, the attempt to embrace the singularity of art while refusing its forms of dis-identification (where the limits between art and non-art dissipate). On the other hand, Badiou's "ultra-Platonism" – which is ultimately indebted to the romantic Platonism of the aesthetic age – reveals his adherence to one of the axioms of the ethical regime: art is of value only insofar as it serves to instruct us on the Idea. Both of these positions have a common goal, which is to construct a philosophic bulwark against the aesthetic regime's dissolution of the "proper" of art. If this bulwark is destined to failure, it is precisely because the proper of "modern" art, according to Rancière, is to be improper, to disturb and unsettle hierarchical distributions of the sensible such as the one that elevates art above the commonplace.

We can add to Rancière's primary criticism of Badiou a list of additional problems that are visible in his work on aesthetics. To begin with, his theoriza-tion of art is largely dependent on a historically specific conception of art that is unique to the modern age. By assuming that art is an iconoclastic gesture refusing the norms of the day in order to venture beyond the givens of the situ-ation, Badiou's working understanding of art is clearly rooted in a romantic ideal proper to the modern age.[42] However, this historical specificity is not recognized and assumed as such, and the iconoclastic conception of art is hegemonically imposed as a universal on the entire history of art. Second, Badiou relies on a simplistic distinction between true art and entertainment that he unquestion-ingly inherits from a hierarchy operative in the social field, which has been analyzed in detail by Pierre Bourdieu in *La Distinction*. Third, Badiou – much like Sartre – doggedly adheres to the principle of genericity while focusing on an era (the past two centuries) in which the distinctions between the arts have been regularly called into question, both in theory and in practice. Finally, Badiou's approach to art is largely dependent on what might be called *illustra-tive hermeneutics*.[43] Like many of his fellow admirers of Jacques Lacan, he tends to "discover" in art an illustration of his own philosophic concepts. It is true, of course, that he has gone to great lengths to try to show that this is not the case.

---

42. On this topic, see the work of Nathalie Heinich, most notably *L'Elite artiste: Excellence et singularité en régime démocratique* (Paris: Gallimard, 2005) and *Être artiste* (Paris: Klincksieck, 1997).

43. Another essential question for Badiou is whether his work in *The Century* has served to supplement his illustrative hermeneutics with a form of *illustrative historiography*: is the supposed "passion for the real" simply a projected illustration of Badiou's concepts in terms of a century-long battle over them? For an extremely pertinent sociological analysis of these illustrative strategies in philosophic discourse, see Pinto's *Les Philosophes entre le lycée et l'avant-garde* (Paris: L'Harmattan, 1987).

He repeatedly affirms, for instance, that art *thinks for itself* and that the philosopher cannot think in its place. However, if we follow Badiou's logic through to the end, we cannot help but wonder if he has done anything other than philosophically colonize the art world. As we have already seen, the distinction between art and non-art, as well as the delimitation and hierarchization of the arts, is based on defining art strictly in terms of thought and reifying the Platonic distinction between Ideas and opinions. In claiming that art *thinks*, has Badiou not already commandeered the very essence of art by making it coterminous with the privileged material of philosophy (thought)? Is the apparent elevation of art (art *thinks* like philosophy) not simply a disguised denigration (art is only of value, and therefore only truly art, if it is elevated – by the philosopher's act of recognition – to the supposedly superior level of philosophy by thinking)? Is art not always secondary to philosophy since artistic practice is of value and interest only insofar as it produces thoughts, which are then humbly welcomed by philosophers into the palace of Ideas? Is this not why assiduous readers such as Rancière cannot help but recognize which artistic "thoughts" actually make it into the realm of Ideas, which are always more or less subtle translations of Badiou's own ideas?[44] If these questions are answered in the affirmative, then Badiou can be legitimately criticized, like his fellow traveler Slavoj Žižek, for using art as an illustration of his own concepts while feigning an illuminating process of discovery.[45] It is important to remind ourselves in this regard that the *illustration* of a philosophic idea in a work of art no more *explains* the work of art than it *proves* the philosophic idea; it simply *extends* a preexistent theory through a rhetorical logic of transubstantiation by which philosophic ideas are translated more or less cunningly into artistic practices.

Rancière's project is equally open to a series of criticisms. To begin with, his descriptive account of the regimes of art is thus far devoid of any developed genetic account that explains *why* these regimes emerged.[46] Part of this is due to his allergy to the social sciences and to "externalist" accounts of the arts that directly engage with the transformation of institutions and artistic practices

---

44. In "Esthétique, inesthétique, anti-esthétique," Rancière writes, concerning Badiou: "The poem only says what philosophy needs it to say and what it feigns to discover in the surprise of the poem" (in *Alain Badiou*, 491).

45. For an excellent critique of Žižek's illustrative hermeneutics, see David Bordwell's "Slavoj Žižek: Say Anything" (www.davidbordwell.net/essays/zizek.php; accessed December 2009). Also see Judith Butler's comments in Judith Butler, Ernesto Laclau, and Slavoj Žižek, *Contingency, Hegemony, Universality: Contemporary Dialogues on the Left* (London: Verso, 2000), esp. 26, 156–7.

46. For a detailed critique of Rancière on this point, see my "Démocratie moderne et révolution esthétique", in *La Philosophie déplacée*, Cornu and Vermeren (eds).

in the modern era.[47] Second, the scope of Rancière's description of the three major artistic regimes needs to be qualified. From the ancient Greeks down through the present, these are apparently the only regimes that have existed, and yet Rancière has still not provided any detailed account of the Middle Ages or the Renaissance. Moreover, although he occasionally makes reference to the "Western tradition," it is unclear to what extent these regimes are unique to a particular geographic or cultural region. Third, his affirmation of the consubstantiality of art and politics is justified only as a historical claim demonstrated through the analysis of specific artistic and intellectual communities. When this assertion is transformed into an ontological constant, it is in dire need of proof in order to be validated. It is arguable that, as things stand, the ontological affirmation of the consanguinity of art and politics is simply based on defining them tautologically as distributions of the sensible. If this is the case, nothing can preclude anyone else from defining art and politics in different ways and drawing alternative conclusions. Affirmation and proof are only equivalent within arguments of authority.

This last problem in Rancière's work points to one of the fundamental issues – and problems, I would argue – that links Rancière and Badiou: the ontologization, or meta-ontologization, of aesthetics.[48] Although Rancière goes to great lengths to show that art is a thoroughly historical phenomenon, his readers cannot help but be struck by at least one level of ontologization. He affirms that works of art have a politics inherent in their very being, which is independent of any explicit political intention on the part of the artist and distinct from the gradual constitution of a work of art through its circulation in the social field. Works of art are produced as a combination of the various "objective politics" inscribed in the distribution of the sensible and manifest in the plastic and narrative field of possibilities at a given moment.[49] As a philosopher of art, Rancière

---

47. Foucault's break with his early position on literature is enlightening in this regard (see Roger-Pol Droit, *Michel Foucault, entretiens* [Paris: Éditions Odile Jacob, 2004]).

48. For another point of view on the ontologization of aesthetics, see Bruno Besana, "Intercession, condition, brouillage: L'œuvre d'art à l'époque de l'ontologie de l'événement," in *Art comme esthétique, éthique et politique* (Paris: UNESCO, forthcoming) (an alternative English version is "From Philosophy of Art to Philosophy with Art: On Some Strategies of Capture," *F.R. David* [Spring 2007]).

49. See Rancière, "The Janus-Face of Politicized Art:" "Commitment is not a category of art. This does not mean that art is apolitical. It means that aesthetics has its own politics, or its own metapolitics. That is what I was saying earlier regarding Flaubert and microscopic equality. There are politics of aesthetics, forms of community laid out by the very regime of identification in which we perceive art (hence pure art as well as committed art). Moreover, a 'committed' work of art is always made as a kind of combination between these objective politics that are inscribed in the field of possibility for writing, objective politics that are inscribed as plastic or narrative possibilities" (in *The Politics of Aesthetics*, Gabriel Rockhill [trans.] [London: Continuum, 2004], 60).

appears to be the only one who has access to this *objective political being of art*. While it is true that he highlights the historical constitution of this political being, there is little or no room for a veritable account of the circulation and reception of works of art in the social field and how this social dimension relates to the political potential of works of art. The very being of art is fixed in relation to the possibilities inherent in the regimes of art. Since Badiou lacks Rancière's historical sensibilities, his theorization of art is founded on a much more explicit aesthetic ontology. As we have seen, the very being of art is defined in terms of an unchanging structural relationship between situations and events: art is a truth procedure that bears the trace of the passage of the event and interrupts the representational situation in which it occurs by naming "the un-nameable." This mode of being of art is precisely what qualifies it – and what has ostensibly always qualified it – as art proper. The discrepancy between these respective forms of aesthetic ontology allows us to conclude by returning to one of the most fundamental differences between Rancière and Badiou: whereas the latter disdains historicism as a sophistic flight from the mighty heights of Platonism, the former insists on the need to situate art theory and practice within the flow of time, including the theory and practice of his Platonist colleague.[50]

---

50. See Badiou's revealing comments on his relation to Rancière at the end of *Logiques des mondes: L'Être et l'événement, 2* (Paris: Éditions du Seuil, 2006), where he claims that they have a common philosophic fidelity to the "red" sequence (1965–80) in spite of their different relation to history (*ibid.*, 586–7).

3

RETHINKING MARXISM

Emily Zakin

In "The Logic of Totalitarianism," Claude Lefort assesses the failure of "the Marxist or quasi Marxist Left"[1] in France to formulate a concept of totalitarianism, allocating the entirety of its theoretical elaboration to the (ostensible) Right and thus leaving its portrayal vulnerable to development and appropriation by the liberal and the conservative movements. Lefort argues that this breakdown of critique can be attributed to a number of interrelated factors, among them the traumatizing effect of Stalinism, an "opposition to liberalism," the illusion of immanent revolution, and the contemptuous view of the state "as a mere organ of society" that expresses the confluence of political and economic forces (LT 278): in short, to Marxism and its fundamental rejection of the state. In place of the fiction of the state, Lefort claims, the Marxist project declares all power to be social power, not political power. In rendering this judgment, Lefort laments the lack of traction that "analyses like those of Hannah Arendt" found.[2] While Slavoj Žižek in *Did Somebody Say Totalitarianism?* agrees that "until two decades ago, Leftist radicals dismissed her as the perpetrator of the notion of 'totalitarianism,'"[3] in contrast to Lefort he assesses the current academic stature of Arendt as a sign of "the theoretical defeat of the Left – of how the Left has accepted the basic coordinates of liberal democracy ('democracy' versus

---

1. Claude Lefort, "The Logic of Totalitarianism," Alan Sheridan (trans.), in *The Political Forms of Modern Society*, John B. Thompson (ed.) (Cambridge, MA: MIT Press, 1986), 276. Hereafter cited as LT followed by the page number.
*2. For a discussion of Hannah Arendt, see the essay by Peg Birmingham in *The History of Continental Philosophy: Volume 5*.
3. Slavoj Žižek, *Did Somebody Say Totalitarianism?* (London: Verso, 2001), 2. Hereafter cited as DSST followed by the page number.

'totalitarianism', etc.)" (DSST 3) and colludes in maintaining the academic and governing status quo.

In charting the space in which Marx has been thought and rethought, and Marxism redeveloped, in current continental philosophy, the dual concepts of the state and totalitarianism, and the concomitant tension between the political and the social that these concepts mark, can be helpfully utilized as a prism through which to appraise the field. There are those, such as Chantal Mouffe and Ernesto Laclau, who explicitly embrace democracy and call for hegemonic rearticulations of the state and the political sphere; and there are those, such as Alain Badiou, Giorgio Agamben, and Žižek, who reject or are ambivalent about democracy, or are apprehensive of the alliance between the state and the political, and who thus call for an articulation of the political outside all state forms. Finally, there is Jacques Rancière, whose sympathies are with democracy although he redefines it as a project wholly incongruent with the state. This essay will attempt to situate these philosophers and their varying connections and divergences. In the first instance, we must begin with how "the political" is defined, since it is on this definition that many of the other aspects of the rethinking of Marx are built.

While Lefort and Arendt locate politics in the division between society and the state, Rancière argues that this division itself is a product of partitioning, of giving a part, or carving up the sensible world into what can and cannot be seen or heard. This work of giving and maintaining order is characterized by Rancière as the sphere of policy or the police. In the preface to *Disagreement*, Rancière explicitly takes up the premise that Marxism has "turned the political into the expression, or mask, of social relationships,"[4] and the conclusion that with its collapse, "the social and its ambiguities" have been abandoned in favor of a purified political philosophy. Rancière counters that the return of political philosophy is belied both by the evacuation of political activity that is concurrent with its supposed resurrection, and by the oxymoronic sterility of the phrase "political philosophy" itself, which, insofar as it theorizes law and order, or the *arkhe* of distribution, might better be called a philosophy of the police. Philosophy, he writes, only "becomes 'political' when it embraces aporia or the quandary proper to politics" (D ix), which is the quandary of equality. While "the self-proclaimed 'restorers' of politics and of 'its' philosophy revel in the opposition of the political and the social" (D 91), Rancière asserts to the contrary that "the 'philosophical' return of politics and its sociological 'end' are one and the same" (D 93).

---

4. Jacques Rancière, *Disagreement: Politics and Philosophy*, Julie Rose (trans.) (Minneapolis, MN: University of Minnesota Press, 1999), vii. Hereafter cited as D followed by the page number.

Rancière elegantly captures the current state of political theory and its various conundrums in both *On the Shores of Politics* and *Hatred of Democracy*. In the former, he is particularly attuned to the glib and self-congratulatory proclamations of a politics that claims to be freed from philosophical hopes for a more perfect world. Declaring the end of "utopian islands and millenarian dreams," these oracles instead reassure us of "more accessible earthly paradises."[5] "One might merely smile," Rancière scoffs, "at the alacrity with which political administrators look forward to the time when politics will be over and they can at last get on with political business undisturbed" (OSP 3). The crux of this overcoming and putting to rest of politics is the demise or ruin of utopian promise, "for the original evil," as this narrative tell us, "was the promise itself," fundamentally "murderous" in its complicity with the future *telos* of a community (OSP 5). Politics has, at last, in this view, abandoned "the programme of liberation and a promise of happiness" (OSP 6) and thus awakened to the insidious transformation of dreams into nightmares (*ibid.*) and the promise of the best into the "promise of the worst" (OSP 9). In the later *Hatred of Democracy*, Rancière further specifies what these supposed terrors are within democracy characterized as the reign of excess; the erosion of borders; the dissolution of politics into limitlessness; the devouring of the state; and "the religion of the collective and the blind fury of the hordes."[6] The haters of democracy, Rancière attests, have falsely characterized "a childish humanity whose dream of engendering itself anew leads to self-destruction" (HD 28). Summed up, these formulations amount to an elegiac mockery of the thesis that "democracy = limitlessness = society," an insistence that the rumors of the death of politics have been greatly exaggerated.

Political philosophy, meanwhile, seems immortal, its death always deferred in the repeated attempts to make the political identical with itself, closing the gap between politics and the police. Rancière conceptualizes the life of political philosophy under three main rubrics: archipolitics, parapolitics, and metapolitics. Archipolitics is associated with Plato and indicates a foundation that is completely realized "with nothing left over" (D 65). In archipolitics, the community is wholly saturated with law such that *physis* and *nomos* are fully identified and contingency has been eliminated (D 68). Parapolitics is associated with Aristotle, and later Hobbes, and indicates a struggle for dominion or the formulation of a social contract that determines sovereignty. And metapolitics is associated with Marx and the idea that political conflict will come to an end when its motor, the economic processes that drive it and produce "a radical surplus

---

5. Jacques Rancière, *On the Shores of Politics*, Liz Heron (trans.) (London: Verso, 1995), 3. Hereafter cited as OSP followed by the page number.
6. Jacques Rancière, *Hatred of Democracy*, Steve Corcoran (trans.) (London: Verso, 2006), 14. Hereafter cited as HD followed by the page number.

of injustice" or "absolute wrong" (D 81), are fully resolved. Insofar as metapolitics conceives of politics as merely a lie or mask, "the social is always ultimately reducible to the simple untruth of politics" (D 83). If the social is "the truth of politics" (*ibid.*), the truth of its lie, then all politics is mere ideology (D 85) and the Marxist withering away of the state produces, or aims to produce, a pure administration that would perfectly map the social body. Metapolitics thereby repeats the archipolitical dream of closure, the end of politics in its "absolutization" (D 86). Rancière, however, distinguishes his own project from the Marxist one insofar as he takes the people to be "different from itself, internally divided" (D 87). Neither the state nor society is a unity, and the people cannot be equated "with a sociologically determinable part" (D 99), since they have no place in the established order. What nonetheless might continue to go by the name of class struggle is the equality "of anyone and everyone" (D 17), an equality that is presupposed by the social order that attempts to deny it.

Rancière thus reconceives class struggle as staging the spectacle of equality. In class struggle, a speech act "subjectifies the part of those who have no part" (D 38) by making possible "a space where they are countable as uncounted" (D 39) or where their status as speakers of the *logos*, of words and not merely noise, can be comprehended as universal. He claims that "the party of the rich has only ever said one thing, which is most precisely the negation of politics: there is no part of those who have no part" (D 14). This party is "antipolitical," policing the parts of a contractual society. But, since the *arkhe* is always premised on a "lie that invents some kind of social nature" (D 16), any social order will be contingent and will always ensure a dispute or disagreement, an "equality that gnaws away at any natural order" (*ibid.*). Hierarchy, the order of the city, is confronted with anarchy, its disordering. Without *arkhe*, the claims of politics to sublimate chaotic nature and produce security, stability, and equal representation are disrupted and politics cannot be identified "with the self of a community" (D 64).

The bedrock of this presupposition of equality lies in the equality of understanding that any speaking being is also a logical being, that the disjunction "between logical animals and speaking animals" (D 22) is itself never a given but always the effect of a social and sensory ordering and thus "the very dispute that institutes politics" (*ibid.*) by establishing domination. The quandary of equality thus presents a disjunction between two logics, the egalitarian logic of politics and the distributive logic of the police, the latter characterized by Rancière as the form of governance that defines the "configuration of the perceptible" (D 29), arranging sensible reality, ordering and allocating "ways of doing, ways of being, and ways of saying" (*ibid.*), giving each body its "particular place and task" (*ibid.*), and pursuing, in utilitarian fashion, the happiness or good of the community. As the name Rancière gives to the rules and policies that govern what can appear and who can be counted, a regime of "total visibility" (D 104), the police are also the order of identity and exchange, negotiating conflicts of interest, defining properties and predicates and determining "a population exactly identical to the counting of its parts" (*ibid.*). Politics, to the contrary, disrupts or challenges the distribution of bodies in social space precisely because it is an activity that springs from "the part of those who have no part" (D 30), that is, those whose placement or configuration is heterogenous to what the police order renders perceptible.

Rancière argues that a "wrong" is perpetuated whenever people are "deprived of *logos*" (D 23), condemned "to the night of silence or to the animal noise of voices expressing pleasure or pain" (D 22), that is, whenever their voices are taken to be of no account, thereby instituting a gap between speech and *logos*. But while social bodies might be subject to an inegalitarian distribution, as speaking beings they can demonstrate their equality.[7] As demonstrable, equality is the "incommensurable" that "ruins in advance the project of the city ordered according to the proportion of the *cosmos* and based on the *arkhe* of the community" (D 19). Foundation, measurement, ratio, the mission of a single logic or principle of unity that could capture the good of all and found the state on its secure basis, is thereby impossible, although its quest is the source of all politics, since "politics such as it is is encountered, always in place already, by whoever tries to found the community on its *arkhe*" (D 18). Equality is thus portrayed, in contrast to the description of order, as, variously, quandary, aporia, heterogeneity, disagreement, antagonism, incommensurability, interruption, polemic, and paradox, that is, as the foreign principle of politics.

Never simply given, neither an essence nor a goal, neither a tool nor a means (D 33), the principle of equality is pure premise, the permanent assumption of politics in its dispute with the police. This premise is activated in its performance, a performance that is simultaneously a subjectification and a disidentification, bringing into being a who that can "measure the gap" (D 36) that it itself manifests, the gap between the acknowledged count of the social and natural order and that which cannot be counted in the given terms of perception, within its frame of reference or field of experience. Rather than a founding or giving form, politics for Rancière is a decomposition and disruption of the regime of appearance. Although the wrong is a miscount, politics is not a better accounting or the providing of an "exact count" (D 28), which would be merely

---

7. For Rancière, women's exclusion from universal suffrage is exemplary of the paradox of excluding some from "the equality of all before the law" (D 41). Women, in this example, is not the group of those who share a set of properties or the name of a collective body or social category; it is instead "the class of the uncounted that only exists in the very declaration in which they are counted as those of no account" (D 38). The demonstration of equality exposes the nonuniversality of universal law, the illogic of the logic of the count. This exhibition of *logos* thereby contradicts and counteracts the ruling order's attempts to deny the *logos* to some.

another policing of demographic categories in administration of particularities; as a response to miscount, "politics exists because those who have no right to be counted as speaking beings make themselves of some account" (D 27).

Politics is thus disagreement or "the practices driven by the assumption of equality between any and every speaking being and by the concern to test this equality" (D 30). This emphasis on process and practice underlines the performative dynamic Rancière attributes to politics, the theatrical or dramatic element of its staging. In its contestation of the partition of the sensible, politics is "*aesthetic* in principle" (D 58, emphasis added). In its subversive presentation of equality, the "act of equality" (D 34) has an *evental* aspect that "cannot consist in any form of social bond whatsoever" (*ibid.*). Politics is "upsetting" (D 49) because its speech act poses the truth of equality against the lie of social reality, contradicting in its *performance* (its *aesthetic event*) the non-count of the speaker as a speaking being. This spectacularity makes apparent what the police render incomprehensible, showing the speaker to be a speaking being. So, while the police create order and form a social bond, politics disrupts established harmony (D 28) and invents "worlds of dissension" (D 58). Politics thus only and always confirms, stages, demonstrates, asserts, dramatizes, and/or occupies equality, and it is this activity, this performance, this speech act, that thereby subverts any social order, a subversion that is not the aftereffect of the demonstration but the demonstration itself. So, whereas the police "can procure all sorts of good" (D 31) and indeed have the good as their *telos* (promoting security and tranquility), political activity secures nothing, stabilizes no social bond, promises no fully realized city; it does nothing but stage over and over again the demonstration of equality, which is its "sole principle" (*ibid.*). And this principle is decidedly not an *arkhe* since it founds no order; it is fundamentally anarchic, "the name of nothing" (D 35). The scandal of politics is "its lack of any proper foundation" (D 61). It has no identity or essence and no remedy that would resolve its difference from itself. The distinction between police and politics, Rancière claims (in one of many departures from Althusser[8]), does not mirror

---

8. For all the authors discussed here, departures and divergences notwithstanding, Althusser appears to have played a decisive role, insofar as his structuralist reading of Marx, his bringing together of Freud (and Lacan) and Marx, and his theory of the subject of ideology, provide the frame of reference (the academic state or situation, we could say) of philosophical Marxism. Both Badiou and Rancière, and for similar reasons, break with Althusser's structuralism as (over)determining the logic of the situation in a way that impedes the possibility of a break with that situation or an irruption from within. For Althusser, whose work rests on a sharp if complicated epistemological distinction between science and ideology, the subject is fundamentally entangled with ideology, is in fact subjectivized by ideology even while constitutive of it; ideology is an identificatory practice. Badiou and Rancière, however, ally subjectivization with truth and with disidentification. [*] For a discussion of Althusser, see the essay by Warren Montag in *The History of Continental Philosophy: Volume 6.*

that between state and society; it does not proclaim the State a dead and rigid machine opposed to the life of society (D 29).

If the people are not equal to themselves, democracy cannot be reduced to social relations nor to any coincidence between form and content, law and spirit, individual and community. This imaginary "idyllic state" of consensus or the "inclusion of all" (D 116), which is always counterposed to totalitarianism, Rancière renames "postdemocracy" (D 95), the nihilistic reassertion of unity and totality, or the identity of humanity with itself, whose image serves as the basis of many critiques of so-called democracy. Against the postdemocratic order of consensus, entangling state and society without residue, Rancière asserts that democracy is the "mode of subjectification" that disrupts or interrupts the "order of distribution of bodies as a community" (D 99). As bodies, the many are doomed to "a purely individual life that passes on nothing to posterity except for life itself, reduced to its reproductive function" (D 23). Rancière thus makes a fundamental distinction between animal being and speaking being. The premise of equality, that is, of equality before the *logos*, although a premise, nonetheless depends for its demonstration on the postulate that "the modern political animal is first a literary animal" (D 37), entangled in the gap "between the order of words and the order of bodies" (*ibid.*), between voice and violence.

Rancière develops this account of the political speech act around mathematical and literary tropes, features that are reinforced by Alain Badiou with his reliance on Lacanian psychoanalysis and Cantorian set theory. Badiou's thought will be treated in the next essay. We can, however, offer a preliminary contrast between these two students of Althusser here. Rancière and Badiou diverge significantly in at least two ways: first, in their assessment of democracy and democratic promise; and second, in their assessment of the rights of man. In the first instance, Badiou accuses Rancière of being too much a democrat,[9] not enough of a militant, and in the end still a political philosopher (M 120), while not *doing* either politics or philosophy (M 115–16). For Rancière, democracy is first of all anarchy (HD 41); it "is neither a society to be governed, nor a government of society, [but] is specifically this ungovernable on which every government must ultimately find out it is based" (HD 49). As neither government nor society, "it is the action that constantly wrests the monopoly of public life from oligarchic governments, and the omnipotence over lives from the power of wealth" (HD 96) and is thus the "vision that even today sustains the hope of a communism or a democracy of the multitude" (*ibid.*). While Badiou concurs that politics is action that disrupts the state, he claims that even democracy, in a formula adopted from Lenin, is merely a "*form of State*" (M 79) or an "exercise

---

9. Alain Badiou, *Metapolitics*, Jason Barker (trans.) (London: Verso, 2005), 120. Hereafter cited as M followed by the page number.

of sovereignty" (*ibid.*). Thus, just as the State must wither away, so too must democracy, which, precisely through its romanticization, devolves into "mass sovereignty" (M 88) or "terroristic-fraternity" (89). Since politics, or communist politics, "strives for its own disappearance" (M 80), Badiou proposes an appeal to "'equality' or 'communism' but certainly not the word 'democracy'" (*ibid.*). "'Democracy' can be retrieved as a political category," Badiou argues, only as "a politics of emancipation [that] does not have the State as its ultimate referent" (M 92); it is then the designation for "the effectiveness of politics" (*ibid.*). Even so, the quarrel with Rancière seems more semantic than fundamental: Badiou writes, in a turn of phrase that could just as well have been written by Rancière, that the work of the "emancipatory process" is toward the impossibility "of every non-egalitarian statement concerning the situation" (M 93).

This divergent appraisal of democracy is echoed, second, in a conflicting verdict on human rights. For Rancière, the demonstration of equality is the staging of a "nonexistent right" (D 25), the right of those who have no rights. A right, for Rancière, "is not the illusory attribute of an ideal subject; it is the arguing of a wrong" (D 89), and thus rights emerge in their declaration, in the demand that lays claim to equality, in the repudiation of the status quo and its count or miscount. Marx's essay "On the Jewish Question" is then the quintessential metapolitical text in Rancière's view, marking a gap between man and citizen, society and state, political and human, whose destiny is to be overcome (M 82, 87). But politics for Rancière takes place in the interplay between police law and its declamatory dispute; Marx's critique of human rights as merely bourgeois rights presupposes an end to the alienating split of subjectivity, the possibility of its being perfectly identical with itself without disjunction. The rights of man, however, are not rights that predicate or belong to the human, but a subjectifying claim that entails disidentification. Rancière offers a formula for rights in his essay "Who is the Subject of the Rights of Man?": "the Rights of Man are the rights of those who have not the rights that they have and have the rights that they have not."[10] In formulating this paradox, Rancière argues that Arendt's critique of human rights renders them either tautological or empty. Rather than viewing the rights of man as either rights of the already politicized citizen or nonexistent, the impasse attributed to Arendt, Rancière contends that this dilemma is itself an artifice of the ruling configuration and that in action that lays claim to rights, this given is disputed and the subject politicizes itself.[11]

---

10. Jacques Rancière, "Who is the Subject of the Rights of Man?" *The South Atlantic Quarterly* 103(2/3) (Spring/Summer 2004), 302. Hereafter cited as WSRM followed by the page number.

11. Lefort makes a similar claim in "Politics and Human Rights" (Alan Sheridan [trans.], in *The Political Forms of Modern Society*, John B. Thompson [ed.] [Cambridge, MA: MIT Press, 1986]), maintaining that human rights are a practice of what is not (yet) real that penetrates and transforms civil society. Challenging Marx's reduction of rights to mere formality

By contrast, Badiou characterizes his work as "a political attack against the ideology of human rights and a defense of antihumanism."[12] In doing so, he claims to be launching a wholesale critique of "democratic totalitarianism" (E lv) and the dominant themes of progressive politics, even and especially those that might appear as most radical. His work begins with two premises that might at first seem irreconcilable, and proceeds from there to develop a series of oppositions. The first premise is that universality entails what he calls "eternal truth," and the second is that such truths are not transcendent but immanent; there is no "heaven of truths" (E 43). These premises are resolved as "an ethics of singular truths" (E lvi), a resolution that requires clear contrasts between truth and knowledge, subjective and objective, event and situation. The event is a singular break with the situation, the subject is induced by truth, and truth remains uncaptured by the order of knowledge that it ruptures. What Badiou means by an ethic, in contrast to the reigning ethics, is continued fidelity to the event of the universal as a break with history and militant adherence to truth.

In *The Sublime Object of Ideology*, Slavoj Žižek distinguishes the Althusserian idea of ideological alienation from the Lacanian one of fundamental antagonism. In the former, still consistent with "the traditional Marxist notion of social antagonism,"[13] there is both a prioritization of a particular antagonism that is considered determinative in the last instance and the possibility of resolving that antagonism within history. By contrast, the Lacanian deadlock does not prioritize a particular antagonism and holds out no hope of final resolution. In this way, according to Žižek, it exemplifies the "post-Marxist" break with utopian logics. The psychoanalytic account of the subject is not accidental to this post-Marxist logic: "the 'death drive,' this dimension of radical negativity, cannot be reduced to an expression of alienated social conditions, it defines *la condition humaine* as such: there is no solution, no escape from it" (SOI 5). The idea of harmonious being, whether within or between human beings, is a dangerous aspiration, even a "totalitarian temptation" (*ibid.*), and the gesture or hope toward reconciliation is the gesture of terrorism. We must instead discover

---

disguising the working of power, Lefort contends that human rights are neither individualist nor unitary, but are a bond of "antagonism" (*ibid.*, 266, 272) or "plurality, fragmentation, heterogeneity" (*ibid.*, 271) that threatens the fantasy of a One and "the loving grip of the good society" (*ibid.*, 272). Lefort's analysis is, however, significantly different from Rancière's insofar as it privileges the limitation of power that the law symbolically enacts (i.e. it privileges the state). Nonetheless, there is a promissory element in Lefort's depiction that is not wholly divergent from Rancière's characterization.

12. Alain Badiou, *Ethics: An Essay on the Understanding of Evil*, Peter Hallward (trans.) (London: Verso, 2001), liv. Hereafter cited as E followed by the page number.

13. Slavoj Žižek, *The Sublime Object of Ideology* (London: Verso, 1989), 3. Hereafter cited as SOI followed by the page number.

a *"modus vivendi"* (a "form-of-life" in Agamben's terms) with this "terrifying dimension" of destruction and impossibility that is inculcated by language.

Crucially, the psychoanalytic theory of antagonism does not derive it from social causes. Antagonism is rather an irreducible element of psychic formation, of a fundamental aggressivity within that no amount of cultural change can dispense with. We must instead reverse the presupposition of social constructionism: social antagonisms are themselves founded on "an original 'trauma,' an impossible kernel which resists symbolization, totalization, symbolic integration" (SOI 6). This traumatic element of "a blind automatism of repetition beyond pleasure-seeking self-preservation" reveals the impossibility built into the pursuit of goods. The project of capitalism, maintaining the circulation of goods in a cycle of generation and degeneration, of expenditure, consumption, exhaustion, and collapse, bringing them into being and passing away, is thus inherently and internally self-destructive, an effect of its own limit.

In understanding this critique of goods, it is useful to bring together, as Žižek does, the Marxist and Freudian notions of "fetish." For Freud,[14] the fetish has a very specific meaning and purpose, serving as a substitute for the mother's missing phallus. The fetish appears where the other's castration is too intense, too traumatic and uncanny, to bear; in place of the missing object, the fetishist installs one that can be made present, thereby exemplifying the psychical mechanism of disavowal whereby a belief is simultaneously retained and given up. Fetishism is thus a very peculiar articulation of the *fort–da* game: a mode of playing with absence and presence in which the replacement object signifies both castration and not castration, the traumatic perceptual presence of an absence (the encounter with castration) and the reassuring absence of a presence (the denial of reality). The fetish is a kind of monument to absence insofar as it both buries and commemorates the horror of castration, thereby testifying to the very reality it denies, its displaced presence. The formula, as Žižek borrows it from Octave Mannoni, of "I know very well but all the same I don't believe it," carries this doubled relation to knowledge, acknowledging reality while nonetheless retaining a belief that runs counter to it.

For Marx,[15] the fetish also serves a veiling function, presenting as magically apparent the commodity that in fact is the objectification of the labor process and dissociating its value from the value of human freedom that this process eradicates. The commodity is thus granted a level of autonomy, independence,

---

14. See Freud's essays "Fetishism" (1927), in *The Standard Edition of the Complete Works of Sigmund Freud, vol. XXI,* James Strachey (ed. and trans.) (London: Hogarth Press, 1968) and "The Splitting of the Ego in the Process of Defense" (1938), in *The Standard Edition, vol. XXIII,* Strachey (ed. and trans.).

15. See Karl Marx, *Capital,* volume 1, chapter 1, section 4, in *The Marx–Engels Reader* (New York: Norton, 1978).

and self-sufficiency that the worker is not. Its displacement of value holds at bay the labor relation that brings it into being, and it thereby takes the place of, substitutes for, the missing social relation. The commodity then appears as transcendent, enigmatic, and mystical, a social thing "whose qualities are at the same time perceptible and imperceptible," fantasmatically replacing "a definite social relation between men."[16]

Both of these types of fetishism, the Marxist and the Freudian, function through mechanisms similar to that of the dreamwork: it is not merely a latent content that is concealed (this attachment to content is itself fetishistic according to Žižek), but rather *"the 'secret' of this form itself"* (SOI 11), its work of condensation and displacement (i.e. of overdetermination) that makes possible its genesis. The real question with regard to both the work that forms the dream and the work that forms "the value of a commodity" (*ibid.*) is how or why this form has been assumed. In the pursuit of goods, the disturbing, strangely familiar secret is less the fundamental lack of a fully harmonious social relation than the very process of disavowal, of knowing and not believing, that gives it form. Through this disavowal of reality (the reality that the social does not exist), fetishism procures the ever-widening circulation of goods, goods that, in keeping consumers attached to objects whose value is misplaced and whose source is not admitted, both reject and retain, pervert and procure, the idea of phallic fullness that never was and can never be: *this* is the object that has the power to fully satisfy me. The free circulation of goods takes the place of human freedom and equality, fills in for their lack, such that the false universalism of bourgeois rights and duties is not simply an inadequacy to live up to its own ideals, but a constitutive fantasy that structures social reality: not a delusion, but a fetish-work that generates and gives shape.

While the discussion of fetishism may have seemed a detour, it is crucial not only to understanding the entanglement of psychoanalysis with contemporary Marxist thought, but also to understanding the critique of democracy and rights developed by the militant Left. For Žižek, democracy is a political fetish and he presses for the courage to abandon "democracy" as the master-signifier of the chain of political signifiers (SOI 78). Crucially for Žižek, the fetish conceals a lack, not a positivity, around which social relations are articulated (SOI 49). The disavowal of absence, the absence of a social relation, explains for Žižek the romanticized attachment to fraternal democracy that nonetheless retains an inability to acknowledge that the father is dead. Fetishism, whether Marxist or Freudian, thereby indicates a fundamental political truth: the splitting of reality that indicates an internal (not external) antagonism, dislocation, and disruption within any perceptual or articulated form of understanding, a gap between

---

16. Karl Marx, *Capital*, in *The Marx–Engels Reader*, 320, 321.

what we know and what we believe. The effect of disavowal is then a habitual vacillation between the vernacular of contingency and the quest for security; without the guarantee of fullness or the fullness of guarantee, the brother–citizen–fetishist reintroduces the paternal function over and over again in the biopolitical gesture of optimization that impedes political action. Sovereignty, or the fear of its absence, is intimately tied to biopower, as both undergird the violence of law and the liberal democratic illusion of freedom and equality.

Žižek pointedly disparages the predominant multiculturalist mode of respecting the "other" that prevails in the "New World Order that poses as the tolerant universe of differences,"[17] just as he mocks the rise of identity politics and its etceteral structure (race, gender, sexuality, etc.). Žižek finds the "underlying ontological vision" of an "irreducible plurality of particular constellations, each of them multiple and displaced in itself" (WDR 65), to be vapid and arid. This vision, the latest variant of nihilism, "masks the underlying monotony of today's global life" (WDR 68), while also encouraging the pseudo-radicalism of taking pleasure in dreaming about and demanding things one does not really want.

But, whereas Žižek sees in democracy the disavowal of social antagonism, Laclau and Mouffe define radical democracy precisely *as* social antagonism. In *Hegemony and Socialist Strategy*, Laclau and Mouffe reflect on the demise of what they characterize as "the Jacobin imaginary."[18] This imaginary had rested on a series of assumptions now in crisis: the epistemological and ontological privilege of the working class, the promise of revolution, and the fantasy of social unity that would "render pointless the moment of politics" (HSS 2). In rethinking Marxism and its stakes, Laclau and Mouffe take the concept of "hegemony" as a "fundamental nodal point of Marxist political theorization" (HSS 3), and moreover one whose logic is heterogenous to other basic Marxist categories (*ibid.*), especially to the rationalism of dialectical materialism and its presumption of historical necessity. Hegemony provides the basis for the development of contingency, as against necessity, and thus for the specificity of a variety of social struggles. Laclau and Mouffe thus describe their project as elaborating a "new conception of politics" (*ibid.*) that is explicitly both "*post*-Marxist" and "post-*Marxist*" (HSS 4), a dual emphasis that marks a trajectory that simultaneously insists on and departs from its Marxist origin. In this joint formulation of radical democracy, Marxism becomes repoliticized (and to some extent de-economized) in a transformation of emancipatory discourse that situates it within the clamor and claims for universality on the part of various particularities.

---

17. Slavoj Žižek, *Welcome to the Desert of the Real: Five Essays on September 11 and Related Dates* (London: Verso, 2002), 94. Hereafter cited as WDR followed by the page number.
18. Ernesto Laclau and Chantal Mouffe, *Hegemony and Socialist Strategy* (London: Verso, 1985), 2. Hereafter cited as HSS followed by the page number.

With Lefort, Laclau and Mouffe assert as well that just as democracy opens the possibility of "hegemonic articulations" (HSS 187), it also carries the immanent possibility of a totalitarian logic that would attempt to reoccupy the space of power, fill in its missing substance, and control its "radical indeterminacy" (HSS 188). Their work thus articulates a fundamental alliance with the Marx of class consciousness and a departure from the Marx of economic determinism and historical materialism, isolating these two strands from one another. In later and separate works, Laclau and Mouffe further pursue the theme of antagonism and democratic struggle. I will focus on just one exemplary essay here.

Laclau's essay "New Reflections on the Revolution of Our Time" perhaps most explicitly clarifies which principles he retains from Marx and which he leaves behind. He calls this work a "manifesto,"[19] and presents the argument of the essay "as a logical sequence of its [Marxism's] categories" (NRRT 4). Laclau here charts a distinction between negativity and objectivity, or between antagonism and contradiction (NRRT 7), affiliating the former with the political and the latter with the social (NRRT 35). With this schema, Laclau articulates the fundamental tension between the political and the social by arguing that while political action seeks a "reconciled and transparent society" (ibid.), such a society would be the annihilation of politics.[20] Politics seeks its own impossibility in the realization of a harmonious social totality, since such a society would no longer be properly political (ibid.). Laclau here adamantly distinguishes between social totality, on the one hand, and politics, on the other. The social is defined as the realm of "the sedimented forms of objectivity" (ibid.) and it is formulated on the model of the *oikos* and its good government with which it is taken to be homologous; the political is defined as the realm of subjectivity and it is formulated on the model of the *polis* or city taken as a site of dissension rather than of good government. The social is the realm of goods as potential or proto-totality (including not only material goods, but most especially the good of the community), and its logic requires ever better management; the political is outside this order of exchange and regulation, and is the realm of freedom. According to Laclau, there is politics because there is "subversion and dislocation of the social" (NRRT 61). And yet, and herein lies the crux of the paradox, the domain of the political founds itself on the creation of some, however imaginative or contentious, vision of ideal closure and reconciliation. Since the social is internally uneven and antagonistic, the subject is "thrown up" (NRRT 44) into a political world of freedom by social and subjective dislocation and incompletion.

---

19. Ernesto Laclau, "New Reflection on the Revolution of Our Time," in *New Reflections on the Revolution of Our Time* (London: Verso, 1990), 5. Hereafter cited as NRRT followed by the page number.
20. Cf. Rancière's claim that "every politics works on the verge of its radical demise" (D 91).

Laclau also distinguishes between subjects and subject-positions or the location of individuals within sedimented social forms. Identities, for Laclau, are established only through relations of difference and are thereby immanently self-sundering; there is no pure externality but instead a "constitutive outside" of identity, such that differences always already inhere in the formation of any identity. Rather than an integrative gesture that inscribes identity in a social whole, as a subject-position, politics in this view is that which interrupts the inscription of particular and predicated subjects into a social whole. While predication and identification particularize us as parts of a whole, members of subsets, thereby divesting us of singularity, interruption singularizes a subject in calling him or her to a task uniquely her own. As the dissemination of the singular rather than the sum total of particulars, the universal cannot be integrated into the whole, a constitutive failure that points to the future possibility of radical democracy since it requires us, as Laclau puts it, "not to understand what society is but what prevents it from being" (NRRT 44). The universal functions through the dislocation of subjects who are not fully placed socially and whose freedom lies in the failure of the structure to fully constitute an identity (*ibid.*). To restate the political paradox, then, we could say, with Laclau, that politics aims toward an "impossible object [society] and thus toward the elimination of the conditions of liberty itself" (*ibid.*). Politics is irreconcilable with the very element that makes politics possible, both because of the paradox earlier discussed – that subjectivity and politics would annihilate their own founding conditions if fully achieved – and also because its possibility lies in the rootless, groundless ground beyond life and history where the signifier emerges.

As Žižek clarifies, the "radical" of radical democracy must be taken in a paradoxical sense, as it does not aim "at a radical solution," but instead acknowledges "a kind of postponing of a fundamental impossibility" (SOI 6). It is thus not a "pure, true democracy; its radical character implies, on the contrary, that we can save democracy only by *taking into account its own radical impossibility*" (*ibid.*). The only solutions are particular ones, and they always entail a radical irresolution, a permanent deadlock. In "An Ethics of Militant Engagement," Laclau writes about his theoretical relation to Badiou, taking up Žižek's claim in *The Ticklish Subject* that Badiou and Laclau share a "deep homology" insofar as both turn away from the Hegelian and Marxist notion of "reconciliation between Universal and Particular."[21] They instead, according to Žižek, assert "a constitutive and irreducible gap," although this gap is different for each. For Laclau it can

---

21. Slavoj Žižek, *The Ticklish Subject: The Absent Centre of Political Ontology* (London: Verso, 2000), 172–3. Hereafter cited as TS followed by the page number. Cited by Ernesto Laclau, "An Ethics of Militant Engagement," in *Think Again: Alain Badiou and the Future of Philosophy*, P. Hallward (ed.) (London: Continuum, 2004), 120–21.

be characterized as "the gap between the Particular and the empty Universal" or as that between "the differential structure of the positive social order … and properly political antagonism." For Badiou, it is "the gap between Being and Event" (*ibid*.). For both, there is a dimension of "decision." While Laclau professes to find Badiou's thought "congenial,"[22] especially in its affirmative and emancipatory commitments, he also questions the ontological and mathematical underpinnings of Badiou's epistemology and its capacity to distinguish truth and disaster. Thus, although Badiou, Žižek, and Laclau can come across as allied insofar as they all borrow fundamental premises from Lacan, Žižek seems a necessary hinge figure here, the one that binds them together.

Agamben is noticeably less psychoanalytic in his perspective, and his work is premised on eminently non-Marxist sources and suppositions, in particular those of Carl Schmitt, Arendt, and Michel Foucault,[23] allying these three together in a remarkable amalgamation of their conceptual leverage. From Schmitt, Agamben takes up the concepts of sovereignty and the state of exception; from Arendt that of totalitarianism and the critique of human rights, as well as the rise of government as administration of an all-encompassing social sphere figured on the order of the *oikos*; and from Foucault the concept of biopower. Were we to situate Agamben within Rancière's rubric, we could perhaps view his work as a version of the modern metapolitical view that sees "the democratic gap as a symptom of untruth" (D 91). Certainly Agamben aims at a certain closure or overcoming of a rift in being. At the same time, his work can be understood as offering a critique of the imbrication of modern parapolitics and archipolitics in a form of sovereignty whose resultant terror aims at establishing an absolute community (D 81). In any case, Rancière also explicitly criticizes Agamben for endorsing Arendt's argument about human rights, as discussed above (WSRM 302).

In *Homo Sacer*, Agamben argues that "the production of a biopolitical body is the original activity of sovereign power,"[24] where this biopolitical body is taken to be "bare life" or *homo sacer*. Whereas Foucault claims that the entrance of *zoe* (natural life) into the polis is the fundamental condition of modernity, Agamben argues that the bond that attaches *zoe* to *bios*, the natural to the political, is "absolutely Ancient" (HS 9). Unlike Foucault, therefore, who charts a historical passage of the primary modes of power and their historical dominance from the reign of sovereignty to juridicality to discipline and biopolitics, Agamben sees

---

22. Laclau, "An Ethics of Militant Engagement," 120.
*23. Michel Foucault is discussed in the essay by Timothy O'Leary in *The History of Continental Philosophy: Volume 6*. For a discussion of Carl Schmitt, see the essay by Chris Thornhill in *The History of Continental Philosophy: Volume 5*.
24. Giorgio Agamben, *Homo Sacer: Sovereign Power and Bare Life*, Daniel Heller-Roazen (trans.) (Stanford, CA: Stanford University Press, 1998), 6. Hereafter cited as HS followed by the page number.

a structural imbrication among these forms of power: the convergence between the juridical and the biopolitical, the law and the body, is the permanent nucleus of sovereignty. If the political history of modernity or the modern history of politics thus charts an increasing "indistinction" between bare life and the law, one also marked by the collapse of democracy into totalitarianism, this confusion is realized in the biopolitical invasion of sovereignty into the everyday activities of the vulnerable body such that the camp rather than the city becomes the site or *nomos* of human (animal) being, the triumph of universal homelessness. Democracy is then defined by its biopolitical condition, allied always already with totalitarianism. The political project that is demanded is a politics that is no longer founded on the exception of bare life (which, precisely as exception, is always included) and its unity with law (HS 11). In the juncture between *homo sacer* and sovereignty, between life and law, sovereignty and biopower are the dirty secret of one another: each liminal, crossing, becoming the other, entailing a confusion between them.

Bare life is neither natural life (*zoe*) nor political life (*bios*), but something that emerges from their "zone of indistinction," just life, nothing but life, sheer life, life itself, life abandoned to itself and to death, neither *zoe* nor *bios*, neither *physis* nor *nomos* (HS 84–5, 88, 106). As sacred, bare life is "life exposed to death" (HS 88) or *homo sacer*, defined by Agamben as the one who can be killed but not sacrificed and who is thus outside all law, human or divine, political or theological, abandoned to and by the law. The double exclusion of *homo sacer* from human and divine law points toward an "originary political structure prior to the distinction between sacred and profane, religious and juridical" (HS 74). Thus, "the sacredness of life, which is invoked today as an absolutely fundamental right in opposition to sovereign power, in fact originally expresses precisely both life's subjection to a power over death and life's irreparable exposure in the relation of abandonment" (HS 83). The sacred is the mark of sovereign excess, its access to and grasp of the body. In bringing sovereignty together with bare life, Agamben writes that "the sovereign is the one with respect to whom all men are potentially *homines sacri*, and *homo sacer* is the one with respect to whom all men act as sovereigns" (HS 84).

In Žižek's view, the liberal–totalitarian state of emergency that Agamben theorizes, a state that produces only survivors, entails an alliance between victimization, humanism, and the pursuit of goods insofar as they are all oriented by the biopolitical project of the optimization of life (WDR 107). Sovereignty and biopower are then the flipside of each other: the bifurcated and dual formation of law that describes the way in which capital, and terror, operates. Žižek thus characterizes the liberal mode of subjectivity as itself *homo sacer* (WDR 71), thereby aligning Agamben with the questioning of democracy (WDR 97). And certainly Agamben's politics cannot be assimilated into the radical–democratic project (WDR 98); he is not interested in renegotiating the limits of inclusion and exclusion or the limit that separates citizen from *homo sacer* (WDR 98, 100). There is no place in Agamben for such a democratic project of renegotiation and there is, in fact, no democratic subject, but only a democratic consumer and survivor. In the postpolitical regime of biopolitics, we are all *homo sacer* (WDR 100). With no democratic way out, a messianic dimension lurks in Agamben's theory, pointing toward a future where mere life would no longer be the ultimate terrain of politics (*ibid.*), simultaneously a suspension of mere life and an embrace of mere life.

In *Means Without Ends,* Agamben argues that Marx's critique of the rights of man and his theses about human emancipation have become archaic: "The Marxian scission between man and citizen is thus suspended by the division between naked life (ultimate and opaque bearer of sovereignty) and the multifarious forms of life abstractly recodified as social–juridical identities."[25] Human rights provide no defense in camps, but simply secure the operation of biopower. Nonetheless, Agamben continues to maintain a discourse of emancipation, one that defines it as overcoming of division and "the possibility of a nonstatist politics" (MWE 8–9) as opposed to state sovereignty. In arguing for a form of life that "must become the guiding concept and the unitary center of the coming politics" (MWE 12), Agamben proposes a new relation between *zoe* and *bios*, one that does not depend on their sacrificial split. Here we have both a conjunction with and a departure from Badiou. Both Badiou and Agamben condemn the biopolitical or bioethical hold on life, the means by which the state keeps the human in its grip. For Badiou, however, the only answer to state policy is a militantly subjective politics, while for Agamben *happiness* itself becomes the source of a revolutionary form of life, a way of closing the gap that permits the zones of indistinction to dispense terror and dispense with life. As Agamben puts it at the conclusion of *Homo Sacer*, the "biopolitical body that is bare life must itself instead be transformed into the site for the constitution and installation of a form of life that is wholly exhausted in bare life and a *bios* that is only its own *zoe*" (HS 188). It might be edifying to read this opaque passage alongside a similarly opaque selection from *State of Exception*, in which Agamben envisages that "one day humanity will play with law just as children play with disused objects" (SE 64). Taking these together, Agamben suggests that the journey before us, embroiled in the enigma of our political plight, will lead to an overcoming and an arrival at justice, or failing that, we will find "unprecedented

25. Giorgio Agamben, *Means Without Ends: Notes on Politics*, Vincenzo Binetti and Cesare Casarino (trans.) (Minneapolis, MN: University of Minnesota Press, 2000), 6. Hereafter cited as MWE followed by the page number.

biopolitical catastrophe" (HS 188). In evading this dire option that he himself has so thoroughly investigated, Agamben reaches for the messianic.

Agamben's political conclusions tend to bifurcate, or combine, the Heideggerian and the Benjaminian. From Heidegger, he adopts the idea of "the end of the history of being" (MWE 110). From Walter Benjamin, he adopts the idea of a uniquely revolutionary form of violence,[26] one that, citing Benjamin, "neither makes nor preserves law, but deposes it" (SE 53). In this combination, Agamben foresees a double end: of the history of being and of the history of the state. This would be a politics of pure means, without ends, a revolutionary politics, and also the coming into history of "anarchic historicity" (MWE 111). If, also with Benjamin, the state of exception has become the rule, fundamental and exemplary, then only an "anomic violence" (SE 54), that is, a violence that does not return to the law, a violence that is "pure" in the sense of being absolved of all attachment to the law, either as constituted by it (i.e. the police) or constitutive of it (i.e. mythical violence), can transform, or better overturn, or even better dissolve, "the relation between violence and law" (SE 63). Because it is neither constitutive nor constituted, pure violence operates as a means without ends (SE 61), an absolute medium or mediation that is thereby also a dissolution. Pure violence would enact a "play with law" (SE 64) such that "the world appears as a good that absolutely cannot be appropriated or made juridical" (*ibid.*). Rather than a politics "contaminated by law," Agamben proposes instead "political action," a revolutionary event "which severs the nexus between violence and law" (SE 88), thereby allying "pure means" with "human praxis" (*ibid.*). Only this absolute violence can break with the order of the state in its homogenizing biopoliticization. Here, as with Badiou, we have a Marxist idea of an anti- or post-state politics, one that does not run from violence. As a politics beyond the law, pure, wholly removed from the violence of law or the law of violence, it is divine.[27]

What seems clear for all the philosophers discussed in this essay is that the social is viewed, if not always as a fetish, at least suspiciously; it does not exist just as the people does not exist, since there is no self-identity. This is a kind of antihumanism, as well as an antideterminism. Thus we see that the opposition between humanism and determinism has been superseded because both are rejected, the one for its argot of victimization, of the sacrificial, suffering human

26. In *State of Exception*, Kevin Attell (trans.) (Chicago, IL: University of Chicago Press, 2005), 54–9, Agamben moderates a debate between Benjamin and Schmitt on "pure" violence. Hereafter cited as SE followed by the page number.
27. There is an obviously theological dimension to much of contemporary Marxism. Badiou, Žižek, and Agamben in any case pay heed and homage to Benjamin's notion of divine violence. And, following a trajectory that seems to radically depart from Benjamin, both Žižek and Badiou treat St. Paul as a crucial figure.

animal, the other for its adherence to the logic of the situation. Instead we have a subjectivization that breaks with its history, a constitutive self-sundering, and a thinking of emancipation as making the claim to equality, via disagreement, dissensus, and antagonism. Disidentification, rather than class consciousness, has become the basic tenet of class struggle. Refusing to acquiesce or collaborate in the demise of politics, pursuing the impossible, and not merely, as Žižek cogently characterizes what passes for radicalism today, embarking on "an unending process which can destabilize, displace, and so on, the power structure" through "endless mocking parody and provocation" (WDR 101), the philosophers discussed here retain a shared fidelity to Marx's legacy by repudiating postpolitical nihilism and adamantly adhering to the task (act, presentation, supposition, appearance) of emancipation and universality.

4

THINKING THE EVENT: ALAIN BADIOU'S PHILOSOPHY AND THE TASK OF CRITICAL THEORY

Bruno Bosteels

There can be no doubt that the notion of the event constitutes one of the core concepts in contemporary philosophy, cutting across the divide between so-called "continental" and "analytic" thought. From Martin Heidegger to Jacques Derrida and from Alfred North Whitehead to Donald Davidson, a modern or contemporary philosopher can be defined as one who develops the conceptual tools necessary to think through the peculiar nature of an event as such. The result of this agreement is actually a striking paradox. The event, which in most versions is supposed to mark an unprecedented break with the status quo, has itself become today a matter of strict consensus. What should be absolutely singular and chance-like is on the verge of being drowned out in the bland unanimity of nonthought. In the words of the late François Zourabichvili: "The theme of the event lies at the center of philosophical preoccupations today, it animates the most daring and the most original projects. But the spirit of the time does not provide in and of itself a philosophy and should not mask irreconcilable differences."[1] To save the event from the risk of complete shipwreck in this process, few endeavors could be more urgent than an overview of the history and theory of the event, or rather of events in the plural, since the uses of this concept are so numerous and variegated as to block nearly all possible

---

1. François Zourabichvili, *Deleuze: Une philosophie de l'événement* (Paris: Presses Universitaires de France, 1996), 20. Badiou himself refers to the ubiquity of the concept of the event in *Logiques des mondes: L'Être et l'événement, 2* (Paris: Éditions du Seuil, 2006), 403, translations of French editions throughout are mine; published in English as *Logics of Worlds: Being and Event, Volume 2*, Alberto Toscano (trans.) (London: Continuum, 2008). Hereafter cited as LW followed by the page number.

comparison. Indeed, there seem to be as many versions of the concept of the event as there are philosophers who claim to stand in its lineage.

Alain Badiou[2] is certainly among the more forceful proponents of a full-bodied doctrine of the event, one polemical and ambitious enough to compete with alternative versions that can be found in the works not only of Heidegger or Derrida but also of Michel Foucault, Gilles Deleuze, or Jean-François Lyotard.[3] It is precisely through the category of the event that Badiou, as he puts it in his *Manifesto for Philosophy*, proposes to take one more step in the reconfiguration of modern philosophy over and against the widespread declarations of its imminent end, crisis, or closure, especially in the guise of Western metaphysics: "A single step. A step within the modern configuration, the one that since Descartes has bound the three nodal concepts of being, truth and the subject to the conditions of philosophy."[4] For Badiou, the event is that which ties these three nodal concepts into a single philosophical knot. How then can we capture the singular force of this use of the concept of the event, if at the same time we want to avoid the generalized state of homonymy that surrounds it in the context of contemporary thought? Wherein lies the pull of Badiou's treatment of being, truth, and subject by way of the event? How can we account for the fact that this pull now seems to have become unstoppable, especially among newer generations of students, artists, scholars, activists, and so on?

I. TRAJECTORIES

In order to highlight the singularity of Badiou's ongoing philosophical project, I propose to mark three trajectories in and out of his thinking of the event. The first one is conceptual and tries to come to grips with the way in which being, event, truth, and subject fit into a unified philosophical system. Badiou in fact is adamant about what he considers to be the necessarily systematic nature of philosophy insofar as "it is of the essence of philosophy to be systematic, and no philosopher has ever doubted this, from Plato to Hegel" (MP 65). On the most general level, we could say that Badiou's system, like Hegel's, remains dialectical

---

2. Alain Badiou (January 17, 1937– ; born in Rabat, Morocco) was educated at the École Normale Supérieure (1956–61) and gained his habilitation in 1989. His influences include Althusser, Canguilhem, Lacan, Mao, Marx, and Sartre. He has held appointments at the University of Reims (1965–69), the University of Paris VIII–Vincennes-St. Denis (1969–99), and the École Normale Supérieure (1999–2006).

*3. The work of Deleuze, Derrida, Foucault, and Lyotard is treated in individual essays in *The History of Continental Philosophy: Volume 6*.

4. Alain Badiou, *Manifesto for Philosophy*, Norman Madarasz (ed. and trans.) (Albany, NY: SUNY Press, 1999), 32. Hereafter cited as MP followed by the page number.

in that it seeks to think both substance and subject at the same time. It does so, however, by splitting each of these terms. Badiou defines the dialectic precisely in terms of a logic of scission, instead of the textbook versions of negation and sublation or the negation of negation: "The dialectic, so to speak, is itself dialectical in that its conceptual operators, which reflect reality, are all equally split."[5] Being itself, to begin with, never amounts to a full substance – say, the substance that ultimately is life itself for the Spinozists Deleuze and Toni Negri. It is true that both Deleuze and Badiou inscribe being in a metaphysics of the multiple, or of multiplicity. Being not only is multiple, but it is actually a multiple of multiples. No matter how far you go, in strictly ontological terms you never reach a substantial halting point, except the void: in Badiou's case, the empty set or null set, marked $\varnothing$. This is one of the possible readings of the death of God, namely, the One "is" not. Being is multiple, not One. But Badiou's ontology more specifically takes as its point of departure an "originary scission" or Two at the very heart of being *qua* multiple, namely, the split between inconsistent and consistent multiplicity. It does so, moreover, by claiming that mathematics *is* the discourse of ontology.

For Badiou, mathematics in its unfolding historicity, from the ancient Greeks to the distinctly modern revolutionary invention of set theory after Georg Cantor, says everything that can be said about being *qua* being. This claim marks the shockingly ambitious opening wager of his undeniable masterpiece *Being and Event*:

> Our goal is to establish the meta-ontological thesis that mathematics is the historicity of the discourse on being qua being. And the goal of this goal is to assign philosophy to the thinkable articulation of two discourses (and practices) which *are not it*: mathematics, science of being, and the intervening doctrines of the event, which, precisely, designate "that-which-is-not-being-qua-being."[6]

Logics of Worlds, as a matter of fact, proposes a theory of appearing (or "great logic," as opposed to logic in the "small" sense of a combination of linguistic or grammatical rules) to supplement the theory of being (philosophy as "metamathematics" or set-theoretical "metaontology") expounded in the first volume of *Being and Event*:

---

5. Alain Badiou, *Théorie de la contradiction* (Paris: Maspero, 1975), 81.
6. Alain Badiou, *Being and Event*, Oliver Feltham (trans.) (London: Continuum, 2005), 13. Hereafter cited as BE followed by the page number.

> If *Logics of Worlds* deserves the subtitle *Being and Event*, 2, it is to the extent that the traversal of a world by a truth, initially grasped in its type of being, this time finds itself objectivated in its appearing, and to the extent that its incorporation into a world unfolds the true in its logical consistency. (LW 38)

Prior to thinking logical consistency, however, the question is how to develop an ontological discourse based on sheer inconsistent multiplicity, when everything that presents itself belongs to consistent multiples.

Badiou thus affirms that even if the One "is" not, "there is" One. This means that oneness is only the effect of an operation that counts-as-one, whatever there is in a given situation. Consistent multiplicity presents multiple ones, counted as so many x's or y's. Whatever precedes the operation of counting itself, the stuff that is pure inconsistency without one, remains strictly speaking out of reach of all presentation. To accomplish the difficult task of thinking inconsistency, therefore, will involve the entire trajectory of Badiou's thinking, from the dialectic of void and excess all the way to the theory of the subject of truth in the final meditations of *Being and Event*. In fact, unlike what happens in *Logics of Worlds,* which begins by positing a metaphysical theory of the subject from the start, there is a principle of retroactive clarification at work in *Being and Event*, insofar as the earlier meditations become effectively thinkable only under the condition of the later ones. The possibility of thinking inconsistency as such thus arrives in actual fact only if and when there happens to be a subject at work who is faithful to an event.

Before reaching this point we must grasp how, in addition to the division between consistent and inconsistent multiplicity, there is a second split central to Badiou's philosophical system: the one that separates presentation from representation, or a given situation from the state of this situation. In set-theoretical terms, presentation counts the elements of a set whereas representation counts the parts or subsets of a set. It is a count of the count, not exactly a recount but a peculiar redoubling of the count. Representation thus operates according to the logic of the power set, $p(\alpha)$, which is the set of all subsets of α. It does for inclusion ($\subset$, or "is a subset of") what presentation does for belonging ($\in$, or "is an element of"), without for a moment undoing the fact that the latter defines the only verb of the ontological discourse for Badiou. It is one thing, for example, to count the members or citizens (elements) of a nation, and another to count them a second time in terms of groups or classes (parts), according to age, race, occupation, sexual orientation, legal status, and so on. In fact, Badiou argues that the political state typically wants nothing to do with singular members but only with classes, or interest groups, which is why the play on the double meaning of the state, both in its strictly political sense, as "State," and in its everyday usage, as in "a state of affairs," is justified. In set theory, the pivotal theorem of excess then holds that there is an inevitable excess of parts over elements, of inclusion over belonging, or of representation over presentation pure and simple: $p(\alpha) > \alpha$. This is not only intuitively clear for finite situations, insofar as anyone can grasp that there are more ways of grouping the elements of a set into subsets than there are elements in the original set: far more importantly, set theory – in an event of its own – also demonstrates formally that, in the cases of infinite sets, there is no way to measure *by how much* the cardinality of the power set exceeds the cardinality of the original set. Badiou calls this the "impasse" or "deadlock" of ontology: "The gap between α (which counts-as-one the belongings, or elements) and $p(\alpha)$ (which counts-as-one the inclusions or parts) is, as we shall see, the point in which the impasse of being resides" (BE 83). This impasse is quite literally the turning point around which pivots the whole conceptual artifice of *Being and Event*.

Thus, in the ontological investigation, any attempt to present being *qua* being, that is, any attempt to present presentation itself, hits an insurmountable obstacle in the guise of the excess of representation over presentation pure and simple. What seems at first to be an utter obstacle, though, quickly turns into an enabling moment that will trigger pure inconsistency itself, so to speak, to come to pass "in person," at least if we keep in mind that *en personne* can also signify "in nobody" or "anonymously" in French. To understand this move, it is essential to add that the excess of representation over presentation that constitutes the impasse of ontology is not in turn a purely structural given. It is not simply of the order of the always-already in the sense of a deconstructive orientation; rather, what seems to be a structural impasse both signals and requires at the same time the exceptional intervention of a subject. The excess of any structure of representation over and above its own resources, in other words, is a question of a rare and contingent occurrence. It appears only where something happens that goes against the state of what is normally given. The event is this something, which is almost nothing, but which suffices to trigger a radical transformation of the situation as a whole: the supplement of *what happens* over and above *what is*. However, an event, too, is in some way split. It is not a miraculous or mystical occurrence coming from beyond but something that always happens, whenever it does happen, within a singular situation in this world. What makes such a happening into an event for a given situation is its eventual site that is symptomatic of the situation as a whole. Thus, on one hand, an event certainly can be seen as purely self-referential; ontologically speaking, self-belonging is even the only feature – condemned in set theory – that describes the event. On the other, though, it is tied to the situation by way of the eventual site whose elements it mobilizes and consequently raises from minimal to maximal existence. And of the eventual site, perhaps symptomatically, there is no matheme.

A truth, then, is the sum of consequences that can be drawn from the faithful investigation of the situation from the point of view of its supplementation by an event. The most important feature of a truth is its generic nature. In set-theoretical terms, a generic set is one without attributes or predicates that would define "what" counts as an element of the set. Badiou, referring to the mathematician Paul Cohen's 1963 proof of the existence of generic sets, names this the one notion that sums up all *Being and Event*. This is because a truth, understood as a process or procedure instead of as a property of logical statements in the narrow sense, investigates and treats a given situation from the point of what is most generic, indistinct, or anonymous about it. Ultimately, taking off from the symptomatic site where a certain miscount or impasse uncovers the point where the state of a situation fails to guarantee its own consistency, this amounts to nothing less than a thinking of the being of that situation as pure generic or indiscernible inconsistency. It is also for this very reason that a truth is strictly speaking universal. Not only does it relate to a given situation from what is most anonymous and generic about it, but precisely because no particular attributes are required, such an investigation is also in principle addressed to all.

It is worth stressing, since this is a common misconception, that Badiou does not treat truth as a revelatory or mystical experience of gaining access to being *qua* being. It is not a question of staring ourselves blind on truth as on the sun in Plato's allegory of the supreme Idea of the Good; sticking to the same allegory, we must also return to the cave of illusory shadows. This is why Badiou introduces both a further scission – this time between truth and truthfulness or veridicality – and a new operation, forcing, which somehow links the two. Forcing, we might say, extending its strictly set-theoretical meaning, is the moment of the putting-to-work of truth: "A term forces a statement if its positive connection to the event forces the statement to be veridical in the new situation (the situation supplemented by an indiscernible truth). Forcing is a relation *verifiable by knowledge*" (BE 403). This is how a truth, which breaks with our current encyclopedia of knowledge, nonetheless produces new knowledges as well.

A subject, finally, is the local instance of fidelity to a truth procedure. "I term *subject* any local configuration of a generic procedure from which a truth is supported" (BE 391). It is the subject who is in charge of investigating the consequences of a truth in the present and forcing its supposed completion back on the situation at hand. For Badiou as for Lacan, the subject is fundamentally split. Unlike Lacan, however, Badiou does not ascribe this split to the individual's subjection to the law of the signifier but rather to the subject's incorporation in a truth process, which usually separates a part that is inscribed in normality (the mortal individual or human animal) from the militant part that is involved in the elaboration of the truth itself (the Immortal).

We are now in a position to understand in what sense Badiou's system can be concentrated in a single formulation from *Being and Event*: "The impasse of being, which causes the quantitative excess of the state to err without measure, is in truth the pass of the Subject" (BE 429). This means that in the end, the task of thinking substance and subject at the same time implies, as it were, a barring of both terms of the dialectic. By the same token, we come to understand in what sense philosophy circulates between a doctrine of being and an intervening doctrine of truth, that is, between ontology and the theory of the subject.

Badiou's philosophical system in *Being and Event*, to put it differently, appears at first to hover around three (and now, with *Logics of Worlds*, four) fundamental concepts: being (and now also appearing), truth, and subject, tied together as if in a Borromean knot by way of a unique doctrine of the event. In actual fact, however, not only are almost all of these concepts subject to a dialectical scission (consistent/inconsistent being, presentation/representation, event/evental site, truth/truthfulness, mortal animal/immortal subject), but there are also a number of intercalated or intermediary concepts (such as the notion of forcing, not to mention points, bodies, and organs, all of which are added in *Logics of Worlds*) without which this philosophy risks lapsing into various forms of idealism or precritical dualism.

Badiou indeed wants his philosophy to be not just dialectical but materialist as well. After having reviewed his teacher Louis Althusser's canonical works under the title "The (Re)commencement of Dialectical Materialism," now in *Logics of Worlds* he seems to square the circle with a plea for nothing less than a renewal of the materialist dialectic against the dominant ideological climate that the book calls democratic materialism: "After much hesitation I have decided to name my enterprise – or, rather, the ideological atmosphere in which it gives vent to its most extreme tension – a *materialist dialectic*."[7] Beyond its latest polemical edge, this materialist side of Badiou's philosophy can be understood on several different levels. Ontologically speaking, for instance, the axiom of separation posits the hypothetical existence of at least one set (the empty set) to which the properties of further operations can be applied. It thus defeats the idealist belief in the all-powerfulness of language that seems to accompany the aftermath of the linguistic turn. In the same vein, logically speaking, the theory of appearing may well amount to a phenomenology but it refuses to give to the subject a constituent role any more so than ontology would to language or to logic in the narrow sense. Badiou also postulates that every appearing is

---

7. Alain Badiou, "Democratic Materialism and the Materialist Dialectic," Alberto Toscano (trans.) *Radical Philosophy* 130 (March–April 2005), 21. Badiou's review of Althusser's *For Marx* and *Reading Capital* appeared as "Le (Re)commencement du matérialisme dialectique," *Critique* 240 (1967).

anchored in a minimal component, or real atom, of being. This runs counter to the whole paradigm of virtuality that runs from Bergson to Deleuze and from Brian Massumi to Elizabeth Grosz. Finally, and perhaps above all, materialism also applies to the concept of philosophy itself. For Badiou, philosophy is never a self-generated speculative discourse but is conditioned from the outside by the nonphilosophical – aside from being threatened from within, as we will see, by an antiphilosophical tendency as well.

Thus, we could say that Badiou's philosophy too presents a "thinking of the outside," albeit in a slightly different sense from what Maurice Blanchot or Deleuze had in mind when they used this expression to describe the work of Foucault. For Badiou, this supposes, against any and all speculative–idealist temptations, that philosophy itself does not produce any truth. To believe otherwise, no matter how flattering it may well seem to the philosopher, always has disastrous consequences for philosophy itself. A truth always originates in an event, but philosophy is strictly speaking unable to give rise to an occurrence of this nature. Events instead happen in the so-called truth procedures, which are also the conditions of philosophy.

The basic materialist principle behind this conception of the philosophical act thus holds that truths in the plural are produced outside philosophy in the four generic procedures of truth that are art, science, politics, and love. What philosophy does rather modestly amounts to developing the conceptual toolbox to think the truths at work in such scientific discoveries, amorous encounters, political sequences, or artistic configurations. The task of philosophy, in other words, consists in creating a conceptual space of compossibility for the various truths produced in its time. "The specific role of philosophy is to propose a unified conceptual space in which naming *takes place* of events that serve as the point of departure for truth procedures," Badiou affirms in his *Manifesto for Philosophy*:

> It does not establish any truth but it sets a locus of truths. It config-
> urates the generic procedures, through a welcoming, a sheltering,
> built up with reference to their disparate simultaneity. Philosophy
> sets out to think its time by putting the state of procedures condi-
> tioning it into a common place. (MP 37)

In the end, this distinction between philosophy and its conditions is only another way of affirming the materialist primacy of practice over theory.

Put otherwise, the truths of art, politics, science, and love stand in themselves as forms of thinking; they need not wait for the philosopher to tell them what counts as "the political" or "the aesthetic" and so on. But philosophy can think through such thinking. Badiou proposes for instance that philosophy become a kind of metapolitics:

By "metapolitics" I mean whatever consequences a philosophy is capable of drawing, both in and for itself, from the notion that real politics are forms of thought. Metapolitics is opposed to political philosophy, which claims that since politics does not think, it falls to the philosophers to think "the" political.[8]

Badiou's proposal for an inaesthetics,[9] likewise, is neither an aesthetic theory nor a philosophy *of* art; and metamathematics, finally, should not be confused with an epistemology or a philosophy *of* mathematics.

II. GENEALOGIES

A second trajectory, which I would call genealogical, could take us in a number of different directions. There is the question, first, of the continuity or discontinuity in Badiou's philosophy: whether his work presents some kind of break between an "early" and a "late" Badiou, as historians of philosophy are so fond of establishing in the cases of Wittgenstein or Heidegger or Lacan. I favor a more continuist line of arguing, but this interpretation is by no means uncontroversial, even now that Badiou seems to have joined his voice to those of us who plead for an ongoing renewal of the materialist dialectic. Second, there is also the question of the relation among Badiou's major works. He himself speaks of "the dialectic between my two 'big' books, the old one and the new one," referring to the two volumes of *Being and Event*, and thus to the dialectic "of *onto*-logy and onto-*logy*, or of being and appearing" (LW 527). But I would make the case that *Theory of the Subject*, which Badiou himself recently described as his "first 'big' book of philosophy,"[10] actually mediates between the other two, insofar as the version of dialectical materialism embraced in this earlier book encompasses a notion of the event – mentioned but not yet fully developed under this name – as both a vanishing cause (the event conceived of ontologically as a flash of self-belonging, an instant that disappears as soon as it appears) and as a new consistency (the event as incorporated logically in a disciplined body that must endure and be able to treat at least a few points). Read in this way, as Badiou's third "major" book, *Theory of the Subject* could serve as the very embodiment of the necessary dialectic between *Being and Event* and *Logics of Worlds*.

---

8. Alain Badiou, *Metapolitics*, Jason Barker (trans.) (London: Verso, 2005), xxxix (translation modified).

*9. Badiou's inaesthetics is discussed in this volume in the essay by Gabriel Rockhill.

10. Alain Badiou, *Pocket Pantheon: Figures of Postwar Philosophy*, David Macey (trans.) (London: Verso, 2009), 289, translation modified.

In addition to such potentially rather scholastic questions, however, I would also like to propose a slightly different take on Badiou's genealogical trajectory. This involves studying how, to put it in Nietzschean terms, "he became who he is" by following a spiraling fidelity to three *maîtres*, meaning both "masters" and "teachers," namely, Sartre, Althusser, and Lacan. Thus, in a rare autobiographical statement, "The Philosopher's Avowal," Badiou writes: "There are the immediate teachers, the ones we meet at school; and then there are the philosophical master-teachers. During the decisive period of my formation, I have had three: Sartre, Lacan, and Althusser."[11] Badiou began by thinking that he would follow in Sartre's footsteps as a novelist, playwright, and committed intellectual. His success as a student of philosophy, however, would decide otherwise for him. Thus, after his entry into the École Normale Supérieure, his encounter with Althusser's Marxism would force him for years to push the investigation of the structure to the point of its immanent breakdown or deadlock. But, as we saw, this impasse is itself the retroactive effect of a subjective intervention. Thus, whereas Althusser was forever unable to perceive in the notion of the subject anything but an effect of ideology, Badiou finds in Lacanian psychoanalysis a theory of the divided subject with which to supplement the basic principles of structuralist Marxism. Fidelity to the event and its consequences then allows for a renewed understanding of the old notion of commitment that Badiou openly inherited from Sartre: his first and most formidable love, both in a literary and a philosophical sense, perhaps on a par only with Stéphane Mallarmé and Samuel Beckett.

To achieve this seemingly impossible triangulation, finally, we must consider the role of Badiou's Maoism. Indeed, as I have argued elsewhere, it is the sequence of Badiou's so-called "red years," roughly from 1968 until the backlash of 1977 with the arrival of the Nouveaux Philosophes, that alone enables his unique articulation of Sartre, Althusser, and Lacan.[12] Thus, it should not come as a surprise if *Logics of Worlds*, in which Badiou forcefully returns to the tradition of dialectical materialism, or the materialist dialectic, also begins and ends with reflections on Mao. This is at least in part due to the fact that Badiou himself in more recent years has come to the realization that an effective transmission of his philosophical system also presupposes the transmission of the experiences – be they political or artistic or otherwise – that make up much of its genealogy.

11. Alain Badiou, "L'Aveu du philosophe." Available at www.lacan.com/badphilo.htm (accessed June 2010).
12. For a more detailed account of Badiou's Maoist years, see my "Post-Maoism: Badiou and Politics," *Positions: East Asia Cultures Critique* 13(3) (2005). This special issue, which is titled "Badiou and Cultural Revolution," also contains a bibliography of Badiou's Maoist group, UCFML, or Union des Communistes de France (marxistes-léninistes).

III. POLEMICS

As Badiou's philosophical system kept spiraling outward, its polemical force also underwent a snowball effect. This then opens up a third trajectory for traversing Badiou's thinking. From the start, in fact, much of his conceptual labor has been determined by his opponents: adversaries, I should say, more so than enemies, even though there is no shortage of the latter and they are not spared either. It is just that they receive little to no philosophical credit. Even his three master-teachers, perhaps with the sole exception of Sartre, have been the object of frontal assaults and partial criticisms, respectively: Althusser, who is targeted most vitriolically in *De l'idéologie*, and Lacan, throughout Badiou's writing but most succinctly in *Theory of the Subject*.

Subsequently, Badiou's polemic with Deleuze, based on a long correspondence and summed up in *Deleuze: The Clamor of Being*, is meant to pinpoint the precise nature of a fundamental divergence – being or life itself as the singular event versus events as breaks with the normal representation of being – in the midst of an overarching convergence regarding philosophy as a metaphysics of infinite multiplicity against the jargon of finitude.[13] In addition, much of *Being and Event* (including its title) represents a coming to terms with the "poetic" hermeneutical ontologies of presencing influenced by the work of Heidegger, as opposed to the "axiomatic" metamathematical ontology that Badiou proposes. This last polemic in particular still deserves to be unpacked in greater detail. Finally, Badiou has never ceased writing models of review articles that usually lead to the clarification of an intimate disagreement, particularly in relation to French philosophy.[14]

Aside from these individually oriented polemics, Badiou's work has also reopened the debates both old and new with the adversaries of the tradition of philosophy as such. First and foremost among these adversaries, of course, we find the sophists, or those who make up the tradition of what Badiou, in his *Manifesto for Philosophy*, calls the "Great Modern Sophistry" (MP 98). This diatribe against the sophists – including Nietzsche or Wittgenstein as the major figures and Richard Rorty or Gianni Vattimo as minor ones – is what we would come to expect from a self-proclaimed Platonist. Indeed, as Badiou writes in an essay on Lacan, "the antisophistic argumentative rage constitutes the 'tumos' of philosophy, i.e., its core of polemical anger, since its origin."[15] Perhaps more

---

13. See further Alain Badiou, *Deleuze. The Clamor of Being*, Louise Burchill (trans.) (Minneapolis, MN: University of Minnesota Press, 2000).

14. Most of Badiou's reviews and notes on French philosophy are collected in the small volume *Pocket Pantheon*. For a general panorama, see Alain Badiou, "The Adventure of French Philosophy," *New Left Review* 35 (September–October 2005).

15. Alain Badiou, "Lacan et Platon: Le mathème est-il une idée?" in *Lacan avec les philosophes*, Bibliothèque du Collège international de Philosophie (ed.) (Paris: Albin Michel, 1991), 136.

interesting than this age-old rage, though, is the fact that in addition to, and partially overlapping with, the sophists, the adversaries of philosophy in the way Badiou seeks to reground it also include a respectable series of so-called "antiphilosophers."

In Badiou's hands, the understanding of antiphilosophy obviously is not limited to the otherwise quite difficult reconstruction of Lacan's usage of the term. Instead, the category emerges as the name for a longstanding tradition of thinkers who, with regard to the dominant philosophical trends of their time, situate themselves in the strange topological position of an outside within or of an internal exteriority, adopting a range of attitudes that typically oscillate between distance and proximity, admiration and blame.

Based on his readings of Nietzsche, Wittgenstein, and Lacan, as well as the occasional reference to Kierkegaard, Rousseau, and St. Paul, Badiou distinguishes a number of features that make antiphilosophy into a coherent tradition in its own right. First, the assumption that the question of being, or of the world, is coextensive with the question of language; second, and as a consequence, the reduction of truth to being little more than a linguistic or rhetorical effect, the outcome of historically and culturally specific language games or tropes that therefore must be judged, or even mocked, in light of a critical–linguistic, discursive, or genealogical analysis; third, an appeal to what lies just beyond language, or at the upper limit of the sayable, as a domain of meaning or sense, irreducible to truth theoretically understood; and, finally, in order to gain access to this domain, the search for a radical act, such as the religious leap of faith or the revolutionary break, the intense thrill of which would disqualify in advance any systematic theoretical or conceptual elaboration. Of course, not all antiphilosophers share these features in their totality, or not to the same extent. Whereas Nietzsche's filiation with the sophists is explicit in his work, for example, by contrast there are certainly many theses in Lacan's conception of truth and meaning that bring him closer to an antisophistic stance that every contemporary philosopher, in Badiou's view, should traverse. In fact, the tension between the first two of these features and the last two produces a characteristic vacillation that, even within the work of a single antiphilosophical thinker, can range from a purely constructivist viewpoint, which reduces truth to what can be discerned in the existing language systems, all the way to the yearning for a mystical beyond, pointing toward the other side of language.

The most important element in the characterization of an antiphilosopher, without a doubt, is the reliance on a radical gesture – the act – that alone has the force of destituting, and occasionally overtaking, the philosophical category of

---

This article is published in a shorter and slightly modified version as "Anti-Philosophy: Plato and Lacan," in *Conditions*, Steve Corcoran (trans.) (London: Continuum, 2008), 228–47.

truth. In the case of Nietzsche, to give but one eloquent example, Badiou qualifies this antiphilosophical act as "archi-political," whereby the prefix is meant to draw a clear line of demarcation between the act for antiphilosophy and the event for philosophy – even though the same "events" in the common sense of the word, for instance, the French Revolution or the Paris Commune, may be at stake. Badiou first posits that Nietzsche's relation to politics, which he sees as significantly overdetermined by 1789 or 1792, is one of rivalry and mimicry. To be more precise, the antiphilosopher is never content with putting his thinking under condition; instead, he will absorb the energy of a given event – in politics or in art or even in love and in science – so as to make it his own. Not only does this entail a significant amount of suturing of philosophy onto the event, but it also goes one step further by turning the ensuing notion – in this case the act that breaks in two the history of the world – into an explosive that can be used both to dethrone traditionally conceived philosophy and to mock really existing politics:

> The philosophical act is, I would say, *archi-political*, in that it proposes itself to revolutionize all of humanity on a more radical level than that of the calculations of politics. From this let us retain that archi-politics does not designate the traditional philosophical purpose of finding a ground for politics. The logic, once again, is a logic of rivalry, and not one of founding oversight. It is the philosophical act itself that is archi-political, in the sense that its historical explosion will show, retroactively, that the political revolution properly speaking has not been truthful, or has not been authentic.[16]

Badiou draws important lessons from this reading of the antiphilosophical act, first and foremost with regard to the necessary restraint and reserve philosophy should show in front of the events that condition it. Otherwise, the risk is great that only an antiphilosopher's personal experience can guarantee the authenticity of the proposed break, as in Nietzsche's *Ecce Homo*, whereas all philosophy for Badiou presupposes the possibility of separating a truth statement from the question "Who is speaking?" In fact, this decisive role of the speaking subject constitutes a final feature that is typical of antiphilosophy. It reveals the extent to which the experience of a radical act can be transmitted only in a near-autobiographical style that is inseparable from the subject of the enunciation. This explains the experimental, writerly side of antiphilosophers,

16. Alain Badiou, "Casser en deux l'histoire du monde?" (Paris: Les Conférences du Perroquet 37, 1992), 11. This lecture, together with Badiou's essays on Kierkegaard and Lacan – who according to him represent our principal modern antiphilosophers – is forthcoming as part of a single volume, *What Is Antiphilosophy? Writings on Kierkegaard, Nietzsche, and Lacan*, Bruno Bosteels (ed. and trans.) (Durham, NC: Duke University Press, forthcoming).

present in Nietzsche's aphorisms, Kierkegaard's diaries, Lacan's seminars, or St. Paul's epistles:

> Why? Because as opposed to the regulated anonymity of science, and against everything in philosophy that claims to speak in the name of the universal, the antiphilosophical act, which is without precedent or guarantee, has only itself and its effects to offer by way of attesting to its value.[17]

In the end, though, the fate of the antiphilosopher may well be to bequeath to the philosopher the task of avoiding the disastrous consequences of claiming truth itself to be within its purview: the disaster, that is, of presenting itself as a truth procedure. As Badiou writes in *Manifesto for Philosophy*:

> The key to this turnabout is that philosophy is worked from within by the chronic temptation of taking the operation of the empty category of Truth as identical to the multiple procedures of the production of truths. Or else: that philosophy, renouncing the operational singularity of the seizing of truths, is *itself* presented as being a truth procedure. Which also means that it is presented as an art, a science, a passion or a policy. (MP 128–9)

Precisely for this reason, however, the philosopher must stay in the closest proximity to the antiphilosopher, who alone keeps him on guard against the temptations of religion, disaster, or the "service of goods" pure and simple:

> I think that all three – but Nietzsche's case is without doubt the most dramatic – in the last instance sacrificed themselves for philosophy. There is in antiphilosophy a movement of putting itself to death, or of silencing itself, so that something imperative may be bequeathed to philosophy. Antiphilosophy is always what, at its very extremes, states the new duty of philosophy, or its new possibility in the figure of a new duty. I think of Nietzsche's madness, of Wittgenstein's strange labyrinth, of Lacan's final muteness. In all three cases antiphilosophy takes the form of a legacy. It bequeaths something beyond itself to the very thing that it is fighting against. Philosophy is always the heir to antiphilosophy. (*Ibid.*)

---

17. Badiou, "Who is Nietzsche?" Alberto Toscano (trans.), *PLI: The Warwick Journal of Philosophy* 11(1) (2001), 10. This is a slightly different and shorter version of the lecture cited in the previous note.

This, in the final instance, would be the legacy that Nietzsche, Wittgenstein, and Lacan bequeathed to all those who seek to (re)affirm the possibility of philosophy today.

IV. PROSPECTS

To conclude, let me now turn to the possibility of thinking *with* Badiou, that is, not just of continuing the exegetical commentary on Badiou's own thinking, but of actually putting his thought to work so as to think the events of our time or of previous times. In the preface to *Being and Event*, Badiou indeed insists that he wants his philosophy to serve as a toolbox to think events in any or all of the four conditions of truth that for him are science, politics, love, and art:

> The categories that this book deploys, from the pure multiple to the subject, constitute the general order of a thought which is such that it can be *practised* across the entirety of the contemporary system of reference. These categories are available for the service of scientific procedures just as they are for those of politics or analysis. They attempt to organize an abstract vision of the requirements of the epoch.   (BE 4)[18]

While seemingly self-effacing, however, the suggestion of practical availability and service also presents us with a number of problems. Perhaps these problems even amount to authentic aporias – otherwise not a very common term in this thinker's personal vocabulary – which somehow would be inherent in Badiou's philosophy: not necessarily shortcomings, but inevitable side-effects of the enormous gravitational pull of his thinking.

If one reads the meditation on Mallarmé in *Being and Event* (Meditation 17), for example, one does not obtain an analysis of Mallarmé as an event in French symbolist or postsymbolist poetry so much as a commentary on Mallarmé as the poet–thinker of the eventfulness (or eventality, *événementialité*) of the event. "A poem by Mallarmé always fixes the place of an aleatory event; an event to be interpreted on the basis of the traces it leaves behind," Badiou posits at the opening of this pivotal meditation (BE 191).

---

18. See also, somewhat less modestly, the end of Badiou's preface to the English translation of *Being and Event*: "I would like this book to be read, appreciated, staked out, and contested as much by the inheritors of the formal and experimental grandeur of the sciences or of the law, as it is by the aesthetes of contemporary nihilism, the refined amateurs of literary deconstruction, the wild militants of a de-alienated world, and by those who are deliciously isolated by amorous constructions" (BE xv).

Of course, it is one thing to read Mallarmé as the poet–thinker of the event-like nature of the event (*l'événementalité de l'événement*) and quite another to read his work as an event in nineteenth-century French poetry. It is almost, though, as if Badiou's meditation, by a strange inward necessity, were unable to preserve the radical innovation in the history of poetry addressed by the second reading except by replacing it with, or displacing it onto, the concentrated rigor and self-contained formalization of the first approach.

Something similar happens in the case of Badiou's sections on Paul Valéry's *Marine Cemetery* at the end of *Logics of Worlds*. Here too the poem is read as a subtle disposition of the different elements and processes involved in the transformative change produced by an event. "This poem is, in our terms, the history of an event," Badiou writes (LW 455); and in a footnote, he adds that Valéry matches Mallarmé's extraordinary skills in this regard:

> It is the question of the "pure event" that connects the Mallarmé of *A Cast of Dice* and the Valéry of *Marine Cemetery*: under which conditions can the poem capture what lies beyond what is, what purely happens? And what then is the status of thought, if it is true that such a happening strikes at thought's corporeal support?
>
> (LW 516, translation modified)

In both of these cases, poetry is not read *as an event* so much as in terms of a poetic *theory* of the event *qua* event.

Badiou's readings of Mallarmé and Valéry demonstrate an almost boundless confidence in the powers of thought to think the event, except that, in the process of this demonstration, most events, which are supposed to give rise to the various truths that condition philosophy from the outside, become transposed into so many theories of the event, of truth, of the body, or of the subject, and so on. In other words, it is as if Badiou's philosophy, instead of serving the truths that are produced outside it in the four conditions or generic procedures, could not avoid looping these instances back onto themselves before tying them in with a strictly intraphilosophical apparatus – namely, his own.[19]

---

19. When I asked Badiou about this in an interview a few years ago, he admitted that this was indeed a real problem, one "which obviously entails a rather large amount of philosophical appropriation of the condition." In fact, he added, it might be the only plausible way to argue that his philosophy carries a dogmatic streak in it, insofar as "I submit the condition to the conditioned." See my "Can Change Be Thought? A Dialogue with Alain Badiou," in *Alain Badiou: Philosophy and Its Conditions*, Gabriel Riera (ed.) (Albany, NY: SUNY Press, 2005), 257. I cannot agree, in this regard, with Alberto Toscano's vote of confidence in Badiou's "inaesthetics," in the translator's note to *Handbook of Inaesthetics* (Stanford, CA: Stanford University Press, 2004), when he writes: "Rather than seeking to welcome (that is, to absorb)

If these strategies may seem justifiable on the part of a philosopher whose thought operations are by definition unique to philosophy even though they are conditioned by events outside it, there comes a point where such selective appropriations and displacements of the condition back onto the conditioned, or of the events back onto the philosophy of the event, can become real obstacles to that philosophy's application. Indeed, it is not difficult to imagine how the available options for such an application are reduced to two mirroring extremes. Either we could privilege the systematicity of the philosopher's conceptual apparatus, in which case the events studied by application actually risk becoming nothing more than illustrations of concepts extrinsic to the events themselves, or we could privilege the radical break introduced by the events in question at the expense of the philosopher's systematization, in which case the events risk becoming the occasion for a typically antiphilosophical appeal to the ineffable singularity of experience, over and above its impoverished conceptualization.

My proposal for renewing the task of theory, as different from philosophy properly speaking, derives from a desire to trace a diagonal across these two extremes so as to produce an effective and applied thinking of the event that can still learn a great deal from Badiou's work. I could phrase this by returning to my initial statement that to be a philosopher today means to think the event. We might then ask: Is this also true the other way around? In other words, does thinking the event always require that one be a philosopher? I would argue that theory has a role of its own to play in this context – one comparable to the role of psychoanalysis for the condition of love, or to the role of inaesthetics for art, or metapolitics for politics, when they are not yet equated with philosophy as such. This also means that a theoretical treatment of events that take place within the various truth procedures need not worry about the simultaneous presence and philosophical reflection of all four of them.

Badiou's requirements for philosophy are perhaps overly demanding if it is our aim to take him up on his offer of applying the conceptual apparatus of *Being and Event*. In his *Manifesto for Philosophy*, for instance, he even goes so far as to suggest that, in the absence of a strict compossibility among the truths produced in all four of these conditions, philosophy also ceases to exist. "We shall thus posit that there are four conditions of philosophy, and that the lack of a single one gives rise to its dissipation, just as the emergence of all four conditioned its

---

the poem into the realm of speculative thinking in a hermeneutic vein, Badiou's approach is committed both to declaring the autonomy of artistic procedures (poetic or literary, cinematic or theatrical) and to registering what he calls their 'intraphilosophical effects'" (*ibid.*, x). Or, rather, Badiou may very well be committed to this ideal, but whether he manages to live up to it in his own work is a different question. I would argue, in particular, that Badiou's *Handbook of Inaesthetics* and *Metapolitics* are not quite examples of the method they are meant to introduce in the philosophical treatment of art and politics, respectively.

apparition" (MP 35). I would argue that we need not follow the philosopher in these exorbitant demands. My proposal is rather to work more closely on the conditions, as it were at the grassroots level, all the while trying to stay clear of the pull by which the philosopher almost inevitably seems to tie the conditions back into the conditioned. This task, by which I would redefine the field of theory or critical theory, involves a precarious balancing act between, on the one hand, the quasi-transcendental if not outright transcendent repetition of the essence of the event and, on the other, the empiricist diluting of the event into the prior conditions or prerequisites that explain away the chance surprise of its emergence.[20]

MAJOR WORKS

Le Concept de modèle: Introduction à une épistémologie matérialiste des mathématiques. Paris: Maspero, 1969. New exp. ed. Paris: Fayard, 2007. Published in English as *The Concept of Model: An Introduction to the Materialist Epistemology of Mathematics*, edited and translated by Zachery Luke Fraser and Tzuchien Tho. Melbourne: re.press, 2007.

Théorie de la contradiction. Paris: François Maspero, 1975.

De l'idéologie (with François Balmès). Paris: François Maspero, 1976.

Théorie du sujet. Paris: Éditions du Seuil, 1982. Published in English as *Theory of the Subject*, translated by Bruno Bosteels. London: Continuum, 2009.

Peut-on penser la politique? Paris: Éditions du Seuil, 1985. Published in English as *Can Politics be Thought?*, translated by Bruno Bosteels. Durham, NC: Duke University Press, forthcoming.

L'Être et l'événement. Paris: Éditions du Seuil, 1988. Published in English as *Being and Event*, translated by Oliver Feltham. London: Continuum, 2005.

Manifeste pour la philosophie. Paris: Éditions du Seuil, 1989. Published in English as *Manifesto for Philosophy*, edited and translated by Norman Madarasz. Albany, NY: SUNY Press, 1999.

Le Nombre et les nombres. Paris: Éditions du Seuil, 1990. Published in English as *Number and Numbers*, translated by Robin Mackay. Cambridge: Polity, 2008.

Conditions. Paris: Éditions du Seuil, 1992. Published in English as *Conditions*, translated by Steve Corcoran. London: Continuum, 2009.

L'Éthique: Essai sur la conscience du mal. Paris: Hatier, 1993. Published in English as *Ethics: An Essay on the Understanding of Evil*, translated by Peter Hallward. London: Verso, 2001.

Beckett: L'increvable désir. Paris: Hachette, 1994. Published in English as part of *On Beckett*, edited and translated by Nina Power and Alberto Toscano. Manchester: Clinamen, 2003.

Deleuze: La Clameur de l'être. Paris: Hachette, 1997. Published in English as *Deleuze: The Clamor of Being*, translated by Louise Burchill. Minneapolis, MN: University of Minnesota Press, 2000.

Saint Paul: La Fondation de l'universalisme. Paris: Presses Universitaires de France, 1997. Published in English as *Saint Paul: The Foundation of Universalism*, translated by Ray Brassier. Stanford, CA: Stanford University Press, 2003.

---

20. A version of this article was first presented as a public lecture at the 2006 School of Criticism and Theory, Cornell University. With thanks to this program's director, Dominick LaCapra, for his kind invitation, and to members of the audience for their numerous questions and objections.

Abrégé de métapolitique. Paris: Éditions du Seuil, 1998. Published in English as *Metapolitics*, translated by Jason Barker. London: Verso, 2005.

Petit manuel d'inesthétique. Paris: Éditions du Seuil, 1998. Published in English as *Handbook of Inaesthetics*, translated by Alberto Toscano. Stanford, CA: Stanford University Press, 2004.

Infinite Thought: Truth and the Return to Philosophy, edited and translated by Oliver Feltham and Justin Clemens. London: Continuum, 2003.

Theoretical Writings. Edited and translated by Alberto Toscano and Ray Brassier. London: Continuum, 2004.

Le Siècle. Paris: Éditions du Seuil, 2005. Published in English as *The Century*, translated by Alberto Toscano. Cambridge: Polity, 2007.

Logiques des mondes: L'Être et l'événement, 2. Paris: Éditions du Seuil, 2006. Published in English as *Logics of Worlds: Being and Event, Volume 2*, translated by Alberto Toscano. London: Continuum, 2008.

Polemics. Translated by Steve Corcoran. London: Verso, 2006.

Petit panthéon portatif. Paris: La Fabrique, 2008. Published in English as *Pocket Pantheon: Figures of Postwar Philosophy*, translated by David Macey. London: Verso, 2009.

De quoi Sarkozy est-il le nom? Circonstances, 4. Paris: Lignes, 2008. Published in English as *The Meaning of Sarkozy*, translated by David Fernbach. London: Verso, 2008.

Seconde Manifeste pour la philosophie. Paris: Fayard, 2009. Published in English as *Second Manifesto for Philosophy*, translated by Louise Burchill. Cambridge: Polity, 2010.

L'Hypothèse communiste. Circonstances, 5. Paris: Lignes, 2009. Published in English as *The Communist Hypothesis*, translated by David Macey. London: Verso, 2010.

Éloge de l'amour. Paris: Flammarion, 2009. Published in English as *In Praise of Love*, translated by Peter Bush. New York: The New Press, 2012.

L'antiphilosophie de Wittgenstein. Caen: Nous, 2009. Published in English as *Wittgenstein's Anti-Philosophy*, translated by Bruno Bosteels. London: Verso, 2011.

Five Lessons on Wagner. Translated by Susan Spitzer. London: Verso, 2010. Published in French as *Cinq leçons sur le 'cas' Wagner*. Caen: Nous, 2010.

La philosophie et l'événement. Meaux: Germina, 2010. Published in English as Philosophy and the Event, translated by Louise Burchill. Cambridge: Polity, 2013.

Cinéma. Edited by Antoine de Baecque. Paris: Nova, 2010. Published in English as *Cinema*, translated by Susan Spitzer. Cambridge: Polity, 2013.

La relation énigmatique entre politique et philosophie. Meaux: Germina, 2011. Published in English as *Philosophy for Militants*, translated by Bruno Bosteels. London: Verso: 2012.

La République de Platon. Paris: Fayard, 2012. Published in English as *Plato's Republic: A Dialogue in 16 Chapters*, translated by Susan Spitzer. Cambridge: Polity, 2012.

The Adventure of French Philosophy. Edited and translated by Bruno Bosteels. London: Verso, 2012. Revised, shortened, and published in French as *L'aventure de la philosophie française depuis les années 1960*. Paris: La Fabrique, 2012.

Mathematics of the Transcendental: Onto-logy and Being-there. Translated by A. J. Bartlett and Alex Ling. London: Continuum, 2013.

What Is Antiphilosophy? Writings on Kierkegaard, Nietzsche, and Lacan. Edited and translated by Bruno Bosteels. Durham, NC: Duke University Press, forthcoming.

5

RETHINKING ANGLO-AMERICAN PHILOSOPHY: THE NEO-KANTIANISM OF DAVIDSON, MCDOWELL, AND BRANDOM

John Fennell

If, as Richard Rorty suggests, there are three seminal works of post-Second World War English speaking philosophy that ushered analytic philosophy into its "post-analytic" phase – W. V. O. Quine's "Two Dogmas of Empiricism" (1951), Wittgenstein's *Philosophical Investigations* (1953), and Wilfrid Sellars's "Empiricism and the Philosophy of Mind" (1956) – what could be called, rather unimaginatively, its "post-postanalytic" phase can usefully be understood as working through a certain naturalism about meaning, mind, and reason common to all three.[1] I use the tentative expression "a certain naturalism" because I think there are two different senses of naturalism lurking in these works that need to be separated and whose separation is crucial to understanding how Donald Davidson, John McDowell, and Robert Brandom take up the legacy of Quine, Wittgenstein, and Sellars.[2]

---

1. Richard Rorty, "Introduction" to Wilfrid Sellars, *Empiricism and the Philosophy of Mind* (Cambridge, MA: Harvard University Press, 1997), 1–2. This reprinting of Sellars's essay contains Rorty's introduction and a study guide by Brandom.
2. Donald Davidson (March 6, 1917–August 30, 2003; born in Springfield, Massachusetts) was educated at Harvard University (BA, 1939; PhD, 1949). Influenced by Anscombe, Kant, C. I. Lewis, Quine, Ramsey, Spinoza, Tarski, and Wittgenstein, he held appointments at Queens College, CUNY (1949–51), Stanford University (1951–67), Princeton University (1967–70), the Rockefeller University (1970–76), the University of Chicago (1976–81), and the University of California, Berkeley (1981–2003). He has written more than a hundred articles, which have been assembled in five volumes of collected papers: *Essays on Actions and Events*; *Inquiries into Truth and Interpretation*; *Subjective, Intersubjective, Objective*; *Problems of Rationality*; and *Truth, Language, and History*.

    John McDowell (March 7, 1942– ; born in Boksburg, South Africa) was educated at New College, Oxford (BA, 1965; MA, 1969), where his influences included Dummett, Evans,

I. NATURALISM AND NEO-KANTIANISM:
QUINE, WITTGENSTEIN, SELLARS

The two forms of naturalism to be distinguished are the *naturalization* of meaning, mind, and reason and the *naturalistic reduction* of them. The first form of naturalism consists in the rejection of transcendent *abstrata*, like Meanings (with a capital "M") that are knowable *a priori*, that bear necessary relations to each other, and that are expressed in analytic statements. Naturalism in this form consists either in rejecting the notion of Meaning as a kind of non-spatiotemporal entity belonging in some extra- or super-natural, Platonic form-like realm or else in rejecting some Cartesian immaterial mind-substance categorically distinct from anything in corporeal nature. Although different, both reject anything beyond the natural and in this respect express a similar form of naturalism: naturalism *qua* anti-super-naturalism. The second form of naturalism amounts to the denial of any normative-rational dimension to human beings and thus denies a normative-rational dimension to the basic human activities of justifying claims to knowledge, holding contentful mental states, and speaking meaningful language. Naturalism in this second sense consists in reducing (or eliminating) the is/ought, cause/reason, fact/norm distinctions. This form of naturalism is reductive naturalism, naturalism *qua* non-normativism. Put positively, anti-super-naturalism is the weaker claim that human beings and their rational activities of making claims to knowledge, holding mental states, and speaking a meaningful language, are natural phenomena that belong to, or form a part of, the larger natural world. As natural objects and phenomena inside this larger natural order, human beings and their activities are *open to* the kind of law-governed explanation that all natural objects are and that natural science strives to uncover. Non-normativism or reductive naturalism is the stronger claim that human beings and their activities are *nothing but* natural objects and phenomena, that not only are they open to being understood in the vocabulary of the natural science and the explanatory apparatus of natural law, but that they can be *exhaustively* explained in such terms. Quine advocates both forms of

---

Hegel, Kant, Rorty, Sellars, Strawson, Wiggins, and Wittgenstein. He began his career as a fellow at University College, Oxford (1966–86), and since 1986 has taught at the University of Pittsburgh. Selected major works include: *Mind and World*; *Mind, Value, and Reality*; and *Meaning, Knowledge, and Reality*.

Robert Brandom (March 13, 1950– ; born in New York) was educated at Yale University (BA, 1972) and Princeton (PhD, 1977). Influenced by Dummett, Frege, Hegel, Heidegger, Kant, David Lewis, Rorty, Sellars, and Wittgenstein, he has spent his career, beginning in 1976, at the University of Pittsburgh. His major works include: *Making It Explicit*; *Articulating Reasons: An Introduction to Inferentialism*; and *Tales of the Mighty Dead: Historical Essays in the Metaphysics of Intentionality*.

naturalism, whereas Wittgenstein and Sellars hold the first but not the second; for them meaning and reason are to be naturalized (de-super-naturalized, de-transcendentalized) without being naturalistically reduced. Their position I term neo-Kantianism since it insists on Kant's distinction between "ought" and "is," on the irreducibility of "norms" to "facts," while denying that this irreducibility requires the positing of another, transcendent realm or immaterial substance wherein such norms exist or subsist. Thus, Wittgenstein and Sellars prise apart the issue of the normativity of meaning and reason from commitment to a two-world/two-self metaphysic, arguing that meaning and reason can be de-transcendentalized without being stripped of their normative character.

Quine's epistemic holism is the basis of his commitment to the first sense of naturalism. Epistemic holism, the thesis that sentences go to experience all at once for confirmation or disconfirmation, has the consequence that *all* sentences are open to revision on the basis of experience; that is, none are analytic, *a priori*, or necessary.[3] In the context of radical translation, this leads to translational indeterminacy: that "There is a rabbit" and "Gavagai" are assented to and dissented from under the same sensory conditions (which is what experience comes to in this context) need not entail they have the same meaning, since this experiential datum is compatible with "Gavagai" meaning "There is an undetached rabbit part" or "There is a stage in the history of a rabbit," and so on.[4] Hence Meanings – what such analytic hypotheses of a translation manual express – are indeterminate. If Quine's holism leads to this weaker sense of naturalism, his scientism commits him to the stronger sense: not just to the elimination of *Meanings* but to the evacuation of *meaningfulness* (intentionality, normative-rationality) from the activities of justifying claims to knowledge, holding contentful mental states, and speaking a meaningful language. Epistemology becomes "naturalized epistemology": the theory of knowledge becomes the merely *descriptive* enterprise of reporting how we *in fact* arrive at our beliefs rather than the *normative* enterprise of determining whether how we arrive at them is how we (rationally) *ought* to. Philosophy of mind becomes behaviorist psychology, where intentional mental

---

3. Willard Van Orman Quine, "Two Dogmas of Empiricism," in *From a Logical Point of View* (Cambridge, MA: Harvard University Press, 1953), 41–2.
4. Willard Van Orman Quine, *Word and Object* (Cambridge, MA: MIT Press, 1960), ch. 2. Quine's adoption of radical translation as the methodological starting-point for inquiring into meaning immediately de-transcendentalizes or pragmatizes it because it holds that all there *is* to the meaning of a sentence or mental state (whether another's or one's own) is whatever the practice of *giving* the meaning, that is, radical translation, can recover of it. This has the effect that conclusions at the level of the *epistemology* of meaning (whether we can *know* the meaning) are immediately conclusions at the level of the *metaphysics* of meaning (whether there *is* any meaning to be known), and that they apply in the first-personal case as well as the third-personal case: "radical translation begins at home" (Willard Van Orman Quine, *Ontological Relativity and Other Essays* [New York: Columbia University Press, 1969], 46).

states, such as beliefs and desires, get understood in purely behaviorist terms of correlations between (dispositions to) gross bodily behaviors and sensory stimulations, and as a consequence their intentionality is eliminated. Philosophy of language becomes a kind of behavioral sociolinguistics: the theory of meaning becomes nothing more than the activity of correlating a translatee's assent/dissent behavior in response to sensory stimulation with a translator's; understanding and speaking a language is no longer considered an essentially meaning-freighted activity; it is just the acquiring of certain regular correlations between sights (stimulations) and sounds (verbal responses), and thus as an activity is no different in kind from a parrot vocalizing or a dog heeling on command.

Wittgenstein and Sellars both embrace the first form of naturalism; they part company with Quine in resisting the second form. For Wittgenstein as for Quine, if the meaning of a term is understood as transcendent to use (i.e. as Meaning), as some kind of rule over and above ordinary use that lays down in advance of use what the term means, then meaning so conceived is indeterminate. Hence, Wittgenstein advocates a use-based account – the meaning of a term depends on how the linguistic community in fact uses the term – which expresses his commitment to the de-transcendentalization of meaning (the elimination of Meaning) since it locates the meaning of a term in the actual *de facto* uses made of it by language users. However, while locating meaning in actual practices of communal linguistic use, Wittgenstein, unlike Quine, does not want to reduce meaning to mere regularities in communal linguistic behavior, for this would rob meaning of its essential normative dimension: if meaning were identified with actual regularities in use, then since actual uses contain mistaken uses, such an account would build mistakes into the meaning of a term, which would in turn mean that there is no such thing as the correct, determinate meaning of a term. To obtain the neo-Kantian position that makes meaning *dependent on* but *not reducible to* regularities in actual communal use, Wittgenstein's key notions of custom, practice, and form of life are conceived in normatively rich rather than naturalistically reduced terms, not as observable regularities in community-wide linguistic behavior resulting from stimulus–response conditioning, but as *normatively structured* regularities instilled through practices in which masters *instruct, evaluate, correct,* and so on, novices in the use of terms.[5] In doing so they point the way to showing how the normativity of meaning can be naturalized (found in actual use) without thereby being naturalistically reduced.

Sellars's attack on the "Myth of the Given" is similarly an attack on reductive–naturalistic accounts of meaning and knowledge, for his problem with "the Given of experience" acting as a foundation for meaning and knowledge is

---

5. Ludwig Wittgenstein, *Philosophical Investigations*, G. E. M. Anscombe (trans.) (Oxford: Blackwell, 1953), §§198, 199, 202, 207, 208, 241.

that it fails to attend to the normative-rational dimension of these phenomena. Although animals and machines, like persons, are sensation-capable, that is, they can register the impacts of the experiential "given," there is a fundamental difference between the person who *says* "This is red" when having a red experience and the parrot trained to produce the *sounds* "T-h-i-s-i-s-r-e-d" when the red light flashes, or the photocell rigged up to a speaker that stutters the same sounds when a red object passes before its sensor. The difference is, he thinks, that the content-bearing (intentional) states of the person essentially bear normative-rational (e.g. logical and epistemological) relations to other content-bearing states: the thought that this is red *entails* the thought that this is colored, is *compatible with* the thought that this is round (and also with the thought that this is not round), is *contradictory with* the thought that this is green, provides *evidence for* the thought that this is not a Granny Smith, and so on. These logical and epistemological relations, which are distinctive of intentional activity, are normative in that if one has the first thought one *ought* (rationally) to have the other thoughts, independently of whether one *does* in fact have them. As such they express relations that cannot be completely captured by natural laws that operate at base with the category of temporal sequence; that is, when this happens that *will* happen, for whether or not one does as a matter of fact have the thought that this is colored after having the thought that this is red, nevertheless the latter thought ought (rationally) to be had. In this way, Sellars argues that what is distinctive of contentful states is that they bear these normative-rational relations to each other, that they have a location in "the logical space of reasons," which cannot be reduced to the natural lawlike relations of before and after, or cause and effect.[6] For Sellars, it is because "the given of experience" can only stand in temporal or causal relations, rather than normative-rational relations, to content-bearing states that it cannot be the foundation of such (normative-rational) content-bearing states, and thus why any attempt to derive content from "the given" would be "of a piece with the naturalistic fallacy in ethics," that is, attempting to derive "ought" from "is".[7] Furthermore, this normative

---

6. Wilfrid Sellars, *Empiricism and the Philosophy of Mind* (Cambridge, MA: Harvard University Press, 1997), 76.

7. *Ibid.*, 19. Sellars readily acknowledges that his critique of "the Given" reprises Hegel's critique of Sense-Certainty in the *Phenomenology*: experiences must be contentless if they are to be certain, but experiences that have no content cannot enter into logical or epistemological relations with beliefs. Hence they are unable to serve as *semantic* or *epistemic* foundations. For example, in the opening section of *Empiricism and the Philosophy of Mind*, Sellars refers approvingly to Hegel as "that great foe of 'immediacy'" and characterizes his work as continuing the assault on "the Given" initiated by Hegel (*ibid.*, 14), and later, he refers to his attack on the given as an "incipient *Méditation Hégélienne*" on the notion (*ibid.*, 42). McDowell and Brandom, who are heavily influenced by Sellars, also see their work having deep affinities with Hegel.

dimension of beliefs and utterances, this locating of a belief or utterance in the logical space of reason, which is constitutive of its being contentful in the first place, is understood by Sellars to be socially achieved. One learns the meaning of color words, and thus grasps color concepts and forms justified beliefs about the colors of things, from others – for example, from those who have already mastered the language game of color predication – through practices of instruction, evaluation, correction, and so on. So for Sellars, as for Wittgenstein, content is constituted by normative-rational relations that in turn are constituted in the actual social practice of language learning where the inferential and epistemological relations that judgments bear to each other are instilled.

A central theme of Davidson's, McDowell's, and Brandom's work is that each in its different way aims to elaborate this Wittgenstein–Sellars-initiated, neo-Kantian middle ground that accepts the Quinean abandonment of a transcendent-to-practice notion of meaning (anti-super-naturalism) while rejecting the elimination of normativity (non-normativism): Davidson in the subtle treatment of the relation between reason and cause that emerges in his charity-constrained, triangulated account of radical interpretation; McDowell in the role that "second nature" plays in his naturalized Platonism; and Brandom in the social-fallibilistic character of his deontic scorekeeping account of meaning.

II. DAVIDSON: CHARITY AND TRIANGULATION

While Davidson has much in common with his teacher, Quine, there are crucial differences between them in their general philosophical outlooks and conclusions. The commonalities concern their shared methodological starting-point of radical translation (or radical interpretation) and their agreement over the core doctrine of holism. These have the effect of committing Davidson to the Quinean conclusions of the rejection of the analytic/synthetic (*a priori/a posteriori*, necessary/contingent) distinction and the elimination of Meanings (meaning indeterminacy). As such, they express Davidson's commitment to a general de-trancendentalization of meaning and reason, and so to naturalism *qua* anti-super-naturalism. Two central differences concern the difference in the data on which radical interpretation/translation is based and the different status that the principle of charity has in radical interpretation/translation. These differences signal Davidson's commitment to the essential normative-rational character of meaning and belief and thus mark his refusal to have the *naturalization* of meaning and reason lead, as it does in Quine, to the *naturalistic reduction* of meaning and reason. Hence, they express his neo-Kantianism: his resistance to naturalism *qua* anti-normativism while at the same time embracing naturalism *qua* anti-super-naturalism.

Even though Davidson more or less adopts the Quinean methodological starting-point of radical translation, at the outset there is a highly significant modification in his conception of the data available to the radical translator, which gets signaled in his terminological shift from "radical translation" to "radical interpretation." As against conceiving of the data as a speaker's assent/ dissent behavior under certain sensory stimulations, Davidson takes the data of radical interpretation to consist in a speaker's *holding a sentence true* when certain conditions obtain *in the world*. That is, not only is there a difference between them over what the speaker is responding *to* (not the experiences of speaker, i.e. states of affairs in the world-*as-they-affect-the speaker*, but states of affairs in the world *itself*), the nature of *what* the response is is also different (not verbal behavior, i.e. mere noise production, but the attitude of holding true). The difference is that the attitude of holding true, as opposed to the mere produc- tion of noise, is minimally contentful; it is not dumb sounds but a state with a content – namely, *that* a certain sentence (whatever it means) is meaningful, is being held true. It signals at the outset of Davidson's account that the data of radical interpretation are not to be understood, as they are for Quine, in the very stripped back, reductive-naturalistic terms of physical noise in response to sensory stimulation, but rather as intentional.

The other major difference between them concerns the status of the principle of charity as a constraint on radical translation/interpretation, and this differ- ence brings to center stage Davidson's irreducibly normative-rational conception of human beings and their activities as against Quine's reductively naturalistic conception. In order to resolve the impasse in translation/interpretation created by the holistic interdependence of meaning and belief, both think that the translator/ interpreter is to employ the principle of charity. The principle of charity obliges the translator/interpreter to make a charitable assumption about what the speaker believes – the charitable assumption being that the translator/interpreter is to attribute true and/or rational beliefs (according to the interpreter) to translatees/ interpretees *in the main*, and on the basis of this, use the speaker's assent/dissent behavior or what the speaker holds true to determine what the speaker's utter- ances mean. The difference between them arises over the force of the obligation to translate/interpret charitably. For Quine, the constraint to translate charitably has at most a pragmatic force: one should translate others charitably (e.g. as not believing contradictions, as holding beliefs about rabbits rather than undetached rabbit parts or time-slices of rabbits) *if* one wants to interact with them in a hassle- free way. For Quine, it is *possible* to translate others as holding mostly false and irrational beliefs by our lights; it is just that pragmatic considerations to do with ease of understanding and facility in communication and interaction counsel one against doing so. For Davidson, on the contrary, this is not possible: interpreting them in a way that has them holding false or irrational beliefs in the main either means that one's interpretation is thereby wrong or the creatures we are inter-preting are not creatures engaged in belief-holding, language-using activities after all.[8] The principle of charity not merely has hypothetical, pragmatic force but is a categorical, constitutive constraint on interpretation: interpreting them so that, for example, their beliefs abide by noncontradiction or that they hold beliefs about whole rabbits rather than about spatial or temporal parts of them, in the main, is required not merely *if* one wants to understand them *more easily*, but if one is to find them understandable *at all*, that is, if they are to be belief holders, creatures capable of meaningful or interpretable activity *period*.[9]

Davidson's theory of belief and meaning attribution, then, gives an essential role to normative-rational considerations, for to insist that charity is constitu-tive of interpretation is just to insist that normative rationality is a constitutive constraint on holding beliefs or speaking a language. It means that for Davidson these human activities are a lot richer than a purely reductive–naturalistic account would have it, involving in addition an irreducible normative-rational dimension. This is Davidson's neo-Kantianism since it insists on the Kantian conception of human beings as essentially rationally autonomous agents and not merely causally determined or law-governed objects. However, this needs to be handled carefully: while distinguishing reason from cause, or the normative from the nomological, Davidson needs to be careful not to completely exile them from each other for this risks making reason completely other to nature and thereby courts a form of super-naturalism about meaning and reason, the avoidance of which is necessary if he is to maintain the Quinean naturalized position on Meanings to which he is also committed. That is, if Davidson is to tread the fine line of holding the first sense of naturalism while denying the second, he owes us an account of how he can have normative-rational relations without positing

---

8. Like radical translation, radical interpretation and the principles that govern it result in meta-physical as well as epistemological claims about meaning (see note 4). Consequently, I move between epistemological formulations of the thesis that charity is constitutive of content (e.g. what it is to *attribute* beliefs or *take* someone to be a belief holder) and metaphysical formu-lations of it (e.g. what it is to *be* a belief or believer).

9. Donald Davidson, "Radical Interpretation," in *Inquiries into Truth and Interpretation* (Oxford: Clarendon Press, 1984), 137. The various features of Davidsonian charity can be seen to mirror some core concepts of Gadamerian hermeneutics. In attributing to inter-pretees what *interpreters* find true or reasonable, and in this attribution being a *condition* of interpretation rather than something interpretation may or may not bear out, charity functions very much like Gadamer's notions of tradition or prejudice: the inescapable back-ground of basic beliefs that an interpreter cannot help but bring with her to any attempt to understand another person or text. In addition, charity in both these respects resem-bles what Gadamer calls a "hermeneutics of trust": the fundamental presupposition or trust that others have a basic sensibleness to them, or that they share a world with us (whatever the differences in beliefs about this world there may be between us), which is necessary for understanding others to be possible in the first place.

an other-worldly realm or substance, or, put conversely, he needs to show us how normative-rational relations are in some sense continuous with ordinary, natural-worldly phenomena and relations, while not thereby being reduced to them. The causal principle of content determination, which gets its full elaboration in the theory of triangulation, is where this subtle position on the relation between reason and cause, the normative and the natural, gets worked out.

On Davidson's fully fledged triangulation account of content determination, the content of a belief and the meaning of an utterance are the result of a process of triangulation between the world, the speaker/interpretee, and the hearer/interpreter. The causal principle forms a part of the triangulated process, and as a constraint on interpretation says that the content of a belief (and thence the meaning of a sentence) is determined by what state of affairs in the world causes it. The basic idea is that an interpreter, by knowing what conditions obtaining in the world cause him to hold true a belief or sentence of his own language, and by noticing that an interpretee holds true an utterance of his own language under the same conditions, puts forward the interpretative hypothesis that the meaning of the interpretee's utterance is the same as the one he utters under those same conditions. In this way an interpreter can figure out the meanings of an interpretee's beliefs and sentences (knowledge of another's mind) by using his knowledge of a common world about which both interpreter and interpretee are speaking and holding beliefs (knowledge of the world) and his knowledge of the language–world relations of his own language (knowledge of his own mind). While this is the *basic* strategy, matters are not nearly so simple: the above account makes it seem as if one *first* had independent knowledge of the contents of one's own mind and language as well as independent knowledge of the external world (by simply being in causal contact with it), from which one *then* gains knowledge of other minds. However, rather than seeing knowledge of other minds as dependent on these other two kinds of knowledge, Davidsonian triangulation contends that knowledge of the content of our own mental states, knowledge of the mental states of others, and knowledge of the external world all come into being together. In particular, knowledge of other minds is implicated in knowledge of one's own mind and knowledge of the external world: the intersubjective is not dependent on the subjective and objective; rather, there is an interdependence between the subjective and the intersubjective and an interdependence between the objective and the intersubjective. I will look at the reasons behind each interdependence and in doing so show how the subtle position on reason and cause emerges.

While the term "triangulation" appears in Davidson's later work,[10] its presence is discernible in his earlier, constitutive charity account. Regarding the

10. It first appears in the 1983 paper, "A Coherence Theory of Truth and Knowledge," after which it gets more constant discussion in, for example, "Epistemology Externalized" (1990),

JOHN FENNELL

interdependence of the subjective and the intersubjective, this is present at the outset in the methodological standpoint of radical translation, for if *in general* whatever there is to the content of mental states and the meaning of sentences is whatever can be recovered from the third-personal position of the radical interpreter, then not only would others not be belief holders or language users unless they were interpretable by one, but also one would not be either unless interpretable by others. Like Quinean radical translation, Davidsonian radical interpretation "begins at home." Davidson's reason is the familiar Wittgensteinian one against the possibility of a private language: if one by oneself were the authority on the contents of one's own mental states and utterances, then whatever *seemed* to one to be their meaning would just *be* their meaning, and therefore they would not mean anything determinate at all. It is only if there is another present to interpret what their content is that there is any chance of an independent check on their having a stable, determinate content, even to oneself. Thus, one's having contentful mental states and one's speaking a meaningful language requires the other; determinate subjective content requires intersubjective interpretation.

Furthermore, being interpretable to another requires a common world that both speaker and hearer are responding to, talking about, holding beliefs concerning. It cannot be based on subjective experience for the reason just outlined, which is why Davidson takes the data of radical translation to be holding sentences true in response to *states of affairs in the world* and not to experience (sensory stimulation). In his later work, this requirement gets expressed in the causal principle: that the contents of others' (and one's own) beliefs and utterances are what cause them in the objective world. Thus, the objective is required for the intersubjective. However, what the objective cause is of each of our mental states and utterances cannot be straightforwardly identified, this time for familiar Quinean–Davidsonian reasons: whenever we are in causal contact with whole, spatiotemporal objects, we are in causal contact with undetached parts of them, time-slices in the histories of them, and so on. Although the requirement that the cause be something objective or common to both of us rules out any subjective causal antecedent in the form of experience, this still leaves a multitude of objective causes to choose among. In order to fasten on whole objects rather than undetached parts or time-slices of them as the cause (and thus the content) of the mental states and utterances, interpreters need to make an assumption about what normative similarities in the world interpretees are responding to: namely, that interpretees respond to the same

---

"Three Varieties of Knowledge" (1991), "The Second Person" (1992), and "The Emergence of Thought" (1997). All these papers are reprinted in *Subjective, Intersubjective, Objective* (Oxford: Oxford University Press, 2001).

98

saliencies in the world that interpreters do, that they live in the same similarity-spaces as interpreters do (e.g. that they notice and respond to whole objects, not undetached parts or time-slices of them). Unless this assumption is made, there is no way for the causal principle alone to determine what the objective cause and thus content of the belief or utterance is. That is, in order to have any determinacy in the identity of the objective cause we need to mobilize the whole intersubjective, charity-constrained apparatus of radical interpretation: that interpretees believe what interpreters do in the main, that interpretees hold obvious (to interpreters) empirical beliefs, that what they are causally responsive to is what we are, namely whole objects rather than spatial or temporal parts of them. Objectivity is thus dependent on intersubjectivity: the objective cause is not something directly identifiable by speakers and hearers, but rather is a construct of the entire intersubjective, triangulated, normative-rational process of interpretation.

Of course with the introduction of the causal principle in triangulation, a question arises about its compatibility with the principle of charity, which is the familiar question of the compatibility of reason and cause. For if content is constitutively constrained by charity, content is determined by normative-rational factors: what one believes is, for the most part, what one rationally ought to believe. However, if the causal principle governs content attribution, content is determined by a causal relation between a belief and the states of affairs in the world that cause it: what one's beliefs are about are what in fact cause them in the world. The first determines the meaning of sentences and the content of beliefs by means of a normative-rational mechanism; the second according to a facto-causal mechanism. The problem is that these mechanisms or principles need not coalesce, which is just to hold that reasons are distinct from causes: the cause of a belief need not provide a good reason for it, and thus the belief attribution demanded by normative-rational considerations need not be the belief attribution suggested by consideration of the causal factors. Davidson's way round the tension involves recognizing the difference between claiming that reason and cause are *distinct* and claiming that reason and cause are *incompatible*: to say they are distinct is merely to say that they *need not* go together, whereas to hold they are incompatible is to hold that they *cannot* go together. The first, unlike the second, allows for the possibility that they *can* go together, that reasons can be causes.[11] Although we cannot infer from the fact that something is a cause of a belief that it provides good reason for it (because of the distinctness of reason and cause), likewise we cannot infer from the fact that something is a cause of a belief that it is thereby not a reason for it (because in being distinct they are not

---

11. This position, that reasons, while distinct from causes, can nevertheless still be causes, is the
    cornerstone of his philosophy of action.

thereby incompatible). Reason and cause, although distinct, are not incompatible; rationality, although distinct from and thus irreducible to causality and the realm of the natural, is capable of coexisting with it: it does not *require* anything super-causal or super-natural. It is this insight on the subtle relation between reason and cause that emerges from Davidson's theory of content, which paves the way for his neo-Kantian middle position: one that allows him to hold that there is an irreducible normative-rational dimension to human beings and their meaning-bearing activities without having to posit anything beyond the natural. This middle position is even more evident in his philosophy of mind: anomalous monism, as the name suggests, is a form of nonreductive physicalism that aims to combine physical monism (i.e. anti-super-naturalism) with the idea that there are no strict type identities obtaining between the mental and the physical (i.e. antireductive naturalism).

III. MCDOWELL: NATURALIZED PLATONISM AND SECOND NATURE

The problem that McDowell explicitly addresses in *Mind and World*, a problem he takes to arise with the modern scientific revolution of the seventeenth century and its attendant "disenchantment" of nature, is the problem we have been focused on: the problem of providing an adequate account of the place of rational, intelligent, meaningful activities in a thoroughgoing natural world. At the outset, McDowell signals his commitment to de-transcendentalization for he refuses to configure the problem in Cartesian "substance" terms of how two categorically distinct substances fit in the same world, preferring instead the de-reified, Kantian–Sellarsian terms of types of processes or "kinds of intelligibility": how rational *processes* (e.g. thinking and speaking a language) fit into a realm of thoroughgoing natural *processes*, or how two different kinds of *intelligibility* – the kind that belongs to "the space of reasons" and the kind that belongs to "the realm of law" – that cannot be reduced to one another can nevertheless apply to one and the same process (thinking or speaking) or thing (human agent). Seeing the problem in these de-reified terms immediately makes space for a middle position between Platonism (or dualism) and reductive naturalism, for rather than there being two metaphysically distinct regions or things, there is just one process or thing, and a natural empirical process or thing at that, which is open to two ways of being understood.

The structuring dilemma of *Mind and World* is the one that structures this essay; indeed, my understanding of the contemporary landscape of Anglo-American philosophy is indebted to McDowell. The horn of the dilemma I call reductive naturalism is McDowell's "bald naturalism," and the horn that I call super-naturalism McDowell refers to as "rampant Platonism." McDowell's term for the middle position between the two horns is "naturalized Platonism." Naturalized Platonism aims to respect rationality, the production and consumption of meaning, as *sui generis* (and thus avoid bald naturalism) while insisting that such states and activities are part of, arise in, and reflect features of our natural way of living (and thus avoid rampant Platonism). His strategy is to link reason and nature not by relocating rational thought and intentional activity within the bounds of the realm of law (*à la* reductive naturalism), but by expanding the bounds of nature to include more than the realm of law.[12] The key concept that is to effect this reconception of the natural, this expansion of nature beyond the realm of law, is the concept of "second nature." This notion of second nature is the notion of normative nature: the idea that the domain of the normative (rational thought or intentional activity generally) is natural. Both parts of the term "second nature" are important for showing how naturalized Platonism is meant to avoid bald naturalism and rampant Platonism. To insist on a *sui generis* domain of the normative or the rational, and hence resist reductive naturalism, seems to force one into rampant Platonism: the postulation of an ideal realm of meanings and normative-rational relations radically disconnected from what goes on in the natural, phenomenal world. In order to avoid the metaphysical postulation of a Platonic other-world of ideal rational relations, the normatively constrained ideal space of reasons must be natural in some way, but not in the way that a rock's falling to the ground is (which might be thought of as a paradigm of a process of "first nature"). If it were, rational processes would be understood in the same general law-governed terms and McDowell would be advocating some form of reductive naturalism. Call this other sense of nature, in which thought and other intentional activities are natural, "second nature." In short, the "nature" part of "second nature" is important in order for McDowell's naturalized Platonism to avoid rampant Platonism; and the "second" part of "second nature" is important for his view to extend the notion of nature beyond objects of first nature (i.e. as coextensive with whatever is susceptible to the kind of law-governed explanations characteristic of natural science) to normative phenomena, and hence to avoid bald naturalism.

To expand nature beyond the realm of law, which is what the notion of second nature is designed to do, produces a problem the avoidance of which is behind the original thought that naturalism and rampant Platonism exhaust the space of possibilities in the modern era; it seems to involve a renunciation of scientific modes of explanation of the natural world, "a crazily nostalgic attempt to re-enchant the world" and be a reversion to a medieval way of thinking about nature that divines meaning in "the movement of the planets or the fall of a

---

12. John McDowell, *Mind and World* (Cambridge, MA: Harvard University Press, 1994), 77–8.

sparrow."[13] What makes bald naturalism and rampant Platonism seem to exhaust the philosophical options for accounting for mind in the natural world in the first place is that any attempt to reconceive or expand nature to include normative phenomena looks like a prescientific re-enchantment of the natural world in which natural objects are understood to be freighted with meaning and purpose. It is therefore incumbent on McDowell to explain this notion of "second nature" that extends without renouncing the modern scientific conception of nature.

While explicitly acknowledging that this concept is drawn from Aristotle's account of the development of ethical character – "the best way I know to work into this different conception of what is natural is by reflecting on Aristotle's ethics"[14] – it also counts as part of its ancestry Hegel's notion of *Sittlichkeit* – "I would like to conceive this work [*Mind and World*] as a prolegomenon to a reading of the *Phenomenology*"[15] – and the Wittgensteinian notions of custom, practice, and form of life.[16] What all these notions have in common is that they take the normative as irreducible to the natural but as nevertheless arising out of ordinary (natural) human phenomena: namely, historically concrete, socially articulated, normatively structured practices of learning, habituation, and enculturation. Each takes rationality to be a normatively rich, not naturalistically reduced, natural phenomenon, thus as not exhaustively explained by similarities in stimulus–response behavior (Quine) but by similarities in normative nature, by agreements in judgments of normative similarity (Wittgenstein–Sellars–Davidson). They are what constitute McDowellian shared "second nature," that is, our nature as normatively governed creatures. Hence second nature is that aspect of ourselves constitutive of (practical) ratio-

---

13. *Ibid.*, 72.

14. *Ibid.*, 78.

15. *Ibid.*, ix. Although McDowell does not explicitly use the Hegelian notion of *Sittlichkeit*, his general sympathy with Hegel and his explicit invocation of the closely related Hegelian notion of *Bildung* make it appropriate. *Sittlichkeit* refers to the customary way of being of a people: their cultural institutions, social mores and roles, and so on. In short, it refers to how a community constructs meaning for itself insofar as this is embodied in historical–social practices and roles. Moreover, in its *ultimate* dialectical form, *Sittlichkeit* refers to a community's norms once they have been subjected to communal question, dispute, rational examination, and reflection, and adopted on the basis of their being authoritative for this historicized formation of reason. With *Sittlichkeit*, then, Hegel introduces a nonmetaphysical, custom-based, historically situated conception of reason that has both the elements McDowell seeks in the notion of second nature: normativity and no metaphysical inflation.

16. An important Wittgenstein scholar, McDowell is responsible for the "normatively laden" interpretation of the notions of custom, practice, and form of life, against Kripke's Humean, reductive-naturalistic reading of them (in *Wittgenstein on Rules and Private Language* [Cambridge, MA: Harvard University Press, 1982]). See in particular John McDowell, "Wittgenstein on Following a Rule," *Synthese* 58 (1984).

nality in Kant's sense, which in being constituted in actual, social practices, is de-transcendentalized.

Similarly, in McDowell's primary source for the concept of second nature – Aristotle's account of how an individual can learn to be moral – we get a model for how a natural entity such as a human being can grasp and participate in normatively structured conduct and develop a second (normative) nature. Aristotle's account of how virtue is acquired explains how ethical demands are recognized as such by ordinary individuals as a result of their exposure to proper upbringing and initiation into the appropriate ethical customs and traditions. Such individuals acquire at the end of this social initiation a reflective awareness of the validity of these ethical demands: not just a recognition of what it is to be virtuous or to have a good character, but also a justification of this (what Aristotle calls "the that" and "the because" of virtue). Ethical requirements are demands of reason that one comes to understand and accept given the right education and socialization (*Bildung*); the right education and socialization enable one to develop a "responsiveness" to the rational-ethical demands (develop "practical wisdom") and in doing so achieve a rational-ethical character. Moral education, socialization into the right form of life, which is an actual occurrence in the ordinary natural world, produces a rational-ethical nature in a flesh and blood, historico-social human being, that is, in a natural (not transcendent) self who, in developing a sensitivity to the rational requirements of ethical character, is not only subject to a natural-law-like process but recognizes and responds to the normative demands of ethical-rationality. Hence a non-super-natural process produces an ethical nature, a capacity to be responsive to normative-rational demands constitutive of ethical character. In this account we have the development in natural individuals of *second* nature, the recognition of what it is to be virtuous and why, which while not to be understood on the model of the lawlike relations between external events (characteristic of first nature), is nevertheless just as much a part of the nature of human beings as getting hungry. Such an account is meant to "naturalize" the space of reasons not in the manner of bald naturalism (i.e. by reducing normative-rational talk to lawlike regularity talk) but by making our normative rationality a perfectly un-special (natural) characteristic of ordinary human development and living, part of the everyday social practices of real human beings.

IV. BRANDOM: DEONTIC SCOREKEEPING

In Brandom's monumental *Making It Explicit*, the middle position between Platonic super-naturalism and reductive naturalism about meaningfulness is also to be won by working out in detail or "making explicit" the Wittgenstein–Sellars social practice-based account of the normativity of meaning and it has three central features: pragmatism, inferentialism, and socialized fallibilism. The pragmatic characteristic of his view consists in his de-transcendentalization of meaning through the adoption of the Quine–Wittgenstein–Sellars practice-centered approach of looking for the normativity of the meaning of a term in our actual use of the term in asserted judgments. On this approach, since the meaning of a term waits on its use in asserted judgments, judgments that express the meaning of terms (what pre-Quine would be analytic statements) are determined by the actual making of judgments employing those terms (synthetic statements). Thus Brandomian pragmatism can be equivalently expressed, as Quine's anti-Platonism can be, as the abandonment of the analytic–synthetic distinction.

Just as Quine's abandonment of the analytic–synthetic distinction is based on holism, Brandom's pragmatism is closely related to *inferentialism* (his Sellarsian term for holism). For Brandom, the thing about judgments is that they are inferentially related to other judgments, and the place a judgment occupies in the web of interrelated judgments is determined by the inferential relations it bears to these other judgments and that they bear to it. So if a term's meaning is determined by its use in asserted judgments, and these are inferentially articulated, then the inferential relations of judgments that the term occurs in constitute its meaning. This inferentialist picture of meaning contrasts with the representationalist account: instead of an assertion, for example, "This is red," meaning what it does in virtue of *referring* to a particular state of affairs in the world, its meaning is a function of its *inferential* relations, for example, relations of implication to other sentences (e.g. "This is colored"), relations of incompatibility to still other sentences (e.g. "This is blue"), and so on. However, these meaning-constitutive inferential relations should not be thought of in the strict formal logical way of deductive consequence and contradiction, but as relations of *material* inference. Importantly for Brandom, material inferences – inferences from, for example, "X is west of Y" to "Y is east of X," from "It is raining in the vicinity of X" to "The roads around X are wet" – are perfectly proper as they stand; their validity does not *derive* from the application of a logical principle (e.g. *modus ponens*) after the addition of a suppressed major premise, for example, "If X is west of Y, then Y is east of X," or "If it is raining in the vicinity of X, then the roads are wet around X."[17] In fact, Brandom suggests the explanatory order is the other way round: the validity of deductive logical principles is based on the self-standing validity of material inferential moves. This explanatory prominence given to the proprieties of material inference means that what-

---

17. Robert Brandom, *Making It Explicit* (Cambridge, MA: Harvard University Press, 1994), 98.

ever normative rationality formal logic has must already be present in material inferential proprieties, and so is in keeping with the pragmatism of looking to actual use and actual inferential proprieties for the foundation of the normative.

These two features of pragmatism and inferentialism naturalize meaning, that is, see it as constituted by actual use and the material inferential relations obtaining in actual use, and in doing so face the usual danger of reductive naturalism (what Brandom calls "regularism"): of identifying meaning with purely *de facto regularities* in assertional use and inferential behavior, and thereby eliminating its normative dimension. In order to preserve the normativity of meaning and remain faithful to his goal of carving out a middle position that naturalizes normativity without naturalistically reducing it, Brandom introduces into his view a third, normatively imbued, *social-fallibilist* feature. The pragmatist and inferentialist characteristics of conceptual content are explicated in the *deontic* (normative) terms of obligation and permission – or as Brandom prefers "commitments" and "entitlements" – that are designed to ensure that actual use and the material-inferential relations obtaining therein are normative from the outset, with the normative element in turn getting a social-fallibilist characterization in the form of *deontic scorekeeping*.[18] This deontic scorekeeping account of meaning normativity involves seeing the material inferential relations between judgments that constitute the meaning of terms occurring in them as commitments and entitlements that a speaker *undertakes* by asserting a judgment and that are instituted socially by a scorekeeper who assesses (keeps score of) these commitments and entitlements by *attributing* them to the speaker and by undertaking the same or different ones himself. Speaking a language is thus understood in Sellarsian terms as taking part in "the game of giving and asking for *reasons*"; indeed, deontic scorekeeping is the attempt to make explicit what goes on in this game, because to make an assertion is to undertake commitments and entitlements, which are things that stand in need of reasons (from other commitments and entitlements) and which can be used as a reason (for still other commitments and entitlements). The normativity of meaning is to be got from this being a reason-giving, reason-requiring activity, where reason in turn is understood in a social, material-inferential way.

The basic idea here is that any given assertion carries with it commitments and entitlements to other assertions: for example, to assert "This is red" is to be committed to "This is colored" and "This is not blue," and also to be entitled to "This is the color of a ripe tomato," but it is incompatible with commitments to "This is blue" and "This is not colored," and so on. This account avoids devolving into a form of reductive naturalism that eliminates normativity because these commitments and entitlements are not identified with those a speaker *in fact*

---

18. *Ibid.*, 180–98.

undertakes but those he *should* undertake, where the ones he should undertake are the ones a scorekeeper attributes to him and undertakes himself. However, in turn, the commitments and entitlements that a speaker should undertake are not identified with those a *given* scorekeeper *in fact* attributes and undertakes, for these latter can be kept score of by another scorekeeper's undertakings of commitments and entitlements, and so on. In this way, the normativity of meaning is preserved, for what commitments and entitlements an assertion should issue in is never identified with what any speaker *or* scorekeeper takes them to be. The possibility of a gap between the commitments and entitlements undertaken by a speaker and a scorekeeper, as well as between scorekeepers, is what supplies the normative ingredient, and it is an ingredient supplied by the social-fallibilist structure of deontic scorekeeping. Brandom's idea here is that to avoid reduction of the normative to the non-normative (naturalistic reductionism), one must have the ability to draw the seeming–being distinction, that is, be able to distinguish between what a speaker or scorekeeper *believes* an assertion commits and entitles the speaker to and what it *does* commit and entitle the speaker to. And what is needed to draw the seeming–being distinction is a *fallibilist* conception of any given speaker's and scorekeeper's undertakings of commitments and entitlements, since fallibilism is just the idea that one may always be wrong, that how things seem to one need not be how they are. Thus what his social account of normativity requires are the resources to fund a fallibilist conception of any given scorekeeper's attributions of commitments and entitlements, and Brandom thinks what is needed to fund fallibilism is that deontic scorekeeping have the structural capability to generate ever new and different scorekeeping perspectives. That is, he thinks that it is deontic scorekeeping's inbuilt fallibilist structure, a structure that guarantees the permanent possibility of further scorekeeping perspectives, that ensures there is a genuine, objective normative dimension to the practice. Objective normative assessment is the result of a structural difference in perspectives between speaker and scorekeeper, and between one scorekeeper and another.[19]

Hence it is this structural feature of deontic scorekeeping – of providing for the permanent possibility of perspectival differences between commitments and entitlements undertaken by speakers and scorekeepers – that allows for fallibilism and stops the normativity of meaning (which is constituted by these undertaken commitments and entitlements) from simply reducing to the *de facto* say-so of any particular speaker or scorekeeper. Further, the normativity thus funded is immanent to the social practice of scorekeeping: the seeming–being distinction is drawn not by invoking some independent-of-*all*-scorekeeping-practices standard of assessment (against which a given scorekeeping assessment

---

19. *Ibid.*, 597.

can be judged, namely, the Meaning), but rather by having a mechanism for constructing an independent-of-*this*-scorekeeping-practice standard of assessment by having the permanent possibility (for any scorekeeping assessment) of *another* scorekeeping assessment against which it can be assessed. Hence the middle position of a naturalized account that at the same time avoids naturalistic reduction is attained: naturalization is achieved by looking for the normativity of meaning, in Wittgenstein–Sellars fashion, solely within the actual social practice of speakers and scorekeepers undertaking and attributing commitments and entitlements in what they assert; and reductive naturalism is eschewed because an objective normative dimension is preserved by the fallibilism of this practice.[20]

V. CONCLUSION: CONTINENTAL CONNECTIONS

One source of the analytic–continental divide was Russell's and Moore's banishing of the British Hegelianism of T. H. Green and F. H. Bradley from its hegemonic position in the British academy in the late nineteenth and early twentieth centuries.[21] The strain of neo-Kantian post-analytic philosophy I have been tracking in this essay welcomes Hegel (at least in the cases of McDowell and Brandom) back into the English-speaking philosophical fold and promises a rapprochement between current Anglo-American and continental philosophy. In endeavoring to delineate a neo-Kantian, neo-Hegelian position that naturalizes (in the sense of socio-historicizing) mind and meaning (*Geist*) without naturalistically reducing them, Davidson, McDowell, and Brandom represent an important counter-current to the reductive naturalism that has generally pervaded English-speaking philosophy after Quine and which helped to keep the divide in place. Interestingly, it is a reductive naturalism that was not a part of the foundations of the analytic tradition – a founding tenet of the tradition was Frege's antipsychologism about logic and meaning – but was a positivist-influenced, Quinean addition, which, once jettisoned, reacquaints the tradition with its neo-Kantian, Fregean origins, allowing it again to take seriously Kant's image of human beings and human activities as essentially rationally autonomous and not merely naturally law-governed. It also brings contemporary Anglo-American philosophy into conversation with the post-Kantian, post-Hegelian traditions in continental philosophy of hermeneutics and phenomenology,

---

20. Robert Brandom argues that deontic scorekeeping reflects Hegel's account of the nature of conceptual norms in *Tales of the Mighty Dead: Historical Essays in the Metaphysics of Intentionality* (Cambridge, MA: Harvard University Press, 2002), ch. VII.
21. See Peter Hylton, *Russell, Idealism, and the Emergence of Analytic Philosophy* (Oxford: Oxford University Press, 1990).

which always took this Kantian point seriously. The fundamental distinction in hermeneutics between *Geisteswissenschaften* and *Naturwissenschaften* is rooted in this Kantian insight: it is because mind and meaning are autonomous in Kant's sense – domains of normative-rational connection rather than simply domains of natural law-governedness – that the "sciences" that study them are different in kind from the sciences of nature. As Davidson might put it, mind and meaning are anomalous (i.e. a-nomological, not reducible to operations describable by natural scientific laws) because they are autonomous (i.e. normative-rational phenomena). Likewise, Husserl's Fregean rejection of psychologism, which is foundational for instituting phenomenology as a discipline, is precisely a critique of naturalistically reductive conceptions of mind.[22] If phenomenology is "philosophy as rigorous science," it is because it is *not* a "rigorous" natural science, but because it rigorously attends, in a way that natural sciences of the mind do not, to the ineliminable intentionality of consciousness, the meaning-laden, normative-rational structures that mediate human encounters with the natural world. In similarly stressing the irreducible normative-rational dimension of human interactions in and with the world, I think it not too much a stretch to speak of Davidson, McDowell, and Brandom as continuing the break-through to hermeneutics and phenomenology (already begun by Wittgenstein and Sellars) within Anglo-American philosophy.[23]

*22. For a discussion of Russell, Frege, Husserl, and the origins of the analytic–continental bifurcation in philosophy, see Michael Friedman and Thomas Ryckman, "Origins of the Two Traditions: Frege, Husserl, Carnap, and Heidegger," in *The History of Continental Philosophy: Volume 3*.

23. It may even be a characterization they would embrace. I have noted already McDowell's and Brandom's affinity for the continental tradition, especially Hegel; in McDowell's case this extends to Gadamer (see e.g. McDowell, *Mind and World*, 115–19), and in Brandom's to Heidegger (e.g. Brandom, *Tales of the Mighty Dead*, chs 10, 11). Even Davidson, who had no great admiration for Hegel, had a well-known regard for Gadamerian hermeneutics; see in particular the closing paragraphs of his contribution to the "Library of Living Philosophers" volume devoted to Gadamer, "Gadamer and Plato's *Philebus*," in *The Philosophy of Hans-Georg Gadamer*, Lewis Edwin Hahn (ed.) (Chicago, IL: Open Court, 1997).

6

RETHINKING SCIENCE AS SCIENCE STUDIES: LATOUR, STENGERS, PRIGOGINE

Dorothea Olkowski

I. BRUNO LATOUR

At the end of *Pandora's Hope: Essays on the Reality of Science Studies*, Bruno Latour[1] sums up, succinctly, both the method and result of his account of social theory and science studies. Science studies, he declares, is not critical or debunking; it simply shifts attention from the theory of science *to its practice*. What looked like different and unconnected theoretical questions turn out, in practice, to be tightly intertwined.[2] This simple formulation is the expression of what has been called Latour's constructivist position with respect to science studies. On the basis of "actor network theory," which describes the manner in which scientific facts are created by and through networks of human and nonhuman actors, Latour proceeds to an examination and refutation of the avowed modernist distinction between nature and culture.[3]

---

1. Bruno Latour (June 22, 1947– ; born in Beaune, France) was educated at the University of Bourgogne and received a *doctorat d'état* from the University of Tours in 1975. His work was influenced by Marc Augé, Harold Garfinkel, Roger Guillemin, Charles Péguy, Michel Serres, and Gabriel Tarde. He has held academic appointments at the Centre de Sociologie de l'Innovation at the École Nationale Supérieure des Mines (1992–2006), the Jonas Salk Institute for the Biological Sciences (1975–76), the London School of Economics, Harvard University, and Sciences Po Paris (2006–).
2. Bruno Latour, *Pandora's Hope: Essays on the Reality of Science Studies* (Cambridge, MA: Harvard University Press, 1999), 293–4. Hereafter cited as PH followed by the page number.
3. David Ingles and John Bone, "Boundary Maintenance, Border Crossing, and the Nature/Culture Divide," *European Journal of Social Theory* 9(2) (2006). Latour's various narratives are formalized in "Actor-Network-Theory" or "ANT." Alluding to relativity physics's "uncertainty principle," ANT reflects the impossibility of deciding whether five crucial aspects of

109

Latour believes that "the only way to understand the reality of science studies is to … pay very close attention to the details of actual scientific practice, the way anthropologists do when they live among 'foreign tribes'" (PH 24).[4] This requires following scientists into the laboratory or into the field, as Latour does when he accompanies four scientists investigating the shifting boundary between savannah and forest in Brazil, where he, indeed, pays close attention to the details of actual scientific practice. But the questions Latour poses in this situation are those he brings to it: How do these scientists pass from what he calls "ignorance to certainty, from weakness to strength, from inferiority in the face of the world to the domination of the world by the human eye?" (PH 30). In contrast to the completely preconstructed universe of the laboratory, the question of whether the Brazilian savannah and forest are advancing or receding with respect to one another establishes a minimalist laboratory. It is demarcated in a grid of coordinates by the botanist to record the emergence of species and variations of growth. The botanist cuts particular specimens and brings them with her to her local university office. Detached from the forest, the specimens are now separated, preserved, classified, and tagged, then reassembled, reunited, redistributed according to principles developed by the botanist and her discipline. "With so many trumps in hand, every scientist becomes a structuralist" (PH 38) and the forest is "reduced to its simplest expression" (PH 39).[5] For their part, the pedologists organize the space of the forest utilizing surveying techniques (PH 43). The land itself is said to be transformed into a "proto-laboratory – a Euclidean world where all phenomena can be registered by a collection of coordinates" (ibid.). As the soil samples are collected, the geo-morphologist records the coordinates of each location, the number of the hole from which they have been extracted, the time, and depth, as well as any available qualitative data. Once they are collected, she sends the samples to laboratories around the world where chemical composition, grain size, and radioactivity can be measured (PH 46).[6] The upshot of this activity is that every studied aspect of the forest belongs both to the world of things and to that of signs. Science studies is to focus precisely on this hybrid, the materiality of the soil and the coding of the sign.

For Latour, all scientific work in the field and in the laboratory, such as that of Louis Pasteur, also extensively profiled by Latour, raises a fundamental question. This is the question of an "alternative to the model of statements that posit

---

the social sciences reside in the observer or in the phenomenon observed. These aspects are: the nature of groups, actions, objects, facts, and the question of the empirical nature of the social sciences. See Latour, *Reassembling the Social: An Introduction to Actor-Network-Theory* (Oxford: Oxford University Press, 2005), 22 n.16.
4. Who, we might ask, is foreign?
5. There is no indication from the botanist herself how she sees this activity.
6. Qualitative considerations include texture, color, and earthworm activity.

a world 'out there' which language tries to reach through a correspondence across the yawning gap separating the two" (PH 141). In the field, as dirt and plant samples are gathered and studied, "each element belongs to matter by its origin and to form by its destination," that is, no rupture appears between things and signs and "elementary *forms* of mathematics … are used to collect *matter* through the mediation of a practice embodied in a group of researchers" (PH 57–8).[7] Mediation produces what Latour calls a *hybrid* consisting of form and matter, skilled bodies, and groups arranged in a *continuous* space-time, a regulated *series* of transformations, transmutations, and translations. This kind of knowledge does not refer to the world "out there" but to an immanent world that keeps "something" constant through a series of transformations, an immanent world of coherence and continuity, the *same meaning* through a series of transformations. For example, matching the color of soil samples with a standardized color chart pierced with holes, the material soil samples can be read literally as a text, as belonging to a color code that can be communicated anywhere in the world (PH 58–60). This test is preceded and followed by a multitude of others that, more radically, put a sign in place of a thing. Finally, the signs are assembled and a diagram is constructed that takes the place of the original situation, revealing otherwise invisible features of the savannah–forest transition.

Latour calls this process translation. He claims, initially, to utilize a semiotic model but semiotics operates only within translation. "All reasoning is of the same form; one sentence follows another. Then a third asserts that these are identical even though they do not resemble one another … the second is used in place of the first, and a fifth affirms that the second and the fourth are identical."[8] In this way, a sentence is displaced and translated, all the while *pretending* not to have moved, to have stayed faithful. Yet as Latour's many diagrams attest, there is a structure here as well as a system. For example, not only do the elements of knowledge exist in *continuous* space-time, but the chain they form conforms to the dictates of dynamical systems as defined by classical physics; it must be reversible, closed, atomistic (consisting of numerous distinct elements or actors in Latour's terminology), and, within limits, deterministic.[9] Like the atoms described in Newton's laws of motion, *truth* must be transportable in either direction along this chain such that "truth-value circulates here like electricity through a wire"; it moves continuously through a *closed* system or area. Although the chain has no limit at either end, whatever gets added on must participate in

---

7. The *elements* referred to here are elements presented in a scientific text that includes Latour as an author (PH 56).

8. Bruno Latour, *The Pasteurization of France*, Alan Sheridan and John Law (trans.) (Cambridge, MA: Harvard University Press, 1988), 176.

9. David J. Depew and Bruce H. Weber, *Darwinism Evolving: Systems Dynamics and the Genealogy of Natural Selection* (Cambridge, MA: MIT Press, 1995), 92.

the series nature of the transformations in accordance with the elements of the immanent system: locality, particularity, materiality, multiplicity, and continuity at one end; compatibility, standardization, text, calculation, circulation, and relative universality at the other. Each stage is thereby matter for what follows and form for what precedes. The two directions represent the limits of the system, the rules of reduction and realism at one end and amplification and relativism at the other. Once such rules are in place, they remain in place, and the phenomena Latour describes well up in the middle between the two limits, then pass up and down the chain of transformations (PH 70–74).[10]

If it can be said that a network of actants all contributed to the scientific phenomenon called savannah–forest encroachment, what can be said of Pasteur's laboratory? "Pasteur encountered a vague, cloudy, gray substance sitting meekly in the corner of his flasks and turned it into the splendid, well-defined, articulate yeast twirling magnificently across the ballroom of the Academy" (PH 145).[11] Doing away with the epistemological–ontological divide, as Latour claims to do, entails granting historicity to the humans doing research as well as to the microorganisms they are researching. So Latour states that Pasteur changed the microorganisms by means of a simple recourse to the idea that rather than two realms there are many. In this, Latour bows in the direction of Idealism, returning to humans the possibility of activity without reopening a subject–object dichotomy between nature and mind or society. In other words, action, far from being a property of humans, belongs to an *association* of actants, human and nonhuman, able to exchange competences and offer one another new possibilities, goals, and functions (PH 182).[12] The actants involved in *Pasteurization* include Pasteur himself, the culture medium, the ferment, the Lille laboratory, the French Academy, and on and on. In place of a single referent, one finds an entire series of transformations that make up the reference, and every change in the series of transformations circulates the reference, as Latour expresses it (PH 147–50). So the claim that a scientific phenomenon exists arises from the claim that it is entrenched in an expensive and massive institution, involving a site, laws, people, and customs that provide the mediations needed for actors to establish, maintain, and substantiate newly emerging entities (PH 157, 307, 311).[13] The implication of this new view of science is that there is no *normal science* and there are no paradigms in the Kuhnian sense because there is no single coherent research program. Instead, there is a vast network consisting

---

10. In his description over these pages, Latour's onto-epistemology clearly resembles that of Gilles Deleuze in that both are modeled on mathematical dynamical systems.
11. Latour refers to Pasteur as Prince Charming and his microbes as Cinderella.
12. Following from this, Latour substitutes the term *collective* for the old word, society. A collective is an exchange of human and nonhuman properties inside a corporate body (PH 193).
13. See PH 303–11 for a full glossary of terms.

of various kinds of "actors" moving both forward and back, undergoing transformations. This is why, if an entity, such as Pasteur's microbes, circulates, the impact can be reversed, extended into the past making "the microbes the *substrate* of other people's unwitting actions" (PH 169).[14]

Latour's analyses of these two exemplary series of actants reveals what is for him a categorial error. Reflecting on the notion of translation, or network, he concludes that the work of those who study society remains incomprehensible if it is segmented into its three habitual categories of nature, politics, and discourse.[15] Each of these points engages in two sets of practices but conceives of them as completely separate from one another. The first of these two practices, "translation" or "mediation," creates mixtures between hybrids of nature and culture, but also between nature, politics, and discourse. The second, "purification," creates and maintains two entirely distinct ontological zones, one consisting of humans and one of nonhumans. It separates and maintains as separate nature, culture, and discourse. In other words, the modern critical stance purifies the networks, but the networks rely on what has been purified to carry out their translations. And yet, "we have never been modern" according to Latour, insofar as we simultaneously direct our attention to both purification and translation and do not separate them (WM 11). Although a certain amount of intellectual effort has been devoted to the study of the opposition between science and discourse, virtually none has been directed to that between science and politics. However, science and politics may be defined by a common text, that of the *constitution*. Just as politicians draft a constitution for states, so scientists draft one for nature, and each constitution has been drafted by excluding the power of the other (WM 14).

If the moderns conceived of hybrids as (impossible) mixtures of radically disconnected pure forms, for example, Nature/Society or Nature/Subject, then let us become premodern, deploying the middle as the point of departure from which point of view the pure extremes are but provisional and partial.[16] Crucially, the place of the object will be modified; no longer the realm of things-in-themselves, it will belong to the community that recognizes how and to what extent objects construct subjects. From now on all actors have historicity and the extremes of Nature and Society can be utilized as relative reference points useful in differentiating intermediaries. In addition, then, to the horizontal (*x*) axis at each end of which the two pure extremes are located, Latour calls for

---

14. See PH 170. Substance here means "the work of *retrofitting* that situates a more recent event as what 'lies beneath' an older one" (*ibid.*).

15. Bruno Latour, *We Have Never Been Modern*, Catherine Porter (trans.) (Cambridge, MA: Harvard University Press, 1993), 3. Hereafter cited as WM followed by the page number.

16. "A mediator, however, is an original event and creates what it translates as well as the entities between which it plays the mediating role" (WM 78).

the addition of a vertical (y) axis, one that registers variations in the stability of entities from event to essence with the assumption that all actants proceed from existence (below the horizontal axis) to essence (above the horizontal axis). However, very little, in fact no activity can be discerned above the horizontal axis in the essential sectors. It appears that all events find their reality in the existential realm, the depths analogous to the depths of the earth itself where magma erupts and forms relatively stable sites. It is, then, by this means that the "ontology of mediators" has a variable geometry, and the so-called essence of an event or actant is simply the trajectory that links each of its manifestations in the x–y plane (WM 86, 83).[17]

II. ISABELLE STENGERS AND ILYA PRIGOGINE

Isabelle Stengers[18] emerged internationally as a philosopher of science, along with coauthor and chemist Ilya Prigogine,[19] on publication of their book, *Order Out of Chaos: Man's New Dialogue with Nature*. There they argue that if "in the classical view, the basic processes of nature were considered to be deterministic and reversible … [t]oday we see everywhere, the role of irreversible processes, of fluctuations."[20] Stengers and Prigogine reformulate this world as open, complex, probabilistic, and temporally irreversible. Thus *Order Out of Chaos* is an account of the conceptual transformation of science from classical science to the present, particularly as it applies to the macroscopic scale, the scale of atoms, molecules, and biomolecules, with special attention to the problem of time, a problem that

17. That this is a dynamical system operating in what is called ideal or mathematical *state space* should by now be evident.

18. Isabelle Stengers (1949– ; born in Belgium) received her degree in chemistry at the Université Libre de Bruxelles, where she is currently a professor in the philosophy of science. Her work has been influenced by Sandra Harding, Serres, Gilbert Simondon, Shirley Strum, and Whitehead.

19. Ilya Prigogine (January 25, 1917–May 28, 2003; born in Moscow, Russia) received a *licence en sciences chimiques* in 1939, a *doctorat en sciences chimiques* in 1941, and was made Agrégé de l'Enseignement Supérieur en Chimie Physique in 1945, all at the Université Libre de Bruxelles. His work was influenced by Bergson, Théophile De Donder, Jean Timmermans, and Alan Turing. Prigogine held appointments at the Université Libre de Bruxelles, the International Solvay Institute in Brussels (1959–2003), as Professor of Physics and Chemical Engineering at the University of Texas at Austin (1967–2003), and as Visiting Professor of Chemistry at the Enrico Fermi Institute for Nuclear Studies and the Study of Metals at the University of Chicago (1961–66). He was Professor of Physics and Chemical Engineering at the University of Texas at Austin (1967–2003), Regental Professor (1977–2003), and Ashbel Smith Professor (1984–2003).

20. Isabelle Stengers and Ilya Prigogine, *Order Out of Chaos: Man's New Dialogue with Nature* (New York: Bantam Books, 1984), xxvii. Hereafter cited as OC followed by the page number.

arose out of the realization that new dynamic states of matter may emerge from thermal chaos when a system interacts with its surroundings. These new structures were given the name *dissipative structures* to indicate that dissipation can in fact play a constructive role in the formation of new states (OC 12).[21] Stengers and Prigogine thus take us from the static view of classical dynamics to an evolutionary view arising with nonequilibrium thermodynamics, based on time irreversibility. Simultaneously, "one of the main themes of this book is that of a strong interaction of the issues proper to culture as a whole and the internal conceptual problems of science in particular" (OC 19).[22] Thus, the reorientation from the classical to the contemporary view is, for them, equally reflected in the conflict between the natural sciences and the social sciences and humanities. If the development of science has been understood to shift away from concrete experience toward abstraction, this is, the authors believe, a consequence of the limitations of classical science, its inability to give a coherent account of the relationship between humans and nature. Many important results were repressed or set aside insofar as they failed to conform to the classical model. In order to free itself from traditional modes of comprehending nature, science isolated and purified its practices in the effort to achieve greater and greater autonomy, leading it to conceptualize its knowledge as universal and to isolate itself from any social context (OC 19–22).

Nevertheless, Stengers and Prigogine are alarmed by contemporary criticisms of science, such as that of the philosopher Martin Heidegger,[23] who levies what they see as an unrestricted condemnation of modern science,[24] insofar as Heidegger seems to identify science with the subjection of nature (OC 32–3).[25] Equally, they are concerned with the contemporary shift away from science toward mysticism. Neither of these alternatives provides the direction they seek. The enthusiasm for modern science that arose in the sixteenth century and, in many respects, continues unabated today, arose, they posit, as an extension of the age-old effort of humankind to organize and exploit the world and to understand

---

21. Equilibrium thermodynamics studies the transformation of energy, and the laws of thermodynamics recognize that although "energy is conserved," when energy is defined as the capacity to do work, nevertheless, nature is fundamentally asymmetrical; that is, although the total quantity of energy remains the same, its distribution changes in a manner that is irreversible. See P. W. Atkins, *The Second Law* (New York: Scientific American Library, 1984), 8–13.

22. The French title of this book, an earlier and slightly less developed version, reflects the "new alliance" between science and culture.

*23. Heidegger's critique of science is discussed in the essay by Dennis J. Schmidt in *The History of Continental Philosophy: Volume 4*.

24. For a nuanced discussion of Heidegger's relation to science and philosophy of science, see Trish Glazebrook, *Heidegger's Philosophy of Science* (New York: Fordham University Press, 2000).

25. Latour picks up this theme from Stengers and Prigogine.

humankind's place in nature. However, while the ancients remained preoccupied with the question of why certain natural processes occur, the moderns ask only *how*, and answering this question involves activity, the manipulation of physical reality rather than its passive observation. Thus, unlike its predecessor, modern science learned to prepare and isolate physical reality to make it conform to an ideal conceptual scheme (OC 37–41). Experiment is an art with no guarantees of success. It requires choosing an interesting question that embodies a theory's implications, abstracting a natural phenomenon from its environment, and staging it to test the theory in a manner that is both reproducible and communicable. Additionally, modern science can engage in a thought experiment, governed entirely by theory (OC 42–3). What is crucial here is that the scientist cannot force nature to respond the way the scientist wishes; there is, in effect, a dialogue between humans and nature, not a dictatorship.

But science writes in a mathematical language, so the world appears to be homogeneous, as a result of which the simple can always explain the complex. Moreover, the scientific view may have arisen, in part, owing to the mutual amplification of theological discourse and science, a resonance located in the medieval insistence on the rationality of God, who could be counted on to provide a basis for the world's intelligibility. Humans, utilizing scientific experiments, sought to view the world from this same divine viewpoint. This is how, Stengers and Prigogine claim, the aim of modern science came to be that of discovering the *unique* truth about the world, one that excludes the observer and reflects the divine point of view (OC 44–52). For modern science, the central theoretical and practical problem was to find a way to define a continuously varying speed, instantaneous changes in position, velocity, and acceleration, and the state of a body at a given instant. The nearly miraculous explanation came in the form of a single force called gravity. Any pair of material bodies, planets or atoms, is linked by the same force of attraction that operates in the universe as a whole, any local variations being too small to have an impact. Given an initial state, the general law deduces the series of states the system will pass through, and a single state is sufficient to define both the future and the past of any system. This is the meaning of reversibility. Classical dynamics required bold assumptions: a world in which all trajectories are reversible. And yet, the active experiments carried out by scientists remained *extraneous* to the idealized, reversible world they describe (OC 57–61).[26] This sort of tension between science and society remains thematically central. Stengers and Prigogine are quite explicit that they look for a convergence between nature and the mind that knows, perceives, and creates science. The ideal of a being who could calculate

---

26. "If the velocities of all the points of a system are reversed … [t]he system would retrace all the states it went through during the previous change" (OC 61).

the future and past of the world, starting from the observation of an instantaneous state, is not an ideal they endorse (OC 77).

This raises the question: What *is* the relation of philosophy to science? Is philosophy the queen of the sciences or only the handmaiden? For Stengers and Prigogine, the answer to this question is closely associated with their understanding of time, which, they claim, can bridge the spiritual and physical aspects of nature, including human nature. To this end, they narrate the rediscovery of the arrow of time by science. Moving from the study of heat to the conservation of energy, the first and second laws of thermodynamics, linear and nonlinear thermodynamics, self-organization, chaos, dissipative structures, evolution, complexity, open systems, relativity, uncertainty, and finally to temporal evolution in quantum systems, leads to the conclusion that the reversibility of classical dynamics is a characteristic of closed dynamic systems only, and that science must accept a pluralistic world in which reversible and irreversible processes coexist.[27] In place of general, all-embracing schemes that could be expressed by eternal laws, there is time. In place of symmetry, there are symmetry-breaking processes on all levels, and yet, temporal irreversibility has become the unifying source of order on all levels. For classical dynamics, time was a geometric parameter; as such, this conception was part of a general drive to eliminate time, to reduce the different and the changing to the identical and permanent. Although Bergson, in 1922, attempted to introduce and defend (against Einstein) the possibility of a multiplicity of coexisting "lived" times, for Einstein, intelligibility remained tied to immutability (OC 293–4). It is precisely this "denial of becoming" that led to the rift between science and philosophy (OC 298).[28] Thus, Stengers and Prigogine propose a structure that takes its orientation from the observer, "who measures coordinates and momenta and studies their change in time," leading to the discovery of unstable dynamic systems, intrinsic randomness, and irreversibility, and proceeding to dissipative structures and from there back to the time-oriented observer (OC 300). All scientific activity is time-oriented and the scientist must come to see herself as part of the universe she describes. Irreversibility is not universal; it requires a minimum of complexity in the dynamical system, such that with an increase of complexity, the role of irreversibility increases (OC 301).[29] If the philosopher and mathematician Gottfried Leibniz's monadology is "the most

---

27. These theories and others along with their philosophical implications are discussed at length in *Order Out of Chaos*.
28. By the time scientists began to consider time irreversibility, philosophy had already been relegated to the sidelines.
29. "The world of classical science was a world in which the only events that could occur were those deducible from the instantaneous state of the system … [T]he objects chosen by the first physicists to explore the validity of a quantitative description … were found to correspond to

consequential formulation of a universe from which all becoming is eliminated," one can look to Charles Sanders Peirce, Bergson, and Lucretius for original and "pioneering step[s] toward the understanding of the pluralism involved in physical laws" (OC 303). Therefore Stengers and Prigogine conclude that, contrary to the model put forward by Thomas Kuhn, change in science does not occur as a result of a crisis, a nearly violent disruption of an otherwise homogeneous and conservative scientific community. Although they concede that crises do occur, science can also be characterized by problems that arise as the consequence of "deliberate and lucid questions asked by scientists who know that the questions had both scientific and philosophical aspects"; in other words, change occurs as a result of both the "internal logic of science" and "the cultural and social context of our time" (OC 309).

Following the publication of *Order Out of Chaos*, Stengers made a concerted effort to go her own way as well as to forge new intellectual ties to other scientists and philosophers. Stengers begins by questioning the concept of complexity in the discourse of science, a concept that comes to the fore when the relevance of a *simple* model and that model's relation to what is complicated, but not necessarily complex, becomes an issue. Just because a phenomenon requires a probability treatment does not imply complexity, which is distinguishable from the *complicated* real, characterized by approximations that limit us, but which can still be identified.[30] Close to but not identical with *emergence*, which refers to a physical genesis of the new, complexity, Stengers argues, implies a *conceptual* genesis, an expression of the limited character of the conceptual tools appropriate to simple models but which cannot be prolonged as relevant (PI 12). Insofar as complexity is conceptual, it sets out problems. For scientists, "complexity arises when they must accept that the categories of understanding that guided their explorations are in question, when the manner in which they pose their questions has itself become problematic" (PI 13).[31] Thus, one does not discover complexity with respect to objects with a history; rather, complexity is constitutive of a *living object* (PI 14). This is especially the case when science studies beings produced by history that are also capable of history; that is, the meaning of this being's interrogation may also present problems for the being itself. The intrinsic complexity of living systems thus imposes the necessity for intelligent

a *unique* mathematical description that actually reproduced the divine ideality of Aristotle's heavenly bodies (OC 305–6).

30. Isabelle Stengers, *Power and Invention*, Paul Bains (trans.) (Minneapolis, MN: University of Minnesota Press, 1997), 7, 10. Hereafter cited as PI followed by the page number.

31. "Complexity is not a theory, an exportable general model. The 'complex' lesson of dissipative structures is … this gravitational factor that, according to circumstances, can be insignificant or 'change everything'" (PI 13).

experimentation, avoiding silencing the interrogated being (PI 17).[32]A related and formidable distinction in physics is that between phenomenological and fundamental laws, the former tied to irreversible evolutions and the latter to reversibility. Laws of physics are fundamental insofar as they go beyond appearances to unify the diversity of physical phenomena. From this perspective, the distinction between before and after is merely phenomenological, and uncertainty regarding the future is an effect of ignorance (PI 21–2). What physicists do not see, according to Stengers, is the existence of two types of deterministic laws. One is a science of movement or dynamics, for which the velocity at a given instant is equal to the cause producing it. The velocity must be sufficient to allow the body to regain the altitude it lost, thereby joining past and future through the sign of identity, which is understood as a *syntactic rule*, a rule defining velocity, force, and acceleration (PI 24, 25).[33] The second, based on the study of unstable dynamic systems, allows a rapprochement of sorts between fundamental laws and phenomenology. In a highly unstable system, starting from quasi-identical states, originally indistinguishable systems will behave dissimilarly and only a God capable of defining the instantaneous state of a system with infinite precision could calculate the trajectories (PI 27). This distinction exposes the *limits* of the physicist's ideal without abandoning fundamental laws. Closely related is the question of change, whether it is imposed from the outside or is immanent to things. Modern science set itself up in opposition to the latter, establishing the dominance of the idea of change as nothing but movement, yet with two possibilities. Either change is due to chance collisions of atoms or there is a force exterior to masses responsible for movement (PI 33). Indeed, such a force was put in place in the form of mathematical universal laws of dynamics, which imply that an object of dynamics can be completely understood, meaning that the totality of its past and future can be deduced. And yet, Joseph Fourier's formulation of the law of heat diffusion, insofar as it characterized an intrinsically irreversible process, the first to be given a mathematical expression, was a scandal for science, since it brought forth the realization that dynamics, describing nature as obedient and controllable, corresponds only to a particular case. The importance of unities such as photons and electrons, whose processes imply irreversible interaction with the world, gradually came to into view (PI 48). Insofar as these transitions are *smooth*, continuous processes, they promote an acceptance of the autonomy of things, and the opening of new alliances with nature and with natural and productive processes of all types (PI 56, 59).

---

32. Insistence on attention to the sensitivities of the interrogated subject is fundamental in Stengers's thinking overall.
33. This is the principle of sufficient reason.

Such transitions and transformations, no matter how smooth and continuous, raise certain important questions. If science had once been understood entirely in terms of fundamental laws, then is it science and scientists that propose changes to this understanding? Or, is it nonscience? Exactly what counts as science can be determined only in a precise context. Innovations and transformations are creations, organizing the examination of phenomena, which "produce the criteria on the basis of which the accepted innovations will be described a posteriori as 'obviously' scientific" (PI 82). The implication Stengers draws is that science is a collective activity producing its own norms and responses to these norms, thereby linking scientists and allowing them to work. It is this collective activity, rather than objectivity, however one defines it, that connects scientists who engage in scientific activities, but only insofar as it attracts their interest (PI 82, 83).[34] This question of what is science and what makes one a scientist haunts Stengers's work. What concerns and worries her is the "condemnation of nature to exploitation, the subject and object to separation," and "the splintered figure of the other of the identity of science" (PI 110–11).[35] Rather than Kuhnian official scientific maps and scientific rationality guaranteeing access to phenomena, Stengers proposes a structure of interconnections and relations of expression between otherwise separated populations, keeping alive the possibility of a certain *jouissance,* that moment when a small detail destroys a grand generalization that the road map had guaranteed.

These considerations culminate in Stengers's *The Invention of Modern Science,* a philosophical work in which she engages directly with the dominant philosophies of science to examine the epistemological and social relations between philosophers and scientists.[36] For scientists, Stengers argues, Kuhn's claim that in *normal science,* scientists do what they have learned to do, that is, utilize a paradigm to study scientific phenomena, preserves what is essential.[37] What is essential is autonomy, the preservation of the community as the norm and as condition of the possibility for a fruitful exercise of science (IMS 5). This is crucial in several respects. Guided and supported by the community, individual scientists are freed from accounting for their choices and research priorities

---

34. "To interest someone means ... to act in such a way that this thing ... can concern the person, intervene in his or her life, and eventually transform it" (PI 83–4).
35. "I would like to express the deep uneasiness aroused in me by the binary characterization that the modern sciences seem to produce, constructing their identity through opposition with an *other*" (PI 111).
36. Isabelle Stengers, *The Invention of Modern Science,* Daniel W. Smith (trans.) (Minneapolis, MN: University of Minnesota Press, 2000). Hereafter cited as IMS followed by the page number.
37. See Thomas Kuhn, *The Structure of Scientific Revolutions* (Chicago, IL: University of Chicago Press, 1970).

and they confidently confront even the most disconcerting phenomena. Such "tacit knowledge" is crucial to the scientist who plays the role of an expert or connoisseur who has the capacity to evaluate research within the domain of her expertise (IMS 6–7).[38] Nevertheless, while the concept of the paradigm guarantees cumulative progress and consensus in the sciences, Kuhn also proposed a principle of symmetry that requires the researcher to be attentive to everything outside the research paradigm, such as relations of force, social games of power, differences of resources, or impure interests (industry, the state). Is it not the case, after all, that scientists do, in fact, draw on all the resources of society (IMS 9)? How could they continue their research without the resources supplied by the social, political, technological, and economic environment? Even so, Stengers maintains, scientists do attempt to conceal their relation to everything outside science. Thus the attacks aimed at technosciences for failing to distinguish between the productions of science and those of technical and technological production, as well as feminist critiques aimed at the identification of scientific rationality with male values, fall short of their goal insofar as, unlike Kuhn, these critiques accept what scientists say about themselves without question. Only Kuhn's questioning of the mode of knowledge, the relation of normal science to what is outside it, opened a wound and fomented a revolt. Scientists might accept the social nature of their discipline, yet they insist that it is more than that, that there is an element of reality, and that if scientists have to justify their actions as socially interested, it will be increasingly difficult for them to pursue minor areas of research. Moreover, they hold out the fear of being overtaken by the interests of those who accuse them of being interested.

In acknowledging this problem, Stengers takes up the cause of science as much as that of philosophy. As she argues,

> the philosophers were requiring of the sciences (which they do not practice) that they justify the practice of the philosophers of science; that sciences illustrate a definition of scientific rationality which the philosophers could then disengage, so as to know better than the scientists, what defines scientists as such. (IMS 14)[39]

To stem the emergence of oppositional forces, Stengers proposes that philosophy should be willing to practice the "Leibnizian Constraint," not to maintain as its *ideal* the reversal of established sentiments since they may be precisely

---

38. For "tacit knowledge," see Michael Polanyi, "The Republic of Science: Its Political and Economic Theory," *Minerva: A Review of Science, Learning and Policy* 1(1) (1962).

39. In fencing, to disengage is to perform a maneuver that changes the line of attack.

what give meaning and interest to one's problem (*ibid.*).[40] What, after all, is the point of studying science if not to try to open scientists to what their established identity led them to refuse, combat, or misunderstand? And if the words we use clash with others, scandalize and provoke hateful misunderstandings, producing greater rigidity in order to protect each one's position, then constructing differences using language that leaves irreducible oppositions is clearly counter to the goal of opening science to its own outside. Thus, a version Latour's "principle of irreduction" will be called into play, that of not putting oneself in the position of a judge who knows what science or politics is and who gives or refuses to give one of these terms the power to explain the other. Neither unveiling the truth behind appearances nor denouncing the appearances that veil the truth, Stengers guards against the *mobilizing* power of language, the formation of antagonistic camps and recruits to populate them. In this way, she hopes to make room in society for the recovery of a taste for an interest in science and technology, a taste that allows one to take them seriously, but also to laugh at them in a way that does not mock and is not ironic. Rather, laughter is directed toward the life of power when power conceals itself behind objectivity or rationality. Can we not laugh *with* the scientists? How, she inquires, can this situation be brought about (IMS 17)?

Stengers formulates a creative proposal. Is it not the case, she asks, that scientific theories require the invention of a world that they then render intelligible and to which they give signification? Such a situation undoubtedly calls for careful description. Does this situation conserve the idea of a pure mathematical and experimental science juxtaposed with an impure external milieu that constantly threatens to invade it? Or, as Stengers suggests, can we take the scientific paradigm to be a manner of intervening in the world, an intervention that creates what it explains in a competent, discussable, and astute manner that constitutes the paradigm as an event (IMS 49)?[41] In such an intervention, *every* fact is an artifact, dictated by experimental conditions that produce observable phenomena. Nevertheless, even if we accept the redefinition of the paradigm as an event, we might ask about the necessity of paradigms. That is, without a paradigm, are the claims of scientists nothing but ideological claims? This inquiry brings us back to the relation between science and its other, its nonscience, and the assertion that science must have autonomy and demarcation. One might, like Hannah Arendt, put into question the false opposition between a truth of which "man" is the measure and a pure rational truth, that is, between *poeisis*

---

40. In spite of her admiration for Deleuze, Stengers is not unwilling to diverge from his philosophy in this and in other key respects.

41. "A great number of actors, all of whom have been, in one way or another, produced by the text, undertake to draw lessons from it. All are situated in the space it has opened; none can claim to have a privileged relation of truth with it" (IMS 67).

and praxis when the latter is understood in the Greek manner as performative speech for the sake of immortality that excludes useful or necessary acts (IMS 61).[42] Indeed, this became an important aspect of the distinction between humans and animals as only those who seek immortal fame do not live and die like animals! In this regard, Stengers's claim that the baboons studied by Shirley Strum *do politics* radically overturns the notions of purity and demarcation and brings to light the disqualification of women, foreigners, and others as political actors. Stengers's goal is not to eliminate the difference between science and sociology but, precisely, to open up a space where the distinction between the two can be constructed; not to deny that there is a difference between science and nonscience but also not to declare that scientists have privileged knowledge of what this difference that singularizes them signifies (IMS 62, 64, 67).

What is called for, according to Stengers, is the construction of a point of view from which modern science can be understood as a contingent process, a process whose statements belong to the order of the possible in the context of scientists working with other scientists. This is a point of view that acknowledges the difference between opinions and what can be demonstrated (IMS 80, 81, 83). So, for example, we might say that Galileo's law of motion is relative to an order of created fact, an artifact of the lab such that the different falling motions and the three concepts of speed that he develops give way to a motion both unique and decomposable in terms of independent variables, controllable by the operator and capable of forcing the skeptic to admit that there is only a single legitimate way to articulate them. This is a world, both fictive and concrete, that yields to one method of interrogation, as only this method has the power to silence critics and rivals. Simultaneously, it is an abstract world: things will have been eliminated if the experimental apparatus does not permit their categories to be defined (IMS 84–5, 90). If the method of science produces truth with regard to a reality it invents *and* discovers, this reality guarantees the production of truth when the constraints of the procedure are respected and the scientist submits to an event that cannot be reduced to the simple possession of knowledge but rather gathers those who are *interested*, who are willing to risk the intervention of this event in their own problematic field of interrogation (IMS 91, 92).[43] Thus, to bring a scientific event, say the theory of the big bang, into existence, specialists must multiply the links between this event and work of scientists who do not

---

42. See Hannah Arendt, *The Human Condition* (Chicago, IL: University of Chicago Press, 1998), 12–21, especially: "The task and potential greatness of mortals lie in their ability to produce things – works and deeds and words – which would deserve to be and, at least to a degree, are at home in everlastingness" (*ibid.*, 19).

43. "Interest derives from *inter-esse*; to be situated between …. Those who let themselves become interested in an experimental statement accept the hypothesis of a link that engages them" (IMS 95).

belong to this specialty. Unlike communicative rationality, which seeks agreement, scientific rationality seeks to make one forget the contingent singularity of the invention of an experimental practice, so as to make the phenomenon available for other work, to make it objective and to theorize it, to make it construct a representation of reality as it exists outside the laboratory (IMS 105, 107).[44]

All of this, of course, crashes up against the rocks of modern science and modern life. Kuhnian paradigms no longer form as science mobilizes rapidly through technological innovation, leaving no time to think data through or search for subtle correlations. Scientists are both drawn to and ruled by the imperative to provide society with useful information. Lead scientists and principal investigators have become "patrons" recruiting allies and financing for their growing laboratories. They speak different languages to different constituents, including the "incompetent" public; they are encouraged by "philosophers who learned in school that science would decipher laws that characterize phenomena objectively and their task would be to think this" (IMS 118), and by the errors of those sociologists who trust the rhetoric addressed to the public, "not realizing that the information they have access to reduces them to impotence" (IMS 124). But it should be the case, Stengers advises, that when these scientists leave the laboratory, the change of milieu implies a change of practices, an acknowledgment that it is part of their scientific, ethical, and political responsibility to affirm the selective character of their knowledge, thereby separating science and power (IMS 128, 134). Silencing rivals in order to assert the power to represent phenomena, declaring nonlaboratory sciences such as evolution impotent, the association of a free subject with one freed of opinion, the stabilization of the subject–object relation: these are some of the unfortunate consequences of confusing the event of science in theoretico-experimental practices with the production in laboratories of allies who fail to recognize the limits of their invention-discovery, who fail to separate science from power (IMS 130, 133). This is echoed in the feminist perspective of Sandra Harding, who endorses the impassioned activity of Galileo and Newton while decrying the discourse on method and objectivity that makes their work authoritative (IMS 133, 21).[45] Additionally, the limits of theoretico-experimental sciences must be established in the face of newly emerging sciences and field sciences such as computer simulation. The latter produces no theory, only models that cannot be constructed in the laboratory, and finds nothing but constraint in mathematical laws. Or, there are the field sciences, which must collect indices and reconstitute concrete

---

44. "Every theory affirms a social power, a power to judge the value of human practices. No theory is imposed without social, economic, or political power being at play, somewhere" (IMS 113).
45. See Sandra Harding, *The Science Question in Feminism* (Ithaca, NY: Cornell University Press, 1986).

situations rather than representing phenomena like functions with independent variables, and which tend to be interdisciplinary and open to uncertain-
ties rather than proofs. And, there are the scientists, like psychoprimatologists
who are faced with creatures (rats, baboons, humans) who are interested in the
questions they are asked, or who have brought new beings into existence that
cannot be sent out into a nature that is no longer a natural environment for
them (IMS 135–46).

Acknowledging this multiplicity of interests makes way for the invention
of a new image of science, one that no longer represents the world as offered
up in order to be deciphered in terms of obstacles to be skirted, reduced, or
ignored. In order for the multiplicity of scientific practices to be represented,
science would have to consider a *slowing down* of its current mobilization, a
slowing down that gives voice to the "Parliament of Things," proposed by Latour.
The Parliament of Things is a space of mediators with room for both Natures
and Societies, where their representatives all speak in the name of some invention, some "object-discourse-nature-society whose new properties astound us
all and whose network extends from my refrigerator to the Antarctic by way of
chemistry, law, the State, the economy, and satellites" (IMS 154).[46] Such a point
of view is neither revolutionary nor reformist, insofar as it puts into question
both the concept of ruptures in the continuum of smooth space and the possibility of continuous progress. In this it is truly paradoxical, proving that even
epistemology requires invention, the invention of the ways that make possible
becoming interested – *inter-esse* – in others, and, in turn, making them interested as well, not via the realm of intersubjective or communicative rationality,
but rather through the invention of links arising as disparities (IMS 153–5).[47]
As Stengers states, the scientist's profile will have to change: neither a patron
nor a practitioner of normal science, lacking any common ground, the scientist
will recognize herself as a representative of the problem that both engages and
situates her. And so, Stengers asks, is not every innovation made on the basis
of a risk, "a quantitative intensification of already-existing putting into relation"
(IMS 158–9)? If so, then let us recognize this risk, let all sensibilities, not just
those of scientists, formulate problems, and let us not forget that our practices
must hold up when put to the test.

---

46. See Bruno Latour, "D'où viennent les microbes?," *Les Cahiers de Science et Vie* 4 (August 1991),
    47.
47. Like Latour, Stengers appears to advocate an onto-epistemology based on that constructed
    by Deleuze. However, in her call for a slow-down and in her problematization of continuous,
    smooth space, she may well be indicating the need for something else. See as well my *The
    Universal (In the Realm of the Sensible)* (Edinburgh: Edinburgh University Press, 2007), ch. 1,
    for a proposal concerning such an alternative onto-epistemology.

7

EUROPEAN CITIZENSHIP: A POSTNATIONALIST PERSPECTIVE

Rosi Braidotti

This essay argues that the establishment of the European Union as a constitutional, political, and cultural project, and, more specifically, the enlargement of the European Union to include former Eastern bloc countries after 1989, constitute a break in the scholarship about Europe as a philosophical concept. This claim does not imply any causal connection between the events, but rather draws new analytic categories, which I will outline and explore in this essay.

The starting premise is that the classical scholarship on the philosophical idea of Europe had settled on the consensus that it coincides with the universalizing powers of self-reflexive reason. This idea, formulated in the eighteenth century and canonized by Hegel's philosophy of history, transforms Europe into a universal attribute of the mind that can lend its quality to any object. The self-reflexivity at stake in this definition of Europe was reasserted by Edmund Husserl in the 1930s as a "historical teleology of the infinite goals of reason."[1] This self-aggrandizing vision assumes that Europe is not just a geopolitical location, but rather a concept unfolding through space and time, which can be applicable anytime and anywhere, provided the essential criteria are met. Europe announces itself as the site of origin of critical reason and self-reflexivity. Equal only to itself, Europe as universal consciousness therefore transcends its specificity or, rather, posits the power of transcendence as its distinctive characteristic and universalism as its particularity. This makes Eurocentrism into more than just a contingent matter of attitude: it is a structural element of

---

1. Edmund Husserl, *The Crisis of European Sciences and Transcendental Phenomenology* (Evanston, IL: Northwestern University Press, 1970), 299.

philosophical thought, which is also embedded in both theory and institutional and pedagogical practices.

I will focus on two features of this Eurocentric paradigm. The first is a universal claim about the structure, value, and function of reason. The second is the importance of the dialectics of self and other, or the binary logic of identity and otherness as the motor for the formation of subjectivity. Central to this universalistic posture and its binary logic is the notion of "difference" as pejoration. Subjectivity is equated with consciousness, universal rationality, and self-regulating ethical behavior, whereas Otherness is defined as its negative and specular counterpart. Insofar as difference spells inferiority, it acquires both essentialist and lethal connotations for people who get branded as "others." These are sexualized, racialized, and naturalized others, who are reduced to the status of disposable bodies. Because their history in Europe has been one of lethal exclusions and fatal disqualifications, they raise issues of both power and exclusion and the need for ethical accountability.

This universalistic self-image has been challenged and displaced by alternative visions of the philosophical status of Europe.[2] These challenges are both internal to philosophy as a corporate discourse with a formidable institutional history and external to it. The internal interrogation line is drawn along the debate about the "crisis of reason" that has occurred since the early days of poststructuralism between its proponents and opponents. The external fault line is drawn by intersecting critiques developed by radical epistemologies such as feminism, environmentalism, and postcolonial, race, and critical legal theories. They are formulated as a response to concrete world-historical events, such as colonialism, fascism, and communist totalitarianism, which exemplify the atrocities that were committed in the name of Europe's universal civilizing mission. These historical events are set off against the self-aggrandizing narratives derived from the Enlightenment. What emerges from this juxtaposition is a variety of new critical and creative modes of addressing the question of Europe as philosophy.

The European Union as the immediate social and political context in which these competing views emerge adds to their political and ethical urgency. It also sets the arena for a contested debate about what kind of political, moral, and legal entity Europe is in the process of becoming. This essay aims at providing an overview of the main trends of thought in this debate.

Before going any further, however, some careful distinctions need to be made between perspectives situated within the European continent itself and the terms of the debate within the Anglo-American world. I find it especially important to

---

*2. Some of these alternative visions are discussed by Eduardo Mendieta in "Postcolonialism, Postorientalism, Postoccidentalism," in this volume.

take distance from the often polemical tone the notion of Europe has acquired in US academic debates centered on French philosophy, especially on issues related to humanism, postmodernism, and relativism. A clear example is Martha Nussbaum's influential statement in *Cultivating Humanity* in favor of two inter-locked ideas that pertain to the classical paradigm of European thought: first, an unquestionable appeal to the authority of the history of European philos-ophy since Greek antiquity; second, the notion that the exercise of philosophical reason is a moral enterprise. This moral universalism concretely results in the liberal American translation of classical European humanism into elitist ideals about higher education, citizenship, and political participation. These beliefs in turn support a transhistorical and ethnocentric civilizational reading of this discipline as a universalistic discourse that is structurally antithetical to any localized, situated perspectives, which are reduced to relativism.

The philosophical opposition to this traditional view confirms the Eurocentric universalistic paradigm, albeit by negation. Recent critiques of the explicit racism of the great continental philosophers are conceived as deconstructions of this Eurocentric and masculinist bias in the teaching of the history of philosophy. Robert Bernasconi's critical analysis of the racist elements within philosophy contests the equation of continental philosophy with Europe as a geographical and historical entity.[3] It rather needs to be extended to include the multiple ethnic others and foreign influences that have nurtured and fueled continental thought. Bernasconi argues also that the institutional racism of philosophy is such that there is hardly any work on the history of African philosophical tradi-tions and the contribution they have made to the discipline. It is therefore urgent to compose alternative, non-Europe-based histories of continental philosophy as a transnational enterprise.

These critiques exemplify a trend that is also alive in European thought today. The operative words here are "situated perspectives." Both the critique of ahis-torical Eurocentrism and the quest for alternative genealogies of thought express a form of ethical and political accountability that requires adequate understand-ings of one's embedded and embodied perspectives. Michel Foucault's cartog-raphies of power provide a conceptual and methodological example of this approach, as do the feminist politics of locations as situated knowledges and Gilles Deleuze's concept of radical immanence. For all these thinkers, to stress the situated structure of philosophical knowledge also means to recognize its partial or limited nature. The immediate consequence of this acknowledgment is both ethical and methodological. It requires a specific form of accountability for the production of philosophical ideas. The critiques of both universalism

3. See Bernasconi's "Introduction," in Robert Bernasconi and Sybil Cook (eds), *Race and Racism in Continental Philosophy* (Bloomington, IN: Indiana University Press, 2003).

and of liberal individualism are fundamental starting-points to rethink the interconnection between the self and society in an accountable manner. This nondualistic situated ethics accounts in a nonrelativistic manner for the complex power mechanisms at play in the enunciation of scientific discourse.

For philosophers situated in Europe today, the European Union project has to do with the sobering experience of taking stock of our specific location. The opposite of the grandiose and aggressive universalism of the past, this is a situated and accountable perspective. Daniel Cohn-Bendit recently stated that for this European project to work, we must start from the assumption that Europe is the specific periphery where we live and that we must take responsibility for it.[4] Imagining anything else would be a repetition of that flight into abstraction for which our culture is (in)famous.

As a consequence, the working definition of Europe adopted in this essay takes a firm and critical distance from the Eurocentric universalism that is taken for granted in the dominant philosophical debates in North America, both by its supporters and by its opponents. I argue that as a result of the European Unification project, but also as a factor that sustains it, the philosophical question about Europe is no longer that of identity, but rather the process of rupture from and transformation of its imperial and undemocratic past. In other words, it is not about who Europeans are, but about what they are capable of becoming. Europe has to become the site of self-criticism and self-transformation on the basis of the hard-won lessons of its rich, dramatic, and complex history. Europe today stands for the ethical obligation to be accountable for its past history and the long shadow it casts on its present politics. In this respect, the political project of the European Union marks a radical redefinition of Europe's relationship to its outside, or its constitutive others. Insofar as this project is ongoing, it is both contested and fraught with internal contradictions. It follows, then, that the consensus about the displacement of the old universalizing notion of Europe produces a range of options regarding the alternatives. That philosophical consensus itself, however, is beyond dispute.

I. THE EUROPEAN UNION AS NEW DISCURSIVE FRAME

Historically, the project of the European Union originates in the defeat of fascism and Nazism after the Second World War and is grounded in antifascism, antinationalism, and antimilitarism. The life and work of one of the initiators

---

4. See Daniel Cohn-Bendit, "Transit Discussion," *Newsletter of the Institute for Human Sciences* 50 (June–August 1995), 1–4.

of the project of European federation – Altiero Spinelli – testifies to this.[5] In the context of the Cold War, however, the new European Community also functioned as a showcase of Western superiority and streamlined the reconstruction of Europe's war-torn economy. The moral and political bankruptcy of European "civilization" was exemplified by the Holocaust, perpetuated against the Jewish and Roma populations, among others, as well as the persecution of homosexuals, communists, and other groups of people by the Nazi and fascist regimes. The legacy of racism, extermination, and violence of European history comes under criticism in the second half of the twentieth century, first in the aftermath of fascism and subsequently as a commentary on the atrocities of communism. The continental Europe that emerged from the war was philosophically impoverished. As a result of Nazi persecution of Jewish intellectuals, the loss was human first and foremost, but some philosophical ideas also perished. Marxism and psychoanalysis were the critical theories that Nazism violently eradicated. The Cold War, which kept Europe and the world split and dichotomized, and demonized Marxism, did not facilitate the resurgence of those critical theories in the continent where they had originated. Their re-implantation back into Europe entailed a self-critical discussion about the role of totalitarian thought in European cultural, political, and intellectual history that took place within the Frankfurt School, the Yugoslav school of Marxism, and the Italian brand of "Euro-communism," as well as within French philosophy, which acted as a regenerator of a self-reflexive and critical continental philosophy of the subject in the post-Second World War period.

It is significant in this respect that the French poststructuralists reappraised the very thinkers – Marx and Freud – whom the Nazis had banned. Unlike the structuralists, who also returned to Marx and Freud, they focused as well on the other totalitarian movement of the twentieth century and analyzed the limitations and the horrors of communism. This generation, however, also rescued the transformative potential of Marx's own philosophical texts against the political conservatism of the institutions that controlled Marxist (and psychoanalytic) dogma. In their view, the crux of the problem was the universalizing theory of the subject that is implicit in these theories: under the cover of historical materialism, or of the unconscious, the subject of critical European theory preserved a unitary, hegemonic, and teleological place as the motor of human history. Accountability for European history therefore took the form of unhinging the subject from unitarian identities, freeing it respectively from the dictatorship of a libido dominated by Oedipal jealousy, and from the linearity of a historical *telos* that had married reason to the revolution, both of them vowing violence.

---

5. Altiero Spinelli, *Diario europeo* (Bologna: Il Mulino, 1992).

A third historical element that affected the critique of the old idea of Europe is colonialism. The persistence of the colonial question in the work of the post-structuralists is visible: they rejected Eurocentrism and the classical definition of European identity in terms of humanism, rationality, and the universal. They stressed instead the need to open it up to the "others within" in such a way as to relocate diversity as a structural component of European subjectivity. Best expressed in Julia Kristeva's idea of becoming "strangers to ourselves,"[6] this deconstructed vision of the European subject is active also in Hélène Cixous's[7] and Jacques Derrida's reappraisal of their Algerian Jewish roots. Other significant contributions that point strongly in this direction are: Gayatri Spivak's[8] vocal advocacy of new postcolonial subjects that asserts the noncentrality of European hegemony; Deleuze's critique of majoritarian European languages;[9] Massimo Cacciari's work on Europe as an archipelago open to the influence of other cultures;[10] Gianni Vattimo's reflections on Europe, Christianity and secularity;[11] and Foucault's involvement in the Iranian revolution.

To conclude, the philosophical generation that proclaimed the "death of man" was simultaneously antifascist, anticolonialist, postcommunist, and post-humanist. They also redefined the philosophical status of the notion of Europe accordingly.

II. THREE BRANDS OF PHILOSOPHICAL EUROSKEPTICISM

Three varieties of Euroskeptic have appeared that also contain vocal elements of doubt about the possibility of redefining Europe as a nonethnocentric,

6. See Julia Kristeva, *Strangers to Ourselves*, Leon S. Roudiez (trans.) (New York: Colombia University Press, 1991).
7. See Hélène Cixous, "Mon Algériance," *Les Inrockuptibles* 115 (August 20, 1997), 70. Published in English as "My Algeriance, in Other Words, to Depart not to Arrive from Algeria," *TriQuarterly* 100 (Fall 1997).
8. See Gayatri C. Spivak, *In Other Worlds: Essays in Cultural Politics* (London: Methuen, 1987).
9. See Gilles Deleuze, "Les Intellectuels et le pouvoir: Entretien Michel Foucault–Gilles Deleuze," *L'Arc* 49 (1972), published in English as "Intellectuals and Power," Donald F. Bouchard and Sherry Simon (trans.), in *Language, Counter-memory, Practice*, Donald F. Bouchard (ed.) (Ithaca, NY: Cornell University Press, 1973); *Spinoza et le problème de l'expression* (Paris: Éditions de Minuit, 1968), published in English as *Expressionism in Philosophy: Spinoza*, Martin Joughin (trans.) (New York: Zone Books, 1990); and Gilles Deleuze and Félix Guattari, "1227: Treatise on Nomadology – The War Machine," in *A Thousand Plateaus*, Brian Massumi (trans.) (Minneapolis, MN: University of Minnesota Press, 1980).
10. See Massimo Cacciari, *Geo-politica dell'Europa* (Milan: Adelphi, 1994) and *L'Arcipelago* (Milan: Adelphi, 1997).
11. See Gianni Vattimo, *After Christianity*, Luce D'Isanto (trans.) (New York: Columbia University Press, 2002).

multileveled concept in today's world. They have developed accordingly into different forms of Euroskepticism.

Politically, on the Continent, the opposition to the European Union is led by the nationalistic center and the authoritarian Right, which is both xenophobic and in denial of the legacy of fascism. As Stuart Hall put it, the great resistance against the European Union, as well as the American suspicion of it, is a defensive response to a process that aims at overcoming the idea of European nation-states.[12] The short-range effect of this process is a nationalist wave of paranoia and xenophobic fears, which is simultaneously anti-European Union and racist. Thus, the expansion of European boundaries coincides with the resurgence of micro-nationalist borders and fictional ethnicities at all levels in Europe today. Unification coexists with the closing down of borders; the common European citizenship and the common currency coexist with increasing internal fragmentation and regionalism; a new, allegedly postnationalist, identity coexists with the return of xenophobia, racism, and anti-Semitism.

Strong opposition to the European Union is also voiced, however, by the nostalgic Left, which seems to miss the topological foundations for international working-class solidarity and refuses accountability for the political violence of communist regimes the world over. The cosmopolitan tradition of socialism militates against the European dimension. This results in the paradox of making the far Left as Euroskeptical as the far Right.

The critique of Eurocentrism by race and postcolonial theory is also negative about Europe's transformative potential for self-renewal through ethical and political accountability. This Euroskepticism is best expressed by Gayatri Spivak, who turns the tables on the deconstruction of ethnocentrism in *A Critique of Postcolonial Reason*. Spivak suggests that this high level of self-reflexivity is merely Europe's exacerbated expression of its discursive hegemony, recast in a weakened mode of decentered subjectivity. For Spivak the "crisis" of European identity has become the preferred *modus vivendi* of continental philosophers and their chosen manner of silencing the vocal minorities that crowd the margins of the globalized world.

I find all three brands of Euroskepticism unconvincing and therefore do not share their cynical dismissal of critiques of Eurocentrism by European philosophers. On the contrary, contemporary continental philosophy has taken apart the notion of Europe, so as to expose its internal fractures. This high degree of complexity highlights one of the central features of the globalized condition,

---

12. See, for example, Stuart Hall, "Minimal Selves," in *Identity – The Real Me: Postmodernism and the Question of Identity*, Homi K. Bhabha (ed.) (London: ICA Documents, 1987), and "Cultural Identity and Diaspora," in *Identity: Community, Culture, Difference*, J. Rutherford (ed.) (London: Lawrence & Wishart, 1990).

namely, the inadequacy of simple binary thinking. How to think the simultaneity of potentially contradictory social effects is the question. The response
to this challenge is neither the exaltation of neo-universalism under the aegis
of American liberal education, nor the retreat into negativity and relativism. It
rather consists in new forms of situated European accountability.

III. SUBJECTIVITY REVISITED: ON EUROPEAN CITIZENSHIP

The primary effects of the unification project and of globalization on the philosophical notion of Europe concern ethical subjectivity and citizenship. The
classical model that linked citizenship to belonging to a territory and a community – a nation-state and a culture – and opposed it to a condition of state-
lessness, is no longer adequate. De-linking the three basic units that compose
citizenship – the ethnic origin or place of birth; the nationality or bond to a
nation-state; and the legal structure or actual citizenship – sets the conditions
for both the radical transformations that are needed in European subjectivity,
and the greatest opposition to them. These three factors are disaggregated and
disarticulated from each other and become rearranged in a number of interesting ways.

First, let me both acknowledge and then immediately leave aside the neoliberal side of this process, which is exclusively concerned with the defense of
advanced capitalism. Insofar as free movement of workers and capital is a central
feature of the global economy, deregulated capitalism promotes constant flows
and displacements. The problem with this position is twofold: first, it restricts
free mobility to capital and data; second, the speed of circulation is such that
capitalism erodes its own foundations and thus undermines the nation-state,
devastates the environment, and wastes human lives. For these reasons, neoliberalism is not very innovative as a philosophical project. As I stated at the start
of this essay, the philosophically interesting projects combine a focused attention
on situated practices with ethical accountability in their social analyses of transnational capitalism. Consequently the effects of the globalized and so-called
"flexible" labor market, including the de-linking of ethnicity and nationality
from citizenship, have to be analyzed in terms of the power differentials and the
patterns of exclusion and discrimination they entail.[13] Similarly, the rebundling
of entitlements and benefits in packages of new citizenship rights has to be
analyzed as political processes.

---

13. See my *Metamorphoses* (Cambridge: Polity, 2002) and *Transpositions: On Nomadic Ethics*
(Cambridge: Polity, 2006).

There is a further problem: The neoliberal definition of the European Union as a global capitalist power expresses a reactive tendency toward a sovereign sense of the Union. This is also known as the "Fortress Europe" syndrome, and has been extensively criticized in that it entails the belief in an ethnically pure Europe. The question of ethnic purity is the germ of Eurofascism and runs the risk of producing a European form of apartheid.[14] Present-day Europe is struggling with alternative models of citizenship at a time of increasing social exclusion, racism, and xenophobia. That the new inclusive sense of citizenship and the tendency toward a reactionary, fortress mentality coexist makes European citizenship into one of the most contested areas of political and social philosophy.

A disaggregated idea of citizenship emerges from the current European Union situation: as a bundle of rights and benefits that can accommodate both nationals and migrants. This project aims to accommodate cultural and ethnic diversity without undermining European liberal democracies, the benefits of the European welfare state, and the universal idea of individual human rights. Let me examine some significant examples of this transformative project.

IV. TRANSNATIONAL EUROPEAN CITIZENS

Étienne Balibar's[15] redefinition of the concept of European citizenship plays a foundational role in the shift of paradigm about Europe as a philosophical idea.[16] Balibar is the most eminent representative of the Spinozist democratic tradition that has proved so influential in shaping continental political philosophy.[17] The main feature of this school of thought is the definition of the subject not in terms of autonomy and individual rights. The emphasis falls instead on

---

14. Étienne Balibar, *We, the People of Europe? Reflections on Transnational Citizenship*, James Swenson (trans.) (Princeton, NJ: Princeton University Press, 2004).

15. Étienne Balibar (1942– ; born in Avallon, France) studied philosophy at the École Normale Supérieure with Louis Althusser (1960–65) and at the Sorbonne in Paris, received his PhD in philosophy from the University of Nijmegen (1987), and his habilitation from the University of Paris I (1993). He began his long career at the University of Paris in 1969, eventually serving as Professor of Political Philosophy at the University of Paris X–Nanterre from 1993 until his retirement in 2002. Currently, he is Emeritus Professor of Moral and Political Philosophy at Nanterre and Distinguished Professor of Humanities at the University of California, Irvine. In addition to his other works cited elsewhere in this essay, his most important works include: *Reading Capital* (with Louis Althusser; 1965), *Masses, Classes, Ideas* (1994), *The Philosophy of Marx* (1995), *Spinoza and Politics* (1998), and *Citoyen Sujet, Essais d'anthropologie philosophique* (forthcoming).

16. See Étienne Balibar, *We, the People of Europe?* and *Politics and the Other Scene*, Christine Jones *et al.* (trans.) (London: Verso, 2002).

*17. For a discussion of French and Italian Spinozism, see the essay by Simon Duffy in *The History of Continental Philosophy: Volume 7*.

multilayered flows of forces that express a subject's quest for freedom through the understanding of the condition (both positive and negative) of one's specific power locations.

Balibar's democratic project starts from the necessity to learn the lesson of the great human tragedies engendered by European history in the twentieth century. This systematic disregard of human rights makes it imperative to learn and re-elaborate the historical memory with renewed ethical urgency. The learning process, according to Balibar, starts from the recognition of the legacy of fascism and of colonialism and proceeds to take in the effects of Europe's global expansion throughout the whole planet. This process of hybridization forces the recognition of the structural importance of Otherness on the constitution of the European subject. This ongoing learning process simultaneously defeats Eurocentrism and elevates the marginal epistemologies of postcolonial and gender theories to a higher philosophical status.

Balibar takes on critically the idea of the universal power of the law and reminds us that rights are the results of historical struggles and contestations, not of deduction from preexisting general principles. Although the new constitution of the European Union shows both supranational elements and cosmopolitan anticipations, Balibar argues that European citizenship needs to be redefined in transnational terms that draw the hard lessons of the past and meet the complexities of the global age. The point for Balibar is neither to relink nationhood and citizenship by transposing them to a supranational level, nor to declare them obsolete. The point is to turn the question of the European political subject and of citizenship into a process, a work-in-progress. The self-evidence that accompanies so much contemporary cultural racism has to be lifted out of this debate. It is a question of redefining community, belonging, and power mechanisms of exclusion.

The process of the European Union is taken as both part of the global economy and an attempt to move beyond the essentialist grounds on which European nationalism has prospered. Balibar redefines Europe as a transnational space of mediation and transformation. This new European identity is internally differentiated and hence nonunitary and committed to transcultural hybrid exchanges. It is a situated perspective based on multiple border crossings, on confrontations with shifting frontiers and borders, and on a deep commitment to pacifism and human rights.

A more militant version of this position has been developed by another neo-Spinozist political philosopher: Antonio Negri, who developed with Michael Hardt the theory of the necessity of the political project of the European Union as an antidote to the sovereign power of the United States. The European Left has reacted with energy to the historical evidence of the dislocation of European supremacy and the coming of a belligerent American empire. Marxist philosophers, however, have been slow to understand the nondialectical and schizophrenic nature of advanced capitalism, as was articulated, for example in Deleuze and Félix Guattari's two volumes of *Capitalism and Schizophrenia: Anti-Oedipus* and *A Thousand Plateaus.* In both *Empire* and *Multitude: War and Democracy in the Age of Empire,* Hardt and Negri combine a monistic Spinozist political economy with a post-Marxian brand of materialist analysis of labor conditions under advanced capitalism. The productive space of becoming-revolutionary is located in the notion of the politically mobilized multitude as the motor of world resistance. The European Social Forum[18] is a good example of a social movement that expresses the democratic mobilization by the people themselves against the hegemony of imperial power.

In terms of European citizenship this means that the constitutive power lies with the people, or the multitude, which has the power to resist state sovereignty and to redefine the public sphere. Peace, multilateral international relations, and multilevel constitutional arrangements are the key features of the Europe of multitudes.

V. COSMOPOLITANISM REVISITED

Considering the complex power relations and internal fractures induced by the globalization process and the European Union, the relevance of contemporary cosmopolitanism as political philosophy, as an ethics of human empathy, and a constitutional and institutional design is thrown open for questioning. And so are its links with its classical and modern predecessors.

Jürgen Habermas's work, in *The Postnational Constellation,* on the universal value of republican institutions and the emphasis on rational argumentation as the precondition for social justice and democratic governance are relevant to the question of Europe.[19] It is also predictable, in keeping with his philosophical agenda centered on rational cosmopolitanism and communicative ethics. Habermas has defended the novelty and relevance of the European Union as a political and philosophical factor in what he calls the postnational constellation. Contrary to the brutal instrumentalism of unbridled capitalism on the

---

18. The European Social Forum is an annual conference held by members of the alter-globalization movement (also known as the Global Justice Movement), which emerged from the World Social Forum and follows its charter of principles. It aims to allow social movements, trade unions, nongovernmental organizations, refugees, peace groups, anti-imperialist groups, and antiracist and environmental movements to come together and discuss themes linked to major European and global issues.

*19. For a detailed discussion of Habermas, see the essay by Christopher F. Zurn in *The History of Continental Philosophy: Volume 6.*

one hand and the Schmittian belligerency of the US on the other, Europe can and, according to Habermas, should become the political incarnation of a moral community that lives by the normative ideals of Kantian neocosmopolitanism. This means the rule by law, not by force, and the principles of hospitality, not of hostility. Habermas calls for a serious European constitution, that is to say, Europe as a political project that would involve the consolidation of a European public sphere that might strengthen the shared political culture of European democracies and welfare states.

Habermas explores the key philosophical issues raised by the event of the European Union: the security of the rule of law; the sovereignty of the territorial state; collective identity and the democratic legitimacy of the nation-state. The focus of Habermas's argument is the critique of the intolerance, xenophobia, and racism that accompany the structural changes in the postnational constellation. This deficit in democratic procedures is as problematic morally as it is urgent politically. The ethnically mixed and multicultural structure of postnational societies exemplifies the de-linking of nationality and cultural identity from citizenship and the workings of the state, which causes both discomfort and great opportunities. Habermas's point is that "to the degree that this decoupling of political culture from majority culture succeeds, the solidarity of citizens is shifted onto the more abstract foundation of a constitutional patriotism."[20] This results in renewing the sense of civil solidarity and of a universalism sensitive to difference. Against the postmodernists and the liberals alike, who, for diametrically opposed reasons refuse universally binding values, Habermas argues that the only way to meet the challenges of the postnational condition is to renew democracy through the framework of the European Union. Egalitarian universalism and constitutional patriotism in a postnational democracy remain the ideal.

Following Habermas, in her recent work on European citizenship, Seyla Benhabib[21] interrogates critically the disjunction between the concepts of nation, the state, and cultural identity. Solidly grounded in her theory of communicative ethics, Benhabib works toward the elaboration of new rules of global democracy within a multicultural horizon. A self-professed Kantian cosmopolitan,[22] Benhabib argues forcefully that "democratic citizenship can be exercised across national boundaries and in transnational contexts" and defends the European Union accordingly.[23] She is especially keen to demonstrate that the distinction between national minority and ethnic group does very little to determine

---

20. Jürgen Habermas, *The Postnational Constellation* (Cambridge: Polity, 2001), 74.
*21. Benhabib's work is discussed in the essay on "Third Generation Critical Theory" by Amy Allen in *The History of Continental Philosophy: Volume 7*.
22. See Seyla Benhabib, *Another Cosmopolitanism* (Oxford: Oxford University Press, 2006).
23. Seyla Benhabib, *The Claims of Culture* (Princeton, NJ: Princeton University Press, 2002), 183.

whether an identity/difference-driven movement is democratic. In its current phase, cosmopolitanism has emerged as the dominant progressive ethos of the globalized world in that it is expected to neutralize the potential conflicts of heterogeneous and fast-changing globalized societies.

More critical thinkers within the poststructuralist tradition, however, challenge this view and investigate the notion that neutralization of differences may not be the most effective way of dealing with contemporary societies. Considering the history of difference as pejoration, this approach runs the risk moreover of perpetuating traditional forms of exclusion and disqualification. What is absolutely clear in a poststructuralist perspective is that the universalistic assumption of one common measure of norms and values based on reason, which is constitutive of classical cosmopolitanism, is untenable nowadays. Diverse forms of thinking pan-human belonging and ethical interconnection are both available and necessary, starting, for instance, from pacifism. Politically, cosmopolitanism promises the end of wars and the dawn of an age of perpetual peace through global trade, "global civil society," and governance. The recent escalation of wars on terror, however, challenges these premises. Important political, normative, and policy implications are involved in this debate between those promoting cosmopolitanism and those who see a return to a new form of warmongering imperialism.

Derrida strikes his own note on the cosmopolitan issue.[24] Starting from the primacy of the Self–Other relation and also from its paradoxical nature, he emphasizes the impossibility for any culture to be self-evident in the sense of coinciding with itself – and with ideals of cultural sameness. Derrida argues that the Other is constitutive of the Self and acts as an irreducible element of otherness within, as an internal fracture or endless differentiation within, which cannot and must not be resolved. In light of its long history of universal posturing, Europe today, argues Derrida, has a moral obligation to turn the question of its identity into the contemplation of the limits of its universality. Simultaneously a very old culture and younger than ever – because it does not quite exist yet – the European Union offers new modes of interrogating the aporetic relationship that ties Self to Other in a productive spiral of contradictions. Neither reducible to the old mastery as a centralizing, hegemonic power, nor dispersed into endless regional and sub-cultural fragments, Europe has to become an event, a process, a self-reflexive contemplation of its own finitude.

---

24. See, in particular, Jacques Derrida, *The Other Heading: Reflections on Today's Europe*, Pascale-Anne Brault and Michael Naas (trans.) (Bloomington, IN: Indiana University Press, 2002) and *On Cosmopolitanism and Forgiveness*, Mark Dooley and Michael Hughes (trans.) (New York: Routledge, 2001).

Faithful to his ethical project, Derrida outlines a list of ethical obligations that Europe must undertake toward its others and hence toward itself. These include: the critique of totalitarianism; the rejection of racism and xenophobia; the duty of hospitality and openness to strangers; and a commitment to democracy as an unfinished project that is still to come and hence requires all our collective dedication. Contemporary cosmopolitanism, for Derrida, must respect these ethical rules and adopt a political stance that implements them.

VI. PLANETARY SELF-REFLEXIVITY

Derrida's contribution to the European debate is not the only one, however, to support a transformative kind of cosmopolitanism. Starting from the definition of Europe as an endless adventure of the human spirit and a process of self-quest, for instance, Zygmunt Bauman's[25] reflections on Europe connect to his criticism of the project of modernity. Bauman acknowledges that the modern age has reached an aporetic moral condition by having functioned under the twin banners of universality and steady-state-bound foundations, the worst examples of which are revolutionary violence and totalitarianism.[26] These threaten the common good and undermine the autonomous responsibility of the moral self, while proclaiming loudly the need for clear and stable values. Lamenting the facile association of the postmodern era with moral relativism, Bauman stresses instead the specific ethical challenge represented by postmodernity. This can be summed up as an increased degree of self-examination, the loss of the grandiose illusions that drove modernity to excess, and a renewed sense of sobriety in setting social and moral goals. Postmodernity is modernity without illusions.

---

25. Zygmunt Bauman (1925–) was born to nonpracticing Jewish parents in Poznan, Poland. In 1939, after the Nazi invasion, he escaped to the Soviet Union with his family. After the war, Bauman returned to Poland and studied sociology and philosophy at the University of Warsaw. He completed his MA in 1954 and became a lecturer in Warsaw, where he remained until 1968. After completing his habilitation, in 1962 he was appointed to the Chair in Social Sciences at the University of Warsaw. In 1968, the anti-Semitic campaign led by the Polish government forced Bauman out of his job and out of the country. Having had to give up Polish citizenship to be allowed to leave, he first went to Israel to teach at Tel Aviv University, before accepting a Chair in Sociology at the University of Leeds, where he is currently an Emeritus Professor. Bauman's published work extends to approximately thirty books and well over a hundred articles. In addition to his other works cited elsewhere in this essay, his most important works include: *Between Class and Elite: The Evolution of the British Labour Movement – A Sociological Study* (1972), *Modernity and The Holocaust* (1989), *Thinking Sociologically: An Introduction for Everyone* (1990), and *Globalization: The Human Consequences* (1998).
26. Zygmunt Bauman, *Postmodern Ethics* (Oxford: Blackwell, 1993).

This sobering loss of illusions is crucial for the process of redefining Europe as a philosophical notion. The civilizing mission formulated in the eighteenth century was betrayed, or rather fulfilled perversely, by modernization narrowly defined as an economic process. Challenging the Kantian equation of moral and legal norms, Bauman stresses the gratuitousness, the lack of self-interest, and hence the profoundly nonrational nature of many moral choices that are made for the good of the world. This essential gratuitousness defeats the logic of means–end, the economist calculations of gains and profits, which is so central to mainstream morality. Bauman's postmodern ethical project stresses instead the primacy of ethics over politics in the constitution of the subject through the rediscovery of a sense of historical accountability. He also attacks the universalizing claims of state powers and the nationalist ideologies that invent traditions and claim territories to real or fictional nation-states. Bauman is equally scathing, however, regarding the neotribalism of the many self-appointed prophets who capitalize on nationalism and other forms of cultural essentialism. Instead of such cast-iron convictions on newly reinvented foundations, he calls for a vision of Europe in line with Balibar's assertion of the need to re-elaborate critically its own past. The new planetary mission that Europe has to share in entails the criticism of narrow-minded self-interests, intolerance, and rejection of otherness. Symbolic of this closure of the European mind is the fate of migrants, refugees, and asylum-seekers, all of whom bear the brunt of xenophobia in contemporary Europe.

The emphasis on the need to reinvent humanity and planetary values while avoiding the pitfalls of Eurocentrism is central to this project. It entails the ability to learn again from one's own mistakes, but also from the rest of the world.[27] Europe has mellowed into an acceptance of a renewed Kantian model of perpetual peace, in opposition to the aggressive Hobbesian project pursued by the US. The European Union is thus mature enough for a self-critical planetary role as the ethical and political subject that has already undergone intense self-scrutiny and has therefore elaborated a new form of cosmopolitanism free of ethnic nationalism.

An analogous project has emerged within Paul Gilroy's[28] work *Against Race* on colonialism and fascism, racism and anti-Semitism. The continuity between

---

27. Zygmunt Bauman, *Europe, An Unfinished Adventure* (Cambridge: Polity, 2004), 69.
28. Paul Gilroy (1956–) was born in the East End of London to Guyanese and English parents, graduated in American Literature at Sussex University in 1978, and received his PhD in Sociology at Birmingham University in 1986 with Stuart Hall. He taught at South Bank University, Essex University, and Goldsmiths College before leaving London to take up a tenured post at Yale University, where he was Professor of Sociology and African American Studies. In 2005 he was appointed as the first holder of the Anthony Giddens Professorship in Social Theory at the London School of Economics. In addition to his works cited in this essay,

these atrocious aspects of European history lies at the heart of Gilroy's case about the coextensivity of European discourses of modernization and racialized discourses and practices of exclusion. Like most postcolonial and race theorists, Gilroy stresses the murderous charge that "difference" has assumed in European history, and hence also the complicity of rationality with domination and terror. Gilroy, however, strikes a radically neohumanist note. He considers colonialism and fascism as a betrayal of the European ideal of the Enlightenment, which he is determined to defend, and thus he holds Europeans accountable for their ethical and political failings. Racism splits common humanity and disengages whites from any ethical sensibility, reducing them to an infra-human moral status. It also reduces nonwhites to a subhuman ontological status that exposes them to murderous violence. Taking a strong stand against the return of fundamentalist appeals to ethnic differences by a variety of white, black, Serbian, Rwandan, Texan, and other nationalists, Gilroy denounces these "micro-fascisms" as the epidemics of our globalized times. He locates the site of the ethical transformation in the critique of each nationalistic category, starting from the Eurocentric ones, not in the assertion of any dominant one. He sets up diasporic mobility and the transcultural interconnections against the forces of nationalism. This is a theory of mixture, hybridity, and cosmopolitanism that is resolutely nonracial. Against the enduring power of nation-states, Gilroy posits instead the affirmative politics of transversal movements, such as antislavery, feminism, Médecins sans Frontières, and the like. He refers to this ideal as "planetary humanism," defined as a "postracial and post anthropological version of what it means to be human" in the age of biopolitics and genetic power.[29]

Gilroy's cosmopolitan neohumanism is a strategic postracial and inclusive neouniversalism. It suggests the possibility of a "distinctive ecology of belonging" that would recompose the relationship between self, territory, individuality, and society through multiple connections.[30] Planetary humanism marks a social and also symbolic recomposition of one's relationship to space, time, and community. It turns hybridity into an ecophilosophical notion. The challenge is not to return to fixed identities, clear boundaries, and an allegedly pure past, but rather to grab the opportunities offered by the cultural intermixture already available within our own postindustrial ethno/gender landscapes, so as to create yet unknown possibilities for bonding and community building.

Non-Western humanists point out the complicity between European enlightened humanism on the one hand and colonial conquest and exploitation on the

his other major works include *The Black Atlantic* (1993) and *After Empire* (2004) (published in the US as *Postcolonial Melancholia*).

29. Paul Gilroy, *Against Race* (Cambridge, MA: Harvard University Press, 2000), 15.

30. *Ibid.*, 55.

other and call for a more inclusive sense of humanism. For instance, the black feminist theorist Patricia Hill Collins reconnects to the tradition of Ubuntu, or African humanism and African-American spirituality.[31] Drucilla Cornell argues along similar lines.[32] Supported by a dialogical system and informed by the notion of care as a collective responsibility for one's community, Afro-centric humanism has become a resource for all who want to resist the attrition and devastation of a process of modernization that is hastily assimilated to coercive Europeanization. Another significant development in the same area is the decolonization strand of the "postcontinental philosophy" movement. This refers to critical theories inspired mostly by Fanon and Sartre, which reject the deconstructive approach to race and ethnicity issues and embrace instead a robust expression of the specific forms of subjectivity developed by those who inhabit the margins, interstices, and diasporic spaces of modernity. These dehumanized others are the agents of powerful epistemic, symbolic, and material decolonizations.[33]

VII. THE BECOMING-MINORITARIAN OF EUROPE

Another radical position inspired by Deleuze and Guattari's political philosophy argues that the new global context provides the ground for a significant relocation of the notion of Europe as a nomadic and nonethnocentric project. Insofar as it unsettles dominant European identity, the European Union marks a process of becoming-minor of the masterful European subject and engenders more inclusive subject-positions.

In this philosophical paradigm, the post-Eurocentric condition combines nomadic subjectivity with flexible citizenship. The starting-point is the rejection of the myth of unitary visions of the subject and essentialized notions of European cultural homogeneity. European history at any point in time provides ample evidence of ethnic hybridity through waves of migration and the continuing presence of Jewish and Muslim citizens, which challenges the identification of Europe with Christianity. Nonetheless, the myth of cultural

---

31. Patricia Hill Collins, *Black Feminist Thought: Knowledge, Consciousness and the Politics of Empowerment* (New York: Routledge, 1991).
32. Drucilla Cornell, "The Ubuntu Project with Stellenbosch University" (2002), www.fehe.org/index.php?id=281 (accessed December 2009).
33. See, for instance, Walter D. Mignolo, "Philosophy and the Colonial Difference"; Gracia, "Ethnic Labels and Philosophy: The Case of Latin American Philosophy"; and Mendieta, "Is There Latin-American Philosophy?" all in *Philosophy Today* 43 (1999), Selected Studies in Phenomenology and Existential Philosophy Supplement "Extending the Horizons of Continental Philosophy," L. Alcoff and W. Brogan (eds); and Nelson Maldonado-Torres, "Césaire's Gift and the Decolonial Turn," *Radical Philosophy Review* 9(2) (2006).

homogeneity is crucial to the tale of European nationalism. In our era, these myths are being exposed and exploded into questions related to entitlement and agency. Thus, the European Union is faced with the issue: can one be European and Black or Muslim? Gilroy's work on black British subjectivity is indicative of the problem of how European citizenship and blackness emerge as contested issues.[34] However, whiteness is also called into play. Being the norm, whiteness is invisible, as if natural, whereas black, of course, is always marked off as a color. The effect of this structured invisibility is that it masks itself off into a "colorless multicoloredness." White contains all other colors and reduces them to social and symbolic visibility. Giving a specific location, historical grounding, and accountability to antiracist whites is one of the aims of critical whiteness theory. The process of becoming-minoritarian or nomadic constructs subjects that are in transit within different identity-formations, but, at the same time, sufficiently anchored to a historical legacy to accept responsibility for it.

A multiply located, nonunitary subject-position and a rhizomic politics of relations are also recommended by the Deleuzian philosopher Edouard Glissant.[35] He develops an effective rhizomatic poetics and politics, taking as point of reference the historical experience and the specific location of Africans and West Indians caught in the transatlantic slave trade. Glissant foregrounds the importance of memory and the productivity of mixity as the centerpieces of his theory of Relation.[36] He argues that even an experience as devastating as slavery produces specific forms of knowledge and subjectivization that transcend the burden of the negative. Glissant actively expresses the becoming-minoritarian or becoming-rhizomatic of blacks, Creoles, descendants of slaves, and colonized peoples. This is described as a spiritual but also logistical shift in the structure of the subject in the direction of openness toward both self and other.

Glissant's position includes a sharp critique of Eurocentrism, which is based on the ontology of sameness or the rule of One. This includes a

---

34. Paul Gilroy, *Ain't no Black in the Union Jack* (London: Hutchinson, 1987).
35. Edouard Glissant (1928–2011) was born in Sainte-Marie, Martinique and left for Paris in 1946. He studied ethnography, history, and philosophy at the Sorbonne, where he received his doctorate. Together with Paul Niger, he established in 1959 the separatist political party "Front Antillo-Guyanais pour l'Autonomie," as a result of which he was barred from leaving France between 1961 and 1965. He returned to Martinique in 1965 and founded the Institut Martiniquais d'études, as well as *Acoma*, a social theory journal. He now divides his time between Martinique, Paris, and New York, where he has been visiting professor of French Literature at CUNY since 1995. As a philosopher, writer, poet and literary critic, Glissant is one of the most influential figures in Caribbean thought and cultural theory, the preeminent critic of the Négritude school and father-figure of the Créolité movement, which emphasizes hybridity as the bedrock of identity and a "creolized" approach to textuality.
36. See Edouard Glissant, *Poetics of Relation*, Betsy Wing (trans.) (Ann Arbor, MI: University of Michigan Press, 1997).

dualistic relationship with the rest of humanity. There exists a dominant mode of nomadism in Western culture, in the form of epic journeys of discovery, which find their historical apogee in colonialism. The power of sameness in the West is best described in terms of monolinguism, or the illusion of a single cultural and linguistic root. Glissant, in a very Deleuzian mode, plays the rhizome against the root and advocates global polylinguism. This includes the deconstruction of the hubris of European master cultures and the arrogance with which they consider their languages as the voice of humanity. This universalistic pretense is one of the mechanisms supporting colonialism. It also entails the reappraisal of minor languages, dialects, and hybrids, in a phenomenon that Glissant describes as creolization.

Glissant offers a striking example of the poetics of relation in his analysis of how, in the Caribbean colonized territories, the French colonists spoke their own homegrown dialects – Norman or Breton – rather than the high and noble language of the French nation. It is this bastardized language that mingles with that of the local population, creating a crossover between two distinct but analogous forms of linguistic nonpurity. Creolization, therefore, cuts both ways and marks the becoming-minoritarian of the former master languages.

VIII. ON FLEXIBLE EUROPEAN CITIZENSHIP

I want to relate this nomadic sense of identity to the political notion of flexible citizenship. A radical restructuring of European identity as postnationalistic can be concretely translated into a set of "flexible forms of citizenship" that would allow for all "others" – all kinds of hybrid citizens – to acquire legal status in what would otherwise deserve the label "Fortress Europe." This would involve dismantling the us–them binary in such a way as to account for the undoing of a strong and fixed notion of European citizenship in favor of a functionally differentiated network of affiliations and loyalties. These could materialize and exemplify, for the citizens of the member states of the European Union, the disconnection of the three elements discussed above: ethnicity, nationality, and citizenship. According to Ulrich Preuss, such a European notion of citizenship, disengaged from national foundations, lays the ground for a new kind of civil society, beyond the boundaries of any single nation-state. Because such a notion of "alienage" would become an integral part of citizenship in the European Union, Preuss argues that all European citizens would end up being "privileged foreigners."[37] In other words, they would function together without reference

---

37. Ulrich K. Preuss, "Two Challenges to European Citizenship," *Political Studies* 44 (1996), 551.

to a centralized and homogeneous sphere of political power.[38] Potentially, this notion of citizenship could therefore lead to a new concept of politics, which would no longer be bound to the nation-state. This is a pragmatic way to develop the progressive potential of the European Union, and also of accounting for the effects of globalization on us all. These effects boil down to one central idea: the end of pure and steady identities, and a consequent emphasis on creolization, hybridization, a multicultural Europe, within which "new" Europeans can take their place alongside their constitutive others.

The project of a nomadic understanding of European citizenship is a historical chance for Europeans to become more situated and more knowledgeable of their own history and hence more self-critical. Nietzsche argued that many Europeans no longer felt at home in Europe.[39] At the dawn of the third millennium, many want to argue that those who do not identify with the dominant and heroic reading of Europe are ideally suited to the task of reframing Europe. This starts by making it accountable for a history in which fascism, imperialism, and domination have played a central role. Nomadic European subjects can lay the postnationalist foundations for a multilayered and flexible practice of European citizenship in the frame of the new European Union.

IX. CONCLUSION: TOWARD A NEW EUROPEAN SOCIAL IMAGINARY

Communities are also imaginary institutions made of affects and desires. Nations are, to a large extent, imaginary tales, which project a reassuring but nonetheless illusory sense of unity over the disjointed, fragmented, and often incoherent range of internal regional and cultural differences that make up a national identity. The project of developing a range of possible postnationalist, transnational, nomadic subject-positions and equivalent forms of citizenship is related to the process of dis-identification from established, nation-bound identities. Balibar argues that dis-identification is the key to democratic politics in that it implies openness toward the other.[40] This is one of the key elements of the learning process that can lead to a positive and affirmative relocation of European identities. It is important to stress both the need for an adequate European social imaginary for this kind of subject-position, and the difficulties involved in developing this. There is no denying that such an enterprise involves

38. Ulrich K. Preuss, "Problems of a Concept of European Citizenship," *European Law Journal* 1(3) (1995), 280.

39. Friedrich Nietzsche, *Beyond Good and Evil* (Cambridge: Cambridge University Press, 2002), pt 8, "Peoples and Fatherlands."

40. Balibar, *We, the People of Europe?*, 68–9.

a large sense of loss and is not without pain; no process of consciousness-raising can ever be without pain.

What is lacking is a social imaginary that adequately reflects the social realities and the lived experience of a postnationalist sense of European identity. Europeans need to develop adequate, positive representations of the new trans-European condition that they inhabit on the continent. This lack of the social imaginary both feeds on and supports the resistance to the European political project. More work is also therefore needed on the role of contemporary global media in both colonizing and stimulating the social imaginary of global cultures. At least some of the difficulty is due to the lack of a specifically European public debate and low involvement by the very intellectuals who represent it, although the lack of vision on the part of European political leaders does not help the situation.

The acknowledgment of a shortage in the collective imaginary of contemporary European social and political philosophy includes humble and sincere accountability for the complex historical aspects of European culture and its problematic legacy. Donna Haraway sums up admirably this mixture of affects:

> Shaped as an insider and an outsider to the hegemonic power and discourses of my European and North American legacies, I remember that anti-Semitism and misogyny intensified in the Renaissance and the Scientific Revolution of early modern Europe, that racism and colonialism flourished in the traveling habits of the cosmopolitan Enlightenment and that the intensified misery of billions of men and women seems organically rooted in the freedoms of transnational capitalism and technoscience. But I also remember the dreams and achievements of contingent freedoms; situated knowledges and relief of suffering that are inextricable from this contaminated triple historical heritage. I remain a child of the Scientific Revolution, the Enlightenment and technoscience.[41]

The progressive and liberatory potential of this process of situated accountability is equally proportional to the imaginary and political efforts it requires of its participants. The recognition of the new multilayered, transcultural, postnationalist, and nomadic idea of Europe is also the premise for the collective development of a new relationship with collective memory. It paves the way for multiple and alternative ecologies of belonging. This kind of embodied genealogical accountability is a major contribution to the philosophical discussions

---

41. Donna Haraway, *Modest_Witness@Second_Millennium. FemaleMan©_Meets_ Oncomouse™: Feminism and Technoscience* (New York: Routledge, 1997), 3.

about Europe. Through the pain of loss and dis-enchantment, "post-Eurocentric Europeans" on both sides of the transatlantic divide are moving continental philosophy into the global era by finding enough creativity and moral stamina to confront the mixed legacy of their history and work toward becoming "just" Europeans.

8

POSTCOLONIALISM, POSTORIENTALISM, POSTOCCIDENTALISM: THE PAST THAT NEVER WENT AWAY AND THE FUTURE THAT NEVER ARRIVED

Eduardo Mendieta

One of the central contentions of so-called continental philosophy is that in order to properly philosophize one must do the history of philosophy, or in other words, that to philosophize is to think through the history of philosophy. In turn, to do the history of philosophy requires a philosophical insight into what gives coherence, unity, and rationality to that history. History, for a philosophical analysis of philosophy's history, is not just the narration of a sequence of person- alities and their thinking, but the insight into the necessity and dependence of their thinking as a narrative.[1] To philosophize, in the continental philos- ophy tradition, demands both a philosophical understanding of history, and an insight into the way in which that history informs and conditions philosophy. The background assumption for such a view is that there is a fundamental inter- dependence between reason, that is *logos*, and history, that is human activity in time. This entwinement of reason and history achieved its highest expression in the thinking of Hegel.[2] Postcolonial, as well as postorientalist and postocci- dentalist, theory carries this fundamental insight of continental philosophy to the outer limits of its conceptual reach. Postcolonial, postorientalist, and post- occidentalist thinking are all unequivocally legitimate children of continental thinking, and faithful servants of its most important insights. The contributions

---

1. See Jorge J. E. Gracia, *Philosophy and Its History: Issues in Philosophical Historiography* (Albany, NY: SUNY Press, 1992) and Richard Rorty, "The Historiography of Philosophy: Four Genres," in *Truth and Progress: Philosophical Papers, Vol. 3* (Cambridge: Cambridge University Press, 1998).
2. See Jürgen Habermas, *The Philosophical Discourse of Modernity: Twelve Lectures*, Frederick Lawrence (trans.) (Cambridge, MA: MIT Press, 1987), lecture II: "Hegel's Concept of Modernity."

of postcolonial theory are as integral to the unfolding and self-reflection of the tradition as have been the contributions of phenomenology, existentialism, pragmatism, postmodernism, and deconstruction. No exaggeration is committed if it is claimed that continental philosophy is advanced and perpetuated through its challenges by devastating critiques such as those of poststructuralism, postmodernism, and deconstruction. Such critiques were enabled by the tradition itself. The tradition is precisely that ceaseless self-reflexivity, and preservation in critique. Similarly, postcolonialism, postorientalism, and postoccidentalism are part of that relentless self-reflexivity and reverential preservation through critique.

In the following we will provide a synoptic overview of the philosophical contributions and thematics that give coherence to postcolonialism as a form of thinking. We will do this by paying particular attention to the metahistorical innovations introduced by Edward Said, Gayatri Spivak's incisive and provocative appropriations of Martin Heidegger's notions of "worlding," as well as her analysis of Hegel's epistemograph, and Homi Bhabha's analysis of the constitutive desiring of the colonizer and colonized as they are implicated in a form of colonial/colonizing governmentality.[3] These philosophical departures, it is claimed, fall under three rubrics: first, the politics of knowledge, or rather the genealogy of the mutual implication of power/knowledge; second, the geography of reason, or the spatializing of temporalizing that always leaves a trace in terms of a territorializing of reason's materialization in history; and third, the technologies of subjectification that are attentive to the psychic life of domination and colonial desiring. It is thus easy to appreciate the extent to which postcolonial thinking is thoroughly engaged with the central philosophemes of the continental philosophy tradition: the historicity of knowledge, the phenomenology of consciousness, and the genealogy of subjectivity and agency.

We will then relate the conceptual gains of postcolonial theory to those claimed by postoccidentalism. The aim is to unsettle and disturb a certain philosophical complacency and insouciance as it pertains to the philosophical claims of both postcolonialism and postoccidentalism inasmuch as they reflect the recent history of continental philosophy, a history that is perforce viewed through the historical lens of a post-Cold War *pax Americana* sensibility, for which the collapse of the Soviet bloc has meant the conceptual bankruptcy of historical materialism and the so-called end of history that assured that liberalism and Western-style democracy had won the historical stage. Postcolonial philosophizing discerns and commands the historicizing of histories, the locating of subjectivities, thus allowing the heterogeneity and plurivocity of

---

*3. Said, Spivak, and Bhabha are also discussed in detail in the essay by Iain Chambers in *The History of Continental Philosophy: Volume 7.*

the "others" to speak in their many languages and histories. Such philosophical attitude turns into the imperative that the philosophical subject name, locate, map, and territorialize his or her locus of enunciation. As subjects, we speak from a particular place and time. As Fernando Coronil, Enrique Dussel, Walter Mignolo, and Anibal Quijano have argued, postoccidentalism relocalizes us in the colonial and imperial histories of the Americas. The project of postcolonialism, therefore, is one-sided, incomplete, colluding and complicit with colonialism so long as it is not territorialized and temporalized through the sobering criticisms of postoccidentalism. This is the subject of the last part of the essay.

Before we proceed, some terminological clarifications are required. The "post" in postcolonialism, postorientalism, and postoccidentalism can be taken as punctuating a temporal marker. Indeed, postcolonialism makes reference to the time after the end of colonialism, *de jure* if not *de facto* colonialism. The "post" here is a temporal, historical, geopolitical indexicalization. It marks a time in geopolitical world-time. The time it marks is the time of the end of Western imperial and colonial domination, and the beginning of a project of decolonization. But already there in the turning of the hands of the geopolitical world-time clock, there is an indication of another sense of "post." This second sense is a philosophical, conceptual, and *weltanschauungliche* meaning and indication. This "post" refers to a way of looking at the world, one that sees not from the no-place of the pretend universality of the West and Europe, but from the differentiated, particularized, historicized, and marked perspective of the colonized-in-the-processes-of-decolonization consciousness. This "post," as a posture and attitude of self-consciousness and historical reflexivity, traces a different temporality, namely the temporality of resistance to colonialism. Postcolonial theory is a relentless engagement with this duality of the "post." On the one hand, it recognizes the processes of decolonization that are registered in the annals of world history, and seeks to formalize and explicate philosophically what they say about formerly colonizer and colonized peoples. On the other hand, postcolonialism is also a historical phenomenology of the insurrected and contesting consciousness of the subaltern and subjugated, who always resisted the will to dominate of every master. Like Hegel's historical phenomenology of the "West," which is caught in the aporia of constituted and constituting consciousness, postcolonial theory is also caught in the aporia of a subjugated but always already insurrected consciousness. Thus, while many commentators hyphenated the "post-colonial" to indicate the geopolitical world-time clock, in the following we dispense with the dash, and opt for the unity in tension of the historical and transhistorical, the constituted and constituting, the subjugated and insurrected. Additionally, dispensing with the bridging dash (should) allow us to disrupt the temporalizing imperative to see the colonial as having become past. Indeed, one of the central philosophemes of postcolonial, as well as postorientalist and postoccidentalist, thinking is that the colonial has never come to an end, that part of thinking the postcolonial is precisely to think through the enduring effects of the colonial, of course, from another perspective, through and with another archive and another memory. The postcolonial is an engagement with what Bhabha called the "on-going colonial present"[4] and Quijano named the "coloniality of power."[5] The postcolonial present is also the enduring and always already present of the past coloniality. The past is never past, not even when it is forgotten and erased by those who benefited from its crimes and the privileges it granted.

With these hermeneutical indications now in place, we can anticipate that postorientalism and postoccidentalism similarly refer to both temporal and conceptual indications. If postcolonialism announces the end of the epistemic privilege of the fictitious subject of world history – the "West" – then it also announces the beginning of the end of certain indispensable, albeit always invidious, inventions, such as the primitive, the savage, the barbarous, the uncivilized and unmodern, in a word, the oriental. Analogously, with the announcement of this process of mental and philosophical decolonization, which is also the decolonization of philosophy, is also announced the end of othering machines, or *dispositifs*, to use that felicitous construct by Michel Foucault, that allow the invention of unassailable images and constructs of and for the West.[6] In other words, if in order to invent the "West" as the best, and highest stage in the unfolding of world-historical consciousness, something like the "Orient" had to be invented, the cessation of such inventing and projecting also entails the cessation of the inventing and projecting of the "Occident." Yet, as much as "Orientalism" and "Occidentalism" are entwined, they have different logic and histories, which have been variously archived and excavated by different philosophical traditions in different loci of epistemic authority and credibility.

Every major philosophical movement and period has been enabled by material conditions of possibility. The Renaissance was enabled by the rise of a wealthy and philanthropic mercantile bourgeoisie; the Enlightenment by the printing press, the emergence of an educated reading public; postmodernism and deconstruction by the information revolution and the globalization of Euro-American media. Postcolonialism similarly names not just a period, but also a movement that was also enabled by certain material conditions. It would be contrary to the spirit of both postcolonialism and postoccidentalism not to properly foreground their enablement by waves of movements and individual

---

4. Homi K. Bhabha, *The Location of Culture* (New York: Routledge, [1994] 2004), 183. Hereafter cited as LC followed by the page number.
5. Anibal Quijano, "Colonialidad del poder, cultura y conocimiento en America Latina," *Anuario Mariateguiano* 9(9) (1997).
6. See Gilles Deleuze, "What is a *dispositif*?" in *Michel Foucault, Philosopher*, T. J. Armstrong (trans.) (New York: Routledge, 1991).

agents of history. Thus a lengthy discussion of the sources of postcolonial and postoccidentalist thinking would have to analyze at least three different waves of precursors, actors, and thinkers. In the first wave, one would have to study the works of Aimé Césaire, Mahatma Gandhi, José Carlos Mariátegui, José Martí, Lamine and Léopold Senghor, Mao Zedong, and, as some postcolonial critics have argued, W. E. B. Du Bois and the work of the Harlem Renaissance, which went on to influence the Negritude movement in the 1950s and 1960s in Africa. Most of this work was produced at the height of European imperialism and colonialism. A second wave of thinking emerges during the most intense periods of anticolonial struggles, after the end of the two world wars and the moral and intellectual bankruptcy of Europe and the consolidation of US global power. In this second wave we would include the works of Amilcar Cabral, Enrique Dussel, Frantz Fanon, Ernesto Ché Guevara, Renato Ortiz, Angel Rama, Roberto Fernández Retamar, and Iris M. Zavala. A third wave includes the works by Dipesh Chakrabarty, Partha Chatterjee, Coronil, Édouard Glissant, Lewis Gordon, Ranajit Guha, Achille Mbembe, Mignolo, Quijano, Said, and Spivak. While the first two waves were more directly linked to postcolonial struggles, and their respective thinkers were dispersed throughout the Third World, this third wave is marked by their almost exclusive localization in the US academy, and their attenuated relation to ongoing decolonizing struggles. The work of this third wave also reflects greater theoretical eclecticism and heterogeneity, as well as a growing self-reflexivity in light of new challenges, such as the emergence of neocolonialism under the flag of globalization and Aesopian multiculturalism, a form of ethnoracial tolerance that does not step beyond the shop windows of affluent malls in the gated communities of the Euro-American cities.[7]

I. ORIENTALIZING TO INVENT THE "WEST"

Orientalism, published in 1978, is unquestionably the single most important text to have defined and given an identifiable shape to postcolonial theory. It should be taken as a manifesto of a new philosophical method and attitude. In contrast to Spivak and Bhabha, two of the other most notable postcolo-

---

7. I developed this periodization partly inspired by Robert J. C. Young, *Postcolonialism: An Historical Introduction* (Malden, MA: Blackwell, 2001); see also Fernando Coronil, "Latin American Postcolonial Studies and Global Decolonization," in *The Cambridge Companion to Postcolonial Literary Studies*, Neil Lazarus (ed.) (Cambridge: Cambridge University Press, 2004). See also the discussion of the "Tricontinental Conference, Havana 1966" in Vijay Prashad, *The Darker Nations: A People's History of the Third World* (New York: New Press, 2007).

nial critics, whose work has been far more episodic and essayistic, Said[8] has produced a corpus that has achieved wide readership, crossing over beyond the narrow confines of the academy into a global readership. A paused consideration of this book's central thesis, as well as methodological innovations, is indispensable for an understanding of the claims and contributions of postcolonial theory.

It must be remarked from the outset that *Orientalism* was not an orphan book, a kind of lucky draw. As Said has made explicit in many subsequent texts and interviews, *Orientalism* was followed very shortly by *The Question of Palestine* and *Covering Islam*.[9] These two books, in fact, sought to further exemplify and document what he had so eloquently elaborated in *Orientalism*. Yet, when Said's work is commented on, whether affirmatively or critically, very few commentators discuss the dependence of the more overtly political works on the more theoretical one. This failure leads to the obscuring and diminishing of the engaged, practical dimension of Said's work. It also conceals the way in which Said's work was never simply or merely denunciatory. In addition, overlooking Said's authorial intent to have these three books read as a trilogy conceals the fact that Said did not philosophize from an undisclosed or unthematized location.[10] And, most importantly, it also contributes to obfuscating the ways in which Said's work was about linking past European forms of Orientalism with more recent US versions of Orientalism. Indeed, not reading these works as a trilogy, which is how Said conceived them, if not at the outset, then as he wrote them and researched them, hinders us from recognizing that Said's overarching methodology was both archeological and genealogical. These terms are used advisedly, for they allude to Foucault's work, which deeply influenced Said, as he himself has noted. Said, however, went beyond Foucault, who nonetheless provided him with a language and a host of metaphors, but not the methodological impetus, nor the critical humanistic outlook, nor certainly what Said called the secular and worldly attitude of the engaged intellectual who speaks truth to power.[11] It must be remembered that Said's conceptual and generative

8. Edward Said (November 1, 1935–September 25, 2003; born in Jerusalem, British Palestine; died in New York City) was educated at Princeton University (BA, 1957) and Harvard University (PhD, 1964). Said spent his career, beginning in 1963, in the Departments of English and Comparative Literature at Columbia University.

9. See Edward W. Said, *Power, Politics, and Culture: Interviews with Edward W. Said*, G. Vishwanathan (ed.) (New York: Pantheon Books, 2001), 171–3. See also his *Covering Islam: How the Media and the Experts Determine How we See the Rest of the World* (New York: Pantheon Books, 1981), xlix.

10. See for instance Robert Young, *White Mythologies: Writing History and the West* (New York: Routledge, 1990), 132–6.

11. In an interview Said notes that Foucault ceased to interest him inasmuch as Foucault appeared to him as merely a scribe of power who celebrated the triumph of power but now did not have

heroes were thinkers such as Césaire, Fanon, and C. R. L. James, but also Erich Auerbach and Ernst Robert Curtius, thinkers who stand far afield of structuralist and posthumanist stances.[12] This aside is necessary because a group of scholars has sought to dismiss Said by aligning him with Foucault and thus imputing to him the kind of antihumanism, cynicism, and political nihilism that plagued Foucault's work.[13] It is also important that we recall the many occasions, both written and spoken, when Said explicitly paid tribute to but also distanced himself from Foucault.[14] Still, even as Said cannot be assimilated to a kind of Foucaultian analytics, it is necessary that we retain the terms "archeology" and "genealogy" to talk about what Said was elaborating in *Orientalism*, for reasons that will become clear as we proceed.

A careful and attentive reading of the introduction to *Orientalism* will reveal first, and most importantly, that Said was quite aware that he was breaking new conceptual and methodological ground. The introduction to this now canonical text of twentieth-century critical thought is a dense "meditation on method." In these pages, Said is at pains to make explicit what it is that he is trying to do, but he is also impatient to get on with the analysis. He is more interested in showing what his method can reveal than in delaying his discoveries with a protracted methodological discussion. In fact, early on in the introduction to *Orientalism*, Said makes reference to Foucault's two most methodological works – *The Archeology of Knowledge* and *Discipline and Punish* – in order to appropriate Foucault's analytics of discourse.[15] The reference to these methodological works also announces that Said himself is laying out a methodological work, whose method is best elucidated by what it accomplishes, what it yields, rather than by how comprehensive and exhaustively it renders explicit its *modus operandi*. A method is what it allows us to discover, uncover, unearth, and elucidate, what the positivism of the evident conceals and buries over with the force of the authority of science and received wisdom. Still, Said unfolds in some densely argued pages what he thinks is generative and innovative, albeit incipient, in his approach.

---

anything to say about how this very power was always under contestation and confrontation. See Said, *Power, Politics, and Culture*, 214.

12. See Edward W. Said, *Humanism and Democratic Criticism* (New York: Columbia University Press, 2003).

13. See, for instance, James Clifford's early review of *Orientalism*, now reprinted in *The Predicament of Culture: Twentieth-Century Ethnography, Literature, and Art* (Cambridge, MA: Harvard University Press, 1988).

14. See, for instance, the pieces on Foucault now collected in Edward W. Said, *Reflections on Exile and Other Essays* (Cambridge, MA: Harvard University Press, 2000). See also the numerous references, both appreciative and critical, to Foucault in *Power, Politics, and Culture*.

15. Edward W. Said, *Orientalism* (New York: Vintage, 1979), 3. Hereafter cited as O followed by the page number.

Said begins by discussing three meanings that he intends to be attached to the term Orientalism. First, it is the collective name for a series of disciplines, and in that sense it refers to the way in which knowledge is both codified and disciplined within a certain epistemological matrix that corresponds to the way in which knowledge is legitimated and authorized within the Western academy. Second, the terms refers to a "corporate institution" that reigns sovereign over an "epistemologically and ontologically" constituted "imaginative geography" that authorizes, augurs, instigates, demands, and interdicts scholarly, literary, legal, aesthetic, geographical pronouncements that make the Orient available, controllable, acquirable. Orientalism, in this sense, is a *dispositif*, that is, a power–knowledge device that converts cultures and their territories into objects for imperial conquest and consumption. A third sense in which Said wants the term to be understood is in its radical Vichian sense, that is, as a term that in its evident contingency and historical indexicality refers us to the fact that these mythologies disguised as geographical markers are products of human history that, once analyzed as historical formations, reveal to us how much the "Orient" and the "Occident" are implicated and complicit in each other's fantasies and dreams of domination. Orientalism, in this third sense, then, should evoke the coproductivity and codetermination of East and West. As Said writes: "Therefore as much as the West itself, the Orient is an idea that has a history and a tradition of thought, imagery, and vocabulary that have given it reality and presence in and for the West. *The two geographical entities thus support and to an extent reflect each other*" (O 5, emphasis added). We cannot think, then, the West without its imagined and abject East; nor can we think the East without thinking how it in turn must fantasize its other, the West. In fact, Said had alluded to this entwinement earlier in the introduction when he wrote: "European culture gained in strength and identity by setting itself off against the Orient as a sort of surrogate and even underground self" (O 3).

Thus far, then, we have said that Orientalism is a disciplinary regime of knowledge production that has very real power effects, power effects that in turn authorize more of its knowledge production and more of its own power gathering and consolidating. At the same time, Orientalism is also, as is quite evident from the two sections quoted, an "identity machine,"[16] a machine that produces and reproduces a certain ontology of the self. Orientalism, as a power–knowledge *dispositif*, is what one could call an epistemo-onto-logical device that produces "self" and "other" in conflictive, hierarchical, and invidious oppositions in such a way that the self, the I or "we" of the Occident, lives in a predatory and parasitic way off its derogation, abjection, and subalternization of its other. At the same

---

16. For a discussion of the term "identity machines," see Anthony Appiah, *In my Father's House: Africa in the Philosophy of Culture* (New York: Oxford University Press, 1992).

time that its other is produced, it must produce for itself a fictive, impossible, alienating self. Thus, already within the first five pages of the introduction to *Orientalism*, Said has announced that Orientalism is not just about the production of an other, the Orient, off which the West lives and from which it derives very material benefits. Orientalism must by definition entail the production and productivity of another meta-geohistorical fiction: the West, the Occident. Orientalism is part and parcel of a process of Occidentalization, the production of an imaginary of and about the West. In turn, the more the Occident constitutes itself through this imaginary, the more it Orientalizes its other.

The critique of Orientalism, then, is not just a critique that seeks to disabuse us of the errors and prejudices about this imagined other, the "Orient," but is also an explicit critique of the errors, prejudices, and fantasies that we have about ourselves, the "I," the self of the "West." In fact, if we conceive of Orientalism as an epistemo-onto-logical mechanism that conditions the horizon of possible existence and experience for historical agents, then the critique of Orientalism must proceed by way of a phenomenology of the imperial self. Indeed, this is what Said accomplishes explicitly and magisterially in the sequel to *Orientalism*, namely *Culture and Imperialism*. Still, already in 1978 in the introduction we are discussing, we find the elements of this critical and reverse phenomenology of imperial agency and subjectivity that surveys the world with petulance, contempt, and unimpeded sovereignty.

What has been here called the *phenomenology of imperial self*, which could also be called an *analytics of the imperial Dasein*, is made explicit in Said's further elucidation of his methodological considerations. After discussing the three senses in which he means Orientalism, Said narrows and refines the sense he wants to attribute to the term Orientalism by making explicit three qualifications. First, while Orientalism refers to a system of ideas and texts that configure and contain an ideology, it would be wrong to "conclude that the Orient was *essentially* an idea." It is more than just an ideology. Second, even as an ideology and a compendium of ideas, these cannot be properly understood without an "analysis of their force and effects, their configurations of power" (O 5). Ideas have power and power produces certain ideas, just as truth has power effects and these power effects produce certain truths, to paraphrase Foucault. Third, the final qualification, the goal is not to engage in a naive act of epistemological cleansing. Even if the truth of Orientalism were told, it would still endure, precisely because Orientalism is less about what is real and more about the kind of truth and power effects it has because of its mythologies about "them" and "us." As Said put it: "I myself believe that Orientalism is more particularly valuable as a sign of European–Atlantic power over the Orient than it is as a veridic discourse about the Orient" (O 6). It is not that Said is not interested in truth, but that to get to what may be "veridic" we have to work through the centuries of sedimented fiction, mythology, and misrepresentations that produced their own truths; and, above all, we have to dismantle the power–knowledge *dispositif* that holds a monopoly on authorizing not just who is to speak but also what can be said about the "other," regardless of who says it.

With these qualifications in hand, Said then argues that we entirely misunderstand Orientalism if we think of it in terms of a nefarious plot by the "West" or "Europe." Instead, we must understand Orientalism as "a *distribution* of geopolitical awareness into aesthetic, scholarly, economic, sociological, historical, and philological texts" (O 12). In other words, it is a way of cognitively mapping the world. Orientalism is also an *elaboration* of the world in accordance with certain tools and aims. Orientalism, then, is a *Gestell*, a way of positing the world in a certain way, in accordance with certain *Gestalts*, figures, and models, which both voice and are the direct expression of a volitional power. Orientalism is the embodiment of, as Said expressed it:

> a certain *will* or *intention* to understand, in some cases to control, manipulate, even to incorporate, what is a manifestly different (or alternative and novel) world; it is, above all, a discourse that is by no means in direct, corresponding relationship with political power in the raw, but rather is produced and exists in an uneven exchange with various kinds of power, shaped to a degree by the exchange with power political (as with a colonial or imperial establishment), power intellectual (as with reigning sciences like comparative linguistics or anatomy, or any of the modern policy sciences), power cultural (as with orthodoxies and canons of taste, texts, values), power moral (as with ideas about what "we" do and what "they" cannot do or understand as "we" do). *Indeed, my real argument is that Orientalism is – and does not simply represent – a considerable dimension of modern political-intellectual culture, and as such has less to do with the Orient than it does with "our" world.* (O 12, emphasis added)

When Said speaks about these different modalities of power – that is, political, cultural, intellectual, and moral – he is refocusing our attention onto the methodological dimension of his analysis of Orientalism. And what he is directing our attention to is that Orientalism is part and parcel of an ontology of selves that are positioned in geographical, social, historical, cultural, moral, political spaces in certain very specific ways: as masters of a world that is to be possessed, controlled, and known sovereignly and indivisibly. The finest and most explicit moment of this brilliant conceptual breakthrough comes toward the end of the introduction when Said writes:

My principal methodological devices for studying authority here are what can be called *strategic location*, which is a way of describing the author's position in a text with regard to the Oriental material he writes about, and *strategic formation*, which is a way of analyzing the relationship between texts and the way in which group of texts, types of texts, even textual genres, acquire mass, density, and referential power among themselves and thereafter in the culture at large. ... Everyone who writes about the Orient must locate himself vis-à-vis the Orient; translated into his text, this location includes the kind of narrative voice he adopts, the type of structure he builds, the kinds of images, themes, motifs that circulate in his text – all of which add up to deliberate ways of addressing the reader, containing the Orient, and finally, representing it or speaking in its behalf ... Additionally, each work on the Orient *affiliates* itself with other works, with audiences, with institutions, with the Orient itself. (O 20)

Orientalism, in short, produces a type of knowledge that seems authoritative. As a result, it excludes other types of knowledge and sites of authority (texts as well as other ways of making claims to knowledge) and, ultimately, the moral authority and political agency of others who work outside those privileged hegemonic sites. This privileged site of authority, determined by the *strategic location*, cleared by the *Gestalt* projected by Orientalism, in turn coordinates, maps, agglutinates, orders, and regiments a whole horizon of truths, narratives, images, even genres that cognitively and ontologically grid the world, making it knowable in very specific ways, which again exclude unauthorized cognitive mappings. It must be noted parenthetically that what Said called in 1978 *strategic location* and *strategic formation* is what in *Culture and Imperialism* he is going to refer to with the phrase "structure of attitude and reference."[17] Here it becomes explicit how Said's work is both archeological and genealogical in ways that cannot be reduced to Foucault's type of genealogy. Yet the terms are helpful because they allow us to anticipate the ways in which Said's analytics and phenomenology of the Imperial and Occidentalist self are a compendium, a catalogue, an inventory, to use the phrase that Said appropriated with gusto from Gramsci, and a genealogy of our contemporary selves. If we properly read *Orientalism* as a genealogy of this Imperial and Occidentalizing and Orientalizing self, then we will discern that Orientalism is a type of discourse that is not just constraining, repressive, but, most importantly, generative, productive, instigating, and prospective. If we discern this, then we can also discern that Said was less interested in gathering a

---

17. Edward W. Said, *Culture and Imperialism* (New York: Knopf/Random House, 1993), 52–3, 111.

catalogue for scholastic reasons and aims than in providing us with the critical tools to liberate ourselves from an Imperial ontology, or what was called earlier an epistemo-onto-logical machine that conditions the ways in which we can live out our moral agency and political subjectivity.

II. WORLDING THE "COLONIAL WORLD"

In *Culture and Imperialism*, Said claims that: "Without empire, ... there is no European novel as we know it."[18] In fact, "imperialism and the novel fortified each other to such a degree that it is impossible ... to read one without in some way dealing with the other."[19] Gayatri Chakravorty Spivak[20] has offered profoundly disquieting and incisive readings of major European novels that seek to render explicit this mutual "fortification" of the novel and imperialism. Spivak in fact has offered another, perhaps more philosophical, understanding of what Said called "structures of attitude and reference" by appropriating Heidegger's notion of "worlding." For Spivak, to understand how imperialism and the novel are implicated in each other, we have to understand how the novel contributes to the "worlding" of the "Third World" inasmuch as it both projects and conceals the world of the colonized other. This worlding, additionally, entails constituting a horizon of representation and a horizon of expectation, in which subject-positions are allowed and disallowed.[21] The point of the kind of "politics of reading" that is advocated by postcolonial theory aims precisely at un-earthing, remembering, and archiving the worlding that gave origin not just to the other of the West, but to the West itself. For in worlding the other, the other as a "Third World," the West constitutes its own world, a world that is suffused by amnesias, privileges, and subject-positions that are always surveying from above the history of a Subject with capital S, the subject of all world history.[22] Spivak's audacious readings of canonical literary text, such as *Jane Eyre, Frankenstein, Wide Sargasso Sea*, and many other such texts, aim to

---

18. *Ibid.*, 70.
19. *Ibid.*, 71.
20. Gayatri Chakravorty Spivak (February 24, 1942– ; born in Calcutta, India) was educated at Calcutta University (BA English, 1959), and Cornell University (PhD Comparative Literature, 1967); She has taught at the University of Pittsburgh and, since 1991, Columbia University, where she is now a university professor and Director of the Center for Comparative Literature and Society.
21. Gayatri C. Spivak, "Three Women's Texts and a Critique of Imperialism," *Critical Inquiry* 12(1) (Autumn 1985).
22. Spivak has developed most of her disquieting reading in a series of dense, lengthy, and demanding essays. See *In Other Worlds: Essays in Cultural Politics* (London: Methuen, 1987) and *Outside In the Teaching Machine* (London: Routledge, 1993).

forge a form of self-reflexive literary analysis that reads these texts in tandem with readings of the "archives of imperial governance."[23] Part and parcel of these archives is the production of silences, of absences, and unexpected apparitions that are constitutive of the agency of both readers and agents who live in and through the kind of subject-positions that are commanded by an imperial ethos. For Spivak, however, these transversal readings do not presuppose some unalloyed, pristine, untouched, and archaic "other." There is no "lost origin," before colonialism and empire. There is no un-colonized consciousness, or subject that has not been misshapen or misrepresented by a voracious and plenipotent sovereignty and autarkic agency. Just as, for Heidegger and Gadamer, there is no getting out of the hermeneutical circle of interpretation, so for Said and Spivak there is no getting outside the circle of the imperial and colonial worlding that worlds the worlds of both the colonized and the colonizer.

The "politics of reading" entailed by this type of analytics of imperial worlding urged by Spivak remits us to a politics of representation. Spivak has offered one of the most generative readings of what such a politics of representation would entail. In one of her most celebrated essays, as well as one of the most important texts of postcolonial philosophizing, "Can the Subaltern Speak?",[24] Spivak engages Foucault and Deleuze's dialogue on the role of the intellectual in contemporary society as a way to show not only how they both conflate what she calls the macrological with the micrological, but also how in their discussion they also conflate two very distinct notions of "representation." Spivak proceeds to rescue Marx's discussion of the two senses of this term in his *The Eighteenth Brumaire of Louis Bonaparte*. There Marx plays the two different German words – *vertreten* (representation within the economy and the state), and *darstellen* (representation within a theory of subjectivity) – off against one another. The former sense refers us to the role of the advocate, or proxy, while the latter refers us to a portrait, representation, putting forth via an image or trope. If the first belongs to the realm of rhetoric, the second belongs to the realm of persuasion. When Foucault and Deleuze fail, according to Spivak, to distinguish between their representation of those represented – their *vertreten* of those they talk about, those *darstellt*, portrayed, and represented – and the represented themselves, this leads them to a position in which, in "representing them [their subalterns], the intellectuals *represent themselves as transparent*."[25] Because they fail to see that speaking for others is not the same as representing them (giving an account of their social position, for instance), they collapse their

---

23. Spivak, "Three Women's Texts," 254.
24. Gayatri C. Spivak, "Can the Subaltern Speak?" in *Marxism and the Interpretation of Culture*, Cary Nelson and Lawrence Grossberg (eds) (Basingstoke: Macmillan, 1988).
25. *Ibid.*, 275, emphasis added.

borrowed authority into their subjective position in such a way that the subaltern's own subject-position is eviscerated and silenced. Yet it this "representing themselves as transparent" that is of primary importance to Spivak, as well as for all postcolonial and postoccidentalist critics. The mythically unsituated, universal, transparent intellectual is but a mechanism to render one's forms of "representing" unassailable and transhistorical. Spivak echoes Said, and calls us to the institutional responsibility of the intellectual. Additionally, this enactment of transparency sets the stage for the "need for 'heroes,' paternal proxies, agents of power." By representing the world of the subaltern and colonized subjects through a disavowal of one's role in that representation, a rhetoric of need and paternalism is also invoked. It is not the interest or subjectivity of the colonial master that stages the world: it is so staged by historical inevitability, the ineluctable iron logic of progress, modernization, and more recently globalization. This "staging of the world in representation"[26] is integral to the worlding of the colonial masters, for through it the proxy of a paternalistic and heroic sovereignty is effaced and occluded behind the grotesque, distorting, haunting, and pitying portrait of the colonized subaltern.

Said described some of his work as a "geographical inquiry into historical experience."[27] Spivak's work can be read as attempts to develop a "geographical inquiry into imperial reason." In her massive and impressive book *A Critique of Postcolonial Reason*, Spivak undertakes an analysis of the interdependence between a certain reading of universal reason, Hegel's in particular, and certain geographical projections and representation.[28] In fact, for Hegel, which for Spivak is a world-historical metonym,[29] the becoming self-conscious of *Geist* must take form through its geographical trajectory across the world and history. Consciousness assumes a geography, and geography in turn becomes the trace of *Spirit*'s own coming to itself. In Hegel's philosophy of art, world history, and consciousness, we find not just an epistemology, or rather a phenomenology of consciousness, but an "epistemography." For Spivak, Hegel's epistemography becomes the alibi for the staging of the world as the struggle for space, over space, but also the staging for the disappearance of that consciousness

---

26. *Ibid.*, 279.
27. Said, *Culture and Imperialism*, 7. See also his "Secular Interpretation, the Geographical Element, and the Methodology of Imperialism," in *After Colonialism: Imperial Histories and Postcolonial Displacements*, Gyan Prakash (ed.) (Princeton, NJ: Princeton University Press, 1995), and "History, Literature, and Geography," in *Reflections on Exile and other Essays*.
28. An earlier version of this analysis was undertaken in "Time and Timing: Law and History," in *Chronotypes: The Construction of Time*, John Bender and David E. Wellbery (eds) (Stanford, CA: Stanford University Press, 1991).
29. Gayatri C. Spivak, *A Critique of Postcolonial Reason: Toward a History of the Vanishing Present* (Cambridge, MA: Harvard University Press, 1999), 47.

that reads its coming into being on the maps of its conquests. If "[t]he task of the Hegelian philosopher of art [but this applies equally to the philosophy of nature, law, history, and the phenomenology of consciousness] is to analyze the cryptonym, decipher the epistemograph, spell the spirit's paraphe, on its way to Europe's signature,"[30] then the task of the postcolonial philosopher is to render explicit the actual and metaphorical production of space onto which putative universal reason writes itself in the name of a civilizing mission, the fulfillment of a fate, a globalizing project. Echoing Henri Lefebvre's materialist analysis of the social production of space, it can be claimed that Spivak's materialist, feminist, deconstructionist, and postcolonial critique also offers an analysis of the imperial and colonial production of planetary space by way of epistemographs and ontographs that are accompanied by bellicose mappings of imperial sovereignty.

III. "PERVERSE PALIMPSEST OF COLONIAL IDENTITY"[31]

In "The Other Question: Stereotype, Discrimination and the Discourse of Colonialism," Homi Bhabha[32] takes Edward Said to task on two important registers. First, Bhabha thinks Said misreads, with tremendously deleterious consequences, Foucault's concept of power–knowledge. For Bhabha the fecundity of Foucault's genealogical analysis of power–knowledge resides in its rejection of any dichotomous disjunction: essence–appearance, ideology–science, normal–pathological, and so on. "Subjects are always disproportionately placed in opposition or domination through the symbolic decentring of multiple power relations which play the role of support as well as target or adversary" (LC 103). In Said's work, however, this leads to the problem that it becomes difficult to

> conceive of the process of subjectification as a placing *within* Orientalist or colonial discourse for the dominated subject without the dominant being strategically placed within it too. The terms in which Said's Orientalist is unified – the intentionality and unidirectionality of colonial power – also unify the subject of colonial enunciation. (LC 103)

---

30. *Ibid.*, 41.

31. LC 63.

32. Homi K. Bhabha (November 1, 1949– ; born in Mumbai, India) was educated at the University of Mumbai (BA), and Christ Church, Oxford University (PhD, English Literature). He has taught in the English Department at the University of Sussex (1978–94), in Humanities at the University of Chicago (1996–2000), and as Professor of English and American Literature and Language at Harvard University (2001–).

In other words, Said not only homogenizes the Orientalist, making his will to dominate the other both univocal and transparent, but in tandem, owing to the juxtaposition of the mutuality of colonized and colonizer, the other of the Orientalist is similarly homogenized and made univocal and transparent. Said fails to face up to the problems as well as the potentially disruptive effects that introducing the concept of "discourse" entails and evokes. Most of Bhabha's work is guided by the overriding preoccupation to develop models of subjectification and identification that give more nuanced, and perhaps proper, insight into the tethering of colonial subjectivity to that of the colonialized. Bhabha's analytics of subjectification are developed through readings of Fanon and Said, but also Freud and Lacan, readings that are so arresting and original that by now they have insinuated themselves within the canon of psychoanalysis and existentialism.

According to Bhabha there are three fundamental conditions that underlie the *process of identification*: first, identities are called into being with reference to a "phantasmic space of possession" that no subject can occupy separately and continuously. Identification takes place through the reaching out to this space where one is not, and once one is there it is no longer the place to be. This is the place so jealously guarded by the settler, who is haunted by the threat that the natives want to take "their place." Second, this very place of identification is a "space of slipping" in which to be different from those that are different makes you the same as the putatively self-same, as in "you are a doctor, you are a scholar, you are *x*, and therefore are different from them and thus you are like us." This "like us" is predicated on a difference that is marked from the other difference. Here identification happens through a difference that is internal. For Bhabha, this difference that makes the colonizer and colonized the same is one that instigates deferral and displacement.

> It is not the colonialist Self or the colonized Other, but the disturbing distance in-between that constitutes the figure of colonial otherness – the white man's artifice inscribed on the black man's body. It is in relation to this impossible object that the liminal problem of colonial identity and its vicissitudes emerges. (LC 64)

Identification is not, as is implied by Said, a process of juxtaposing, mirroring onto another what is not oneself; it is rather a process of having to negotiate in between, within one's own subjectivity, this otherness, the otherness of the self, which is always already different by the way it marks itself off through an identifying sameness. Third, identification is not about affirming a pregiven identity, nor about accomplishing something that was already inchoate. Identity is always achieved in its mis- and re-identification through the assuming of a projected image. Identity is always the staging of misrecognition.

> The demand of identification – that is, to be *for* an Other – entails the representation of the subject in the differentiating order of otherness. Identification … is always the return of an image of identity that bears the mark of splitting in the Other place from which it comes.
>
> (LC 64)

There are two distinctive forms these slippings and deferrals take within the discourse of colonialism. The colonial subject is constituted, but also dismantled, through discourses that articulate forms of difference. The central issue for colonial discourses is the "mode of representation of otherness." One such mode is that of the "stereotypical discourse." Colonial discourse constitutes the otherness of the subaltern through a stereotypical discourse that projects a fixity, discernibility, legibility, calculability, and already-knowingness of the other. The colonial subject is always already known through the stereotypes. The colonial discourse renders the colonial reality thoroughly known and visible through its stereotypes. But by its very structure as a stereotype, it requires that it be continuously reconfirmed, re-enacted, relived At the heart of the stereotype there is lack, a horrifying vacuum, namely that it will not be confirmed. This self-cancellation of the stereotype is confirmed through a reading of the stereotype as a fetish. The stereotype acts as a fetish, takes the place of the fetish of colonial subjectivity. "The fetish or stereotype gives access to an 'identity' which is predicated as much on mastery and pleasure as it is on anxiety and defense, for it is a form of multiple and contradictory belief in its recognition of difference and disavowal of it" (LC 107).

The other discourse for the constitution of difference that is central to the discourse of colonialism is that of mimicry. At the heart of colonial discourse is the desire for the educated, domesticated, recognizable other that is *"a subject of a difference that is almost the same, but not quite"* (LC 122). The paternalistic, self-abnegating, and self-sacrificing colonial subject is to be met halfway by a colonized subject who will be just like itself, *but* not quite. The *telos* of the colonial discourse is to educate others into its own best image of itself. Mimicry, however, like the stereotypes, is unstable. The mimicry expected of the colonial other, like every iteration, is however liable to be faulty, challenging, mocking, and displacing. While colonial discourse demands this replication, imitation, it also fears it. It is undone by it, in fact.

> The effect of mimicry on the authority of colonial discourse is profound and disturbing.
>
> It is as if the very emergence of the 'colonial' is dependent for its representation upon some strategic limitation or prohibition *within* the authoritative discourse itself. The success of colonial

> appropriation depends on a proliferation of inappropriate objects
> that ensure its strategic failure, so that mimicry is at once resem-
> blance and menace.   (LC 123)

Together, stereotypical and mimetic colonial discourse participate in the constitution of a form of governmentality that "is informed by a productive splitting
in its constitution of knowledge and exercise of power" (LC 118). Through its
mobilization of stereotypes in the form of racisms with their prejudicial and
mystifying ideologies, it sanctions and commands deployment of power, while
it disavows its source and necessity. The discourses that represent difference in
terms of stereotypes and mimicry underwrite a form of governmentality that
foists on its colonial subject both the cause and effect of the excesses of its power.
Their own instability, furthermore, demands the vigilance and anarchical or
arbitrary enactment of its violence.

What makes Bhabha's analysis distinctive is precisely the way in which it
destabilizes Said's and Spivak's sometimes too rigid representation of the identity
of the colonizer, and perforce, of the colonized. Bhabha's work combines productively Lacanian psychoanalysis with Foucaultian genealogy in order to make
more nuanced Said's and Spivak's analyses of the discourses of imperialism and
colonialism. For Bhabha, the ongoing colonial present is not an issue just of the
endurance and efficacy of the colonial past, but also of the ways in which forms
of identification and subject formation have been constituted in the crucible of
colonial domination.

IV. THE WEST'S "OCCIDENT"

Postcolonialism is a form of materialist cultural critique that aims to articulate
the interdependence between cultural expressions and their material underpinnings. Imperialism both presupposed and produced the novel. The novel, in turn,
gave expression to the kind of subjective positions that enabled and condoned an
imperial ethos. Already during the early 1970s Latin American liberation philosopher Enrique Dussel[33] had sought to articulate a similar materialist reading of
the complicity of Western philosophy with the imperial and colonial practices of
the "West." According to Dussel, the great philosophemes of Western philosophy
(such as Descartes's *cogito*, Kant's *ich denke*, and Hegel's *absolutes Wissen*) find

---

33. Enrique Dussel (December 24, 1934– ; born in La Paz, Argentina) was educated at the
National University of Cuyo, Argentina, the Sorbonne, and the Catholic Institute in Paris.
From 1968 to 1975 he taught at his alma mater. In 1975, after an assassination attempt, he
and his family were exiled in Mexico. He has been teaching since then at the Autonomous
Metropolitan University and the Autonomous National University of Mexico, in Mexico City.

their genesis and material condition of possibility in the *ego conquiro* expressed by Hernán Cortés and Francisco Pizarro.[34] "Before the *ego cogito* there is an *ego conquiro*; 'I conquer' is the practical foundation of 'I think.'"[35] Like Said and Spivak, Dussel is also supremely conscious of the relationship between philosophy and geography. In fact, his 1975 *Philosophy of Liberation* – a work that summarized over a decade of philosophizing, written in exile in Mexico – opens with a section entitled "Geopolitics and Philosophy." In his 1992 Frankfurt Lectures, Dussel returns to the relationship between geography and philosophy, but this time to unmask the myth of modernity. Part of the mythology of modernity is to rewrite history and to segregate and marginalize spatially those who are in pursuit of modernity. These lectures were published in English under the title *The Invention of the Americas: Eclipse of "the Other" and the Myth of Modernity.*[36] At the center of these lectures was a challenge to the then-in-fashion debates about modernity and postmodernity. The challenge issued by Dussel was that Charles Taylor, Jürgen Habermas, Gianni Vattimo, and Richard Rorty, each name standing in for a particular philosophical tradition within these debates, did not properly understand the crisis of modernity because they did not understand its sources. They did not understand modernity's sources because they had willfully adopted a chronology of modernity that occluded its sixteenth-century origins and its material conditions of possibility in the conquest of the New World. Dussel, in fact, argued that the crisis of modernity was but the crisis of a project that began in the last decades of the fifteenth century, but that only took proper form in the sixteenth century with the expulsion of the Moors and Jews from the Iberian peninsula. Modernity was the mythological name for another project that had a different name in earlier centuries. This early project had the name of evangelization. Later, before the German and French enlightenments, and surely before the ascendancy of Britain to world empire, the Spanish and Portuguese had been the imperial centers of a Christianizing and evangelizing project. Dussel had, in fact, articulated a counter-narrative of modernity, one that recentered the project of modernity within a longer, most encompassing project, the project of the "Occidentalization" or "Westernization" of the world. Implicit in Dussel's unmasking of the myth of modernity was also a critique of two other philosophical fashions of the later 1980s and early 1990s:

---

34. Enrique Dussel, *Philosophy of Liberation*, Aquilina Martinez and Christine Morkovsky (trans.) (Maryknoll, NY: Orbis Books, [1975] 1985), 8.

35. *Ibid.*, 3.

36. See also Enrique Dussel, *The Underside of Modernity: Apel, Ricoeur, Rorty, Taylor and the Philosophy of Liberation*, Eduardo Mendieta (ed. and trans.) (Atlantic Highlands, NJ: Humanities Press, 1996) and "Beyond Eurocentrism: The World-System and the Limits of Modernity," in *The Cultures of Globalization*, Frederic Jameson and Masao Miyoshi (eds) (Durham, NC: Duke University Press, 1998).

postcolonialism and postmodernism. Curiously, Dussel had called his philosophy of liberation a form of "postmodern" philosophy, just as he had also called
it "barbarian" philosophy. What he meant partly was that the critiques articulated by these movements have been part of the intellectual and philosophical
canon in Latin America already for over a century. In Dussel's work, however,
the issue of the relationship among modernity, globalization, the West, and the
Orient had already been articulated as a philosophical problem. As Said's work
became a point of convergence and departure for postcolonial thinkers, so has
Dussel's.[37]

Fernando Coronil,[38] working from within the social sciences, gave a more
explicit articulation of the problematic anticipated by Dussel. In a programmatic essay entitled "Beyond Occidentalism: Toward Nonimperial Geohistorical
Categories," Coronil presents one of the clearest analysis of Occidentalism and
how it relates to the Orientalist project.[39] He finds Said's analysis in *Orientalism*
indispensable, but also lacking. In fact, according to Coronil, Said presupposes
an unthematized understanding of the West, whereas part of the project of a
critique of all colonial discourse is to give an account not just of a culture's
misrepresentation of its alleged others, but also of how it conceives itself in such
a way that it authorizes itself to view others in a particular light. Coronil does
not want to dispense with Said, but rather urges us to redirect our attention.

> I wish to take a step in this direction by relating Western represen-
> tation of "Otherness" to the implicit construction of "Selfhood" that
> underwrites them. This move entails reorienting our attention from
> the problematic of "Orientalism," which focuses on the deficiencies
> of the West's representations of the Orient, to that of "Occidentalism,"
> which refers to the conceptions of the West animating these repre-
> sentations. It entails relating the observed to the observers, products

---

37. See Linda Martin Alcoff and Eduardo Mendieta (eds), *Thinking From the Underside of History:
    Enrique Dussel's Philosophy of Liberation* (Lanham, MD: Rowman & Littlefield, 2000) and
    Eduardo Mendieta (ed.), *Latin American Philosophy: Currents, Issues, Debates* (Bloomington,
    IN: Indiana University Press, 2002). The debates have been brought home, and now the issue
    is about the role of Latin Americans in the US. See Ramón Grosfoguel *et al.* (eds), *Latin@s
    in the World-System: Decolonization Struggles in the 21st Century US Empire* (Boulder, CO:
    Paradigm Publishers, 2005).
38. Fernando Coronil (November 30, 1944– ; born in Caracas, Venezuela), was educated
    in Venezuela, emigrated to the United States in 1963, and received his BA from Stanford
    University in 1967, and his PhD from the University of Chicago in 1987. He is Associate
    Professor of History and Anthropology, and Director of the Latin American and Caribbean
    Studies Center at the University of Michigan.
39. Another indispensable text in understanding the debates around postoccidentalism is
    Coronil, "Latin American Postcolonial Studies."

to production, knowledge to its sites of formation … This perspective does not involve a reversal of focus from Orient to Occident, from Other to Self. Rather, by guiding our understanding toward the relational nature of representations of human collectivities, it brings out into the open their genesis in asymmetrical relations of power, including the power to obscure their genesis in inequality, to sever their historical connections, and thus to present as the internal and separate attributes of bounded entities what are in fact historical outcomes of connected peoples.

Occidentalism, as I define it here, is thus not the reverse of Orientalism but its condition of possibility, its dark side (as in a mirror). A simple reversal would be possible only in the context of symmetrical relations between "Self" and "Other" – but then who would be the "Other"?[40]

Occidentalism, then, is an identity machine that constructs the self-same in terms of how it: (i) separates the world into discretely bounded geopolitical units; (ii) disaggregates and de-links their entwined histories; (iii) turns difference into hierarchies; (iv) naturalizes representations of otherness; and (v) intervenes in the perpetuation of asymmetrical power relations. The Occident, therefore, constitutes itself through the abrogation of the epistemic, political, geographical authority to do this unto others.

Walter Mignolo[41] will adopt Coronil's formulations, but give them greater historical specificity. Linking Coronil's critiques of Said with Dussel's critique of the philosophers of the discourses of modernity and postmodernity, Mignolo argues that the key word for understanding the material and historical underpinnings of modernity is in fact Occidentalism. Mignolo notes that in the sixteenth century the Americas were in fact called the "Indias Occidentales." The Occidentalist project is not one of the juxtaposition of a radical other, as in Orientalism, but rather the incorporation, assimilation, evangelization, and conversion of the "Indians." In the first stage, the Occidentalist project was one of incorporation and Christianization. Later, the Occidentalist project will become one of civilization and enlightenment; and much later one of modernization and

40. Fernando Coronil, "Beyond Occidentalism: Towards Postimperial Geohistorical Categories," *Cultural Anthropology* 11 (1996), 56.
41. Walter Mignolo (January 5, 1945– ; born in Isla Verde, Argentina) was educated in Argentina at the National University of Cordoba, where he received his BA and MA from the Faculty of Letters and Philosophy. He received his Doctorate in 1974 from the École des Hautes Études in Paris, France. He has taught at the Université de Toulouse, Indiana University, and the University of Michigan. Since 1993, he has been the William H. Wannamaker Professor of Literature and Romance Languages at Duke University.

globalization. Each version or stage of the Occidentalist project has been advocated and shouldered by a different imperial power within Europe. Each imperial seat has left its imprint on what it means to be the West, what it means to be European in relationship to the West.[42] For Mignolo, postoccidentalism is the name for the critique of the project of modernity in particular, but also of the bankruptcy of the Occidentalist project in general, from and in Latin America. The crisis of modernity has been expressed in four different "posts": the "postmodern" project, which was articulated from Europe itself (Arendt, Baudrillard, Lyotard, Vattimo) and the United States (Jameson); the "postcolonial" project, which was articulated in and from India (Bhabha, Guha, Spivak, the Subaltern Studies Group); the "postorientalist" project, which was articulated from the US looking at the Middle East (Said); and the "postoccidentalist" project, articulated in and from Latin America (Dussel, Kusch, Retamar, Silvia Rivera).[43] What these four different "post" projects articulate is the rupture between different cultural areas, traditions, histories, and the locales of the production of knowledge.[44] When Mignolo articulates the differences, but also relationships among these different post projects, he is also recentering our attention on the central philosophical idea of all forms of postcolonial, postorientalist and postoccidentalist critique and analysis, namely that the layering and interlocking of the politics of knowledge with the politics of reading produce for us a geopolitics of knowledge that is attentive to the locus of enunciation of knowledge and how that claimed knowledge is or is not related to those about whom it speaks and seeks to "represent." In Foucault's language, knowledge is always an effect of power and power produces certain knowledges. This is what Quijano called the "coloniality of power," by which he meant that all social relations, including knowledge relations, cannot but be imbricated with and refracted by the power differentials established, reconstituted, and renewed after the onset of colonial relations.[45]

In a 1985 essay entitled "Orientalism Reconsidered," Said, referring to all the kinds of philosophical and intellectual projects that shared in the spirit of his own *Orientalism*, wrote "They are, therefore, planes of activity and praxis, rather than one topography commanded by a geographical and historical vision locatable in

---

42. See Walter Mignolo, "Posoccidentalism: el argumento desde América Latina," in *Teorías sin disciplina: Latinoamericanismo, poscolonialidad y globalización en debate*, Santiago Castro-Gómez and Eduardo Mendieta (eds) (México: Miguel Angel Porrua, 1998).

43. *Ibid.*, 42.

44. See Walter Mignolo, *Local Histories/Global Designs: Coloniality, Subaltern Knowledges and Border Thinking* (Princeton, NJ: Princeton University Press, 1999), esp. ch. 2; see also under the index word "postoccidentalism."

45. Anibal Quijano, "Coloniality of Power, Eurocentrism and Latin America," *Nepantla: Views from the South* 1(3) (2000).

a known center of metropolitan power."[46] Said underscores here the decentered topography of knowledge that is not tethered to the commanding leash of an imperial and metropolitan authorizing power. Like Mignolo, he underscores the different and differentiated geopolitical histories of knowledge productions and knowledge–power circuits. The "posts" in postcolonialism, postorientalism, postoccidentalism are not about marking chronologically a moment of crisis and rupture, but rather about announcing an epistemological, hermeneutical, semiotic turning from a form of knowledge production to another that is attentive to local histories. These "posts" announce a past that is never past, and a future that is still to arrive. These "posts" also call us to acknowledge the always disavowed mutuality that makes it impossible to think the West without the Orient, Europe without its others. Postcolonialism, postorientalism, and post-occidentalism are neither anti-Western, nor anti-Occidentalist. This would only perpetuate the kind of amnesia and blindness that the original critiques sought to remedy. At the beginning of the dismantling of the edifice of colonial philosophy and its attendant mentalities is what Chakrabarty calls an "anticolonial spirit of gratitude,"[47] because philosophy conscious of its origins and effects is a gift from all to all.

46. Said, *Reflections on Exile*, 214.
47. Dipesh Chakrabarty, *Provincializing Europe: Postcolonial Thought and Historical Difference* (Princeton, NJ: Princeton University Press, 2000), 255.

9

CONTINENTAL PHILOSOPHY AND THE ENVIRONMENT

Jonathan Maskit

I. A COMPLEX HISTORY

The history of continental philosophy and the environment brings to the fore some nagging questions: Who counts as a continental philosopher and what is the relationship between geographical location and philosophical approach? Given the embrace of "analytic" philosophy in continental European since the 1970s, philosophy in Europe is now just as divided between "continental" and "analytic" approaches as is philosophy in the English-speaking world. Environmental philosophy in German and French is more likely to engage with English environmental philosophy than with the traditions of French and German philosophy. By far the most productive locale for continentally inspired environmental philosophy is the United States. The situation is further complicated by the fact that continental environmental philosophy has, by and large, developed independently in French, German, and English, so that contributions in one place often remain unnoticed in others. It is the purpose of this essay to present this complicated history, at least in overview. This history has three largely distinct trajectories. English-language continental philosophers have, by and large, sought to show how various European thinkers' work can be used in addressing environmental issues. Interestingly, with the exception of Martin Heidegger and Félix Guattari,[1] the thinkers chosen have not themselves

---

1. Pierre-Félix Guattari (March 30, 1930–August 29, 1992; born in Villeneuve-les-Sablons, France; died in Cour-Cheverny, France) studied pharmacy at Bécon-les-Bruyères (1948–49) and philosophy at the Sorbonne (1950–55). He later trained as a psychoanalyst with Jacques Lacan, and worked with Jean Oury at La Borde Psychiatric Clinic from 1955 on. In addition

been particularly interested in environmental issues (and even Heidegger is an interesting case, since his interest seems to run more toward nature; whatever place environment [*Umwelt*] played in his earlier work, he did not have in mind there what we mean by environment when we talk about environmentalism). Simultaneously, and largely unremarked on by English-language continental philosophers, there has been ongoing interest among the French in various environmental issues. A third trajectory can be traced in Germany, where Heidegger and some of early members of the Frankfurt School were exercised by questions having to do with nature, culture, and technology. While, given the relative strength of the Green Party in Germany, one might have expected German philosophers to show an interest in environmentalism, this has not, by and large, been the case. Contemporary German (and, for that matter, Dutch, Belgian, and Italian) contributions have, for the most part, been largely limited to an engagement with environmental ethics as practiced in the English-speaking world. What is distinctive about continental approaches to environmental philosophy, wherever they occur, is a willingness to call into question *all* the relevant terms, in particular "nature" and "humanity." In distinction, what I am here calling, for lack of a better term, analytic approaches have tended to hold fast their conception of the human being while, at most, being willing to question what nature is, although even this inquiry often does not take place.

While we can find ruminations about nature in the work of Kant, Schiller, Hegel, Nietzsche, and many others, it is really not until Heidegger that thought about nature comes to have what we might term an environmentalist bent. Nevertheless, coming as it does before the events of the 1960s that gave birth to environmentalism, we must characterize Heidegger's work more as proto-environmentalist. This means that Heidegger's interest in the environment remains always rather circumspect, requiring the work of interpreters to bring it to the fore.

Interestingly, while Heidegger's thought has been influential on a number of American interpreters, it has been less clearly influential in the European (and this means primarily French) tradition of environmental philosophy. Here we find an approach to environmental issues that is, in a sense, more radical than anything undertaken in English, whether influenced by the work of nonenvironmentalist continental thinkers or not. What characterizes contemporary French thought about the environment is that, unlike English-language environmental philosophy, it begins not with the assumption of a split between nature and culture, but with the view that nature and culture cannot be thought except in relationship to one another. The reasons for this difference in approach

to his works cited here, Guattari authored *Psychanalyse et transversalité: Essais d'analyse institutionnelle, La Révolution moléculaire,* and *L'Inconscient machinique: Essais de schizo-analyse.*

are many, but have largely to do not with the history of European philosophy but with European land-use practices, and developments in fields such as psychoanalysis and anthropology.[2]

While some well-known continental thinkers have addressed environmental issues, either directly or circumspectly – Michel Serres, Bruno Latour, and Guattari – they have had their environmental work almost entirely ignored by the English-speaking world. Simultaneously, thinkers such as Maurice Merleau-Ponty, Michel Foucault, Gilles Deleuze, and Jacques Derrida, whose work by and large either pays no attention to environmental issues or does so only in passing, have been embraced by English-speaking philosophers. What is unfortunate about this oversight on the part of English-language environmental philosophers is that many of the issues addressed by Serres, Latour, and Guattari – primarily the importance of thinking nature and culture not in opposition but as codeterminants – are only now coming to be recognized as essential to environmental philosophy. However, even in this situation, the groundbreaking work of the French continues to be ignored, which means that English-language environmental philosophers must retread ground that, unbeknown to them, has already been covered.

The following treats the history sketched above in three sections. The first covers Germany (with passing consideration of Belgium, the Netherlands, and Italy); the second addresses English-language developments; the third concerns itself with France.

II. GERMANY AND ELSEWHERE

Much of Heidegger's later work addresses questions having to do with nature, humanity's place in the world, and how human practices allow or force nature to show itself one way rather than another. Such themes clearly have an environmental cast to them, even if Heidegger was writing before there was such a thing as environmentalism. For the later Heidegger, humanity's technological relationship with the world became a central topic of concern. Corollary to this was his interest in what he termed a "new beginning" that would allow human beings to dwell upon the earth, that is, to allow the earth to show itself in a human world in a way shaped not by the terms of science and technology but by the freeing play of poetry. Although such themes in Heidegger's thought now appear

---

2. For an excellent treatment of this history see Kerry Whiteside, *Divided Natures: French Contributions to Political Ecology* (Cambridge, MA: MIT Press, 2004). Since Whiteside's interest is in tracing French political ecology rather than ecological philosophy, he treats not only philosophers but also anthropologists, political theorists, and others.

to have an environmentalist cast to them, this is more due to a change in the times. That is, it is not at all clear that Heidegger conceived of himself as really being engaged in philosophy of nature, never mind environmental philosophy. I return to Heidegger below when I discuss English-language contributions to environmental philosophy.

Several members of the early Frankfurt School are also important here. In *Dialectic of Enlightenment*,[3] Theodor Adorno and Max Horkheimer focus, to a great degree, on enlightenment modernity's relation to nature.[4] While the project of enlightenment sought to free humanity from nature's domination by, as it were, turning the tables on nature so that it would now be dominated by us, the end result turned out to be, at the same time, a new form of domination of humanity by itself. Adorno and Horkheimer argue that enlightenment was unable to establish any legitimate goals or purposes to which humanity's new-found powers could be turned, and, in the absence of such purposes, the tools of domination that so effectively freed humanity from nature's control were open to being turned to the domination of humanity as well. Enlightenment thus turns out to be a double-edged sword, whose end result is to obtain human-ity's freedom from nature only at the cost of the domination of both nature and humanity by the forces of instrumental reason. For Adorno and Horkheimer it is not only the loss of human freedom that indicts enlightenment but also, if we may put it thus, the loss of nature's freedom as well. Missing from Adorno and Horkheimer's work, however, is a response to the situation they analyze.

Unlike Adorno and Horkheimer, whose conclusions are clearly pessimistic, Herbert Marcuse saw in revolutionary politics the possibility to transform technology in such a way that not only humanity, but nature as well, could be freed from the repressive distortions of modernist technological mastery.[5] For Marcuse, it is only through a nondominating technology (a new technology he remains vague in describing) that humanity can recover from the distortions of its nature *and* nature can become what it always could have been. While Marcuse is clearly optimistic, he does not fulfill his promise with detailed proposals and may, as critics such as Jürgen Habermas[6] have argued, have fallen into an unjus-tifiable romanticism.[7]

---

*3. Adorno and Horkheimer's *Dialectic of Enlightenment* is discussed in the essay by Deborah Cook in *The History of Continental Philosophy: Volume 5*.

4. See also Steven Vogel, *Against Nature* (Albany, NY: SUNY Press, 1996), 51–68.

5. See, for example, Herbert Marcuse, *One Dimensional Man: Studies in the Ideology of Advanced Industrial Society* (Boston, MA: Beacon Press, 1964).

*6. Habermas's work is discussed in the essay by Christopher F. Zurn in *The History of Continental Philosophy: Volume 6*.

7. Jürgen Habermas, "Technology and Science as 'Ideology,'" in *Toward a Rational Society*, Jeremy Shapiro (trans.), 81–122 (Boston, MA: Beacon Press, 1970); originally published in

One might have expected that Germany, with its comparatively powerful Green Party (until 2005 the second player in the governing coalition with the Social Democrats), would have continued to produce *continental* environmental philosophers. Such, however, has not generally been the case. Perhaps in part because of the revelations about Heidegger's involvements with National Socialism or because of the turn away from Marxism and the embrace of a revivified Kantian humanism in the thought of Habermas, German philosophers have, by and large, focused their concerns elsewhere. To these speculations should also be added the not inconsiderable fact that philosophers in Germany today are as likely to be interested in Anglo-American analytic philosophy as they are in their homegrown philosophical traditions. Thus, when we look for contemporary German contributions to environmental philosophy (and this is true in the Netherlands and Italy as well), most of what we find are engagements with English-language environmental ethics. We find, for example, investigations of the suitability of utilitarianism as an environmental ethic,[8] a turn to ecology to ground ethics,[9] or various engagements with economic analysis.[10]

That having been said, there have been several recent contributions to environmental philosophy from a continental perspective in Germany (I treat France separately below). Hans Jonas, in the context of his argument for responsibility as the central ethical concept in a technological age, discusses the importance of humanity's taking responsibility for our use of technology not only for ourselves but for nature's sake as well. After suggesting this idea, however, Jonas immediately retreats into the position that "responsibility for man" is sufficient, since his view of humanity includes our "worldly home"; that is, we need to care for where we live, broadly conceived, as part of our responsibility to ourselves and to each other.[11] Jonas thus remains not so much an environmental philosopher as a philosopher of technology.

Technik und Wissenschaft als "Ideologie" (Frankfurt: Suhrkamp, 1968), 48–103. See also Vogel, *Against Nature*, 101–43.

8. Jean-Claude Wolf, "Utilitaristische Ethik als Antwort auf die ökologische Krise," *Zeitschrift für philosophische Forschung* 44 (1990); Dieter Birnbacher, "Landschaftsschutz und Artenschutz: Wie weit tragen utilitaristische Begründungen," in *Naturschutz–Ethik–Ökonomie: Theoretische Begründungen und praktische Konsequenzen*, Hans G. Nutzinger (ed.) (Marburg: Metropolis, 1996).

9. Kutz Bayertz, "Naturphilosophie als Ethik: Zur Vereinigung von Natur- und Moralphilosophie im Zeichen der ökologischen Krise," *Philosophia Naturalis* 24 (1987); Rainer Stuhlmann-Laeisz, "Ökologische Ethik," *Kriterion: Zeitschrift für Philosophie* 1 (1991).

10. Otto Neumaier *et al.* (eds), *Angewandte Ethik im Spannungsfeld von Ökologie und Ökonomie* (Sankt Augustin: Academia, 1994); Anton Leist, "Ökologische Ethik II: Gerechtigkeit, Ökonomie, Politik," in *Angewandte Ethik: Die Bereichsethiken und ihre theoretische Fundierung*, Julian Nida-Rümelin (ed.) (Stuttgart: Alfred Kröner, 1996).

11. Hans Jonas, *The Imperative of Responsibility: In Search of an Ethics for the Technological Age*, Hans Jonas with David Herr (trans.) (Chicago, IL: University of Chicago Press, 1984), 136.

More promising is the work of Hans-Martin Schönherr-Mann, who reinvigorates the tradition of Adorno and Horkheimer (now developing it in the direction of a "negative ecology") by adding to it insights drawn from the work of Nietzsche, Heidegger, and Gianni Vattimo.[12] Writing in the late 1980s, Schönherr-Mann argued that ecological debates in Europe had reached a stalemate between the proponents of technical modernization and those who argued for a "return to nature." For Schönherr-Mann, this situation requires a metaphysical analysis *à la* Nietzsche or Heidegger. In other words, what needs to be seen is that both positions are rooted in modernity's will to master, the former as will to master nature, the latter as will to master that selfsame will to master, that is, a desire for mastery of mastery. Instead of these alternatives, Schönherr-Mann proposes what he calls, following Vattimo, "weak thinking"[13] (often translated "weak theory"), in which thought attempts neither to master the world nor to master itself. Rather, the goal of philosophical engagement is to criticize the ways in which the will to mastery manifests itself so that it can be seen as what it is – a metaphysical position rooted in a particular historical moment with particular ramifications – thus at least opening the way to thinking, and perhaps being, otherwise. That is, weak thinking, rather than offering an alternative conceptualization of the world, endeavors to make evident the contingency of current modes of thought as well as the ways in which they instantiate a will to mastery. This weak thinking risks the same charge of quietism that is often leveled against Heidegger, but constitutes, argues Schönherr-Mann, the only way forward, since all other alternatives simply reinscribe modernity's will to mastery which, as we saw with Adorno and Horkheimer, leads only to further repression of humanity and nature.

III. THE UNITED STATES

As we saw above, some of Heidegger's work can be fairly characterized as proto-environmentalist. It was not, however, until recently that those strands in his thought were teased out by some English-language commentators. Early environmentalist commentators on Heidegger focused on *Gelassenheit* (letting be) as a way of relating to nature and natural beings that Heidegger contrasted with a technical enframing (*Ge-stell*) that forces the world to appear as what he terms standing reserve (*Bestand*), that is, as resources that wait to be used

---

12. See Hans-Martin Schönherr-Mann, *Von der Schwierigkeit, Natur zu Verstehen: Entwurf einer negativen Ökologie* (Frankfurt: Fischer Taschenbuch, 1989) and *Die Technik und die Schwäche: Ökologie nach Nietzsche, Heidegger und dem "schwachen" Denken* (Vienna: Passagen, 1989).

*13. Vattimo's "weak thinking" is discussed in the essay on Italian philosophy by Silvia Benso and Brian Schroeder in *The History of Continental Philosophy: Volume 7*.

and used up.[14] What these commentators found in Heidegger was a thinker who took Kant's insight that how nature appeared to us is dependent on our own categories and Hegel's insight that those categories are historically variable, and combined it with Nietzsche's view that such categories could themselves be criticized as either affirming or destructive. For Heidegger, the categories of technical enframing, which force the world to appear as a set of resources – what he termed standing reserve – had pernicious consequences both for nature and for humanity since, as Heidegger saw, such a form of revealing could not but be applied to humanity as well. Thus, the very same set of practices – scientific, technical, philosophical, and so on – that prevent nature from appearing as free also prevent humanity from encountering itself as free. Finally, commentators have found in Heidegger's proposal of a new or other beginning the possibility that we might come to reveal the world (allow the world to reveal itself) not as forced into rigid categories with which it must conform, but as free.[15] Such revealing for Heidegger will happen, as does technical revealing, primarily in and through linguistic practices. However, freeing revealing will (may) happen through poetizing, in which the poet gives voice to nature itself, so that nature, in a sense, is allowed to show itself to us in language.

Of late there has been a growing tide, led by Michael Zimmerman, one of the earliest proponents of Heidegger as an environmental philosopher, arguing that Heidegger may not be as fruitful a figure as was previously believed.[16] Zimmerman now argues that Heidegger's involvement with National Socialism is deeply implicated in his philosophy and that, as a result, any Heideggerean environmental philosophy, even one presenting itself as having to do with freedom, runs the risk of finding itself endorsing fascism, which is a risk that Zimmerman is unwilling to take. (Part of this hesitation no doubt stems from the fact that it was under the National Socialists that Germany enacted the world's first far-reaching laws for the protection of nature at a time when they were showing precious little regard for the protection of human beings.[17]) While

---

14. For example, Laura Westra, "Let It Be: Heidegger and Future Generations," *Environmental Ethics* 7 (1985).
15. See Bruce V. Foltz, *Inhabiting the Earth: Heidegger, Environmental Ethics, and the Metaphysics of Nature* (Atlantic Highlands, NJ: Humanities Press, 1995).
16. Michael E. Zimmerman, "Implications of Heidegger's Thought for Deep Ecology," *Modern Schoolman* 64 (1986); "Rethinking the Heidegger–Deep Ecology Relationship," *Environmental Ethics* 15 (1993); *Contesting Earth's Future: Radical Ecology and Postmodernity* (Berkeley, CA: University of California Press, 1994); and "What Can Continental Philosophy Contribute to Environmentalism?" in *Rethinking Nature: Essays in Environmental Philosophy*, Bruce V. Foltz and Robert Frodeman (eds) (Bloomington, IN: Indiana University Press, 2004).
17. For a recent discussion of German environmental policy in the 1930s and 1940s, see F.-J. Brüggemeir, M. Cioc, and T. Keller (eds), *How Green were the Nazis? Nature, Environment, and Nation in the Third Reich* (Athens, OH: Ohio University Press, 2005).

Zimmerman does not believe that there is any surefire antidote to fascism, the one most likely to succeed is a commitment to democracy. The privileged position Heidegger gives to poets, argues Zimmerman, is simply inconsistent with a view that holds that environmental decisions must be made democratically. Still, Heidegger's insight that we cannot discuss nature without doing so in relation to humanity is one that we will see fruitfully developed later.

Merleau-Ponty's detailed investigations of human experience, particularly those he developed in his later works, in which he argued that we can make sense of human experience of the world only under the conditions that the world and our bodies are made up of the same "flesh," have been taken up by some commentators as a fruitful path to making sense of the human place in the environment. While it has long been the case that environmentalists have depended on accounts of our experience of nature, they have often done so in relation to the languages of science or religion (the two great traditional languages for discussing nature).[18] Phenomenology, on the other hand, provides the resources for elaborating on experience from out of itself, which makes possible both descriptions and valorizations of that experience in a way that legitimizes them even when they have no grounding in either science or religion.[19] Merleau-Ponty's work thus helps validate the aesthetic component of everyday experience and helps make sense of environmentalist intuitions.

Although Foucault at first blush seems an unlikely candidate to be an environmental philosopher (he famously responded to natural beauty by turning his back on it), if we recall Heidegger's insights – that nature and culture must be thought together and that human practices shape what nature can be for us – then Foucault seems more plausible. Beginning with Thomas Birch, who argued that wilderness areas are little more than prisons for nature, there has been a steady stream of environmental philosophy drawing on Foucault.[20] Éric Darier has argued that three aspects of Foucault's genealogical period "can be particularly helpful for an environmental critique: 'governmentality,' 'biopower' and 'space.'"[21] These three concepts, taken together, give the environmental philosopher powerful tools for making sense of government power and its tendencies,

---

18. This is true, for example, of Aldo Leopold (*A Sand County Almanac*) and Holmes Rolston III (*Earth Ethics: Duties to and Values in the Natural World* and *Philosophy Gone Wild: Essays in Environmental Ethics*).
19. See for example Charles S. Brown and Ted Toadvine (eds), *Eco-phenomenology: Back to the Earth Itself* (Albany, NY: SUNY Press, 2003), as well as David Abram, *The Spell of the Sensuous: Perception and Language in a More-than-Human World* (New York: Vintage, 1997).
20. Thomas H. Birch, "The Incarceration of Wilderness: Wilderness Areas as Prisons," *Environmental Ethics* 12 (1990).
21. Éric Darier, "Foucault and the Environment: An Introduction," in *Discourses of the Environment*, Éric Darier (ed.) (Oxford: Blackwell, 1999), 21. This collection's essays are all environmental applications of Foucault's thought.

in particular as that power is deployed on living (for Foucault human) bodies arrayed in space. We can even see, despite Foucault's protestations to the contrary, a certain sort of environmentalism in his work on biopower, in particular when he turned to issues having to do with public health.[22] For it was here that Foucault showed how the state has sought to control the health of populations by controlling the movement of individuals, foods, substances, and so on; by instituting rules as to appropriate and inappropriate behavior; by setting standards for cleanliness of work places and concerning agriculture; and so on. While such regulations and laws did not concern themselves with nature, they certainly did concern themselves with the human environment, as do many contemporary environmental regulations, such as those addressing agriculture or clean air and water. Foucault's analyses are useful for they show how the object of such measures is not always so much individual health as it is the health of the social body as disciplined body that must be ready to appear for work or warfare.

Deleuze too, although politically more sympathetic to "green" causes (perhaps because of his connection with Guattari) than was Foucault, was no more engaged with them in his philosophy. Nevertheless, commentators on his work have found rich resources there for thinking through environmental issues. As early as 1997, Patrick Hayden sought to apply Deleuze's work to environmental issues, arguing that Deleuze's emphasis on becoming provided resources for thinking about nature as flux rather than as static, a view that Hayden argues is fully compatible with the findings of contemporary ecology.[23] More or less simultaneously with Hayden's work, I argued that Deleuze and Guattari's distinction between smooth and striated space could profitably be applied to clarify what we mean by wilderness. In particular, I argued that the idea of wilderness as a place untouched by human activity is incoherent, and that we would be better off distinguishing between spaces that were smoother, that is, had seen less human activity, including even being mapped, and those that were more striated, that is, developed, paved, controlled, and so on. I also argued for a distinction between types of human activity, following Deleuze and Guattari in finding those activities associated with the modern, capitalist state as being of a different

---

22. See the following, all in Michel Foucault, *Dits et écrits II, 1976–1988* (Paris: Gallimard, 2001): "La politique de la santé au XVIIIe Siècle," #168, and, in revised form, #257 (the earlier text is translated as "The Politics of Health in the Eighteenth Century," Colin Gordon [trans.], in *The Essential Foucault*, Paul Rabinow and Nikolas Rose [eds] [New York: New Press, 2003]); "Crise de la médecine ou crise de l'antimédecine?," #170; and "La naissance de la médecine sociale," #196 (translated as "The Birth of Social Medicine," in *The Essential Foucault*).

23. See Patrick Hayden, "Gilles Deleuze and Naturalism: A Convergence with Ecological Theory and Politics," *Environmental Ethics* 19 (1997), and *Multiplicity and Becoming: The Pluralist Empiricism of Gilles Deleuze* (New York: Lang, 1998).

order than those associated with other forms of social organization.[24] At this time, too, Verena A. Conley invoked Deleuze, although more for his interest in radical democracy and as a coauthor with Guattari than anything else.[25]

One final development in North America needs to be accounted for: ecofeminism, whose roots are in France. As Trish Glazebrook points out, "It was Simone de Beauvoir who first saw that in the logic of patriarchy, both women and nature appear as other. In 1974, Françoise d'Eaubonne coined the term *l'éco-féminisme* to point to the necessity for women to bring about ecological revolution."[26] Despite these continental beginnings, most subsequent ecofeminism has been explicitly hostile to the traditions of continental philosophy, in particular to the idea of postmodernism. While most ecofeminists argue that there are important links between the oppression of women and the exploitation of nature, they do so in different ways, many of them stressing either women's greater spiritual affinity for nature or greater capacity for an environmental ethic. Still others criticize modern, patriarchal, dualistic thinking for its role in the oppression of women and nature. While such critiques might have developed using the resources of continental philosophy, they have largely not done so (although Glazebrook argues that Heidegger ought to be a resource drawn on by ecofeminists, while D. Bruce Martin does the same for Adorno[27]). Indeed, many ecofeminists, while criticizing dualistic thinking and the androcentrism of Western philosophy, dismiss what they term "postmodernism" or "deconstructive postmodernism," which they see as a dangerous form of social constructivism that undercuts any attempt to find real differences between men and women, while also making nature a social rather than a real category of analysis. Mary Mellor makes this claim most forcefully, writing that "ecofeminism is … incompatible with a radically social constructivist position, whether from a phenomeno-

---

24. See my "Something Wild? Deleuze and Guattari and the Impossibility of Wilderness," *Philosophy & Geography* 3 (1998). A revised version of this essay can be found as "Something Wild? Deleuze and Guattari, Wilderness, and Purity," in *The Wilderness Debate Rages On: Continuing the Great New Wilderness Debate*, J. Baird Callicott and Michael Nelson (eds) (Athens, GA: University of Georgia Press, 2008).

25. See Verena A. Conley, *Ecopolitics: The Environment in Poststructuralist Thought* (New York: Routledge, 1997). See also Mark Halsey, *Deleuze and Environmental Damage: Violence of the Text* (Burlington, VT: Ashgate, 2006) and *Deleuze/Guattari and Ecology* (New York: Palgrave Macmillan, 2009).

26. Trish Glazebrook, "Heidegger and Ecofeminism," in *Feminist Interpretations of Martin Heidegger*, N. J. Holland and P. Huntington (eds) (University Park, PA: Pennsylvania State University Press, 2001), 222.

27. *Ibid.*; D. Bruce Martin, "Mimetic Moments: Adorno and Ecofeminism," in *Feminist Interpretations of Theodor Adorno*, Renée Heberle (ed.) (University Park, PA: Pennsylvania State University Press, 2006).

logical, socialist–Marxist or postmodern perspective."[28] That having been said, there are several other ecofeminists who are not only sympathetic to, but explicit advocates of, a continental approach (although not always of the same type) including Jim Cheney, Patricia Jagentowicz Mills, and Ariel Salleh. Mills argues that Adorno and Horkheimer can offer an important corrective to much of the ecofeminist literature linking the domination of women and the domination of nature, since Adorno and Horkheimer do not romanticize nature (or women) the way many contemporary ecofeminists do.[29] Salleh draws more on Marx than on later Marxists to argue that women constitute, if not the revolutionary class that Marx predicted the proletariat would be, at least the central agent for social and environmental change.[30] Finally, Cheney embraces the sort of postmodern philosophical perspective most ecofeminists have eschewed, drawing on Heidegger, Richard Rorty, and Sandra Harding, as well as Biddy Martin and Chandra Mohanty to critique masculinist, totalizing discourse and open up a space for the development of what he terms "bioregional narratives" that are grounded in a place and the practices appropriate thereto.[31]

IV. FRANCE

One way to characterize what we have seen so far is that all of those working in this area have treated nature and humanity as two distinct terms. The question has always been: How ought these two stand in relation to one another? With developments in France, we see the development of a line of thought that rejects the strict dichotomy between humanity and nature and thus paves the way for a philosophy that is far more thoroughgoing in its environmentalism. We might characterize the work of thinkers such as Serres, Guattari, and Latour as being committed to the idea of putting multiple variables in play at once. We will see this type of thinking repeatedly here, albeit in different ways. Before doing so, we should note that the general philosophical climate in France

---

28. Mary Mellor, *Feminism & Ecology* (New York: New York University Press, 1997), 7. Similar antagonisms to postmodernism are voiced by Val Plumwood (*Feminism and the Mastery of Nature* [New York: Routledge, 1993], 61), and Marti Kheel (*Nature Ethics: An Ecofeminist Perspective* [Lanham, MD: Rowman & Littlefield, 2008], 8).

29. Patricia Jagentowicz Mills, "Feminism and Ecology," in *Ecological Feminist Philosophies*, Karen J. Warren (ed.) (Bloomington, IN: Indiana University Press, 1996).

30. Ariel Salleh, *Ecofeminism as Politics: Nature, Marx and the Postmodern* (New York: Zed Books, 1997).

31. Jim Cheney, "Postmodern Environmental Ethics: Ethics as Bioregional Narrative," in *Postmodern Environmental Philosophies*, Max Oelschlaeger (ed.) (Albany, NY: SUNY Press, 1995), and "Nature/Theory/Difference: Ecofeminism and the Reconstruction of Environmental Ethics," in *Ecological Feminist Philosophies*, Karen J. Warren (ed.).

(and French-speaking Belgium), at least as far as environmental philosophy is concerned, is little different from Germany. The single most visible book of environmental philosophy, Luc Ferry's *New Ecological Order*, takes as its target not contemporary developments in France (of which Ferry seems largely unaware) but developments abroad, which Ferry characterizes as a threat to French society and democracy.[32] Among French philosophers who have made their names exclusively as environmental thinkers, none has taken a continental approach.[33] Even as recently as 1998, editors of books or special journal issues dedicated to environmental themes (there remains no philosophical journal dedicated to environmental philosophy in French or German; the English-speaking world now has six) have felt the need to include an introductory essay on the terrain of English-language environmental philosophy.[34]

Part of what makes the thought of Serres, Latour, and Guattari stand out is that they begin by thinking of environmental problems not as ethical but as political. That is, they are problems to be addressed through collective rather than individual action. They thus do not engage in what we might term the meta-ethical investigation so common in English-language environmental ethics, where questions as to the moral standing of nature and whether our concern should be directed toward nature as a whole, ecosystems, species, or individual plants and animals, and so on have all been so central. Such investigations assume a fixed pole – that of human beings – who then must decide how they will act. Even those working from a continental perspective in Germany, the UK, Australia, and the US have tended to follow this model, although they have radicalized it to a degree, asking not how we should act toward nature but how we want nature to be.[35] Part of what makes the work of these French thinkers different is that they begin with a very different conception of nature from that of English-language environmental philosophers. Following the tradition of John Muir, American environmental philosophers have historically shown a

32. Luc Ferry, *The New Ecological Order*, C. Volk (trans.) (Chicago, IL: University of Chicago Press, 1995); originally published as *Le Nouvel ordre écologique: L'Arbre, l'animal et l'homme* (Paris: B. Grasset, 1992). Trained as a philosopher, Ferry served from 2002 to 2004 as the Minister of Education in the cabinet of conservative Prime Minister Jean-Pierre Raffarin.

33. See, for example, Dominique Bourg, *Les Scénarios de l'écologie* (Paris: Hachette, 1996); Catherine Larrère, *Les Philosophies de l'environnement* (Paris: Presses Universitaires de France, 1997); and Catherine Larrère and Raphaël Larrère, *Du bon usage de la nature: Pour une philosophie de l'environnement* (Paris: Aubier, 1997).

34. Angelika Krebs, "Ökologische Ethik I: Grundlagen und Grundbegriffe," in *Angewandte Ethik*, Julian Nida-Rümelin (ed.); A. Gosseries, "L'Éthique environnementale aujourd'hui," *Revue Philosophique de Louvain* 96 (1998). Krebs's article is available in an expanded English version as *Ethics of Nature: A Map* (Berlin: de Gruyter, 1999).

35. See, among others, Steven Vogel, "Environmental Philosophy After the End of Nature," *Environmental Ethics* 24 (2002).

great interest in wilderness.[36] With the possible exceptions of the highest peaks of the Alps, there is no wilderness in France and has not been for many centuries. As Latour puts it, "in the 'geopolitics' of the philosophy of nature, France benefits from a comparative advantage because the notion of an ahuman nature that ought to be protected has never taken root here."[37] This "advantage," of course, only gets us so far, since it is certainly possible to conceive of nature as cultural without also taking on the counter-movement that sees culture as (at least partially) natural. That is, while someone such as Steve Vogel argues forcefully for nature as a social construction, he remains committed to humanity's autonomy from nature. Serres, Latour, and Guattari all agree that such a position is untenable. To see how they arrive at their view, we need to look briefly at the social scientists who influenced their work. I focus here on only one, the social psychologist Serge Moscovici,[38] although one could also mention Denis Duclos, René Dumont, and Edgar Morin, among others.[39]

Moscovici's 1968 *Essai sur l'histoire humaine de la nature* (Essay on the human history of nature) seeks to show how changes in science, technology, social organization, and so on have manifested themselves not in new understandings of the same nature, but in changes in nature itself. Such a view is not surprising, at least not from today's standpoint, when we acknowledge that so much of what we take to be natural is at least as much, if not more, artifactual than natural. This view too is consistent, if not identical, with Heidegger's view

---

36. See, for example, Michael Nelson and J. Baird Callicott (eds), *The Great New Wilderness Debates* (Athens, GA: University of Georgia Press, 1998), and Baird Callicott and Nelson (eds), *The Wilderness Debate Rages On*.

37. Bruno Latour, *Politics of Nature: How to Bring the Sciences into Democracy*, Catherine Porter (trans.) (Cambridge, MA Harvard University Press, 2004), 7 n.3; *Politiques de la nature: Comment faire entrer les sciences en démocratie* (Paris: Éditions la Découverte, 1999), 17 n.3.

38. Serge Moscovici (1925– ; born in Braila, Romania, into a Jewish family) emigrated to France in 1948, where he began studying psychology at the Sorbonne. Cofounder, in 1975, of the Laboratoire Européen de Psychologie Sociale (European Laboratory of Social Psychology), Moscovici has taught in the US and UK in addition to his position at the École Pratique des Hautes Études.

39. See, in particular, Denis Duclos, *Les Industriels et les risques pour l'environnement* (Paris: L'Harmattan, 1991); René Dumont, *Utopia or Else …*, V. Menkes (trans.) (New York: Universe, 1975), originally published as *l'Utopie ou la mort!* (Paris: Editions du Seuil, 1973); Edgar Morin, *Le Paradigme perdu: La Nature humaine* (Paris: Éditions du Seuil, 1973) and *The Nature of Nature*, J. L. Roland Bélanger (trans.) (New York: Peter Lang, 1992), originally published as *La Méthode I: La Nature de la nature* (Paris: Éditions du Seuil, 1977); and Serge Moscovici, *Essai sur l'histoire humaine de la nature* (Paris: Flammarion, 1968). For a more detailed survey of this history, albeit from the perspective of a political theorist, see Whiteside, *Divided Natures*, 47–79. Despite the overall value of his book, Whiteside, perhaps because of his interest in politics, takes no notice of the work of Catherine Larrère and Raphaël Larrère.

that changes in human practice necessitate changes in the world.[40] Moscovici's view, however, is more radical, for it entails that humanity is both the "creator and subject of nature."[41] Thus, we see here already the key insight of French environmental philosophy: it is insufficient to hold one pole (humanity) stable while allowing the other (nature) to evolve. Instead, both poles must be allowed to codetermine each other, and this in a historically mediated fashion. Moscovici conceives of a series of "states of nature": "organic nature," the "universe of forces and movements," and "cybernetic nature."[42] The first of these, from late Neolithic times to the dawn of the Renaissance, is characterized by artisans working on materials such as wood, stone, or metal solely with hand tools. Nature here is conceived as a fixed set of materials, each with its own "nature," that can be complemented by the work of a skilled artisan.[43] The artisan, then, is the one who follows nature's lead and seeks not to impose on it, but to work with it. The mechanistic stage conceives of nature as a set of forces and materials that are, by and large, interchangeable. This nature is made up of quantifiable forces and substitutable materials. Moscovici thus finds the origin of Bacon's and Descartes's mechanized view of nature in the technology of their day. That is, it is the changes in human practice that lead the way for changes in our conceptualization of the world. But this new nature then makes possible a corresponding shift in humanity, whose skilled artisans are no longer needed, to be replaced by unskilled workers fulfilling tasks set them by engineers and others trained in the ways of the new nature. That is, and here Moscovici's argument echoes Adorno and Horkheimer, the new mechanized nature gives birth to a new mechanized humanity. The age of cybernetic nature begins when, as Kerry Whiteside puts it, "we see nature as the combination of elements into self-sustaining systems. Knowledge of the properties of these systems allows us to create new forms of matter, not merely to shape or transform what is given."[44] The engineer is now displaced by the scientist while the distinction between the natural and the non-natural collapses. Nature's processes are seen as alterable and, at least at times, in need of human intervention to keep them going.[45] Here too the changes in

---

40. At its most extreme, Heidegger's view entails such changes leading to fundamentally different worlds. See "The Origin of the Work of Art," in *Poetry, Language, Thought*, Albert Hofstadter (trans.) (New York: Harper & Row, 1971), originally published as "Der Ursprung des Kunstwerkes," in *Holzwege* (Frankfurt: Klostermann, 1950); "The Age of the World Picture," in *Question Concerning Technology and Other Essays*, William Lovitt (trans.) (New York: Harper & Row, 1977), originally published as "Die Zeit des Weltbildes," in *Holzwege*. One might think here too of Foucault's idea of *epistēmē* as worked out in *The Order of Things*.

41. Moscovici, *Essai sur l'histoire humaine de la nature*, 21.

42. *Ibid.*, 76–119.

43. This is Aristotle's nature.

44. Whiteside, *Divided Natures*, 52.

45. We thus find classes in "ecosystem management" and the like.

nature bring about changes in humanity, as those who are empowered to speak and to make decisions shift and as social structures evolve to accommodate the new nature.

While Moscovici's account is compelling, it is descriptive rather than normative. That is, it describes how things have happened, without taking a stance on how we ought to move forward from here. We thus need to turn to the work of Serres, Latour, and Guattari, who will, each in his own way, seek to develop the thesis of the interrelatedness of nature and humanity into a compelling philosophico-political position. One of the difficulties all three face in crafting a normative position is that there is what we might term a cultural time-lag, so that even while our material practices, science, technology, and so on, have moved forward, thus bringing about transformations in nature and ourselves, we cling to older models of *both* humanity and nature. Our solutions thus are often inappropriate to the sort of people that we are and to the world in which we live.

If one accepts Moscovici's thesis that humanity and nature must be conceived of as codeterminants, it follows from this that even if one is concerned only with humanity, one must, *ipso facto*, also concern oneself with nature. However, in *The Natural Contract*, Serres argues for a more forceful position: nature must become part of our political structure, not as a set of passive objects or even vibrant systems, but as a partner with humanity.[46] For Serres, humanity has, for most of its history, not thought much about nature. We have been too concerned with our human projects, only noticing nature when it has made itself unavoidable. Today nature has made itself ubiquitous and has done so in response to human actions and conceptions.

Serres reminds us that humanity has a long juridical tradition of reshaping conflicts in order to make them less deadly. Even war has a set of laws and rules governing it; even when we are intent on killing each other, we must follow the rules. War, like other human institutions, is governed by a sort of contract. In the liberal tradition from Hobbes onward, the grandest of all contracts is the so-called social contract, in which we (tacitly) agree to give up some of our rights in exchange for others being bound to respect the remainder. Yet this contract, argues Serres, has always been predicated on our making common cause with our fellow human beings in the project of turning nature into property. The social contract thus brings into being a certain sort of nature. Yet, if this contractually created nature – a nature that can be seen to overlap to some degree Moscovici's mechanized and cybernetic natures – will not stand passively by as it is turned into products and property, then we need to rethink the human–nature relationship. Such a rethinking, however, is insufficient if

---

*46. Serres's work is the focus of the essay by David F. Bell in *The History of Continental Philosophy: Volume 6.*

it is not accompanied by a reconceptualization of how we relate to our fellow human beings. As Serres puts it, "we must decide on peace among ourselves to protect the world, and peace with the world to protect ourselves."[47] For the idea of making peace with the world to make sense, it would seem that the world would have to be capable of "signing" a contract with us, that is, the world must be a subject. Serres writes,

> What is nature? First, all the conditions of human nature itself, its global constraints of rebirth or extinction, the hostelry that gives us lodging, heat, and food. But nature also takes them away from us as soon as we abuse them. It influences human nature, which, in turn, influences nature. Nature behaves as a subject.[48]

We can see here quite clearly Serres's commitment to the heritage of Moscovici. Yet the idea that nature is a subject is not without its problems. However, Serres reminds us that the intrahuman social contract is already virtual, in that none of us has ever actually consented to it and expect reciprocity from others only in some sort of ideal way. The natural contract too, Serres insists, is also only virtual. That is, we must act as if nature is a party to this contract, even if our motivation for doing so might be purely selfish, which only makes his position more like that of classical contract theorists such as Locke or Hobbes. Just as in classical contract theory, in which my desire for security requires that I respect others in their persons and property, our desire for clean air and water demands that we respect the only "being" capable of furnishing us with those things. Our failure to abide by the natural contract will have negative consequences not only for nature but for us as well.

Latour's view that in the sciences we need to account for the agency not only of human beings but also of the entities studied can clearly be applied to the domain of environmental thought.[49] Latour, in works such as *We Have Never Been Modern*, argues that modern thought has so strictly divided the domains of nature (the domain of scientific discovery) and humanity (the realm of politics) that it has blinded us to the various hybrids that have arisen in between the two domains.[50] When Latour discusses hybrids, he means things such as the hole in

47. Michel Serres, *The Natural Contract*, Elizabeth MacArthur and William Paulson (trans.) (Ann Arbor, MI: University of Michigan Press, 1995), 25; *Le Contrat naturel* (Paris: Éditions François Bourin, 1990), 47.
48. Serres, *The Natural Contract*, 36; *Le Contrat naturel*, 64.
*49. Latour is also discussed in the essay by Olkowski in this volume.
50. Bruno Latour, *We Have Never Been Modern*, Catherine Porter (trans.) (Cambridge, MA: Harvard University Press, 1993); originally published as *Nous n'avons jamais été modernes: Essais d'anthropologie symétrique* (Paris: La Découverte, 1991).

the ozone layer over Australia (we might add the world's climate), which can be described neither as purely natural nor as purely cultural phenomena. Rather, they occupy a middle ground. Politics and science have, since the sixteenth century, been so thoroughly separated from one another that we are either blind to hybrids or do not know what to do with them. Indeed, it is the habit of thought of modernity to insist that there could be no such thing, since the domains of the human and the nonhuman are thought to be distinct and incapable of mixing. Much of Latour's work has been dedicated to showing how and why these domains cannot be kept distinct, either theoretically or practically.

We need to be careful here, for part of the value of Latour's work is that it is not "merely" philosophy but also sociology. Thus, while philosophers now generally agree that the fact–value distinction is incoherent, it remains an important part of political and public discourse. Science (with a capital S) takes on the role in this discourse of determining what is true (what is a fact) and what is not. No matter that practitioners of any individual science do not recognize themselves as having such a role or their science(s) as having such a power. The problem for Latour is how to demythologize Science so that we will see that nonhuman things too are players on the political scene and that human beings shape what those things are. That is, just as we saw with Serres, the problem becomes one of conceptualizing how humanity and nature can be codeterminants of one other. Where Latour goes beyond Serres's position is in his greater emphasis on the relationship between science and politics, thus making the relationship between humanity and nature one that plays itself out not in some abstract realm, but in the very concrete interactions we find in these domains, reconceived, of course, so that they no longer stand in stark opposition to one another.

The grand thrust of Latour's work is to destabilize the opposition between humanity and nature. This move undercuts, on the one hand, appeals by environmentalists to what is best or right for nature and, on the other, appeals by industrialists or politicians that nature is inconsiderable. Latour, finally, argues that what is needed in order to overcome the modern nature–culture divide is a parliament of things in which human and natural actors and hybrids would all have a say. However, as Whiteside points out, it remains unclear just what deliberations in such a parliament are supposed to look like as well as how it is expected to come to a decision.[51] Nevertheless, the idea that we must attempt to rethink nature and culture in relationship is an important one, as is Latour's argument that there is neither apolitical science nor ascientific politics.

---

51. Whiteside, *Divided Natures*, 139.

Guattari adds a third element that is lacking in both Serres and Latour: human subjectivity.[52] While both Serres and Latour argue for the importance of our reconceptualizing both nature and human society, Guattari argues also for the need to account for human subjectivity, in particular in relation to desire.[53] We thus find in his work a sketch of three ecologies: of nature, of society, and of the subject. As with Serres and Latour, although now developed on three axes, these three ecologies are all seen by Guattari as interrelated. For Guattari, and this is partly due to his earlier involvement with communist politics as well as his later involvements with both green politics and alternative forms of psychiatric practice, modern forms of socioeconomic organization – what he terms "integrated world capitalism" – have had strongly deleterious effects for all three ecologies. Nature has become nothing but a set of resources and pollution sinks, society has become nothing but a guarantor of stability for purposes of assuring economic growth, and subjectivity has become a structure of desire in the service of material consumption.

Guattari's insight that one must also address questions having to do with subjectivity is important (and remains, to this day, little discussed among environmental philosophers). Subjectivity, for Guattari (and here he is indebted to his work with Deleuze, particularly in the two volumes of *Capitalism and Schizophrenia*[54]), is always structured out of desire.[55] The problem as he sees it is that our current form of subjectivity is one where the structuration happens in and through the workings of social institutions that are not democratically controlled and whose end is the production of subjects who will be docile, productive, and, most importantly, good consumers. If such is the form of subjectivity with which we (mostly) find ourselves, how might we (i) think subjectivity otherwise and (ii) envision a transition from our current to the alternative form of subjectivity? The second task is no less important than the first since a reorganization of current societal structures without a concomitant reorganization of subjectivity is likely to constitute an unacceptable form of violence to human subjects as we now find them. That is, we Westerners find

52. Félix Guattari, *The Three Ecologies*, Ian Pindar and Paul Sutton (trans.) (London: Athlone, 2000) and *Chaosmosis: An Ethico-Aesthetic Paradigm*, Paul Bains and Julian Pefanis (trans.) (Bloomington, IN: Indiana University Press, 1995). For a brief summary of Guattari's position see Hayden, "Gilles Deleuze and Naturalism," 202–4. See also Hayden, *Multiplicity and Becoming*, 103–32.
53. See on this topic my "Subjectivity, Desire, and the Problem of Consumption," in *Deleuze/Guattari and Ecology*, Herzogenrath (ed.).
54. Gilles Deleuze and Félix Guattari, *Anti-Oedipus: Capitalism and Schizophrenia*, Mark Seem *et al.* (trans.) (New York: Viking Press, 1977), and *A Thousand Plateaus: Capitalism and Schizophrenia*, Brian Massumi (trans.) (Minneapolis, MN: University of Minnesota Press, 1987).
*55. Guattari and Deleuze's account of desire is discussed in detail in the essay by Rosi Braidotti and Alan D. Schrift in *The History of Continental Philosophy: Volume 6*.

ourselves with apparently insatiable desires for material things (desires that are – absurdly – presented in political and economic rhetoric as "natural"). These desires will not simply go away, even if we want them to. We must thus work to conceive of ourselves not as free of desire but as having alternatively structured desires. For example, rather than desiring corporate foodstuffs, we might desire knowing who raised our food, so that we could feel ourselves part of a community. To be only of necessity, rather than primarily, a consumer is to desire otherwise, that is, to be otherwise. We must also work to conceive how we can move from how we are now to that other form of subjectivity, lest proposed changes in societal structure be, as they are commonly thought, hardships imposed on individual subjects for the sake of some abstract "nature."

10

RETHINKING THE NEW WORLD ORDER: RESPONSES TO GLOBALIZATION/ AMERICAN HEGEMONY

Todd May

Continental philosophy has never been reticent about engaging with contemporary political situations. From Kant's and Hegel's reflections on the French Revolution, through Sartre's and Merleau-Ponty's debates about communism, up to Badiou's recent reflections on the character of the twentieth century[1] and Rancière's critique of antidemocratic currents in Europe,[2] continental thinkers have addressed themselves to politics, not only in the abstract, but as it has unfolded around them. In contrast to their analytic counterparts, continental thinkers have held situated political reflection to be an intrinsic part of philosophical practice.[3]

Chief among the political parameters of our time that have held the interest of continental thinkers, particularly in recent years, has been the emergence of what might be called *globalization*. Of course, globalization is a term of common currency. It is a truism to say that we live in an increasingly globalized world. But truisms are where philosophers intervene, either to buttress, to question, or to overturn them. Globalization has been no different. What globalization is, and how to respond to it, have constituted the core of a number of political reflections.

Even the term itself can carry hidden, questionable assumptions. When we refer to globalization, we seem to be referring to the increasing interconnectedness

---

1. Alain Badiou, *The Century*, Alberto Toscano (trans.) (Cambridge: Polity, 2007).
2. Jacques Rancière, *Hatred of Democracy*, Steve Corcoran (trans.) (London: Verso, 2006).
3. For one, albeit controversial, view of analytic philosophy's resistance to political engagement, see John McCumber, *Time in the Ditch: American Philosophy and the McCarthy Era* (Evanston, IL: Northwestern University Press, 2001). McCumber argues that philosophy in the US accommodated itself to the rise of McCarthyism by abandoning political reflection.

of the world in some fashion or another. Whether it be through increased electronic communications, the spread of transnational capitalism, or the movement of peoples and the breakdown of national borders, the idea of globalization carries with it the decline of the integrity of national entities. But is this true? Is what we are witnessing today a decline of nationality in favor of a more fluid transnationality? Perhaps it is something else altogether. Perhaps, instead of globalization, what we have been witnessing over the past several decades is the rise of a particular national hegemony, that of the United States. From this point of view, our world is less one of globalization than of American imperialism. This imperialism, it is true, is far more economic than political, and in that way differs from the colonialisms of the past two centuries. The US infiltrates other countries with its economic and cultural exports rather than governing them politically (with current exceptions, such as Iraq). Although it might be argued that, at least over the past several years, US hegemony, inasmuch as it did exist, is now on the wane, some might nevertheless argue that it would misdescribe the current global political situation to see it as a new phenomenon of globalization rather than a continuity of the type of national dominations that have long been with us.

Of course, these two explanations are not exclusive. There may be an intertwining of the two. In order to address this issue, however, one must begin to get behind the terms *globalization* and *hegemony* and begin to reflect more rigorously on the situation we occupy. Such a reflection would have two related parts: an assessment of the current political character and suggestions for how to intervene in it. In what follows, there is sometimes an emphasis on one or the other of these parts. However, the assessment one provides is not divorced from the kind of responses one sees as appropriate or possible. Conversely, the suggestions one makes for action and intervention depend on what one sees as the salient aspects of the contemporary context.

There have been numerous reflections on what might be called globalization. I will divide these, somewhat arbitrarily, into four categories. My only defense of this division is that it offers a practical categorization. There are, to be sure, transversal lines of influence and similarity: elements of a particular thinker's approach may be closer to elements of a thinker in another category. If some readers consider that another division better facilitates understanding, they should help themselves to it. The four categories are these:

I   Critiques of media and the rise of electronic interaction. Here the primary thinkers are Jean Baudrillard, Paul Virilio, and, to a lesser extent, Slavoj Žižek.

II Conceptions of multitude. In this category fall the work of Michael Hardt and Antonio Negri, as well as Paulo Virno.

III Reconceptualizations of democracy. This would include the work of Jacques Derrida, Ernesto Laclau, and Chantal Mouffe, and part of the recent writings of Judith Butler.

IV Renewal of the anarchist tradition. This is the most recent of the responses, and includes the work primarily of myself and Saul Newman.

I

Reflections on and critiques of the media have a long standing. We might date the background for current approaches to Guy Debord's classic book *The Society of the Spectacle* (1967). Debord argues, in an update of Marxist thought, that current social relations are no longer mediated by relations of production, but rather through what he calls "the spectacle." The spectacle consists of the ubiquitous images – in advertising, on television, in the movies, and (postdating Debord's work) on the internet – through which we relate to ourselves and one another. Debord, though, insists that the spectacle is not simply a matter of the images themselves: "The spectacle is not a collection of images; rather, it is a social relationship between people that is mediated by images."[4]

The idea that our relationships have been mediated by images is at the core of the thought of Jean Baudrillard.[5] In his early work, Baudrillard, like Debord, shifts the frame of Marxist thought away from its focus on productive relations. For Baudrillard, the proper focus is, instead, on consumption.[6] He argues that we must abandon the focus on productivism and begin to ask about consumption: how it occurs and what codes it follows. Over the course of his career, Baudrillard radicalizes this idea until he argues that, because of the role various media play in constituting our world, we no longer live in a world of reality. Instead, our world is one of hyperreality or simulation.

We might think of the emergence of simulation this way. Human relations have always been mediated to some extent, at least through primitive signs and signals. The rise of language constitutes an important moment in the mediatization of those relationships, as does the appearance of the printing press. However, with the explosion of media through which people interact with one another and their world – television, internet, email – social relationships have become dominated by the media through which they occur. In fact, as media

---

4. Guy Debord, *The Society of the Spectacle*, Donald Nicholson-Smith (trans.) (Cambridge: Zone Books, 1994), 12.

*5. Baudrillard's work is also discussed in the essay on postmodernism by Simon Malpas in *The History of Continental Philosophy: Volume 7*.

6. See, for instance, Jean Baudrillard, *The Mirror of Production*, Mark Poster (trans.) (St. Louis, MO: Telos Press, 1975).

195

begin to replace face-to-face interaction and engagement with the world, the world as a referent of those relationships and engagement begins to drop out. It no longer matters whether there is an outside world to which the images and media refer. Reality shifts, from referent of images to the images themselves. Images simulate rather than referring to reality. As Baudrillard puts the point, "To dissimulate is to feign not to have what one has. To simulate is to feign to have what one hasn't."[7]

Simulation is the co-optation of reality by media. Whether or not an event occurs outside that co-optation is irrelevant. There is an impact on our experience only inasmuch as something arises within the ambit of the simulated world. What we encounter is given to us solely through the images that are the ether of our lives. This means that if an event takes place outside of that ether, it is as though it did not take place. It will not register; it will not encrust itself into reality, or at least that hyperreality in and through which we live. Alternatively, there need be no event that takes place in order for it to be experienced as real. An event could be entirely fabricated by the press, or arise as a rumor on the internet, and be experienced with all the reality formerly accorded to the "real" world.

Baudrillard analyzes the attacks of 9/11 in terms of the images that were disseminated.[8] He does not deny, of course, the horror of the attacks. However, he finds that the reality that persisted in them was through images as they unfolded in the media. He argues that the goal of the attackers was to undermine the society of the spectacle through an excess of its own spectacularity. In that sense, the terrorist attacks were played out entirely within hyperreality.

In Baudrillard's view, then, globalization is the creation of simulation. He rarely offers anything that could be considered a response to it, for two reasons. First, Baudrillard is not a nostalgic thinker. He does not seem to miss the real world that has been left behind. Second, it is not entirely clear he could coherently offer a critique of our simulated world. If it is as encompassing as he claims, then there seems no place from which critique could occur. All critical positions have already been absorbed into hyperreality. What might be read as his only sustained response to simulation is offered in his 1979 book *Seduction*, where he paints a picture of politics as an ongoing seduction. This seduction is never consummated; rather, it is a game of symbolic feints where nothing is ever captured because there is nothing to be captured. "The law of seduction takes the form of an uninterrupted ritual exchange where seducer and seduced constantly

---

7. Jean Baudrillard, *Simulations*, Paul Foss *et al.* (trans.) (New York: Semiotext(e), 1983), 5.
8. Jean Baudrillard, *The Spirit of Terrorism and Requiem for the Twin Towers*, Chris Turner (trans.) (New York: Norton, 2002).

raise the stakes in a game that never ends."[9] In a world without reality, it is difficult to conceive how else politics might occur.

If Baudrillard's view of the rise of the media is playful and ironic, Paul Virilio[10] sees a darker mechanism at work. Like Baudrillard, Virilio focuses his work on the way electronic media have reshaped our world. However, Virilio sees media not only as the creation of a new reality but also as an intervention into our own reality. On the one hand, the rise of electronic media has made us unrecognizably different. On the other hand, we have not entered a hyperreality in which the real world no longer matters. We have become subject to forces that are reshaping us for the worse.

In his early works, Virilio focuses on the emergence of what he calls *speed*, and in particular the military uses of speed. We might think of speed as instantaneity of communication and intervention, an instantaneity that replaces both space and time. Formerly, military intervention was a matter of controlling space: having more territory, fighting from higher ground, and so on. Then it became a matter of time: who could get where faster. This is signaled by the importance of faster weapons and the development of military airplanes. Now, military intervention is approaching the instantaneous. One no sooner sees the target than one can destroy it. Moreover, this instantaneity is not only a matter of advanced weaponry. It also concerns the control of societies. The rise of electronic communication has created a system in which we can conduct our lives away from public space, but in a space that can be continuously monitored: by cameras, by electronic surveillance, through the monitoring of the computers at which many of us work, by tracking our purchases, and so on.

What this creates is a militarization of society, but in a particular way. It is not that everyone in society is mobilized in a military effort. Rather, there emerges a new class division. No longer is the class rupture between Marx's capitalists and proletariat. Now the divide runs between the military and the civilians. "The military class is turning into an internal super-police. Moreover, it's logical. In the strategy of deterrence, military institutions, no longer fighting among themselves, tend to fight only civilian societies – with, of course, a few skirmishes in the Third World."[11] This military class should be understood not only as the uniformed military; it also includes political and business leaders and anyone

---

9. Jean Baudrillard, *Seduction*, Brian Singer (trans.) (New York: Palgrave Macmillan, 1991), 22.

10. Paul Virilio (1932– ; born in Paris) grew up in Brittany, where he experienced and was marked by the German occupation and Allied bombings of Nantes. A cultural theorist and urbanist, he was trained in architecture at the École des Métiers d'Art and also studied philosophy with Vladimir Jankélévitch, Raymond Aron, and Maurice Merleau-Ponty at the Sorbonne. He served as Professor and Director at the École Spéciale d'Architecture in Paris from 1968 to 1998.

11. Paul Virilio, *Pure War*, Sylvère Lotringer (trans.) (New York: Semiotext(e), 1997), 94.

else who is aligned with the controlling class, that is, who utilizes speed in order to control part or all of a population.

More recently, Virilio has turned his attention away from the military uses of speed and toward the encrustation of human beings into technology. This encrustation is largely corporeal: the body is monitored, plugged into various technologies, trained to become a relay in the digital infrastructure. Where once the idea of being merely a cog in a machine was a metaphor for alienation, Virilio sees this as becoming a literal truth. Moreover, given the instantaneity of networks of control, our corporeal attachment to technology ensures that we are constantly monitored and manipulated.

> The generalized arrival of transmission has taken over from the restricted arrival of transport ... A "freeze frame" whereby the interactive experience of generalized teleaction will soon prolong the life sentence of the expanse of the space-world, to the exclusive advantage of the time-world of the real instant.[12]

Unlike Baudrillard, Virilio does not see our immersion in technology as benign. He is concerned about its environmental impact, but also about its alienating effects. Where for Baudrillard we are simply becoming something else, for Virilio we have lost what it is to be fully human, and this is to be lamented. Although he calls for resistance to this loss, Virilio does not offer a programmatic response. Rather, he seeks, through the starkness of his descriptions, to recall for us the dangerous technological drift of our current situation.

Although he does not fit neatly into the category of critiques of media and electronic interaction (or, for that matter, into any other category), Slavoj Žižek should at least be mentioned in this regard since his work intersects with the concerns of Baudrillard and Virilio. For Žižek, there is always a Hegelian irony in play, and it occurs in technology as it does elsewhere in the contemporary world. In "Cyberspace, Or, The Unbearable Closure of Being,"[13] he argues that we use the internet in order to pretend to ourselves that the desires we fulfill through it or the online personalities we create are merely that: pretend. That is, we project our real desires onto electronic media the more effectively to deny that they are indeed our real desires. More recently, in *Welcome to the Desert of the Real*, a response to the events of 9/11, Žižek has claimed that the past century, which involved purported attempts to touch the Lacanian Real, has, in that very attempt, found itself more mediatized than ever. He points out the irony of the Islamic fundamentalists who destroyed the World Trade Center in an attempt

---

12. Paul Virilio, *Open Sky*, Julie Rose (trans.) (London: Verso, 1997), 143.
13. In Slavoj Žižek, *The Plague of Fantasies* (London: Verso, 1997).

to strike at the heart of the modern, Western world, and whose success was had through the media impact of the attacks. This is, he argues, "the fundamental paradox of the 'passion for the Real': it culminates in its apparent opposite, in a *theatrical spectacle* – from the Stalinist show trials to spectacular terrorist acts."[14] Alternatively, the US, which sees itself as the bastion of democracy, supports undemocratic regimes around the world in the name of the very democracy it forecloses.

II

Turning to the next analysis of and response to globalization, those involving conceptions of the multitude, we should note that there are themes these thinkers share with those we have just discussed. There is no denial of the importance of the role of the media or of electronic communication in the formation of the contemporary scene. However, the emphasis is elsewhere. The accent in this approach is placed on the political and economic rather than on the technological.

The most important and influential book oriented around the multitude is Michael Hardt and Antonio Negri's *Empire* (2000). The framework of the book is complex, and much of its philosophical background derives from the work of Gilles Deleuze (especially the idea of the multitude as a virtuality, a point we can only gloss here). Regarding globalization, Hardt and Negri argue that we have entered a period characterized not so much by colonialism or imperialism but by the imperial. The imperial is immanent. Instead of a colonial project of taking over another country, entering it from the outside, as it were, the globalized world is, in their view, all inside. There is a single global economic–political order rather than an order of nation-states transcendent to one another. This new order may be conceived as a pyramid in which, at the top or first tier, the US holds a dominant position among a set of nation-states that can engage in economic regulation through such instruments as the G7 and the World Bank. The second tier contains transnational corporations. The third tier consists in various groups, including nongovernmental organizations, which represent the *multitude*, a term we will return to in a moment. In the end, then, the world is not divided simply into nation-states but more importantly into networks of flows of information, production, and so on. There is no transcendent power,

---

14. Slavoj Žižek, *Welcome to the Desert of the Real: Five Essays on September 11 and Related Dates* (London: Verso, 2002), 9. It should perhaps be noted that in *The Century*, Badiou also argues that the twentieth century exhibited a passion for the real. However, Žižek's Real and Badiou's real are not exactly the same. For Žižek, the Real is the Lacanian unreachable Real; moreover, he believes that this passion for the Real is ambivalent. For Badiou, in contrast, the real is more diffuse than the Lacanian Real, and those whose passion was for it were not ambivalent.

as in modern sovereignty, but only the power of Empire in the immanence of the networks.

This view has elements in common with that of Baudrillard and Virilio, specifically in its emphasis on networks and on the important role of electronic media in those networks. However, Hardt and Negri's analysis is more encompassing. The media are part of Empire, but they do not exhaust it. There is a decline of nation-states, but not their disappearance. There can be tensions and resistances, but these resistances are immanent to Empire rather than transcendent. Resistance does not arise from those who are left outside, because there is no outside. Rather, it arises from the creative power that exists within Empire. This is where Hardt and Negri invoke the multitude.

The multitude is not the proletariat, nor is it any other particular identity. In fact, one of the crucial characteristics of the multitude is precisely its lack of such an identity. Because of this, the multitude is not a specific group of people. The multitude is fluid, without strict borders. Essentially, the multitude consists in the creative power of everything that can resist the control of Empire, a virtuality within Empire that has not been caught in the net of its controlling practices and institutions. As they write in their follow-up to *Empire*, appropriately entitled *Multitude* (2004), the multitude, like Empire, "too might thus be conceived as a network: an open and expansive network in which all differences can be expressed freely and equally, a network that provides the means of encounter so that we can work and live in common."[15] Invoking the perspective of Deleuze, the multitude is a network of differences rather than a uniformity of identity.

This conception of the multitude allows for a variety of political alliances. Since those alliances are not predicated on particular identities, there is no question of who can or cannot participate in the struggle. The multitude is beyond identity politics, and is, in Hardt and Negri's view, the only way to conceive resistance to Empire, that is, to the immanence of power and control in a globalized world.

At around the same time that Hardt and Negri published *Empire*, the Italian thinker and activist Paolo Virno gave a series of lectures (in 2001) that would eventually be collected in *A Grammar of the Multitude*. Virno and Negri come from the same background – the Italian *autonomia* movement[16] – but their conception of the multitude is divergent. If for Hardt and Negri the multitude is a creative virtuality, for Virno it is an empirical product of what he calls "Post-Fordism": a mode of production that involves not only manual but also intellectual labor. In Virno's view, the multitude is, as it is for Hardt and Negri, a mass

---

15. Michael Hardt and Antonio Negri, *Multitude: War and Democracy in the Age of Empire* (London: Penguin, 2004), xiii–xiv.
*16. For a discussion of Virno, Negri, and *autonomia*, see the essay on Italian Philosophy by Silvia Benso and Brian Schroeder in *The History of Continental Philosophy: Volume 7*.

that is not exactly a class. But, in contrast to their view, for Virno the multitude is not only the basis for social production, but also the product of a particular productive context. The multitude can be revolutionary, but it is not revolutionary in its essence. In his introduction to *A Grammar of the Multitude*, Sylvère Lotringer sums up this distinction trenchantly when he writes, "*Empire* involves an original kind of class struggle: *a struggle looking for a class*. For Virno it would be just the reverse: a class looking for a struggle."[17]

As Hardt and Negri make clear in *Multitude*, their conception of the multitude is that of a new democracy. In the context of globalization, the question of democracy has assumed a new importance. There is, on the one hand, the official discourse of democracy, a discourse that arises from the corridors of power in developed countries, and especially in the US. This discourse emphasizes two elements as constitutive of democracy: elections and capitalism. The first ensures political representation; the second free economic activity. However, among many progressive thinkers, the combination of elections and democracy does not seem always to yield a political and economic order that merits the honorific *democratic*. This is because both elections and capitalism individually, and even more so in their combination, lend themselves to manipulation and control by elites. This point seems an obvious one, but its implications are often missed. Do we really want to label as democratic political and economic orders that work to the benefit of the few, and that, to one extent or another, leave those who are not well placed outside real political and economic participation? Moreover, do such orders not tend toward a stifling homogenization in which certain styles of living and interacting are privileged and anything alternative marginalized? A number of thinkers have argued, as we will see in the next section, that we need to reconceive democracy, particularly in an age where globalization can lend itself to exploitation, oppression, and marginalization on a much greater scale than we have seen previously.

III

Hardt and Negri's *Multitude* can be seen as one approach to this reconceptualization. Recent political texts by Derrida, Laclau and Mouffe, and, to a lesser extent, Judith Butler, provide others. Turning first to Derrida, it is perhaps not surprising that he wants to reconceive democracy in terms of the other that is often excluded. Deconstruction has always been a project of thinking the outside, not as outside but as constitutive of the inside. Where the inside (however that

---

17. Sylvère Lotringer, "Introduction," in *A Grammar of the Multitude*, Isabella Bertoletti *et al.* (trans.) (New York: Semiotext(e), 2004), 16.

inside is defined) sees itself in contrast to the outside, deconstruction shows that the outside is never entirely outside. The outside is also inside, and the inside is also outside.[18] For our purposes, the political importance of this has to do with Derrida's project of thinking democracy deconstructively.

In one of his earlier attempts to do so, *The Other Heading* (1992), Derrida focuses his energies on Europe. This is not surprising, and not only because Derrida lived in France (although he was born in Algeria). For the past twenty years, Europe has been in the throes of integrating non-European populations into national entities that have traditionally seen themselves as culturally homogeneous. As the 2005 riots in France – as well as the increase of racism and xenophobia across Europe – have shown, this process is not going smoothly. Thinking about this situation deconstructively at the time of German reunification, Derrida reflects:

> that there is another heading, the heading being not only ours but the other, not only that which we identify, calculate, and decide upon, but the *heading of the other*, before which we must respond, and which we must *remember, of which* we must *remind ourselves*, the heading of the other being perhaps the first condition of an identity or identification that is not an ego-centrism destructive of oneself and the other.[19]

Europe has long seen itself as the exemplar of where the world is "heading." However, Derrida argues, that exemplarity must itself come into question. Or better, in order for Europe to remain exemplary, its exemplarity must come into question. Europe can no longer think of itself as a unity (or a group of unities) characterized by particular identities. It must instead head in another direction, a direction characterized by the other that it has excluded from its sense of itself. "And what if Europe were this ... [a]n opening and a non-exclusion for which Europe would in some way be responsible?"[20] Thus the identity of Europe must be bound to its no longer thinking of itself as resting on particular identities.

This idea, which is carried forward in a series of works, among them *The Politics of Friendship* (1994), which seeks to undercut the friend–enemy distinction in Carl Schmitt, might be said to culminate in his reflections on democracy in his 2003 book *Rogues*. In this work, Derrida articulates most fully his concept of democracy-to-come. One way to approach this concept would be through his

---

*18. How this works is discussed by Samir Haddad in his essay on Derrida in *The History of Continental Philosophy: Volume 6*.

19. Jacques Derrida, *The Other Heading: Reflections on Today's Europe*, Pascale-Anne Brault and Michael Naas (trans.) (Bloomington, IN: Indiana University Press, 2002), 15.

20. *Ibid.*, 17.

reflections on the other heading. If Europe is to become an opening or a nonexclusion, to what is it supposed to open itself? If we try to categorize that *what*, then we have limited the opening. It becomes no longer an opening, but instead an enclosure for a defined other. And is there not something contradictory about a "defined other"? To be open, then, is to remain receptive to what is to come, without knowing exactly what that might be.

In *Rogues*, Derrida points out the aporia, the gap, necessarily associated with such a thinking of democracy. On the one hand, there must be an openness to an other that cannot be defined. On the other hand, for there to be democracy there must also be a kind of sovereignty, a self-rule, that is necessarily exclusive, since it involves the creation of a legal structure of specific rights that is protected by force. A democracy-to-come must bring together this paradox of sovereignty and openness. Because of this,

> [t]he "to-come" not only points to the promise but suggests that democracy will never exist, in the sense of a present existence: not because it will be deferred but because it will always remain aporetic in its structure (force *without* force, incalculable singularity *and* calculable equality ...[21]

To endorse a democracy-to-come, however, is not a passive affair. It does not involve waiting. One must act toward a democracy-to-come, embracing both sides of the paradox. Otherwise, the force of sovereignty that is supposed to protect democracy threatens to undercut the very democracy it is designed to protect.

Reconceiving democracy from a different angle, Laclau and Mouffe have followed a thread that is similar to Derrida's in avoiding closure, but that hews more closely to the radical tradition of Marx and especially the Italian Marxist Antonio Gramsci. In their groundbreaking book from 1985, *Hegemony and Socialist Strategy*, Laclau and Mouffe argue that the problem with the socialist projects of the twentieth century was that they were, in some form or another, reductive. The differences that constitute different classes and segments of those classes were reduced to simple unities. When those simple unities did not appear in reality, steps were taken to force reality into the simplicity of the vision. In short, radical politics became totalitarian.

Since the publication of *Hegemony and Socialist Strategy*, Laclau and Mouffe have followed distinct but related intellectual paths. For Laclau, the thinking of politics has never been far from radical politics. In his 2007 book *On Populist*

---

21. Jacques Derrida, *Rogues: Two Essays on Reason*, Pascal-Anne Brault and Michael Naas (trans.) (Stanford, CA: Stanford University Press, 2004), 86.

Reason, Laclau turns to a rethinking of populism to sharpen his view of radical democracy.[22] As he notes, populism, like the radical political projects discussed in *Hegemony*, often descends into a political reductionism. However, it is not necessary that this be so. Populism often appeals to people at a variety of levels, depending on their different positions within society. The question, then, is one of how to bring unity to these different levels, without forcing them into a narrowly conceived political program.

In order to do this, Laclau proposes the concept of the empty signifier, a signifier that is at once specific and universal.[23] For instance, the central category of populism is *the people*. However, in populism, under the umbrella of *the people* is not a homogeneous class, but a variety of classes that are united by their exclusion from a political order or their experience of exploitation or oppression. Specific demands may be made or specific groups identified, but those demands or identities are expressions of a group defined not by its having a particular signification but rather by the "equivalential links" that are drawn from a variety of sources. In this sense, the empty signifier is at once a specific identity or series of demands or opposition that at the same time takes up other identities or demands or oppositions that become "equivalent" to it. So the signifier *the people* is two-sided: it may refer to specific people in one sense, but in another sense those people lose their specificity since they become representatives of a larger group of which they are not the only members.

In Laclau's view, globalization requires the construction of a populism of the sort he analyzes, a politics of the empty signifier.

> There has been a multiplication of dislocatory effects and a proliferation of new antagonisms, which is why the anti-globalization movement has to operate in an entirely new way: it must advocate the creation of equivalential links between deeply heterogeneous social demands while, at the same time, elaborating a common language.[24]

Thus, while Derrida focuses on a deconstructive play between sovereignty and openness in order to keep a politics of the other alive and avoid political reductionism, Laclau works to a similar end through a particular reading of populist reason.

Mouffe's more recent work has affinities with that of Laclau, but its theoretical references have more to with the German (and Nazi) theorist Carl Schmitt, who

---

*22. For a discussion of radical democracy, see the essay by Lasse Thomassen in *The History of Continental Philosophy: Volume 7*.
23. Laclau defines the empty signifier in an earlier essay, "Why Do Empty Signifiers Matter to Politics?" in *Emancipation(s)* (London: Verso, 1996), 36–46.
24. Ernesto Laclau, *On Populist Reason* (London: Verso, 2007), 231.

posits a sharp distinction between friend and enemy, us and them.[25] Mouffe wants to introduce a third category, that of adversaries on a common ground, "adversaries being defined in a paradoxical way as 'friendly enemies,' that is, persons who are friends because they share a common symbolic space but also enemies because they want to organize this common symbolic space in a different way."[26] Rather than resolving this tension in terms of friends (as would a consensus model of the kind Habermas advocates) or enemies (which would require war and suppression, in accordance with Schmitt's thought), Mouffe envisions keeping alive this adversarial space. She does not seek to eliminate further conflict about the character of that shared space. Instead, it must remain open for disagreement about its character and norms. For Mouffe, as for Derrida, democracy is not ever achieved in any final way: "the condition of possibility of a pluralist democracy is at the same time the condition of impossibility of its perfect implementation."[27]

In thinking about reconceptualizations of democracy, we should note in passing that a recent work by Butler orients such thought around the work of Emmanuel Levinas. *Precarious Life*, a response to the global situation particularly in the wake of 9/11, argues, as do Mouffe, Laclau, and Derrida, for a nonreductionist view of politics that takes the other into account. And this work, like Derrida's, emphasizes a vulnerability to the other that must characterize any adequate politics. This is, in Butler's view, a particularly urgent task in the wake of American belligerence after the attacks of September 2001.

> "Precarious Life" approaches the question of a non-violent ethics, one that is based on an understanding of how easily human life is annulled. Emmanuel Levinas offers a conception of ethics that rests upon an apprehension of the precariousness of life … [H]is view is … useful for those cultural analyses that seek to understand how best to depict the human, human grief and suffering, and how best to admit the "faces" of those against whom war is waged into public representation.[28]

What draws these views together as responses to globalization is their common project of thinking diversity without reducing it to a simple identity. This common project, although realized in different ways, might be said to

---

*25. For a discussion of Schmitt, see the essay by Christopher Thornhill in *The History of Continental Philosophy: Volume 5*.

26. Chantal Mouffe, *The Democratic Paradox* (London: Verso, 2000), 13.

27. *Ibid.*, 16.

28. Judith Butler, *Precarious Life: The Power of Mourning and Violence* (London: Verso, 2006), xvii–xviii.

address a "postnationalist" world, a world in which people are no longer isolated into distinct "nationalities," be they cultural, linguistic, religious, or national in the traditional sense. The question faced by these thinkers is that of conceiving democracy in a world defined as much by its differences as by its similarities. Although each has its own orientation, all these projects of reconceptualization are characterized by a concern for the integrity of the other in the democratic process.

IV

The final category of response to globalization has been more marginal theoretically than the previous three. However, it has intersected with a growing trend among progressive political activists. Since the fall of the Berlin Wall, Marxism as a framing doctrine for the political Left has been in steady decline. It is not that Marx's writings are considered irrelevant; rather, they no longer command the power of framing political action. After a century during which the Left could not escape the terms of Marxism in defining itself and its goals, Marx has finally lost his grip on the political framework of the Left. If we can consider another framework to have taken its place, particularly since the World Trade Organization protests in 1999, it would be that of anarchism. With its rejection of the avant-gardism and hierarchical character of Leninism, anarchism emphasizes inclusion, equality, and, to the extent possible, consensus. It has recently made a return to the political scene. This does not mean that anarchism now plays the dominant role that Marxism played during the twentieth century. Far from it. Instead, in the theoretical void of the activist Left that emerged after the fall of the Soviet Union, anarchism has come to be one of the major contenders, perhaps the major contender, for conceiving leftist politics.

However, the world is much changed from the time of the writings of the classical anarchists of the nineteenth and early twentieth centuries:[29] Pierre-Joseph Proudhon, Mikhail Bakunin, and Peter Kropotkin.[30] In particular, the development of French theory in the post-May '68 period has offered tools for a rethinking of anarchism that offers a more contemporary approach to anarchist theory and practice. Where classical anarchism was often marked by the

---

29. This is not to claim that no interesting anarchist theory has occurred for the past hundred years. Although the theoretical tradition has been thin, it has not been utterly bereft. Among those who identify themselves as anarchists, the British thinker Colin Ward (1924–2010) is particularly noteworthy, especially since his approach anticipates much of the poststructuralist approach discussed here. See, for instance, Colin Ward, *Anarchy in Action* (London: Freedom Press, 1982).

*30. For a discussion of Pierre-Joseph Proudhon in the context of French utopian socialism, see the essay by Diane Morgan in *The History of Continental Philosophy: Volume 1*.

humanist optimism and utopianism of the nineteenth century, an incorporation of some of the more sober political viewpoints characteristic of recent continental thinkers opens vistas for a less anachronistic development of anarchist themes. Although work in this area has been as yet sporadic, interest in it, particularly among progressive political activists, continues to grow.

The earliest attempt in this area is my *The Political Philosophy of Poststructuralist Anarchism* (1994). I argue that classical anarchism is characterized by two theoretical commitments: that human nature is inherently good and that power works solely by suppression. These two commitments combine to give rise to the idea that if one eliminates all relations of power, then a utopian society will naturally arise. However, recent thought has abandoned the idea of a benign human nature in favor of the idea that human nature is more plastic. In addition, under the influence of Michel Foucault, the idea that power is creative rather than simply suppressive has gained traction. Therefore, if we combine the egalitarian impulse of anarchism with a recognition of the multiple and irreducible character of power struggles, we arrive at a poststructuralist anarchism, an anarchism that is at once radical and politically supple.

Another project of intersecting recent continental thought with anarchism is Saul Newman's Lacanian postanarchism. Whereas May orients his thought around Foucault, for Newman, Lacan is the major touchstone. In ways that are similar to the work of Laclau, Newman seeks to avoid the essentialism of traditional political categories by appealing to an emptiness rather than an identity at the center of political resistance. "Lacan's notion of the lack as a gap, a radical emptiness produced by signification, was used here to theorize a nonessentialist outside to power."[31] Lacan, then, provides a way to combine the antiauthoritarianism characteristic of anarchism with the nonreductive views of the subject of resistance envisioned by recent French thought.

Anarchist thought has been embraced by the Left during the period of globalization in part because its radical egalitarianism provides a way to conceive solidarity across national borders. For those involved in what was called the "anti-globalization" movement, which is really a globalized anti-authoritarian and anti-transnational capitalist movement, the idea of equality allows one to link the struggles of the Malaysian sweatshop worker, the indigenous farmer in Chiapas, and the illegal immigrant in California. The introduction of recent continental thought into anarchist theory furthers this project, allowing it to abandon the anachronistic commitments of its nineteenth-century founders.

We have canvassed a number of analyses of and responses to globalization. Although they diverge in important ways, they share the belief that the globalized

---

31. Saul Newman, *From Bakunin to Lacan: Anti-Authoritarianism and the Dislocation of Power* (Lanham, MD: Lexington Books, 2001), 160.

world has introduced fundamental changes into both our collective and individual lives, and that these changes require a new conception of where we find ourselves today. Moreover, none of these proposals endorses the idea that what appears to be globalization is really another form of imperialist hegemony, this time under the direction of the US economy. While Hardt and Negri allot the US a place on the first tier of Empire, and while the reconceptualizations of democracy and poststructuralist anarchism do not deny the importance of the US role in the world, the emphasis in all these analyses is on the global character of political, economic, and media change rather than on the domination of a particular national entity. This is perhaps in keeping with the more theoretical character of these approaches. If our world is nothing more than a twenty-first-century repeat of colonialism, with an economic accent rather than a political one and a new country at its center, there is not much to theorize about. However, to the extent that these approaches have theoretical merit, it is because, even if the US does have a dominant role to play in the current geopolitical arena, there are other changes – more important or more lasting – that require our reflection.

Little has been said in this essay about criticisms of these analyses and responses. There are those who might accuse Baudrillard and Virilio of a technological reductionism; others who would likely find the idea of the multitude to be empty or unhelpful; some who may see the reconceptualizations of democracy offered here as too abstract for practical politics; and finally some who may accuse a poststructuralist approach to anarchism of retaining too much utopianism. Moreover, regardless of the criticisms one could make, there remain questions of how to combine elements among the various projects there. What, if any, relation could be drawn between the multitude and anarchist equality? How might Mouffe's adversarial space fare in the face of the simulated society sketched by Baudrillard? Can one combine Laclau's politics of the empty signifier with Derrida's democracy-to-come, or undercut the technological/military dominance that concerns Virilio with a politics of vulnerability of the type Butler endorses?

Much of the work of these thinkers has been coextensive with the rise of globalization itself. They are attempting to understand and to respond to changes through which they – and we – are living. It remains the task of the rest of us, or at least those among us who are concerned with the shape of our world, to think alongside them. We must comprehend and act within and on an increasingly globalized world, in order that we may be subjects of that world and not merely its objects.

11

APPROACHING THE REAL

Ian James

I. THE TURN TO THE REAL

In *Philosophies of Difference*, first published in French in 1986, François Laruelle wrote that "Thinking cannot begin except with and by the real."[1] Published two years before Alain Badiou's *Being and Event* and Jean-Luc Nancy's *The Experience of Freedom* and three years before Jean-Luc Marion's *Reduction and Givenness*, Laruelle's book is one of a handful of groundbreaking philosophical texts published in France in the latter half of the 1980s that aim to mark a decisive break from the philosophies of difference that came to prominence in the late 1960s and 1970s. Largely associated with the categories of text and writing, with the order of the symbolic, and with a linguistic or discursive paradigm, these philosophies perhaps became best known by the loose and often rather unhelpful labels of poststructuralism and postmodernism. Laruelle's affirmation that it is the "real" from which all thinking must begin is indicative of a broad shift within the field of recent and contemporary French philosophy away from the textual, discursive, and linguistic paradigms of structuralism and poststructuralism. Within the context of this shift, the real comes to be figured in various philosophically complex ways. It can, however, be broadly aligned with what might be termed "material immanence," that is to say, a dimension of materiality that is anterior to the order of language and discourse, or to the work of the concept or of representation. This shift toward a central preoccupa-

---

1. François Laruelle, *Philosophies of Difference: A Critical Introduction to Non-Philosophy*, Rocco Gangle (trans.) (London: Continuum, 2011), 152; originally published as *Les Philosophies de la différence: Introduction critique* (Paris: Presses Universitaires de France, 1986), 169.

tion with material immanence has, as John Mullarkey has pointed out, marked a realignment of French thought with naturalism and with the life sciences, with mathematics, and with the reaffirmation of "philosophy as a worldly and materialist thinking."[2] Within this context the challenge that has been taken up by French thinkers in the wake of poststructuralism and postmodernism is one that Laruelle has recently described as that of giving the real the "thought that it merits."[3] The challenge here, a challenge that is arguably ongoing within the field of French philosophy today, is that of finding the best technique by which thinking might "approach" the material real and do justice to it.

The origins of this shift can in fact be discerned in some of the earliest writing by Laruelle, Badiou, and Nancy dating from the 1970s and also in the early thought of Jacques Rancière. In a seminar given originally in November 1977, Badiou, for instance, launches a polemic against the discursive paradigm of structuralist thought.[4] This paradigm, he argues, is a form of "linguistic idealism" and states: "the world is discourse: this argument in contemporary philosophy would deserve to be rebaptized 'idealinguistery.'"[5] This polemic against structuralism is motivated by a clearly articulated demand for a philosophical re-engagement with materiality: "it is materialism," Badiou affirms, "that we must found anew with the renovated arsenal of our mental powers."[6] Three years earlier, Rancière also attacked the notion of "discourse" and does so within the context of a critique of the Althusserian (structuralist–Marxist) conception of ideology: "Ideology," he writes, "is not simply a collection of discourses or a system of representation."[7] Like, Badiou, Rancière is rejecting any understanding of the world as discursively constructed, and is doing so in order to think worldly existence in terms of a more radical materiality than that of language or of signifying processes. Both Laruelle and Nancy also published important works in the 1970s that seek to mark a distance from, or a break with, structuralism. This is evident in the very title of Laruelle's 1977 work *Le Déclin de l'écriture* (The decline of writing). Specifically, the "decline of writing" signaled in the title of this work is aligned with "a materialist critique of textual and linguistic codes"[8] and with a full-frontal polemic against the category of "textuality." "Text," Laruelle writes, "must be stripped of the ontico-ontological primacy with which structuralist

2. John Mullarkey, *Post-Continental Philosophy: An Outline* (London: Continuum, 2006), 2.
3. François Laruelle, *Philosophie non-standard* (Paris: Éditions Kimé, 2010), 99, my translation.
4. Published in French in 1982 in *Théorie du sujet* (Paris: Éditions du Seuil); *The Theory of the Subject*, Bruno Bosteels (trans.) (London: Continuum, 2009).
5. Badiou, *The Theory of the Subject*, 188 (*Théorie du sujet*, 204).
6. Badiou, *The Theory of the Subject*, 182 (*Théorie du sujet*, 198).
7. Jacques Rancière, *La Leçon d'Althusser* (Paris: Gallimard, 1974), 252–3, my translation.
8. François Laruelle, *Le Déclin de l'écriture* (Paris: Aubier-Flammarion, 1977), 14, my translation.

ideology and the majority of 'textual' ideologues comfort themselves."[9] Similarly, in his 1979 work *Ego sum*, Nancy is sharply critical of what he understands to be a contemporary return of the traditional subject of metaphysics in the instances of "Structure, Text, or Process."[10] In *Ego sum* Nancy attempts to reconfigure subjective agency in bodily terms. He aims to think or uncover a bodily site of the production of sense or meaningfulness that would be in excess of any symbolic chain or textual economy and this sets his thinking against the structuralism of Lacan in particular.

This challenge to the discursive and linguistic paradigm of structuralism is taken up by a number of younger thinkers whose work comes to prominence in the 1980s or 1990s. Jean-Luc Marion's *Reduction and Givenness* has already been mentioned but one might also cite in this context the work of Bernard Stiegler on technology and temporality in his *Technics and Time* trilogy and Catherine Malabou's thinking around the concept of plasticity in her work on Hegel.[11] What is striking about all the thinkers mentioned in this context is that, in their common attempt to reconfigure the concerns of philosophical thought by orientating it toward the material immanence of a pre-discursive and pre-textual real, they come to think of this real in variable, and sometimes quite distinct, ways. By the same token, the divergent ways in which the real comes to be thought or figured in turn dictate, or give rise to, very different modes or techniques by means of which it is approached philosophically or, in Laruelle's words, "given the thought that it merits."[12]

These divergences, both in philosophical figurations of the real and in the techniques by means of which philosophy seeks to do justice to it, can best be highlighted by way of two separate comparisons. First, Marion's thinking of givenness and Nancy's philosophy of sense shed light on a phenomenological

9. *Ibid.*, 222.
10. Jean-Luc Nancy, *Ego sum* (Paris: Flammarion, 1979), 11, my translation.
11. See Bernard Stiegler, *La Technique et le temps 1. La Faute d'Épiméthée* (Paris: Éditions Galilée, 1994), published in English as *Technics and Time 1: The Fault of Epimetheus*, Richard Beardsworth and George Collins (trans.) (Stanford, CA: Stanford University Press, 1998); *La Technique et le temps 2. La Désorientation* (Paris: Éditions Galiliée, 1996), published in English as *Technics and Time 2. Disorientation*, Stephen Barker (trans.) (Stanford, CA: Stanford University Press, 2009); *La Technique et le temps 3. Le Temps du cinéma et la question du mal-être* (Paris: Éditions Galilée, 2001), published in English as *Technics and Time 3. Cinematic Time and the Question of Malaise*, Stephen Barker (trans.) (Stanford: Stanford University Press, 2011). For Malabou's work on Hegel, see Catherine Malabou, *L'Avenir de Hegel: Plasticité, temporalité, dialectique* (Paris: Vrin, 1996), published in English as *The Future of Hegel: Plasticity, Temporality, and Dialectic*, Lisabeth During (trans.) (London: Routledge, 2005). Neither Stiegler nor Malabou are discussed at any length here. For a full account of their work within this context, see Ian James, *The New French Philosophy* (Cambridge: Polity, 2012).
12. Laruelle, *Philosophie non-standard*, 99, my translation.

and post-phenomenological trajectory within contemporary French thought. Second, a comparison of Badiou and Rancière reveals divergent paths taken from within the legacy of Althusserian philosophy in France.

II. JEAN-LUC MARION AND JEAN-LUC NANCY

Marion's[13] important contribution to the development of the phenomenological tradition in France owes much to the influence of thinkers such as Michel Henry (1922–2002)[14] and to the way he applies insights yielded from his scholarly work on Descartes to his readings of German philosophers such as Edmund Husserl (1859–1938)[15] and Martin Heidegger (1889–1976).[16] The key insight of *Reduction and Givenness* and of Marion's phenomenology more generally is its identification of "the uniquely dative character of originary phenomenality."[17] The real breakthrough of Husserlian phenomenology, Marion argues, is not its ability to isolate or reduce the appearance of phenomena to the sphere of originary intuition. Nor is it to describe that appearance by way of the phenomenological reduction and in terms of the intentional directedness or signifying logic of the consciousness that constitutes phenomena as phenomena. Rather, phenomenology's most fundamental insight is that, before it is given to intuition, signification, or the intentional directedness of a constituting consciousness, phenomenal appearance is first and, as it were, primordially or originarily *given*. Marion engages very closely with the language and status of originary "giving" and "givenness" in both Husserlian and Heideggerian thought in order

---

13. Jean-Luc Marion (July 3, 1946– ; born in Meudon, France) was educated at the Lycée Condorcet (1964–67), École Normale Supérieure (1967–70), and University of Paris IV-Paris-Sorbonne (1970–74), and received from the Sorbonne a *doctorat du troisième cycle* in 1974 and a *doctorat d'état* in 1981. His influences include Alquié, Balthasar, Derrida, Descartes, Heidegger, Henry, Husserl, Levinas, Nietzsche, and Wittgenstein, and he has held appointments at the University of Paris IV-Paris-Sorbonne (1973–81), University of Poitiers (1981–88), University of Paris X-Nanterre (1988–95), University of Paris IV-Paris-Sorbonne (1995–), and University of Chicago (1994–).

*14. Michel Henry is discussed in the essay on continental philosophy of religion by Bruce Ellis Benson in *The History of Continental Philosophy: Volume 7*.

*15. Husserl is discussed in an essay by Thomas Nenon in *The History of Continental Philosophy: Volume 3*.

*16. Heidegger is discussed in essays by Miguel de Beistegui in *The History of Continental Philosophy: Volume 3*, and Dennis J. Schmidt in *The History of Continental Philosophy: Volume 4*.

17. Jean-Luc Marion, *Réduction et donation* (Paris: Presses Universitaires de France, 1989), 55; published in English as *Reduction and Givenness: Investigations of Husserl, Heidegger and Phenomenology*, Thomas A. Carlson (trans.) (Evanston, IL: Northwestern University Press, 1998), 34. [*] Marion is also discussed in the essay by Benson in *The History of Continental Philosophy: Volume 7*.

to argue that phenomenology must more fully embrace the radicality of its foundational insight. Thus he argues that the "givenness" of phenomenal appearance is not only more primordial than the "objectness" of phenomena disclosed in the Husserlian reduction, but also more originary than, and anterior to, any horizon of being or of ontological difference.

This insistence on the primordial status of givenness lays the basis for Marion's highly original, yet also at times controversial, transformation of phenomenological thought.[18] In what amounts to a reversal of the post-Kantian character of phenomenology, givenness, as the most primordial character of phenomenal appearance, is not constituted *by* consciousness but rather is constitutive *of* consciousness. Marion identifies the material instance of corporeality, or of what he more precisely comes to call "flesh," as the site of givenness: appearance is always given to, and in the corporeality of, flesh. It is on the basis of this givenness of appearance *to* and in the "flesh" that consciousness and intentionality are constituted, and phenomenal objects revealed or disclosed. The primordiality of givenness also, and decisively, allows all those elements given in phenomena that might be radically in excess of the horizons of intentionality, objectness, or ontic being to be phenomenologically circumscribed and described. Thus modes of experience or appearing that are indeterminate, unforeseeable, and ontically unverifiable can now be taken seriously phenomenologically. Radically new historical sequences, artistic, erotic, and religious experience are all placed by Marion under the sign of "saturated phenomena," that is, phenomena in which "*more, indeed immeasurably more*, than intention would ever have aimed at or foreseen."[19]

Marion's transformed phenomenology therefore allows him to reconfigure the real as that which is given immanently to, and within, the material immanence of flesh, to rethink agency in corporeal terms, and then finally to extend the domain of phenomena beyond that which is strictly determinable in appearance according to objectness or "beingness" (*étantité*). All this becomes possible by way of an extension of the phenomenological technique of reduction. It was the phenomenological reduction that allowed Husserl to isolate the appearance

---

18. For texts relating to the critique of Marion and the controversy in France about recent developments in phenomenology see Dominique Janicaud, *Le Tournant théologique de la phénoménologie française* (Paris: Éditions de l'Éclat, 1991); *Phenomenology "Wide Open": After the French Debate*, Charles N. Cabral (trans.) (New York: Fordham University Press, 2005); and Janicaud *et al.*, *Phenomenology and the "Theological Turn": The French Debate* (New York: Fordham University Press, 2000).

19. Jean-Luc Marion, *Being Given: Towards a Phenomenology of Givenness*, Jeffrey L. Kosky (trans.) (Stanford, CA: Stanford University Press, 2002), 197; originally published in French as *Étant donné: Essai d'une phénoménologie de la donation* (Paris: Presses Universitaires de France, 1997), 277.

of phenomena within the immanence of consciousness and therefore within the sphere of originary intuition (thus making phenomenology possible). Perhaps the most important innovation of *Reduction and Givenness* is Marion's discovery of the "third reduction." Where Husserl uses the reduction to isolate phenomena as "objects," Heidegger's phenomenological and ontological thinking reduces phenomena to "beings." These reductions, to objectness and beingness, respectively, need to be superseded by a third reduction to "givenness." It is only on the basis of this innovation or radicalization of the phenomenological technique of reduction that Marion can figure the real as givenness to, and within, the flesh. The reconfiguration of the real and the possibility of thinking it philosophically depend entirely on the technique of the third reduction.

Nancy's[20] philosophy and ontology of "sense" also seek to approach or circumscribe the real in material and corporeal terms but do so in a way that moves beyond the orbit of phenomenology and the question of the appearance of phenomena. One of his most important texts is *The Sense of the World*. Here Nancy argues that "sense" needs to be understood as an order of meaning that unfolds prior to any symbolic dimension or signifying chain and therefore prior to any relation of signifier to signified. When he speaks of "the sense of the world," he is not speaking of the sense or meaning that the world *has* but rather argues that the world is always disclosed to us in, and as, sense. What he calls our "being-towards-the-world" is "caught up in sense well before all signification. It makes, demands or proposes sense this side of or beyond all signification. ... Thus, *world* is not merely the correlative of *sense*, it is structured as *sense*, and reciprocally, *sense* is structured as *world*."[21] Sense thus takes on an ontological status, the being of the world always arrives to us *as* sense, and it does so in a way that exceeds any mode or logic of phenomenal appearance: "world," Nancy writes, "invites us to no longer think on the level of the phenomenon ... but on the level, let us say for the moment, of disposition (spacing, touching, contact, crossing)."[22] The emphasis placed by phenomenology on an ocular register, on the language of appearance, seeing, lighting, and so on, is displaced here in favor

20. Jean-Luc Nancy (July 26, 1940– ; born in Caudéran, France) studied at the Sorbonne, where he obtained his degree in 1973 under the supervision of Paul Ricoeur. In addition to Ricoeur, major influences include Blanchot, Derrida, Hegel, Heidegger, and Nietzsche. He taught philosophy at the University of Strasbourg from 1968 until his retirement in 2008, during which time he worked closely and collaborated frequently with Philippe Lacoue-Labarthe (1940–2007).
21. Jean-Luc Nancy, *The Sense of the World*, Jeffrey S. Librett (trans.) (Minneapolis, MN: University of Minnesota Press, 1997), 7–8; originally published in French as *Le Sens du monde* (Paris: Éditions Galilée, 1993), 17–18.
22. Nancy, *Le Sens du monde*, 34 n.19 (*The Sense of the World*, 176).

of a haptic register, that of tact, contact, touching, and sensing.[23] The corporeal or the bodily plays a key role in the Nancean thinking of sense. For if it can be understood as a "*coming* into presence" of the world, then this is so only insofar as sense is also a "transitivity, as passage to presence – and therewith as passage *of* presence."[24] The site of this transitivity or passage is the material sensing body or, more precisely, the multiplicity of bodies that, in sensing, are exposed to each other. The being of the world, therefore, arrives always as the sharing of sense between bodies and does so in their touch and contact with each other in bodily sensing.

Sense in Nancy, therefore, is comparable to Marion's givenness. It has a material and bodily status and its "passage," "sharing," or "exposure" in the contact or touching of bodies is situated prior to any conscious intentionality or order of signification. Yet where givenness, for Marion, is primordially phenomenal and is primordial to the extent that it is anterior to any horizon of being, sense, for Nancy, is primordially ontological, and as a mode of bodily contact, touch, and spacing, exceeds the phenomenological horizon of appearance or luminescence. This difference between givenness and sense is the basis for a very clear divergence between Marion and Nancy in relation to philosophical technique. For if Nancean sense means we can no longer think "on the level of the phenomenon," then the technique of reduction, no matter how enhanced or radicalized, will no longer allow thought to approach the real. The key thing to note here is that Nancy's sense, as a transitivity or passage *between* bodies, is always a multiplicity or plurality and, *as transitivity*, is always also in excess of what can be held in reserve, disclosed, or reduced to any given instance. If sense is being, therefore, it is so, as Nancy argues in another of his most important works, *Being Singular Plural*,[25] as a kind of infinite multiplicity, a singular plurality of the passage of sense as the coming to presence of a world. Sense, therefore, is not presentable as such but is always in excess of any presentation.

This means that where Marion has to radicalize a technique of thought that allows justice to be done to the absolute unconditionality of phenomenal givenness (the third reduction), Nancy has to engage a practice of thought that allows him to do justice to the infinite excess of sense. Sense is that which can be approached only *at* the limits of finite bodily experience or philosophical thinking, but must also be thought as an infinite excess *over* those limits. Nancy's philosophical technique therefore comes to be one of a practice of writing that

23. See, in this regard, Jacques Derrida, *On Touching – Jean-Luc Nancy*, Christine Irizarry (trans.) (Stanford, CA: Stanford University Press, 2005).
24. Nancy, *Le Sens du monde*, 25 (*The Sense of the World*, 12).
25. Jean-Luc Nancy, *Être singulier pluriel* (Paris: Éditions Galilée, 1996); published in English as *Being Singular Plural*, Anne E. O'Byrne and Robert D. Richardson (trans.) (Stanford, CA: Stanford University Press, 2000).

thinks at the limit of thought in order to circumscribe that point at which sense is exposed in excess of the limit. Nancy calls this technique "ex-scription," a mode of writing by which that which is inscribed as meaning or signification is also marked as an excess over both instances. Nancy's thinking of the real as sense necessitates a technique of thought that is almost diametrically opposite to that of Marion. Where the third reduction allows givenness to be circumscribed and delimited phenomenologically, the Nancean practice of ex-scription means that the being that sense *is*, is always dispersed outside of any discursive limit and is always exterior to the very discourse of being (onto*logy*) that seeks to inscribe it.

III. ALAIN BADIOU AND JACQUES RANCIÈRE

In Marion and Nancy, the philosophical techniques of the third reduction and of "ex-scription" are necessitated by the primordial status of givenness and by the infinitely excessive status of sense respectively. A similar correlation of thought and technique can be found in the philosophies of Badiou[26] and Rancière. From the 1970s onwards, and following on from the late Lacan, Badiou insists that the discourse of mathematics is the only means by which the real can be thought. In a seminar given in May 1977, he affirms quite clearly that "mathematics is the science of the real and its signifiers, whatever they may be, are accountable for it."[27] Given the abstraction of mathematical discourse, it may seem strange that the same philosopher who, also in 1977, insists that "materialism must be founded anew," comes to designate mathematics as the "science of the real." Badiou makes the case for mathematics being the sole discourse able to present or "speak" the material real in his most important philosophical work – *Being and Event*.

Since its Greek origin, Badiou argues, Western philosophy has been fundamentally caught up with the question of the one and the many, and has consistently sought to subordinate the multiplicity of being to figures of unity, be they theological, philosophical and conceptual, or anthropological and social. Badiou's fundamental philosophical decision from which all his thinking flows is that the being of all that is *is* infinite multiplicity. Since any one identifiable thing or situation of things can always be decomposed into ever smaller parts (*ad infinitum*), its being is ultimately to be located *only* in its multiplicity, a multiplicity that can never be determined or counted in terms of a totality or

---

26. For Badiou's biographical information, see note 2 in the essay by Bruno Bosteels in this volume.
27. Badiou, *The Theory of the Subject*, 154 (*Théorie du sujet*, 171).

overarching unity. It is this insight that leads Badiou to Cantorian set theory as the sole means of speaking the being or the real of all that is. Specifically, the mathematical presentation of inconsistent (that is, non-countable) multiplicity and the ability of set theory to adequately think or present infinity and different orders of infinity means that mathematical discourse, for Badiou, will always have the sole privilege of "speaking" being. Only mathematics, therefore, can give us ontology and all of philosophy's thinking must begin with this insight and remain faithful to it.

From this founding insight Badiou derives a new axiomatic method of philosophical thinking, itself borrowed from mathematics, but also his "renovated arsenal" of key concepts such as truth, universality, the subject, and, of course, the event. It is the ability of mathematics to think multiplicities that are inconsistent (or that cannot be counted) that allows Badiou to formulate his understanding of any event as the emergence of the radically new (uncounted multiplicity) from within known and determinate historical situations (counted multiplicity). Not only, therefore, does the discourse of mathematics allow Badiou to think and present the real of being adequately in the way no other discourse can; it also allows thought to discern and enact radical possibilities of transformation and change.

Rancière[28] is also concerned to circumscribe the materiality of the real in order to discern possibilities of change and transformation. Unlike Badiou, however, he is not interested in approaching the real in terms of its countable or non-countable multiplicity and in the subtraction of its qualitative aspects (that is, as pure number). Rather, in a gesture that can be diametrically opposed to Badiou's subtractive mathematical approach, Rancière is concerned with the sensible and with the aesthetic (understood as sense experience in general). To this extent he can be closely aligned with a thinker like Nancy. Like Nancy, Rancière understands the aesthetic as a fundamental dimension of sense experience that orders collective and shared existence. However, whereas Nancy understands the "sharing" of sense in terms of a primordial unfolding of a world in sense's "transitivity" or passage between bodies, Rancière's aesthetic is understood in terms of a "distribution of the sensible" that orders bodies and corporeal spacing in terms of separation and division and in terms of hierarchical relations of inclusion and exclusion. The aesthetic, or "distribution of the sensible," for Rancière is "the system of self-evident facts of sense perception that simultaneously discloses the existence of something in common and the delimita-

---

28. For Rancière's biographical information, see note 1 in the essay by Gabriel Rockhill in this volume.

tions that define the respective parts and positions within it."²⁹ It is, therefore, an "apportionment of parts and positions ... based on a distribution of spaces, times and forms of activity that determines the very manner in which something in common lends itself to participation in a way that various individuals have a part in this distribution."³⁰ Unlike Nancy, Rancière identifies forms of exclusion and hierarchical ordering as being organized at the most fundamental level of sense experience. This means that the political practice of change and transformation that his thinking articulates is concerned always with those occupying material sites of sense experience that are subject to modes of exclusion and hierarchical subordination. Politics, for Rancière, therefore exists *as such* only in the interruption of an order of domination and in the emergence or institution of a "part of those who have no part"³¹ that is then included in a newly configured distribution of the sensible.

The aesthetic or the sensible in Rancière is therefore always that which is distributed according to an ordering of shared participation *and* exclusion. Yet it is also at the very same time an unstable and heterogeneous element in such a way that any existing order or distribution of the sensible is always vulnerable to interruption and transformation since the multiplicity of marginalized and excluded elements will always be the source of political claims and contestation. This material heterogeneity and instability of ordering or classification finds its correlate in Rancière's practice of writing. He does not, strictly speaking, offer a purely philosophical discourse or ontology of the sensible. His writing situates itself in the indeterminate interstices of philosophy, history, aesthetics, and politics. In so doing it responds to the heterogeneity of sense and its distribution, a heterogeneity that cannot be contained within the limits of any one specific discourse (philosophical, ontological, political, etc.). Once again a practice of writing is determined or necessitated in its specificity by the very conception of the material real that is being thought.

IV. PHILOSOPHY AS TECHNOLOGY

The turn to the "material real" in recent French thought therefore also and necessarily gives rise to a sustained and variable engagement with the materiality of

29. Jacques Rancière, *The Politics of Aesthetics: The Distribution of the Sensible*, Gabriel Rockhill (trans.) (London: Continuum, 2004), 12; originally published in French as *La Partage du sensible: esthétique et politique* (Paris: La Fabrique, 2000), 12.

30. *Ibid.*

31. Jacques Rancière, *La Mésentente: politique et philosophie* (Paris: Éditions Galilée, 1995), 31; published in English as *Disagreement: Politics and Philosophy*, Julie Rose (trans.) (Minneapolis, MN: University of Minnesota Press, 1998), 11.

thought itself. Comparing the different techniques adopted by Marion, Nancy, Badiou, and Rancière in their attempt to approach the real allows philosophical writing to be understood as a mode of material "technicity." Laruelle,[32] with whom this discussion began, goes even further than these thinkers insofar as he comes to characterize philosophical writing *per se* as a form of technology. He does so in negative terms consistently aligning philosophy as a whole with the Heideggerian account of onto-theology and nihilism, and of modern technology as "enframing."[33]

In fact, Laruelle approaches the technique of philosophical writing from a structural or formal perspective arguing that, as a technique predicated on conceptual abstraction, and as an attempt to confer upon the totality of existence some kind of discursive and theoretical unity, philosophy is always an articulation of transcendence *over* immanence. The transcendence of philosophical thought can never do justice to the immanence of the real. Indeed, it is, structurally speaking, a totalizing and violently reductive gesture in relation to the real. Philosophy necessarily divides the real in its abstract conceptual operations, since it is both a discursive and therefore secondary *reflection* of it, and, at the same time, it sets itself up as a *presentation* of the real *as* real. That is to say, it fraudulently tries to substitute the conceptual representation or reflection of the real for the real itself and claims a unity or identity between the two. For Laruelle the real is only ever an entirely autonomous and indivisible dimension of materiality, one that can never be reflected into, divided by, or represented in the transcendence of conceptual language. It is a grounding Laruellian axiom that "The Real excludes any possibility of it being seized or captured like a thing in a mirror that would alienate it in an image or an intention *of* it."[34] The real, therefore, is in and by itself entirely autonomous and indivisible in relation to that technology of transcendence and abstraction that philosophy always is.

The result of this is that Laruelle, from the 1980s on, comes to designate the entirety of his thinking as "non-philosophy" and makes his project one of a "global change of ground."[35] This change of ground from philosophy to non-philosophy begins, therefore, with Laruelle taking the indivisible "One" of the real as his sole starting point. He then develops various non-philosophical

---

32. François Laruelle (1937– ; born in Chavelot, France) studied philosophy at the École Normale Supérieure at Fontenay-Saint-Cloud, completed his doctorate under the direction of Paul Ricoeur, and taught for most of his career until his retirement in 2006 at the University of Paris X-Nanterre. Influences include Derrida, Heidegger, and Nietzsche.

33. François Laruelle, *Principes de la non-philosophie* (Paris: Presses Universitaires de France, 1996), 9–10, 52, 259; *En tant qu'un* (Paris: Aubier, 1991), 10.

34. Laruelle, *Principes de la non-philosophie*, 165, my translation.

35. *Ibid.*, 4.

practices throughout his career and does so by subjecting the technical materials of philosophical discourse to complex operations. Non-philosophy extracts the discursive material forms of philosophy and then deploys them in such a way that they are shorn or stripped of their operational transcendence and then placed back into a relation to the real that is not one of conceptual division, reflection, or splitting. In so doing, non-philosophical thought, for Laruelle, adopts a "posture of immanence" and not a philosophical stance of transcendence.[36]

What is perhaps most important and innovative in the "posture of immanence" adopted by Laruelle's non-philosophy is the way in which it comes to align itself with science. He is not interested in aligning the speaking of the real solely with mathematics as does Badiou. Badiou's decision in favor of mathematics is, for Laruelle, rather an arbitrary one. It is instead science, according to Laruelle, that shares non-philosophy's posture of immanence. Scientific practice does not seek conceptual unities or forms of totalization that encompass the entirety of "Being." Laruelle is interested in the way in which experimental and theoretical science seek to articulate the real in non-conceptual terms. This would include the discourse of mathematics but would also encompass other means by which scientific discourse "receives" the real or is determined by it. As key commentators of Laruelle such as Ray Brassier have pointed out, the aim of non-philosophy is nothing less than a reversal of Kantianism whereby the real ceases to be shaped and ordered by human conceptual categories and, as it were, bend itself towards them. Rather, the conceptual categories of human thought will now be ordered and shaped by the real, will incline themselves towards and will be determined by it.[37]

A logic of "determination-in-the-last-instance" of and by the real comes to order all of Laruelle's non-philosophical thinking. The correlation that was seen in Marion, Nancy, Badiou, and Rancière between the philosophical configuration of the real and the various techniques deployed to do justice to that real finds its most radical expression or development in Laruelle's non-philosophy. In each case something like a reversal of Kantianism has occurred insofar as thought is developing a material technique that is determined, as it were, by way of an immanent cause, by the real itself. In the case of Laruelle, a conception of immanent materiality as radically indivisible and autonomous necessitates the abandonment of philosophy *per se* and the creation of an entirely different discursive form.

---

36. Laruelle, *En tant qu'un*, 49–50.
37. See Ray Brassier, *Nihil Unbound: Enlightenment and Extinction* (Basingstoke: Palgrave Macmillan, 2010).

V. BEYOND POST-KANTIANISM

The shift away from the linguistic and discursive paradigm of (post)structur-alism that was identified at the beginning of this discussion has therefore been accompanied by a perhaps even more radical break or rupture within the trajec-tory of post-Kantian European philosophy. The material real that is thought by each of these thinkers is one that would determine thought itself and would no longer, as Kant's Copernican revolution would have it, be determined by the categories of thought. Out of this come renewed materialist conceptions of subjective agency and collective experience as well as renewed forms of polit-ical thinking and engagement. It is not surprising within this context that a number of French thinkers, like Badiou and Laruelle, have turned towards science, technology, and mathematics. Philosophers such as Bernard Stiegler[38] have sought to rethink the human experience of time in relation to technology and have done so by drawing on the earlier scientific thought of figures such as, among others Gilbert Simondon (1924–89), Georges Canguilhem (1904–95), and André Leroi-Gourhan (1911–86). Catherine Malabou[39] has engaged with recent discoveries in neuroscience and with the work of prominent figures such as Antonio Damasio (1944–), Joseph Ledoux (1949–), and Marc Jeannerod (1935–).[40] Quentin Meillassoux, a young philosopher influenced to some degree by Badiou, has also championed the scientific approach and the privileging of mathematics in particular.[41] It is arguable, therefore, that, within the field of recent French thought, the discursive and linguistic anti-foundationalism of

---

38. Bernard Stiegler (1952–) received his doctorate from the École des Hautes Études en Sciences Sociales in 1992. Influences include Derrida, Freud, Heidegger, Husserl, and Nietzsche. He has held posts at the Collège Internationale de Philosophie, the Institut de Recherche et Coordination Acoustique/Musique (IRCAM), and currently serves (since 2006) as Director of the Department of Cultural Development and Director of the Institut de Recherche et d'Innovation at the Centre Pompidou in Paris, as Professorial Fellow at Goldsmiths College, University of London, and as Professor at the University of Technology at Compiègne.

39. Catherine Malabou (1959–) studied at the École Normale Supérieure at Fontenay-Saint-Cloud before writing her doctoral dissertation on Hegel under the supervision of Jacques Derrida at the École des Hautes Etudes en Sciences Sociales. She taught at the University of Paris X-Nanterre before moving to her present position at the Centre for Modern European Philosophy at Kingston University, UK.

40. See Catherine Malabou, *Que faire de notre cerveau ?* (Paris: Bayard, 2004), published in English as *What Should We Do with Our Brain?* Sebastian Rand (trans.) (New York: Fordham University Press, 2008); *Les Nouveaux blessés: De Freud à la neurologie, penser les trauma-tismes contemporains* (Paris: Bayard, 2007), published in English as *The New Wounded: From Neurosis to Brain Damage*, Steven Miller (trans.) (New York: Fordham University Press, 2012).

41. See Quentin Meillassoux, *Après la finitude* (Paris: Éditions du Seuil, 2006), published in English as *After Finitude: An Essay on the Necessity of Contingency,* Ray Brassier (trans.) (London: Continuum, 2010).

poststructuralism and postmodernism has given way to reinvented forms of materialist realism. This is not a return of philosophy to straightforwardly solid and traditional metaphysical foundations. In Laruelle's terms, it could be said that philosophy, in the aftermath of the destruction or deconstruction of metaphysics, has left the illusory ground of traditional thought in order to incline itself toward and to approach "a real base – the only real base," that of the real itself.[42]

---

42. Laruelle, *En tant qu'un*, 193.

CHRONOLOGY

	PHILOSOPHICAL EVENTS	CULTURAL EVENTS	POLITICAL EVENTS
1620	Bacon, *Novum organum*		
1633		Condemnation of Galileo	
1634		Establishment of the Académie Française	
1637	Descartes, *Discourse on Method*		
1641	Descartes, *Meditations on First Philosophy*		
1642		Rembrandt, *Nightwatch*	English Civil War begins
1651	Hobbes, *Leviathan*		
1662	*Logique du Port-Royal*		
1665		Newton discovers calculus	
1667		John Milton, *Paradise Lost*	
1670	Pascal, *Les Pensées* (posthumous) Spinoza, *Tractatus theologico-politicus*		
1675		Leibniz discovers calculus	
1677	Spinoza, *Ethics*		
1687		Newton, *Philosophiae naturalis principia mathematica*	
1689	Locke, *A Letter Concerning Toleration* (–1690) Locke, *An Essay Concerning Human Understanding* and *Two Treatises of Civil Government*		

	PHILOSOPHICAL EVENTS	CULTURAL EVENTS	POLITICAL EVENTS
1695		Bayle, *Dictionnaire historique et critique*, vol. I	
1714	Leibniz, *Monadologie*		
1739	Hume, *A Treatise of Human Nature*		
1742		Handel, *Messiah*	
1748	Hume, *An Enquiry Concerning Human Understanding*		
1751	Diderot and D'Alembert, *Encyclopédie, vols 1 & 2*		
1755	Rousseau, *Discours sur l'origine et les fondements de l'inégalité parmi les hommes*		
1759		Voltaire, *Candide*	
1762	Rousseau, *Du contrat social* and *Émile ou de l'éducation*		
1774		Goethe, *Sorrows of Young Werther*	
1776	Death of Hume	Adam Smith, *Wealth of Nations*	American Declaration of Independence
1781	Kant, *Kritik der reinen Vernunft*		
1783	Kant, *Prolegomena zu einer jeden künftigen Metaphysik*		
1784	Kant, "Beantwortung der Frage: Was ist Aufklärung?"		
1785	Kant, *Grundlegung zur Metaphysik der Sitten*		
1787			US Constitution
1788	Birth of Arthur Schopenhauer Kant, *Kritik der praktischen Vernunft*	Gibbon, *The Decline and Fall of the Roman Empire*	
1789	Death of d'Holbach	Adoption of *La Déclaration des droits de l'Homme et du citoyen*	French Revolution and the establishment of the First Republic
1790	Kant, *Kritik der Urteilskraft*		
1791		Tom Paine, *The Rights of Man* Mozart, *The Magic Flute*	
1792	Mary Wollstonecraft, *Vindication of the Rights of Woman*		
1794		Creation of the École Normale Supérieure	Death of Robespierre
1795	Schiller, *Briefe über die ästhetische Erziehung des Menschen*		

PHILOSOPHICAL EVENTS	CULTURAL EVENTS	POLITICAL EVENTS
1797 Schelling, *Ideen zu einer Philosophie der Natur als Einleitung in das Studium dieser Wissenschaft*		
1798 Birth of Auguste Comte	Thomas Malthus, *Essay on the Principle of Population*	
1800 Fichte, *Die Bestimmung des Menschen* Schelling, *System des transcendentalen Idealismus*	Beethoven's First Symphony	
1804 Death of Kant		Napoleon Bonaparte proclaims the First Empire
1805	Diderot, *Le Neveu de Rameau*	
1806 Birth of John Stuart Mill	Reinstatement of the Sorbonne by Napoleon as a secular university	Napoleon brings the Holy Roman Empire to an end
1807 Hegel, *Die Phänomenologie des Geistes*		
1812 (–1816) Hegel, *Wissenschaft der Logik*		
1815	Jane Austen, *Emma*	Battle of Waterloo; final defeat of Napoleon
1817 Hegel, *Encyclopedia*	Ricardo, *Principles of Political Economy*	
1818 Birth of Karl Marx	Mary Shelley, *Frankenstein, or, The Modern Prometheus*	
1819 Schleiermacher, *Hermeneutik* Schopenhauer, *Die Welt als Wille und Vorstellung*	Byron, *Don Juan*	
1821 Hegel, *Grundlinien der Philosophie des Rechts*		Death of Napoleon
1823	Beethoven's Ninth Symphony	
1830 (–1842) Auguste Comte, *Cours de philosophie positive* in six volumes	Stendhal, *The Red and the Black*	
1831 Death of Hegel	Victor Hugo, *The Hunchback of Notre Dame*	
1832 Death of Bentham	Clausewitz, *Vom Kriege*	
1833 Birth of Wilhelm Dilthey	Pushkin, *Eugene Onegin*	Abolition of slavery in the British Empire
1835	The first volume of Alexis de Tocqueville's *Democracy in America* is published in French	
1837	Louis Daguerre invents the daguerreotype, the first successful photographic process	

PHILOSOPHICAL EVENTS	CULTURAL EVENTS	POLITICAL EVENTS
1841 Feuerbach, *Das Wesen des Christentums* Kierkegaard, *On the Concept of Irony with Constant Reference to Socrates*	R. W. Emerson, *Essays: First Series*	
1842	Death of Stendhal (Marie-Henri Beyle)	
1843 Kierkegaard, *Either/Or* and *Fear and Trembling* Mill, *A System of Logic*		
1844 Marx writes *Economic-Philosophic Manuscripts*	Alexandre Dumas, *The Count of Monte Cristo*	
1846 Kierkegaard, *Concluding Unscientific Postscript*		
1847 Boole, *The Mathematical Analysis of Logic*	Helmholtz, *On the Conservation of Force*	
1848	Publication of the *Communist Manifesto*	Beginning of the Second Republic
1851	Herman Melville, *Moby Dick* Herbert Spencer, *Social Statics* The Great Exhibition is staged at the Crystal Palace, London	
1852		Napoleon III declares the Second Empire
1853		(–1856) Crimean War
1854	H. D. Thoreau, *Walden*	
1855	Walt Whitman, *Leaves of Grass*	
1856 Birth of Sigmund Freud		
1857 Birth of Ferdinand de Saussure Death of Comte	Charles Baudelaire, *The Flowers of Evil* Gustav Flaubert, *Madame Bovary*	
1859 Birth of Henri Bergson, John Dewey, and Edmund Husserl Mill, *On Liberty*	Charles Darwin, *Origin of Species*	(–1860) Italian Unification, except Venice (1866) and Rome (1870)
1861	Johann Jakob Bachofen, *Das Mutterrecht*	Tsar Alexander II abolishes serfdom in Russia
1863 Mill, *Utilitarianism*	Édouard Manet, *Olympia*	Abraham Lincoln issues the *Emancipation Proclamation*
1865	Premiere of Richard Wagner's *Tristan und Isolde* (–1869) Leo Tolstoy, *War and Peace*	The surrender of General Robert E. Lee signals the conclusion of the American Civil War
1866	Fyodor Dostoevsky, *Crime and Punishment*	The Peace of Prague ends the Austro-Prussian War
1867 Marx, *Das Kapital, vol. I*		

226

PHILOSOPHICAL EVENTS	CULTURAL EVENTS	POLITICAL EVENTS
1868 Birth of Émile Chartier ("Alain")	Birth of W. E. B. Du Bois Creation of the École Pratique des Hautes Études (EPHE)	
1869 Mill, *The Subjection of Women*	(–1870) Jules Verne, *Twenty Thousand Leagues Under the Sea* (–1976) Wagner, *Der Ring des Nibelungen*	Completion of the Suez Canal
1870		(–1871) Franco-Prussian War Establishment of the Third Republic
1871 Lachelier, *Du fondement de l'induction*	Darwin, *The Descent of Man* Eliot, *Middlemarch*	Unification of Germany: Prussian King William I becomes Emperor (*Kaiser*) of Germany and Otto von Bismarck becomes Chancellor
1872 Nietzsche, *Die Geburt der Tragödie*		
1873 Death of Mill	(–1877) Tolstoy, *Anna Karenina*	End of German Occupation following France's defeat in the Franco-Prussian War
1874 Birth of Max Scheler Émile Boutroux, *La Contingence des lois de la nature* Brentano, *Psychologie vom empirischen Standpunkt*	First Impressionist Exhibition staged by the Société anonyme des peintres, sculpteurs et graveurs (Cézanne, Degas, Guillaumin, Monet, Berthe Morisot, Pissarro, Renoir, Sisley)	
1877	Henry Morton Stanley completes his navigation of the Congo River	
1878		King Leopold II of Belgium engages explorer Henry Morton Stanley to establish a colony in the Congo
1879 Frege, *Begriffsschrift*	Henrik Ibsen, *A Doll's House* Georg Cantor (1845–1918) becomes Professor of Mathematics at Halle Thomas Edison exhibits his incandescent light bulb	
1883 Birth of Karl Jaspers and José Ortega y Gasset Death of Marx (–1885) Nietzsche, *Also Sprach Zarathustra* Dilthey, *Einleitung in die Geisteswissenschaften*	Cantor, "Foundations of a General Theory of Aggregates"	

	PHILOSOPHICAL EVENTS	CULTURAL EVENTS	POLITICAL EVENTS
1884	Birth of Gaston Bachelard Frege, *Die Grundlagen der Arithmetik*	Mark Twain, *Adventures of Huckleberry Finn*	
1886	Nietzsche, *Jenseits von Gut und Böse*		
1887	Nietzsche, *Über der Genealogie der Moral*		
1888	Birth of Jean Wahl		
1889	Birth of Martin Heidegger, Gabriel Marcel, and Ludwig Wittgenstein Bergson, *Essai sur les données immédiates de la conscience*		
1890	William James, *Principles of Psychology*		
1892	Frege, "Über Sinn und Bedeutung"		
1893	Xavier Léon and Élie Halévy cofound the *Revue de métaphysique et de morale*		
1894			Captain Alfred Dreyfus (1859–1935), a Jewish-French army officer, is arrested and charged with spying for Germany
1895	Birth of Max Horkheimer	The Lumière brothers hold the first public screening of projected motion pictures Wilhelm Conrad Röntgen discovers X-rays	
1896		Athens hosts the first Olympic Games of the modern era	
1897	Birth of Georges Bataille		
1898	Birth of Herbert Marcuse	Zola article, "J'accuse," is published in defense of Dreyfus	
1899			Start of the Second Boer War
1900	Birth of Hans-Georg Gadamer Death of Nietzsche and Félix Ravaisson (–1901) Husserl, *Logische Untersuchungen*	Freud, *Interpretation of Dreams* Planck formulates quantum theory	
1901	Birth of Jacques Lacan		
1903	Birth of Theodor W. Adorno and Jean Cavaillès	Du Bois, *The Souls of Black Folk*	
1904	(–1905) Weber, *Die protestantische Ethik und der Geist des Kapitalismus*		

	PHILOSOPHICAL EVENTS	CULTURAL EVENTS	POLITICAL EVENTS
1905	Birth of Raymond Aron and Jean-Paul Sartre	Einstein formulates the special theory of relativity	Law of separation of church and state in France
1906	Birth of Hannah Arendt and Emmanuel Levinas	Birth of Léopold Sédar Senghor	The Dreyfus Affair ends when the French Court of Appeals exonerates Dreyfus of all charges
1907	Birth of Jean Hyppolite Bergson, *L'Evolution créatrice*	Pablo Picasso completes *Les Demoiselles d'Avignon*	
1908	Birth of Simone de Beauvoir, Claude Lévi-Strauss, Maurice Merleau-Ponty, and W. V. Quine		
1911	Victor Delbos publishes the first French journal article on Husserl: "Husserl: Sa critique du psychologisme et sa conception d'une Logique pure" in *Revue de métaphysique et de morale*	The Blaue Reiter (Blue Rider) group of avant-garde artists is founded in Munich	
1913	Birth of Albert Camus, Aimé Césaire, and Paul Ricoeur Husserl, *Ideen*	Marcel Proust (1871–1922), *Swann's Way*, the first volume of *Remembrance of Things Past* First performance of Stravinsky's *Rite of Spring*	
1914			Germany invades France
1915	Birth of Roland Barthes	Franz Kafka, *Metamorphosis*	
1916	Publication of Saussure's *Cours de linguistique générale*	James Joyce, *A Portrait of the Artist as a Young Man*	
1917	Death of Durkheim		Russian Revolution
1918	Birth of Louis Althusser Death of Georg Cantor and Lachelier		Proclamation of the Weimar Republic First World War ends
1919		German architect Walter Gropius (1883–1969) founds the Bauhaus School	
1920			Ratification of the 19th amendment to the US Constitution extends suffrage to women
1922	Birth of Karl-Otto Apel Wittgenstein, *Tractatus Logico-Philosophicus* Bataille begins his twenty-year career at the Bibliothèque Nationale	T. S. Eliot, *The Waste Land* Herman Hesse, *Siddhartha* James Joyce, *Ulysses*	
1923	Institut für Sozialforschung (Frankfurt School) is founded	Kahil Gibran, *The Prophet*	

PHILOSOPHICAL EVENTS	CULTURAL EVENTS	POLITICAL EVENTS
1924 Birth of Jean-François Lyotard Raymond Aron, Georges Canguilhem, Daniel Lagache, Paul Nizan, and Sartre enter the École Normale Supérieure	André Breton, *Le Manifeste du surréalisme* Thomas Mann, *The Magic Mountain*	Death of Vladimir Lenin
1925 Birth of Gilles Deleuze	Franz Kafka, *The Trial* First Surrealist Exhibition at the Galerie Pierre, Paris	
1926 Birth of Michel Foucault Jean Hering publishes the first French text to address Husserl's phenomenology: *Phénoménologie et philosophie religieuse*	The film *Metropolis* by German director Fritz Lang (1890–1976) premieres in Berlin The Bauhaus school building, designed by Walter Gropius (1883–1969), is completed in Dessau, Germany	
1927 Heidegger, *Sein und Zeit* Marcel, *Journal métaphysique*	Virginia Woolf, *To the Lighthouse*	
1928 Birth of Noam Chomsky The first work of German phenomenology appears in French translation: Scheler's *Nature et formes de la sympathie: Contribution à l'étude des lois de la vie émotionnelle*	Bertolt Brecht (1898–1956) writes *The Threepenny Opera* with composer Kurt Weill (1900–1950) The first television station begins broadcasting in Schenectady, New York	
1929 Birth of Jürgen Habermas Heidegger, *Kant und das Problem der Metaphysik* and *Was ist Metaphysik?* Husserl, *Formale und transzendentale Logik* and "Phenomenology" in *Encylopedia Britannica* Wahl, *La malheur de la conscience dans la philosophie de Hegel* Husserl lectures at the Sorbonne	Ernest Hemingway, *A Farewell to Arms* Erich Maria Remarque, *All Quiet on the Western Front*	
1930 Birth of Pierre Bourdieu, Jacques Derrida, Félix Guattari, Luce Irigaray, and Michel Serres Levinas, *La Théorie de l'intuition dans la phénoménologie de Husserl*	(–1942) Robert Musil, *The Man Without Qualities*	
1931 Husserl's *Ideas* is translated into English	Pearl Buck, *The Good Earth* Gödel publishes his two incompleteness theorems	

	PHILOSOPHICAL EVENTS	CULTURAL EVENTS	POLITICAL EVENTS
1931	Heidegger's first works appear in French translation: "Was ist Metaphysik?" in *Bifur*, and "Vom Wesen des Grundes" in *Recherches philosophiques* Levinas and Gabrielle Peiffer publish a French translation of Husserl's *Cartesian Meditations*		
1932	Birth of Stuart Hall Bergson, *Les Deux sources de la morale et de la religion*	Aldous Huxley, *Brave New World* BBC starts a regular public television broadcasting service in the UK	
1933	(–1939) Alexandre Kojève lectures on Hegel at the École Pratique des Hautes Études University in Exile is founded as a graduate division of the New School for Social Research	André Malraux, *Man's Fate* Gertrude Stein, *The Autobiography of Alice B. Toklas*	Hitler becomes Chancellor of Germany
1935		Penguin publishes its first paperback	
1936	Husserl, *Krisis der europäischen Wissenschaften und die transzendentale Phänomenologie* Sartre, "La Transcendance de l'égo" in *Recherches philosophiques*	Benjamin, "The Work of Art in the Age of Mechanical Reproduction"	(–1939) Spanish Civil War
1937	Birth of Alain Badiou, Hélène Cixous, Françoise Laruelle	Picasso, *Guernica*	
1938	Death of Husserl	Sartre, *La Nausée*	
1939	Establishment of Husserl Archives in Louvain, Belgium (–1941) Hyppolite publishes his translation into French of Hegel's *Phenomenology of Spirit*	Joyce, *Finnegans Wake*	Nazi Germany invades Poland (September 1) and France and Britain declare war on Germany (September 3)
1940	Birth of Jean-Luc Nancy and Jacques Rancière Death of Benjamin	Richard Wright, *Native Son*	
1941	Death of Bergson	Death of Joyce Arthur Koestler, *Darkness at Noon?*	Japan attacks Pearl Harbor, and the US enters the Second World War Germany invades the Soviet Union
1942	Birth of Étienne Balibar Camus, *L'Étranger* and *Le Mythe de Sisyphe: Essai sur l'absurde*		

	PHILOSOPHICAL EVENTS	CULTURAL EVENTS	POLITICAL EVENTS
1942	Merleau-Ponty, *La Structure du comportement* Lévi-Strauss meets Roman Jakobson at the École Libre des Hautes Études in New York		
1943	Death of Simone Weil Farber, *The Foundation of Phenomenology* Sartre, *L'Être et le néant*	Herman Hesse, *The Glass Bead Game* Ayn Rand, *The Fountainhead*	
1944		Jorge Luis Borges, *Ficciones* Jean Genet, *Our Lady of the Flowers*	Paris is liberated by the US Army (August 25) Bretton Woods Conference and establishment of the International Monetary Fund (IMF)
1945	Merleau-Ponty, *Phénoménologie de la perception*	George Orwell, *Animal Farm* Sartre, Beauvoir, and Merleau-Ponty begin as founding editors of *Les Temps modernes*	End of the Second World War in Germany (May); atom bombs dropped on Hiroshima and Nagasaki; end of the war in Japan (September) Establishment of the United Nations
1946	Birth of Jean-Luc Marion Hyppolite, *Genèse et structure de la "Phénoménologie de l'esprit" de Hegel* Sartre, *L'Existentialisme est un humanisme*	Eugene O'Neill, *The Iceman Cometh* Bataille founds the journal *Critique*	Beginning of the French Indochina War Establishment of the Fourth Republic
1947	Adorno and Horkheimer, *Dialektik der Aufklärung* Beauvoir, *Pour une morale de l'ambiguïté* Heidegger, "Brief über den Humanismus"	Camus, *The Plague* Anne Frank, *The Diary of Anne Frank* Thomas Mann, *Doctor Faustus*	(–1951) Marshall Plan
1948	(–1951) Gramsci, *Prison Notebooks* Althusser is appointed *agrégé-répétiteur* ("caïman") at the École Normale Supérieure, a position he holds until 1980	Nathalie Sarraute, *Portrait of a Man Unknown* Debut of *The Ed Sullivan Show*	The United Nations adopts the Universal Declaration of Human Rights
1949	Beauvoir, *Le Deuxième sexe* Lévi-Strauss, *Les Structures élémentaires de la parenté* Heidegger's *Existence and Being* is translated	Arthur Miller, *Death of a Salesman* Orwell, *1984* Cornelius Castoriadis and Claude Lefort found the revolutionary group and journal *Socialisme ou Barbarie*	Foundation of NATO

PHILOSOPHICAL EVENTS	CULTURAL EVENTS	POLITICAL EVENTS
1950 Ricoeur publishes his translation into French of Husserl's *Ideas I*		Beginning of the Korean War
1951 Death of Alain and Wittgenstein Arendt, *The Origins of Totalitarianism* Quine, "Two Dogmas of Empiricism"	J. D. Salinger, *The Catcher in the Rye* Marguerite Yourcenar, *Memoirs of Hadrian*	
1952 Birth of Bernard Stiegler Death of Dewey and Santayana Merleau-Ponty is elected to the Chair in Philosophy at the Collège de France	Samuel Beckett, *Waiting for Godot* Ralph Ellison, *Invisible Man*	
1953 Wittgenstein, *Philosophical Investigations* (posthumous) Lacan begins his public seminars	Lacan, together with Daniel Lagache and Françoise Dolto, founds the Société française de psychanalyse Crick and Watson construct the first model of DNA	Death of Joseph Stalin Ceasefire agreement (July 27) ends the Korean War
1954 Lyotard, *La Phénoménologie* Scheler, *The Nature of Sympathy* appears in English translation	Huxley, *The Doors of Perception*	Following the fall of Dien Bien Phu (May 7), France pledges to withdraw from Indochina (July 20) Beginning of the Algerian revolt against French rule
1955 Marcuse, *Eros and Civilization* Cerisy Colloquium *Qu'est-ce que la philosophie? Autour de Martin Heidegger*, organized by Jean Beaufret	Vladimir Nabokov, *Lolita*	
1956 Sartre's *Being and Nothingness* appears in English translation		Hungarian Revolution and Soviet invasion The French colonies of Morocco and Tunisia gain independence
1957 Chomsky, *Syntactic Structures* Founding of *Philosophy Today*	Jack Kerouac, *On the Road* Camus receives the Nobel Prize for Literature	Rome Treaty signed by France, Germany, Belgium, Italy, the Netherlands, and Luxembourg establishes the European Economic Community The Soviet Union launches *Sputnik 1*, the first man-made object to orbit the Earth
1958 Lévi-Strauss, *Anthropologie structurale*	Chinua Achebe, *Things Fall Apart* William S. Burroughs, *Naked Lunch*	Charles de Gaulle is elected president after a new constitution establishes the Fifth Republic

	PHILOSOPHICAL EVENTS	CULTURAL EVENTS	POLITICAL EVENTS
1958		Elie Wiesel, *Night*	
		The Sorbonne's "Faculté des Lettres" is officially renamed the "Faculté des Lettres et Sciences Humaines"	
		(–1960) The first feature films by directors associated with the French "New Wave" cinema, including, in 1959, *Les Quatre Cent Coups* (*The 400 Blows*) by François Truffaut (1932–84) and, in 1960, *A bout de souffle* (*Breathless*) by Jean-Luc Godard (1930–)	
1959	Birth of Catherine Malabou	Günter Grass, *The Tin Drum*	
	Lévi-Strauss is elected to the Chair in Social Anthropology at the Collège de France	Gillo Pentecorvo, *The Battle of Algiers*	
1960	Death of Camus	Marguerite Duras, *Hiroshima, Mon Amour*	
	Gadamer, *Wahrheit und Methode*	Harper Lee, *To Kill a Mockingbird*	
	Sartre, *Critique de la raison dialectique*	First issue of the journal *Tel Quel* is published	
	Spiegelberg, *The Phenomenological Movement*	The birth control pill is made available to married women	
1961	Death of Merleau-Ponty	Alain Robbe-Grillet and Alain Resnais, *Last Year at Marienbad*	Erection of the Berlin Wall
	Derrida, Introduction to *Edmund Husserl: L'Origine de la géométrie*	Joseph Heller, *Catch 22*	Bay of Pigs failed invasion of Cuba
	Frantz, *Les Damnés de la terre*, with a preface by Sartre		
	Foucault, *Histoire de la folie à l'âge classique*		
	Heidegger, *Nietzsche*		
	Levinas, *Totalité et infini: Essai sur l'extériorité*		
1962	Death of Bachelard	Rachel Carson, *Silent Spring*	France grants independence to Algeria
	Deleuze, *Nietzsche et la philosophie*	Ken Kesey, *One Flew Over the Cuckoo's Nest*	Cuban Missile Crisis
	Thomas Kuhn, *The Structure of Scientific Revolutions*	Doris Lessing, *The Golden Notebook*	
	Lévi-Strauss, *La Pensée sauvage*		
	Heidegger, *Being and Time* appears in English translation		
	Merleau-Ponty, *Phenomenology of Perception* appears in English translation		

	PHILOSOPHICAL EVENTS	CULTURAL EVENTS	POLITICAL EVENTS
1962	First meeting of SPEP at Northwestern University		
1963	Arendt, *Eichmann in Jerusalem*	Betty Friedan, *The Feminine Mystique* Sylvia Plath, *The Bell Jar* Alain Robbe-Grillet, *For a New Novel* The first artificial heart is implanted	Imprisonment of Nelson Mandela Assassination of John F. Kennedy
1964	Barthes, *Eléments de sémiologie* Marcuse, *One-Dimensional Man* Merleau-Ponty, *Le Visible et l'invisible* (posthumous)	Saul Bellow, *Herzog* Lacan founds L'École Freudienne de Paris The Beatles appear on *The Ed Sullivan Show*	US Civil Rights Act outlaws discrimination on the basis of race, color, religion, sex, or national origin Gulf of Tonkin Incident
1965	Death of Buber Althusser, *Pour Marx* and, with Balibar, *Lire "Le Capital"* Ricoeur, *De l'interprétation: Essai sur Freud* Foucault, *Madness and Civilization* appears in English translation	Truman Capote, *In Cold Blood* Alex Haley, *The Autobiography of Malcolm X*	Assassination of Malcolm X
1966	Adorno, *Negative Dialektik* Deleuze, *Le Bergsonisme* Foucault, *Les Mots et les choses: Une archéologie des sciences humaines* Lacan, *Écrits*	Alain Resnais, *Hiroshima Mon Amour* (film) Jacques-Alain Miller founds *Cahiers pour l'analyse* Johns Hopkins Symposium "The Languages of Criticism and the Sciences of Man" introduces French theory to the American academic community *Star Trek* premieres on US television	(–1976) Chinese Cultural Revolution Foundation of the Black Panther Party for Self-Defense by Huey P. Newton and Bobby Seale
1967	Derrida, *De la grammatologie, La Voix et le phénomène*, and *L'Écriture et la différence*	Gabriel Garcia Marquez, *One Hundred Years of Solitude* William Styron, *Confessions of Nat Turner*	Confirmation of Thurgood Marshall to the US Supreme Court
1968	Deleuze, *Différence et répétition, Spinoza et le problème de l'expression* Habermas, *Erkenntnis und Interesse*	Carlos Castaneda, *The Teachings of Don Juan: A Yaqui Way of Knowledge* Stanley Kubrick, *2001: A Space Odyssey* The Beatles release the White Album	Events of May '68, including closure of the University of Nanterre (May 2), police invasion of the Sorbonne (May 3), student demonstrations and strikes, and workers' occupation of factories and general strike Prague Spring

235

	PHILOSOPHICAL EVENTS	CULTURAL EVENTS	POLITICAL EVENTS
1968			Assassination of Martin Luther King Tet Offensive
1969	Death of Adorno and Jaspers Deleuze, *Logique du sens* Foucault, *L'Archéologie du savoir* Paulo Freire, *Pedagogy of the Oppressed*	Kurt Vonnegut, *Slaughterhouse-Five* Woodstock Music and Art Fair Neil Armstrong is the first person to set foot on the moon	Stonewall riots launch the Gay Liberation Movement
1970	Death of Carnap Adorno, *Ästhetische Theorie* Foucault, *The Order of Things* appears in English translation Husserl, *The Crisis of European Philosophy* appears in English translation Founding of the *Journal of the British Society of Phenomenology* Foucault is elected to the Chair of the History of Systems of Thought at the Collège de France Ricoeur beings teaching at the University of Chicago	Millett, *Sexual Politics* Founding of *Diacritics* First Earth Day	Shootings at Kent State University Salvador Allende becomes the first Marxist head of state to be freely elected in a Western nation
1971	Lyotard, *Discours, figure* Founding of *Research in Phenomenology*	Reorganization of the University of Paris	End of the gold standard for US dollar
1972	Death of John Wild Bourdieu, *Esquisse d'une théorie de la pratique* Deleuze and Guattari, *Capitalisme et schizophrénie. 1. L'Anti-Oedipe* Derrida, *La Dissémination, Marges de la philosophie,* and *Positions* *Radical Philosophy* begins publication Colloquium on Nietzsche at Cerisy	Italo Calvino, *Invisible Cities* Hunter Thompson, *Fear and Loathing in Las Vegas*	Watergate break-in President Richard Nixon visits China, beginning the normalization of relations between the US and PRC
1973	Death of Horkheimer Lacan publishes the first volume of his *Séminaire* Derrida, *Speech and Phenomena* appears in English translation	Thomas Pynchon, *Gravity's Rainbow* (–1978) Aleksandr Solzhenitsyn, *The Gulag Archipelago* Roe *v.* Wade legalizes abortion	Chilean military coup ousts and kills President Salvador Allende

PHILOSOPHICAL EVENTS	CULTURAL EVENTS	POLITICAL EVENTS
1974 Derrida, *Glas* Irigaray, *Speculum: De l'autre femme* Kristeva, *La Révolution du langage poétique* Levinas, *Autrement qu'être ou au-delà de l'essence*	Erica Jong, *Fear of Flying* Founding of *Critical Inquiry* Creation of the first doctoral program in women's studies in Europe, the Centre de Recherches en Études Féminines, at the University of Paris VIII–Vincennes, directed by Hélène Cixous	Resignation of Nixon
1975 Death of Arendt Foucault, *Surveiller et punir: Naissance de la prison* Irigaray, *Ce sexe qui n'en est pas un* Derrida begins teaching in the English Department at Yale Foucault begins teaching at the University of California–Berkeley Foundation of GREPH, the Groupe de Recherches sur l'Enseignement Philosophique	Cixous and Clément, *La Jeune née* *Signs* begins publication The Sixth Section of the EPHE is renamed the École des Hautes Études en Sciences Sociales	Death of Francisco Franco Andrei Sakharov wins Nobel Peace Prize Fall of Saigon, ending the Vietnam War First US–USSR joint space mission
1976 Death of Bultmann and Heidegger Foucault, *Histoire de la sexualité. 1. La Volonté de savoir* Derrida, *Of Grammatology* appears in English translation Barthes is elected to the Chair of Literary Semiology at the Collège de France	Alex Haley, *Roots: The Saga of an American Family* Foundation of the International Association for Philosophy and Literature	Death of Mao Zedong Uprising in Soweto
1977 Death of Ernst Bloch Deleuze and Guattari, *Anti-Oedipus* appears in English translation Lacan, *Ecrits: A Selection* appears in English translation	240 Czech intellectuals sign Charter 77 The Centre Georges Pompidou, designed by architects Renzo Piano (1937–) and Richard Rogers (1933–), opens in Paris	Egyptian president Anwar al-Sadat becomes the first Arab head of state to visit Israel
1978 Death of Gödel Arendt, *Life of the Mind* Derrida, *La Vérité en peinture*	George Perec, *Life: A User's Manual* Edward Said, *Orientalism* Birmingham School, Centre for Contemporary Culture releases *Policing the Crisis* Louise Brown becomes the first test-tube baby	Camp David Accords
1979 Death of Marcuse	Calvino, *If on a Winter's Night a Traveler*	Iranian Revolution

PHILOSOPHICAL EVENTS	CULTURAL EVENTS	POLITICAL EVENTS
1979 Bourdieu, *La Distinction: Critique sociale du jugement* Lyotard, *La Condition postmoderne: Rapport sur le savoir* Rorty, *Philosophy and the Mirror of Nature* Prigogine and Stengers, *La Nouvelle alliance*	Francis Ford Coppola, *Apocalypse Now* Edgar Morin, *La Vie de La Vie* Jerry Falwell founds Moral Majority The first cognitive sciences department is established at MIT	Nicaraguan Revolution Iran Hostage Crisis begins Margaret Thatcher becomes prime minister of the UK (the first woman to be a European head of state)
1980 Death of Barthes and Sartre Davidson, *Essays on Actions and Events* Deleuze and Guattari, *Capitalisme et schizophrénie. 2. Mille plateaux* Derrida, *La Carte postale* Kristeva, *Pouvoirs de l'horreur: Essai sur l'abjection* Foucault, *The History of Sexuality, vol. 1* appears in English translation	Umberto Eco, *The Name of the Rose* Murder of John Lennon Lacan officially dissolves the École Freudienne de Paris Cable News Network (CNN) becomes the first television station to provide twenty-four-hour news coverage	Election of Ronald Reagan as US president Solidarity movement begins in Poland Death of Yugoslav president Josip Broz Tito
1981 Death of Lacan Habermas, *Theorie des kommunikativen Handelns* Bourdieu is elected to the Chair in Sociology at the Collège de France	First cases of AIDS are discovered among gay men in the US Debut of MTV	Release of American hostages in Iran François Mitterrand is elected as the first socialist president of France's Fifth Republic Confirmation of Sandra Day O'Connor, first woman Justice, to the US Supreme Court
1982 Badiou, *Théorie de sujet* Marion, *Dieu sans l'être* Foundation of the Collège International de Philosophie by François Châtelet, Jacques Derrida, Jean-Pierre Faye, and Dominique Lecourt	Debut of the Weather Channel in the US	Falklands War
1983 Death of Aron Lyotard, *Le Différend* Sloterdijk, *Kritik der zynischen Vernunft*	Alice Walker, *The Color Purple* Founding of *Hypatia*	
1984 Death of Foucault Davidson, *Inquiries into Truth and Interpretation* Irigaray, *Éthique de la différence sexuelle* Lloyd, *The Man of Reason*	Marguerite Duras, *The Lover* Milan Kundera, *The Unbearable Lightness of Being*	Assassination of Indira Gandhi Year-long strike of the National Union of Mineworkers in the UK
1985 Habermas, *Der philosophische Diskurs der Moderne*	Don Delillo, *White Noise*	

PHILOSOPHICAL EVENTS	CULTURAL EVENTS	POLITICAL EVENTS
1985 First complete translation into French of Heidegger's *Sein und Zeit* Irigaray's *Speculum of the Other Woman* and *This Sex Which is Not One* appear in English translation	Donna Haraway, *Cyborg Manifesto* Gabriel Garcia Marquez, *Love in the Time of Cholera*	Mikhail Gorbachev is named General Secretary of the Communist Party of the Soviet Union
1986 Death of Beauvoir Deleuze, *Foucault* Establishment of the Archives Husserl de Paris at the École Normale Supérieure	Art Spiegelman, *Maus I: A Survivor's Tale*	Chernobyl nuclear accident in USSR Election of Corazon Aquino ends Marcos regime in Philippines
1987 Derrida begins his appointment as Visiting Professor of French and Comparative Literature at the University of California, Irvine	Toni Morrison, *Beloved* Discovery of Paul de Man's wartime journalism damages the popularity of deconstruction in the US	Gorbachev inaugurates *perestroika* (restructuring), leading to the end of the USSR The First Intifada begins in the Gaza Strip and West Bank
1988 Badiou, *L'Être et l'événement*	Salman Rushdie, *The Satanic Verses*	Benazir Bhutto becomes the first woman to head an Islamic nation Pan Am Flight 103, en route from London to New York, is destroyed by a bomb over Lockerbie, Scotland
1989 Death of Sellars Guattari, *Les Trois Écologies* Marion, *Réduction et donation* Žižek, *The Sublime Object of Ideology* Publication of Heidegger's *Beiträge zur Philosophie (Vom Ereignis)*	*Exxon Valdez* oil spill in Alaska Tim Berners-Lee submits a proposal for an information management system, later called the World Wide Web	Fall of the Berlin Wall Students protest in Tiananmen Square, Beijing
1990 Death of Althusser Butler, *Gender Trouble*	The World Health Organization removes homosexuality from its list of diseases Beginning of the Human Genome Project, headed by James D. Watson	Nelson Mandela is released from prison Lech Walesa is elected president of Poland Reunification of Germany Break-up of the former Yugoslavia and beginning of the Yugoslav Wars Sandinistas are voted out of power after ten years of war against the US-backed Contras
1991 Deleuze and Guattari, *Qu'est-ce que la philosophie?* Laruelle, *En tant qu'un*	Fredric Jameson, *Postmodernism, or, The Cultural Logic of Late Capitalism*	First Gulf War begins Election of Jean-Bertrand Aristide as president of Haiti

	PHILOSOPHICAL EVENTS	CULTURAL EVENTS	POLITICAL EVENTS
1991		The World Wide Web becomes the first publicly available service on the internet	
1992	Death of Guattari		Dissolution of the Soviet Union
			Guattari runs unsuccessfully as a regional Green Party candidate in France
			Maastricht Treaty is signed, creating the European Union
1993	Gilroy, *Black Atlantic*		Vaclav Havel is named the first president of the Czech Republic
	Nancy, *Le Sens du monde*		Pablo Escobar, Colombian drug lord, is killed
1994	Death of Karl Popper	Death of Ralph Ellison and Eugène Ionesco	Genocide in Rwanda
	Brandom, *Making it Explicit*	Bhabha, *The Location of Culture*	End of apartheid in South Africa; Nelson Mandela is sworn in as president
	McDowell, *Mind and World*		
	Publication of Foucault's *Dits et écrits*	The Channel Tunnel opens, connecting England and France	North American Free Trade Agreement (NAFTA), signed in 1992, goes into effect
1995	Death of Deleuze and Levinas	Mignolo, *The Darker Side of the Renaissance*	End of Bosnian War
			World Trade Organization (WTO) comes into being, replacing GATT
1996	Laruelle, *Principes de la non-philosophie*	Cloning of Dolly the sheep (died 2003)	Death of Mitterrand
	Nancy, *Être singulier pluriel*		
1997	Marion, *Étant donné: essai d'une phénoménologie de la donation*		
1998	Death of Lyotard		Socialist–Green Coalition under Helmut Schmidt in Germany
	Dussel, *Ética de la liberación en la edad ded la globalización y la exclusión*		
1999	Spivak, *A Critique of Postcolonial Reason*	Death of Iris Murdoch	Introduction of the Euro
	Badiou leaves Vincennes to become Professor and Head of the Philosophy Department at the École Normale Supérieure		Antiglobalization forces disrupt the WTO meeting in Seattle
2000	Death of Quine		Second Intifada
	Negri and Hardt, *Empire*		
	Rancière, *La Partage du sensible: esthétique et politique*		

PHILOSOPHICAL EVENTS	CULTURAL EVENTS	POLITICAL EVENTS
2001 Balibar, *Nous, citoyens d'Europe? Les Frontières, l'État, le peuple*		Terrorist attack destroys the World Trade Center
2002 Death of Bourdieu and Gadamer		Luiz Inacio Lula da Silva is elected president of Brazil
2003 Death of Blanchot and Davidson	Completion of the Human Genome Project	Start of the Second Gulf War Beginning of conflict in Dafur
2004 Death of Derrida and Leopoldo Zea Malabou, *Que faire de notre cerveau?*	Asian tsunami	Madrid train bombings
2005 Death of Ricoeur	Hurricane Katrina	Bombings of the London public transport system
2006 Badiou, *Logiques des mondes. L'Être et l'événement, 2* Quentin Meillassoux, *Après la finitude. Essai sur la nécessité de la contingence*		Evo Morales is elected president of Bolivia Bombings of the Mumbai train system
2007 Death of Jean Baudrillard and Rorty		
2008 Publication of first of Derrida's Seminars: *La Bête et le souverain*	Death of Robbe-Grillet, Aimé Césaire, Aleksandr Solzhenitsyn	Election of Barack Obama, the first African American president of the US International banking collapse
2009 Death of Lévi-Strauss, Leszek Kolakowski, Marjorie Grene	Death of Frank McCourt and John Updike	
2010 Death of Pierre Hadot and Claude Lefort	Death of Tony Judt and J. D. Salinger Mario Vargas Llosa wins Noble Prize in Literature	Arab Spring uprisings begin in Tunisia BP oil spill in Gulf of Mexico
2011 Death of Michael Dummett and Elizabeth Young-Bruehl SPEP celebrates 50th anniversary	Death of Friedrich Kittler and Christa Wolf	Death of Václav Havel US special forces kill Osama Bin Laden Capture and assassination of Muammar Gaddafi Occupy movement
2012	Death of Eric Hobsbawm and Adrienne Rich	

BIBLIOGRAPHY

Major works of individual philosophers are collected at the end of the relevant essay in the text.

Abram, David. *The Spell of the Sensuous: Perception and Language in a More-than-Human World.* New York: Vintage, 1997.

Adorno, Theodor W., and Max Horkheimer. *Dialectic of Enlightenment.* Translated by John Cumming. New York: Continuum, 1972 Originally published as *Dialektik der Aufklärung: Philosophische Fragmente.* Frankfurt: Fischer, 1969.

Agamben, Giorgio. *Homo Sacer: Sovereign Power and Bare Life.* Translated by Daniel Heller-Roazen. Stanford, CA: Stanford University Press, 1998.

Agamben, Giorgio. *Means Without Ends: Notes on Politics.* Translated by Vincenzo Binetti and Cesare Casarino. Minneapolis, MN: University of Minnesota Press, 2000.

Agamben, Giorgio. *State of Exception.* Translated by Kevin Attell. Chicago, IL: University of Chicago Press, 2005.

Alcoff, Linda Martin, and Eduardo Mendieta, eds. *Thinking From the Underside of History: Enrique Dussel's Philosophy of Liberation.* Lanham, MD: Rowman & Littlefield, 2000.

Appiah, Anthony. *In My Father's House: Africa in the Philosophy of Culture.* New York: Oxford University Press, 1992.

Arendt, Hannah. *The Human Condition.* Chicago, IL: University of Chicago Press, 1998.

Arendt, Hannah. *Origins of Totalitarianism.* New York: Harcourt, 1968.

Atkins, P. W. *The Second Law.* New York: Scientific American Library, 1984.

Badiou, Alain. "The Adventure of French Philosophy." *New Left Review* 35 (September–October 2005): 67–77.

Badiou, Alain. "L'Age des poètes." In *La Politique des poètes,* edited by Jacques Rancière, 21–38. Paris: Albin Michel, 1992.

Badiou, Alain. "L'Aveu du philosophe." Available online at http://www.ciepfc.fr/spip.php?article70 (accessed June 2010).

Badiou, Alain. *Casser en deux l'histoire du monde?* Paris: Les Conférences du Perroquet 37, 1992.

Badiou, Alain. "Democratic Materialism and the Materialist Dialectic." Translated by Alberto Toscano. *Radical Philosophy* 130 (March–April 2005): 20–24.

Badiou, Alain. "Dialectiques de la fable." In *Matrix: Machine philosophique*, Alain Badiou, Thomas Benatouil, Elie During *et al.*, 120–29. Paris: Ellipses, 2003.

Badiou, Alain. "Fifteen Theses on Contemporary Art". *Lacanian Ink* 23 (2004), www.lacan.com/frameXXIII7.htm (accessed December 2009).

Badiou, Alain. "Lacan et Platon: Le mathème est-il une idée?" In *Lacan avec les philosophes*, edited by the Bibliothèque du Collège international de Philosophie, 135–54. Paris: Albin Michel, 1991.

Badiou, Alain. "The Lessons of Jacques Rancière: Knowledge and Power After the Storm." In *Jacques Rancière: History, Politics, Aesthetics*, edited by Gabriel Rockhill and Phil Watts. Durham, NC: Duke University Press, 2009. Published in French as "Les leçons de Jacques Rancière, savoir et pouvoir après la tempête," in *La Philosophie déplacée: Autour de Jacques Rancière*, edited by Laurence Cornu and Patrice Vermeren. Paris: Horlieu Éditions, 2006.

Badiou, Alain. *Petit panthéon portatif*. Paris: La Fabrique, 2008.

Badiou, Alain. "Rancière and Apolitics." In *Metapolitics*, translated by Jason Barker, 114–23. London: Verso, 2005.

Badiou, Alain. "Rancière and the Community of Equals." In *Metapolitics*, translated by Jason Barker, 107–113. London: Verso, 2005.

Badiou, Alain. "Le (Re)commencement du matérialisme dialectique." *Critique* 240 (1967): 438–67.

Badiou, Alain. "Who is Nietzsche?" Translated by Alberto Toscano. *PLI: The Warwick Journal of Philosophy* 11(1) (2001): 1–11.

Baird Callicott, J., and Michael Nelson, eds. *The Wilderness Debate Rages On: Continuing the Great New Wilderness Debate*. Athens, GA: University of Georgia Press, 2008.

Balibar, Étienne. *Citoyen sujet, Essais d'anthropologie philosophique*. Paris: Presses Universitaires de France, forthcoming.

Balibar, Étienne. *Masses, Classes, Ideas: Studies on Politics and Philosophy Before and After Marx*. Translated by James Swenson. New York: Routledge, 1994.

Balibar, Étienne. *The Philosophy of Marx*. Translated by Chris Turner. London: Verso, 1995. Originally published as *La Philosophie de Marx*. Paris: Éditions la Découverte, 1993.

Balibar, Étienne. *Politics and the Other Scene*. Translated by Christine Jones, James Swenson, and Chris Turner. London: Verso, 2002. Originally published as *Droit de cité*. La Tour-d'Aigues: Éditions de l'Aube, 1998.

Balibar, Étienne. *Spinoza and Politics*. Translated by Peter Snowdon. London: Verso, 1998. Originally published as *Spinoza et la politique*. Paris: Presses Universitaires de France, 1985.

Balibar, Étienne. *We, the People of Europe? Reflections on Transnational Citizenship*. Translated by James Swenson. Princeton, NJ: Princeton University Press, 2004. Originally published as *Nous, citoyens d'Europe? Les Frontières, l'état, le peuple*. Paris: Éditions la Découverte, 2001.

Balibar, Étienne, and Louis Althusser. *Reading Capital*. Translated by Ben Brewster. London: New Left Books, 1970. Originally published as *Lire "Le Capital,"* 2 vols. Paris: F. Maspero, 1965.

Baudrillard, Jean. *The Mirror of Production*. Translated by Mark Poster. St. Louis, MO: Telos Press, 1975.

Baudrillard, Jean. *Seduction*. Translated by Brian Singer. New York: Palgrave Macmillan, 1991.

Baudrillard, Jean. *Simulations*. Translated by Paul Foss, Paul Patton, and Philip Beitchman. New York: Semiotext(e), 1983.

Baudrillard, Jean. *The Spirit of Terrorism and Requiem for the Twin Towers*. Translated by Chris Turner. New York: Norton, 2002.

Bauman, Zygmunt. *Between Class and Elite: The Evolution of the British Labour Movement. A Sociological Study*. Manchester: Manchester University Press, 1972.

Bauman, Zygmunt. *Europe: An Unfinished Adventure*. Cambridge: Polity, 2004.

Bauman, Zygmunt. *Globalization: The Human Consequences*. New York: Columbia University Press, 1998.

Bauman, Zygmunt. *Modernity and the Holocaust*. Ithaca, NY: Cornell University Press, 1989.

Bauman, Zygmunt. *Postmodern Ethics*. Oxford: Blackwell, 1993.

Bauman, Zygmunt. *Thinking Sociologically: An Introduction for Everyone*. Oxford: Blackwell, 1990.

Bayertz, Kurt. "Naturphilosophie als Ethik: Zur Vereinigung von Natur- und Moralphilosophie im Zeichen der ökologischen Krise." *Philosophia Naturalis* 24 (1987): 157–85.

Benhabib, Seyla. *Another Cosmopolitanism*. Oxford: Oxford University Press, 2006.

Benhabib, Seyla. *The Claims of Culture*. Princeton, NJ: Princeton University Press, 2002.

Benjamin, Walter. "Critique of Violence." In *Reflections: Essays, Aphorisms, Autobiographical Writings*, translated by Edmund Jephcott, 277–300. New York: Harcourt Brace Jovanovich, 1978.

Bernasconi, Robert, and Sybil Cook, eds. *Race and Racism in Continental Philosophy*. Bloomington, IN: Indiana University Press, 2003.

Besana, Bruno. "From Philosophy of Art to Philosophy with Art: On Some Strategies of Capture," *F. R. David* (Spring 2007): 127–39. Published in French as "Intercession, condition, brouillage: L'œuvre d'art à l'époque de l'ontologie de l'événement," in *Art comme esthétique, éthique et politique*. Paris: UNESCO, forthcoming.

Bhabha, Homi K. *The Location of Culture*. New York: Routledge, [1994] 2004.

Bhabha, Homi K. "The Other Question: Stereotype, Discrimination and the Discourse of Colonialism." In *The Location of Culture*, 94–120. New York: Routledge, [1994] 2004.

Birch, Thomas H. "The Incarceration of Wildness: Wilderness Areas as Prisons." *Environmental Ethics* 12 (1990): 3–26.

Birnbacher, Dieter. "Landschaftsschutz und Artenschutz: Wie weit tragen utilitaristische Begründungen." In *Naturschutz–Ethik–Ökonomie: Theoretische Begründungen und praktische Konsequenzen*, edited by Hans G. Nutzinger, 49–71. Marburg: Metropolis, 1996.

Bordwell, David. "Slavoj Žižek: Say Anything." www.davidbordwell.net/essays/zizek.php (accessed June 2010).

Bosteels, Bruno. "Can Change Be Thought? A Dialogue with Alain Badiou." In *Alain Badiou: Philosophy and Its Conditions*, edited by Gabriel Riera, 237–61. Albany, NY: SUNY Press, 2005.

Bosteels, Bruno. "Post-Maoism: Badiou and Politics." *Positions: East Asia Cultures Critique* 13(3) (2005): 575–634.

Bourg, Dominique. *Les Scénarios de l'écologie*. Paris: Hachette, 1996.

Braidotti, Rosi. *Metamorphoses*. Cambridge: Polity, 2002.

Braidotti, Rosi. *Transpositions: On Nomadic Ethics*. Cambridge: Polity, 2006.

Brandom, Robert. *Making It Explicit*. Cambridge, MA: Harvard University Press, 1994.

Brandom, Robert. *Tales of the Mighty Dead: Historical Essays in the Metaphysics of Intentionality*. Cambridge, MA: Harvard University Press, 2002.

Brassier, Ray. *Nihil Unbound: Enlightenment and Extinction*. Basingstoke: Palgrave Macmillan, 2010.

Brown, Charles S., and Ted Toadvine, eds. *Eco-phenomenology: Back to the Earth Itself*. Albany, NY: SUNY Press, 2003.

Brüggemeier, F.-J., M. Cioc, and T. Keller, eds. *How Green were the Nazis? Nature, Environment, and Nation in the Third Reich*. Athens, OH: Ohio University Press, 2005.

Butler, Judith. "Against Proper Objects." *Differences: A Journal of Feminist Cultural Studies* 6(2–3) (Summer–Fall 1994): 1–27.

Butler, Judith. *Antigone's Claim: Kinship Between Life and Death*. New York: Columbia University Press, 2000.

Butler, Judith, with Gary A. Olson and Lynn Worsham. "Changing the Subject: Judith Butler's Politics of Radical Resignification." In *The Judith Butler Reader*, edited by Judith Butler and Sarah Salih, 325–56. Oxford: Blackwell, 2004.

Butler, Judith. *Gender Trouble*. New York: Routledge, 1993.

Butler, Judith. *Giving an Account of Oneself*. New York: Fordham University Press, 2005.

Butler, Judith. "Imitation and Gender Insubordination." In *The Lesbian and Gay Studies Reader*, edited by Henry Abelove, Michèle Aina Barale and David M. Halperin, 307–20. New York: Routledge, 1993.

Butler, Judith. "Performative Acts and Gender Constitution: An Essay in Phenomenology and Feminist Theory." In *Writing on the Body: Female Embodiment and Feminist Theory*, edited by Katie Conboy, Nadia Medina, and Sarah Stanbury, 401–17. New York: Columbia University Press, 1997.

Butler, Judith. "Performativity's Social Magic." In *Bourdieu: A Critical Reader*, edited by Richard Shusterman, 113–28. Oxford: Blackwell, 1999.

Butler, Judith. *Precarious Life: The Power of Mourning and Violence*. London: Verso, 2006.

Butler, Judith. *The Psychic Life of Power*. Stanford, CA: Stanford University Press, 1997.

Butler, Judith. "Reply from Judith Butler to Mills and Jenkins." *differences* 18(2) (2007): 180–95.

Butler, Judith. "Sex and Gender in Simone de Beauvoir's *Second Sex*." *Yale French Studies* 72, *Simone de Beauvoir: Witness to a Century* (1986): 35–49.

Butler, Judith. *Subjects of Desire: Hegelian Reflections in Twentieth-Century France*. New York: Columbia University Press, 1987.

Butler, Judith. *Undoing Gender*. New York: Routledge, 2004.

Butler, Judith. "Variations on Sex and Gender." In *The Judith Butler Reader*, edited by Judith Butler and Sarah Salih, 21–38. London: Blackwell, 2004.

Butler, Judith, and Gayle Rubin. "Sexual Traffic: Interview." In *Feminism Meets Queer Theory*, edited by Elizabeth Weed and Naomi Schor, 68–108. Bloomington, IN: Indiana University Press, 1997.

Butler, Judith, Ernesto Laclau, and Slavoj Žižek. *Contingency, Hegemony, Universality: Contemporary Dialogues on the Left*. London: Verso, 2000.

Cacciari, Massimo. *L'Arcipelago*. Milan: Adelphi, 1997.

Cacciari, Massimo. *Geo-politica dell'Europa*. Milan: Adelphi, 1994.

Chakrabarty, Dipesh. *Habitations of Modernity: Essays in the Wake of Subaltern Studies*. Chicago, IL: University of Chicago Press, 2002.

Chakrabarty, Dipesh. *Provincializing Europe*. Princeton, NJ: Princeton University Press, 2000.

Cheney, Jim. "Nature/Theory/Difference: Ecofeminism and the Reconstruction of Environmental Ethics." In *Ecological Feminist Philosophies*, edited by Karen J. Warren, 158–78. Bloomington, IN: Indiana University Press, 1996.

Cheney, Jim. "Postmodern Environmental Ethics: Ethics as Bioregional Narrative." In *Postmodern Environmental Philosophies*, edited by Max Oelschlaeger, 23–42. Albany, NY: SUNY Press, 1995.

Cixous, Hélène. "My Algeriance, in Other Words, to Depart not to Arrive from Algeria." *Tri-Quarterly* 100 (Fall 1997): 259–79. Originally published as "Mon Algériance," *Les Inrockuptibles* 115 (August 20, 1997): 70–74.

Clifford, James. *The Predicament of Culture: Twentieth-Century Ethnography, Literature, and Art*. Cambridge, MA: Harvard University Press, 1988.

Cohn-Bendit, Daniel. "Transit Discussion." *Newsletter of the Institute for Human Sciences* 50 (June–August 1995): 1–4.

Conley, Verena A. *Ecopolitics: The Environment in Poststructuralist Thought*. New York: Routledge, 1997.

Cornell, Drucilla. "The Ubuntu Project with Stellenbosch University" (2002), www.fehe.org/index.php?id=281 (accessed December 2009).

Cornu, Laurence, and Patrice Vermeren, eds. *La Philosophie déplacée: Autour de Jacques Rancière*. Paris: Horlieu Éditions, 2006.

Coronil, Fernando. "Beyond Occidentalism: Towards Postimperial Geohistorical Categories." *Cultural Anthropology* 11 (1996): 51–87.

Coronil, Fernando. "Latin American Postcolonial Studies and Global Decolonization." In *The Cambridge Companion to Postcolonial Literary Studies*, edited by Neil Lazarus, 221–40. Cambridge: Cambridge University Press, 2004.

Danto, Arthur C. *After the End of Art: Contemporary Art and the Pale of History*. Princeton, NJ: Princeton University Press.

Danto, Arthur C. *Beyond the Brillo Box: The Visual Arts in Post-Historical Perspective*. New York: Farrar, Straus & Giroux, 1992.

Darier, Éric. "Foucault and the Environment: An Introduction." In *Discourses of the Environment*, edited by Éric Darier, 1–33. Oxford: Blackwell, 1999.

Davidson, Donald. "A Coherence Theory of Truth and Knowledge." In *Subjective, Intersubjective, Objective*, 137–57.

Davidson, Donald. "The Emergence of Thought." In *Subjective, Intersubjective, Objective*, 123–34.

Davidson, Donald. "Epistemology Externalized." In *Subjective, Intersubjective, Objective*, 193–204.

Davidson, Donald. "Gadamer and Plato's *Philebus*." In *The Philosophy of Hans-Georg Gadamer*, edited by Lewis Edwin Hahn, 421–32. Chicago, IL: Open Court, 1997.

Davidson, Donald. *Inquiries into Truth and Interpretation*. Oxford: Clarendon Press, 1984.

Davidson, Donald. "Radical Interpretation." In *Inquires into Truth and Interpretation*, 125–39.

Davidson, Donald. "The Second Person." In *Subjective, Intersubjective, Objective*, 107–21.

Davidson, Donald. *Subjective, Intersubjective, Objective*. Oxford: Oxford University Press, 2001.

Davidson, Donald. "Three Varieties of Knowledge." In *Subjective, Intersubjective, Objective*, 205–20.

Debord, Guy. *The Society of the Spectacle*. Translated by Donald Nicholson-Smith. Cambridge: Zone Books, 1994.

Deleuze, Gilles. *Cinema I: The Movement-Image*. Translated by Hugh Tomlinson and Barbara Habberjam. Minneapolis, MN: University of Minnesota Press, 1986. Published in French as *Cinéma I: L'Image-mouvement*. Paris: Éditions de Minuit, 1983.

Deleuze, Gilles. *Cinema II: The Time-Image*. Translated by Hugh Tomlinson and Robert Galeta. Minneapolis, MN: University of Minnesota Press, 1989. Published in French as *Cinéma II: L'Image-temps*. Paris: Éditions de Minuit, 1985.

Deleuze, Gilles. *Cinéma*, 6 CDs. Paris: Gallimard, 2006.

Deleuze, Gilles. *Expressionism in Philosophy: Spinoza*. Translated by Martin Joughin. New York: Zone Books, 1990. Published in French as *Spinoza et le problème de l'expression*. Paris: Éditions de Minuit, 1968.

Deleuze, Gilles. "Intellectuals and Power." Translated by Donald F. Bouchard and Sherry Simon. In *Language, Counter-memory, Practice*, edited by Donald F. Bouchard, 205–17. Ithaca, NY: Cornell University Press, 1973. Published in French as "Les Intellectuels et le pouvoir: Entretien Michel Foucault–Gilles Deleuze," *L'Arc* 49 (1972): 3–10.

Deleuze, Gilles. "What is a *dispositif?*" In *Michel Foucault, Philosopher*, translated by T. J. Armstrong, 159–68. New York: Routledge, 1991.

Deleuze, Gilles, and Félix Guattari. "1227: Treatise on Nomadology – The War Machine." In *A Thousand Plateaus*, translated by Brian Massumi, 351–423. Minneapolis, MN: University of Minnesota Press, 1980.

Deleuze, Gilles, and Félix Guattari. *Anti-Oedipus: Capitalism and Schizophrenia*. Translated by Mark Seem, Robert Hurley, and Helen R. Lane. New York: Viking Press, 1977. Originally published as *L'Anti-Oedipe: Capitalisme et schizophrénie I*. Paris: Éditions de Minuit, 1972.

Deleuze, Gilles, and Félix Guattari. *A Thousand Plateaus: Capitalism and Schizophrenia*. Translated by Brian Massumi. Minneapolis, MN: University of Minnesota Press, 1987. Originally published as *Mille plateaux: Capitalisme et schizophrénie II*. Paris: Éditions de Minuit, 1980.

Deleuze, Gilles, and Félix Guattari. *What is Philosophy?* Translated by Hugh Tomlinson and Graham Burchell. New York: Columbia University Press, 1994. Originally published as *Qu'est-ce que la philosophie?* Paris: Éditions de Minuit, 1991.

Depew, David J., and Bruce H. Weber. *Darwinism Evolving: Systems Dynamics and the Genealogy of Natural Selection*. Cambridge, MA: MIT Press, 1995.

Derrida, Jacques. *On Cosmopolitanism and Forgiveness*. Translated by Mark Dooley and Michael Hughes. New York: Routledge, 2001. Originally published as *Cosmopolites de tous les pays, encore un effort!* Paris: Éditions Galilée, 1997.

Derrida, Jacques. *On Touching – Jean-Luc Nancy*. Translated by Christine Irizarry. Stanford, CA: Stanford University Press, 2005. Originally published as *Le Toucher, Jean-Luc Nancy*. Paris: Éditions Galilée, 2000.

Derrida, Jacques. *The Other Heading: Reflections on Today's Europe*. Translated by Pascale-Anne Brault and Michael Naas. Bloomington, IN: Indiana University Press, 2002. Originally published as *L'Autre cap*. Paris: Éditions de Minuit, 1991.

Derrida, Jacques. *Rogues: Two Essays on Reason*. Translated by Pascale-Anne Brault and Michael Naas. Stanford, CA: Stanford University Press, 2004.

Droit, Roger-Pol. *Michel Foucault, entretiens*. Paris: Éditions Odile Jacob, 2004.

Duclos, Denis. *Les Industriels et les risques pour l'environnement*. Paris: L'Harmattan, 1991.

Dumont, René. *Utopia or Else …*. Translated by Vivienne Menkes. New York: Universe, 1975. Originally published as *L'Utopie ou la mort!* Paris: Éditions du Seuil, 1973.

Dussel, Enrique. "Beyond Eurocentrism: The World-System and the Limits of Modernity." In *The Cultures of Globalization*, edited by Fredric Jameson and Masao Miyoshi, 3–31. Durham, NC: Duke University Press, 1998.

Dussel, Enrique. *The Invention of the Americas: Eclipse of "the Other" and the Myth of Modernity*. Translated by Michael D. Barber. New York: Continuum, 1995.

Dussel, Enrique. *Philosophy of Liberation*. Translated by Aquilina Martinez and Christine Morkovsky. Maryknoll, NY: Orbis Books, [1975] 1985.

Dussel, Enrique. *The Underside of Modernity: Apel, Ricoeur, Rorty, Taylor and the Philosophy of Liberation*. Edited and translated by Eduardo Mendieta. Atlantic Highlands, NJ: Humanities Press, 1996.

Ferry, Luc. *The New Ecological Order*. Translated by Carol Volk. Chicago, IL: University of Chicago Press, 1995. Originally published as *Le Nouvel ordre écologique: L'Arbre, l'animal et l'homme*. Paris: B. Grasset, 1992.

Focillon, Henri. *Vie des formes*. Paris: Presses Universitaires de France, 1943.

Foltz, Bruce V. *Inhabiting the Earth: Heidegger, Environmental Ethics, and the Metaphysics of Nature*. Atlantic Highlands, NJ: Humanities Press, 1995.

Foucault, Michel. "The Birth of Social Medicine." In *The Essential Foucault*, edited by Paul Rabinow and Nikolas Rose, 319–37. New York: New Press, 2003. Originally published as "La Naissance de la médecine sociale," in *Dits et écrits II*, 207–28, #196. Paris: Gallimard: 2001.

Foucault, Michel. "Crise de la médecine ou crise de l'antimédecine?" In *Dits et écrits II*, 40–58, #170. Paris: Gallimard: 2001.

Foucault, Michel. *The History of Sexuality, Vol. 1*. Translated by Robert Hurley. New York: Vintage, 1978.

Foucault, Michel. *The Order of Things*. New York: Pantheon Books, 1971. Originally published as *Les Mots et les choses*. Paris: Gallimard, 1966.

Foucault, Michel. "The Politics of Health in the Eighteenth Century." Translated by Colin Gordon. In *The Essential Foucault*, edited by Paul Rabinow and Nikolas Rose, 338–50. New York: New

Press, 2003. Originally published as "La Politique de la santé au XVIIIe Siècle," in *Dits et écrits II*, 13–27, #168. Paris: Gallimard: 2001. A revised version of this text can be found in *Dits et écrits II*, 725–42, #257.

Freud, Sigmund. "Fetishism." In *The Standard Edition of the Complete Works of Sigmund Freud, vol. XXI*, edited and translated by James Strachey. London: Hogarth Press, 1968.

Freud, Sigmund. "Splitting of the Ego in the Process of Defense." In *The Standard Edition of the Complete Works of Sigmund Freud, vol. XXIII*, edited and translated by James Strachey. London: Hogarth Press, 1968.

Gilroy, Paul. *After Empire*. London: Routledge, 2004. Published in the US as *Postcolonial Melancholia*. New York: Columbia University Press, 2006.

Gilroy, Paul. *Against Race*. Cambridge, MA: Harvard University Press, 2000.

Gilroy, Paul. *Ain't no Black in the Union Jack*. London: Hutchinson, 1987.

Gilroy, Paul. *The Black Atlantic: Modernity and Double Consciousness*. London: Verso, 1993.

Glazebrook, Trish. "Heidegger and Ecofeminism." In *Feminist Interpretations of Martin Heidegger*, edited by N. J. Holland and P. Huntington, 221–51. University Park, PA: Pennsylvania State University Press, 2001.

Glazebrook, Trish. *Heidegger's Philosophy of Science*. New York: Fordham University Press, 2000.

Glissant, Edouard. *Poetics of Relation*. Translated by Betsy Wing. Ann Arbor, MI: University of Michigan Press, 1997. Originally published as *Poétique de la Relation* (Paris: Gallimard, 1990).

Gosseries, Axel. "L'Éthique environnementale aujourd'hui." *Revue philosophique de Louvain* 96 (1998): 395–426.

Gracia, Jorge J. E. "Ethnic Labels and Philosophy: The Case of Latin American Philosophy." *Philosophy Today* 43 (1999): 42–9.

Gracia, Jorge J. E. *Philosophy and Its History: Issues in Philosophical Historiography*. Albany, NY: SUNY Press, 1992.

Grosfoguel, Ramón, Nelson Maldonado-Torres, and José David Saldíva, eds. *Latin@s in the World-System: Decolonization Struggles in the 21st Century US Empire*. Boulder, CO: Paradigm Publishers, 2005.

Guattari, Félix. *Cartographies schizoanalytiques*. Paris: Éditions Galilée, 1989.

Guattari, Félix. *Chaosmosis: An Ethico-Aesthetic Paradigm*. Translated by Paul Bains and Julian Pefanis. Bloomington, IN: Indiana University Press, 1995. Originally published as *Chaosmose*. Paris: Éditions Galilée, 1992.

Guattari, Félix. *L'Inconscient machinique: Essais de schizo-analyse*. Fontenay-sous-Bois: Recherches, 1979.

Guattari, Félix. *Psychanalyse et tranversalité: Essais d'analyse institutionelle*. Paris: Maspero, 1972.

Guattari, Félix. *La Révolution moleculaire*. Fontenay-sous-Bois: Recherches, 1977.

Guattari, Félix. *The Three Ecologies*. Translated by Ian Pindar and Paul Sutton. London: Athlone, 2000. Originally published as *Les Trois écologies*. Paris: Éditions Galilée, 1989.

Habermas, Jürgen. *The Philosophical Discourse of Modernity: Twelve Lectures*. Translated by Frederick Lawrence. Cambridge, MA: MIT Press, 1987.

Habermas, Jürgen. *The Postnational Constellation*. Cambridge: Polity, 2001.

Habermas, Jürgen. "Technology and Science as 'Ideology.'" In *Toward a Rational Society*, translated by Jeremy Shapiro, 81–122. Boston, MA: Beacon Press, 1970. Originally published as *Technik und Wissenschaft als "Ideologie"*. Frankfurt: Suhrkamp, 1968.

Hahn, Lewis Edwin, ed. *The Philosophy of Hans-Georg Gadamer*. Chicago, IL: Open Court, 1997.

Hall, Stuart. "Cultural Identity and Diaspora." In *Identity: Community, Culture, Difference*, edited by J. Rutherford, 222–37. London: Lawrence & Wishart, 1990.

Hall, Stuart. "Minimal Selves." In *Identity – The Real Me: Postmodernism and the Question of Identity*, edited by Homi K. Bhabha, 44–6. London: ICA Documents, 1987.

Hallward, P., ed. *Think Again: Alain Badiou and the Future of Philosophy*. London: Continuum, 2004.

Halsey, Mark. *Deleuze and Environmental Damage: Violence of the Text*. Burlington, VT: Ashgate, 2006.

Haraway, Donna. "'Gender' for a Marxist Dictionary: The Sexual Politics of a Word." In her *Simians, Cyborgs and Women: Feminism and the Reinvention of Nature*, 127–48. New York: Routledge, 1991.

Haraway, Donna. *Modest_Witness@Second_Millennium. FemaleMan©_Meets_Oncomouse™: Feminism and Technoscience*. New York: Routledge, 1997.

Harding, Sandra. *The Science Question in Feminism*. Ithaca, NY: Cornell University Press, 1986.

Hardt, Michael, and Antonio Negri. *Empire*. Cambridge, MA: Harvard University Press, 2000.

Hardt, Michael, and Antonio Negri. *Multitude: War and Democracy in the Age of Empire*. London: Penguin, 2004.

Hayden, Patrick. "Gilles Deleuze and Naturalism: A Convergence with Ecological Theory and Politics." *Environmental Ethics* 19 (1997): 185–204.

Hayden, Patrick. *Multiplicity and Becoming: The Pluralist Empiricism of Gilles Deleuze*. New York: Lang, 1998.

Heidegger, Martin. "The Age of the World Picture." In *The Question Concerning Technology and Other Essays*, translated by William Lovitt, 115–54. New York: Harper & Row, 1977. Originally published as "Die Zeit des Weltbildes," in *Holzwege*, 73–110. Frankfurt: Klostermann, 1950.

Heidegger, Martin. "The Origin of the Work of Art." In *Poetry, Language, Thought*, translated by Albert Hofstadter, 17–87. New York: Harper & Row, 1971. Originally published as "Der Ursprung des Kunstwerkes," in *Holzwege*, 1–72. Frankfurt: Klostermann, 1950.

Heinich, Nathalie. *L'Elite artiste: Excellence et singularité en régime démocratique*. Paris: Gallimard, 2005.

Heinich, Nathalie. *Être artiste*. Paris: Klincksieck, 1997.

Herzogenrath, Bernd, ed. *Deleuze/Guattari and Ecology*. New York: Palgrave Macmillan, 2009.

Hill Collins, Patricia. *Black Feminist Thought: Knowledge, Consciousness and the Politics of Empowerment*. New York: Routledge, 1991.

Husserl, Edmund. *The Crisis of European Sciences and Transcendental Phenomenology*. Evanston, IL: Northwestern University Press, 1970.

Hutchings, Kimberly. *Hegel and Feminist Philosophy*. Cambridge: Polity, 2003.

Hylton, Peter. *Russell, Idealism, and the Emergence of Analytic Philosophy*. Oxford: Oxford University Press, 1990.

Ingles, David, and John Bone. "Boundary Maintenance, Border Crossing, and the Nature/Culture Divide." *European Journal of Social Theory* 9(2) (2006): 272–87.

James, Ian. *The New French Philosophy*. Cambridge: Polity, 2012.

Janicaud, Dominique. *Phenomenology "Wide Open": After the French Debate*. Translated by Charles N. Cabral. New York: Fordham University Press, 2005. Originally published as *La Phénoménologie éclatée*. Paris: Éditions de l'Éclat, 1998.

Janicaud, Dominique. *The Theological Turn of French Phenomenology*. Translated by Bernard G. Prusak. In Dominique Janicaud *et al. Phenomenology and the "Theological Turn": The French Debate*, 16–103. New York: Fordham University Press, 2000. Originally published as *Le Tournant théologique de la phénoménologie française*. Paris: Éditions de l'Éclat, 1991.

Jenkins, Fiona. "Toward a Nonviolent Ethics: Response to Catherine Mills." *differences* 18(2) (2007): 157–79.

Jonas, Hans. *The Imperative of Responsibility: In Search of an Ethics for the Technological Age*. Translated by Hans Jonas with David Herr. Chicago, IL: University of Chicago Press, 1984. Originally published as *Das Prinzip Verantwortung: Versuch einer Ethik für die technologische Zivilisation*. Frankfurt: Insel, 1979.

Kheel, Marti. *Nature Ethics: An Ecofeminist Perspective*. Lanham, MD: Rowman & Littlefield, 2008.

Krebs, Angelika. *Ethics of Nature: A Map*. Berlin: de Gruyter, 1999. Expanded translation of "Ökologische Ethik I: Grundlagen und Grundbegriffe," in *Angewandte Ethik: Die Bereichsethiken und ihre theoretische Fundierung*, edited by Julian Nida-Rümelin, 346–85. Stuttgart: Alfred Kröner, 1996.

Kripke, Saul. *Wittgenstein on Rules and Private Language*. Cambridge, MA: Harvard University Press, 1982.

Kristeva, Julia. *Strangers to Ourselves*. Translated by Leon S. Roudiez. New York: Columbia University Press, 1991. Originally published as *Etrangers à nous-mêmes*. Paris: Fayard, 1988.

Kuhn, Thomas. *The Structure of Scientific Revolutions*. Chicago, IL: University of Chicago Press, 1970.

Lacan, Jacques. *The Seminar of Jacques Lacan. Book VII: The Ethics of Psychoanalysis*. Translated by Dennis Porter. New York: Norton, 1986.

Laclau, Ernesto. *Emancipation(s)*. London: Verso, 1996.

Laclau, Ernesto. "An Ethics of Militant Engagement." In *Think Again: Alain Badiou and the Future of Philosophy*, edited by Peter Hallward, 120–37. London: Continuum, 2004.

Laclau, Ernesto. "New Reflections on the Revolution of Our Time." In *New Reflections on the Revolution of Our Time*, 3–85. London: Verso, 1990

Laclau, Ernesto. *On Populist Reason*. London: Verso, 2007.

Laclau, Ernesto. "Why Do Empty Signifiers Matter to Politics?" In *Emancipation(s)*, 36–46. London: Verso, 1996.

Laclau, Ernesto, and Chantal Mouffe. *Hegemony and Socialist Strategy*. London: Verso, 1985.

Larrère, Catherine. *Les Philosophies de l'environnement*. Paris: Presses Universitaires de France, 1997.

Larrère, Catherine, and Raphaël Larrère. *Du bon usage de la nature: Pour une philosophie de l'environnement*. Paris: Aubier, 1997.

Laruelle, François. *Le Déclin de l'écriture* [The decline of writing]. Paris: Aubier-Flammarion, 1977.

Laruelle, François. *En tant qu'un*. Paris: Aubier, 1991.

Laruelle, François. *Philosophie et non-philosophie*. Liège: Pierre Mardaga, 1989.

Laruelle, François. *Philosophie non-standard*. Paris: Éditions Kimé, 2010.

Laruelle, François. *Principles of Non-Philosophy*. Translated by Nicola Rubczak and Anthony Paul Smith. New York: Bloomsbury Academic, 2013. Originally published as *Principes de la non-philosophie*. Paris: Presses Universitaires de France, 1996.

Laruelle, François. *Philosophies of Difference*. Translated by Rocco Gangle. London: Continuum, 2011. Originally published as *Les Philosophies de la différence: Introduction critique*. Paris: Presses Universitaires de France, 1986.

Latour, Bruno. *Aramis, or the Love of Technology*. Translated by Catherine Porter. Cambridge, MA: Harvard University Press, 1966.

Latour, Bruno. "D'où viennent les microbes?" *Les Cahiers de science et vie* 4 (August 1991): 36–62.

Latour, Bruno. *Pandora's Hope: Essays on the Reality of Science Studies*. Cambridge, MA: Harvard University Press, 1999.

Latour, Bruno. *The Pasteurization of France*. Translated by Alan Sheridan and John Law. Cambridge, MA: Harvard University Press, 1988.

Latour, Bruno. *Politics of Nature: How to Bring the Sciences into Democracy*. Translated by Catherine Porter. Cambridge, MA Harvard University Press, 2004. Originally published as *Politiques de la nature: Comment faire entrer les sciences en démocratie*. Paris: Éditions la Découverte, 1999.

Latour, Bruno. *Reassembling the Social: An Introduction to Actor-Network-Theory*. Oxford: Oxford University Press, 2005.

Latour, Bruno. *We Have Never Been Modern*. Translated by Catherine Porter. Cambridge, MA:

Harvard University Press, 1993. Originally published as *Nous n'avons jamais été modernes: Essais d'anthropologie symmétrique*. Paris: La Découverte, 1991.

Latour, Bruno, and Stephen Woolgar. *Laboratory Life: The Social Construction of Scientific Facts*. Beverly Hills, CA: Sage, 1979.

Lefort, Claude. *Democracy and Political Theory*. Translated by David Macey. Minneapolis, MN: University of Minnesota Press, 1988.

Lefort, Claude. "The Logic of Totalitarianism." Translated by Alan Sheridan. In *The Political Forms of Modern Society*, edited by John B. Thompson, 273–91. Cambridge, MA: MIT Press, 1986.

Lefort, Claude. "Politics and Human Rights." Translated by Alan Sheridan. In *The Political Forms of Modern Society*, edited by John B. Thompson, 239–72. Cambridge, MA: MIT Press, 1986.

Leist, Anton. "Ökologische Ethik II: Gerechtigkeit, Ökonomie, Politik." In *Angewandte Ethik: Die Bereichsethiken und ihre theoretische Fundierung*, edited by Julian Nida-Rümelin, 386–456. Stuttgart: Alfred Kröner, 1996.

Leopold, Aldo. *A Sand County Almanac*. New York: Oxford University Press, 1949.

Lloyd, Moya. *Judith Butler: From Norms to Politics*. Cambridge: Polity, 2006.

Malabou, Catherine. *The Future of Hegel: Plasticity, Temporality, and Dialectic*. Translated by Lisabeth During. London: Routledge, 2005. Originally published as *L'Avenir de Hegel: Plasticité, temporalité, dialectique*. Paris: Vrin, 1996.

Malabou, Catherine. *The New Wounded: From Neurosis to Brain Damage*. Translated by Steven Miller. New York: Fordham University Press, 2012. Originally published as *Les Nouveaux blessés: De Freud à la neurologie, penser les traumatismes contemporains*. Paris: Bayard, 2007.

Malabou, Catherine. *What Should We Do with Our Brain?* Translated by Sebastian Rand. New York: Fordham University Press, 2008. Originally published as *Que faire de notre cerveau?* Paris: Bayard, 2004.

Maldonado-Torres, Nelson. "Césaire's Gift and the Decolonial Turn." *Radical Philosophy Review* 9(2) (2006): 111–37.

Marcuse, Herbert. *One Dimensional Man: Studies in the Ideology of Advanced Industrial Society*. Boston, MA: Beacon Press, 1964.

Marion, Jean-Luc. *Being Given: Towards a Phenomenology of Givenness*. Translated by Jeffrey L. Kosky. Stanford, CA: Stanford University Press, 2002. Originally published as *Étant donné: essai d'une phénoménologie de la donation*. Paris: Presses Universitaires de France, 1997.

Marion, Jean-Luc. *Reduction and Givenness: Investigations of Husserl, Heidegger and Phenomenology*. Translated by Thomas A. Carlson. Evanston, IL: Northwestern University Press, 1998. Originally published as *Réduction et donation*. Paris: Presses Universitaires de France, 1989.

Martin, D. Bruce. "Mimetic Moments: Adorno and Ecofeminism." In *Feminist Interpretations of Theodor Adorno*, edited by Renée Heberle, 141–72. University Park, PA: Pennsylvania State University Press, 2006.

Marx, Karl. *The Marx–Engels Reader*. New York: Norton, 1978.

Maskit, Jonathan. "Something Wild? Deleuze and Guattari and the Impossibility of Wilderness." *Philosophy & Geography* 3 (1998): 265–83. Revised as "Something Wild? Deleuze and Guattari, Wilderness, and Purity," in *The Wilderness Debate Rages On: Continuing the Great New Wilderness Debate*, edited by J. Baird Callicott and Michael Nelson, 461–84. Athens, GA: University of Georgia Press, 2008.

Maskit, Jonathan. "Subjectivity, Desire, and the Problem of Consumption." In *Deleuze/Guattari and Ecology*, edited by Bernd Herzogenrath, 129–44. New York: Palgrave Macmillan, 2009.

May, Todd. *The Political Philosophy of Poststructuralist Anarchism*. University Park, PA: Penn State University Press, 1994.

McCumber, John. *Time in the Ditch: American Philosophy and the McCarthy Era*. Evanston, IL: Northwestern University Press, 2001.

McDowell, John. *Mind and World*. Cambridge, MA: Harvard University Press, 1994.

McDowell, John. "Wittgenstein on Following a Rule." *Synthese* 58 (1984): 325–63.

Meillassoux, Quentin. *After Finitude: An Essay on the Necessity of Contingency*. Translated by Ray Brassier. London: Continuum, 2010. Originally published as *Après la finitude*. Paris: Éditions du Seuil, 2006.

Mellor, Mary. *Feminism & Ecology*. New York: New York University Press, 1997.

Mendieta, Eduardo. "Is There Latin-American Philosophy?" *Philosophy Today* 43 (1999): 50–61.

Mendieta, Eduardo, ed. *Latin American Philosophy: Currents, Issues, Debates*. Bloomington, IN: Indiana University Press, 2002.

Mignolo, Walter D. *The Darker Side of the Renaissance: Literacy, Territoriality and Colonization*. Ann Arbor, MI: University of Michigan Press, 1995.

Mignolo, Walter D. *Local Histories/Global Designs: Coloniality, Subaltern Knowledges and Border Thinking*. Princeton, NJ: Princeton University Press, 1999.

Mignolo, Walter D. "Philosophy and the Colonial Difference." *Philosophy Today* 43 (1999): 36–41.

Mignolo, Walter D. "Posoccidentalismo: el argumento desde América Latina." In *Teorías sin disciplina. Latinoamericanismo, poscolonialidad y globalización en debate*, edited by Santiago Castro Gómez and Eduardo Mendieta, 31–58. Mexico: Miguel Angel Porrua, 1998.

Mills, Catherine. "Normative Violence, Vulnerability, and Responsibility." *differences* 18(2) (2007): 133–56.

Mills, Patricia Jagentowicz. "Feminism and Ecology." In *Ecological Feminist Philosophies*, edited by Karen J. Warren, 211–27. Bloomington, IN: Indiana University Press, 1996.

Morin, Edgar. *The Nature of Nature*. Translated by J. L. Roland Bélanger. New York: Peter Lang, 1992. Originally published as *La Méthode I: La Nature de la nature*. Paris: Éditions du Seuil, 1977.

Morin, Edgar. *Le Paradigme perdu: La Nature humaine*. Paris: Éditions du Seuil, 1973.

Moscovici, Serge. *Essai sur l'histoire humaine de la nature*. Paris: Flammarion, 1968.

Mouffe, Chantal, ed. *The Challenge of Carl Schmitt*. London: Verso, 1999.

Mouffe, Chantal. *The Democratic Paradox*. London: Verso, 2000.

Mouffe, Chantal. *On the Political*. New York: Routledge, 2005.

Mullarkey, John. *Post-Continental Philosophy: An Outline*. London: Continuum, 2006.

Nancy, Jean-Luc. *Being Singular Plural*. Translated by Anne E. O'Byrne and Robert D. Richardson. Stanford, CA: Stanford University Press, 2000. Originally published as *Être singulier pluriel*. Paris: Éditions Galilée, 1996.

Nancy, Jean-Luc. *Ego sum*. Paris: Flammarion, 1979.

Nancy, Jean-Luc. *The Sense of the World*. Translated by Jeffrey S. Librett. Minneapolis, MN: University of Minnesota Press, 1997. Originally published as *Le Sens du monde*. Paris: Éditions Galilée, 1993.

Nelson, Michael, and J. Baird Callicott, eds. *The Great New Wilderness Debates*. Athens, GA: University of Georgia Press, 1998.

Neumaier, Otto, Gerhard Schurz, and Alfons Süssbauer, eds. *Angewandte Ethik im Spannungsfeld von Ökologie und Ökonomie*. Sankt Augustin: Academia, 1994.

Newman, Saul. *From Bakunin to Lacan: Anti-Authoritarianism and the Dislocation of Power*. Lanham, MD: Lexington Books, 2001.

Nietzsche, Friedrich. *Beyond Good and Evil*. Cambridge: Cambridge University Press, 2002.

Nussbaum, Martha. *Cultivating Humanity· A Classical Defense of Reform in Liberal Education*. Cambridge, MA: Harvard University Press, 1999.

Olkowski, Dorothea. *The Universal (In the Realm of the Sensible)*. Edinburgh: Edinburgh University Press, 2007.

Pinto, Louis. *Les Philosophes entre le lycée et l'avant-garde*. Paris: L'Harmattan, 1987.

Plumwood, Val. *Feminism and the Mastery of Nature*. New York: Routledge, 1993.

Polanyi, Michael. "The Republic of Science: Its Political and Economic Theory." *Minerva: A Review of Science, Learning and Policy* 1(1) (1962): 54–73.

Prashad, Vijay. *The Darker Nations: A People's History of the Third World*. New York: New Press, 2007.

Preuss, Ulrich K. "Problems of a Concept of European Citizenship." *European Law Journal* 1(3) (1995): 267–81.

Preuss, Ulrich K. "Two Challenges to European Citizenship." *Political Studies* 44 (1996): 534–52.

Quijano, Anibal. "Colonialidad del poder, cultura y conocimiento en America Latina." *Anuario Mariateguiano* 9(9) (1997): 113–21.

Quijano, Anibal. "Coloniality of Power, Eurocentrism and Latin America." *Nepantla: Views from the South* 1(3) (2000): 533–80.

Quine, Willard Van Orman. *From a Logical Point of View*. Cambridge, MA: Harvard University Press, 1953.

Quine, Willard Van Orman. *Ontological Relativity and Other Essays*. New York: Columbia University Press, 1969.

Quine, Willard Van Orman. "Two Dogmas of Empiricism." In *From a Logical Point of View*, 20–46. Cambridge, MA: Harvard University Press, 1953.

Quine, Willard Van Orman. *Word and Object*. Cambridge, MA: MIT Press, 1960.

Ramond, Charles, ed. *Alain Badiou: Penser le multiple*. Paris: L'Harmattan, 2002.

Rancière, Jacques. "Aesthetics, Inaesthetics, Anti-Aesthetics." Translated by Ray Brassier. In *Think Again: Alain Badiou and the Future of Philosophy*, edited by Peter Hallward, 218–31. London: Continuum, 2004. Published in French as "Esthétique, inesthétique, anti-esthétique." In *Alain Badiou: Penser le multiple*, edited by Charles Ramond, 477–96. Paris: L'Harmattan, 2002.

Rancière, Jacques. *Althusser's Lesson*. Translated by Emiliano Battista. (London: Continuum, 2011. Originally published as *La Leçon d'Althusser*. Paris: Éditions Gallimard, 1974.

Rancière, Jacques. *Disagreement: Politics and Philosophy*. Translated by Julie Rose. Minneapolis, MN: University of Minnesota Press, 1999. Originally published as *La Mésentente: politique et philosophie*. Paris: Éditions Galilée, 1995.

Rancière, Jacques. "Les Écarts du cinéma." *Trafic* 50 (Summer 2004): 159–66.

Rancière, Jacques. *La Fable cinématographique*. Paris: Éditions du Seuil, 2001.

Rancière, Jacques. *Hatred of Democracy*. Translated by Steve Corcoran. London: Verso, 2006.

Rancière, Jacques. "Literature, Politics, Aesthetics." *SubStance* 29(2) (2000): 3–24.

Rancière, Jacques. "The Method of Equality." In *Jacques Rancière: History, Politics, Aesthetics*, edited by Gabriel Rockhill and Phil Watts. Durham, NC: Duke University Press, 2009.

Rancière, Jacques. *La Parole muette*. Paris: Hachette Littératures, 1998.

Rancière, Jacques. *The Politics of Aesthetics*. Translated by Gabriel Rockhill. London: Continuum, 2004. Originally published as *La Partage du sensible: esthétique et politique*. Paris: La Fabrique, 2000.

Rancière, Jacques. *Politique de la littérature*. Paris: Éditions Galilée, 2007.

Rancière, Jacques. *On the Shores of Politics*. Translated by Liz Heron. London: Verso, 1995.

Rancière, Jacques. "Who is the Subject of the Rights of Man?" *The South Atlantic Quarterly* 103(2/3) (Spring/Summer 2004): 297–310.

Robinet, André. *Le Langage à l'âge classique*. Paris: Éditions Klincksieck, 1978.

Rockhill, Gabriel. "Le Cinéma n'est jamais né." In *Le Milieu des appareils*, edited by Jean-Louis Déotte. Paris: L'Harmattan, forthcoming.

Rockhill, Gabriel. "Démocratie moderne et révolution esthétique." In *La Philosophie déplacée: Autour de Jacques Rancière*, edited by Laurence Cornu and Patrice Vermeren. Paris: Horlieu Éditions, 2006.

Rockhill, Gabriel, and Phil Watts, eds. *Jacques Rancière: History, Politics, Aesthetics*. Durham, NC: Duke University Press, 2009.

Rolston, Holmes, III. *Earth Ethics: Duties to and Values in the Natural World.* Philadelphia, PA: Temple University Press, 1988.

Rolston, Holmes, III. *Philosophy Gone Wild: Essays in Environmental Ethics.* Buffalo, NY: Prometheus Books, 1986.

Rorty, Richard. "The Historiography of Philosophy: Four Genres." In *Truth and Progress: Philosophical Papers, Vol. 3,* 247–73. Cambridge: Cambridge University Press, 1998.

Rorty, Richard. "Introduction". In Wilfrid Sellars, *Empiricism and the Philosophy of Mind,* 1–12. Cambridge, MA: Harvard University Press, 1997.

Rouse, Joseph. *Engaging Science: How to Understand Its Practices Philosophically.* Ithaca, NY: Cornell University Press, 1996.

Rubin, Gayle. "Thinking Sex." In *The Lesbian and Gay Studies Reader,* edited by Henry Abelove, Michèle Aina Barale, and David M. Halperin, 3–44. New York: Routledge, 1993.

Rubin, Gayle. "The Traffic in Women: Notes on the 'Political Economy' of Sex." In *Toward an Anthropology of Women,* edited by Rayna Reiter, 157–210. New York: Monthly Review Press, 1975.

Said, Edward W. *Covering Islam: How the Media and the Experts Determine How We See the Rest of the World.* New York: Pantheon Books, 1981.

Said, Edward W. *Culture and Imperialism.* New York: Knopf/Random House, 1993.

Said, Edward W. *Humanism and Democratic Criticism.* New York: Columbia University Press, 2003.

Said, Edward W. *Orientalism.* New York: Vintage, 1979.

Said, Edward W. *Power, Politics, and Culture: Interviews with Edward W. Said,* edited by Gauri Vishwanathan. New York: Pantheon Books, 2001.

Said, Edward W. *Reflections on Exile and Other Essays.* Cambridge, MA: Harvard University Press, 2000.

Said, Edward W. "Secular Interpretation, the Geographical Element, and the Methodology of Imperialism." In *After Colonialism: Imperial Histories and Postcolonial Displacements,* edited by Gyan Prakash, 21–38. Princeton, NJ: Princeton University Press, 1995.

Salleh, Ariel. *Ecofeminism as Politics: Nature, Marx and the Postmodern.* New York: Zed Books, 1997.

Schönherr-Mann, Hans-Martin. *Die Technik und die Schwäche: Ökologie nach Nietzsche, Heidegger und dem "schwachen" Denken.* Vienna: Passagen, 1989.

Schönherr-Mann, Hans-Martin. *Von der Schwierigkeit, Natur zu Verstehen: Entwurf einer negativen Ökologie.* Frankfurt: Fischer Taschenbuch, 1989.

Schrift, Alan D. "Judith Butler: Une Nouvelle Existentialiste?" *Philosophy Today* 45(1) (Spring 2001): 12–23.

Sellars, Wilfrid. *Empiricism and the Philosophy of Mind.* Cambridge, MA: Harvard University Press, 1997.

Serres, Michel. *The Natural Contract.* Translated by Elizabeth MacArthur and William Paulson. Ann Arbor, MI: University of Michigan Press, 1995. Originally published as *Le Contrat naturel.* Paris: Éditions François Bourin, 1990.

Soulié, Charles. "Le Destin d'une institution d'avant-garde: Histoire du département de philosophie de Paris VIII." *Histoire de l'éducation* 77 (January 1998): 47–69.

Spinelli, Altiero. *Diario europeo.* Bologna: Il Mulino, 1992.

Spivak, Gayatri C. "Can the Subaltern Speak?" In *Marxism and the Interpretation of Culture,* edited by Cary Nelson and Lawrence Grossberg, 271–313. Basingstoke: Macmillan, 1988.

Spivak, Gayatri C. *A Critique of Postcolonial Reason: Toward a History of the Vanishing Present.* Cambridge, MA: Harvard University Press, 1999.

Spivak, Gayatri C. *In Other Worlds: Essays in Cultural Politics.* London: Methuen, 1987.

Spivak, Gayatri C. *Outside in the Teaching Machine.* London: Routledge, 1993.

Spivak, Gayatri C. "Three Women's Texts and a Critique of Imperialism." *Critical Inquiry* 12(1) (Autumn 1985): 243–61.

Spivak, Gayatri C. "Time and Timing: Law and History." In *Chronotypes: The Construction of Time*, edited by John Bender and David E. Wellbery, 99–117. Stanford, CA: Stanford University Press, 1991.

Stengers, Isabelle. "Another Look: Relearning to Laugh." Translated by Penelope Deutscher. *Hypatia* 15(4) (Fall 2000): 41–50.

Stengers, Isabelle. *The Invention of Modern Science*. Translated by Daniel W. Smith. Minneapolis, MN: University of Minnesota Press, 2000.

Stengers, Isabelle. *Power and Invention, Situating Science*. Translated by Paul Bains. Minneapolis, MN: University of Minnesota Press, 1997.

Stengers, Isabelle, and Bernadette Bensaude-Vincent. *A History of Chemistry*. Cambridge, MA: Harvard University Press, 1996.

Stengers, Isabelle, and Leon Chertok. *A Critique of Psychoanalytic Reason: Hypnosis as a Scientific Problem from Lavoisier to Lacan*. Stanford, CA: Stanford University Press, 1992.

Stengers, Isabelle, and Ilya Prigogine. *Order Out of Chaos: Man's New Dialogue with Nature*. New York: Bantam Books, 1984.

Stengers, Isabelle, and Judith Schianger. *Les Concepts scientifiques: Invention et pouvoir*. Paris: Gallimard. 1987.

Stiegler, Bernard. *Technics and Time 1: The Fault of Epimetheus*. Translated by Richard Beardsworth and George Collins. Stanford: Stanford University Press, 1998. Originally published as *La Technique et le temps 1. La Faute d'Épiméthée*. Paris: Éditions Galilée, 1994.

Stiegler, Bernard. *Technics and Time 2. Disorientation*. Translated by Stephen Barker. Stanford: Stanford University Press, 2009. Originally published as *La Technique et le temps 2. La Désorientation*. Paris: Éditions Galiliée, 1996.

Stiegler, Bernard. *Technics and Time 3. Cinematic Time and the Question of Malaise*. Translated by Stephen Barker. Stanford: Stanford University Press, 2011. Originally published as *La Technique et le temps 3. Le Temps du cinéma et la question du mal-être*. Paris: Éditions Galilée, 2001

Stuhlmann-Laeisz, Rainer. "Ökologische Ethik." *Kriterion: Zeitschrift für Philosophie* 1 (1991): 2–7.

Vattimo, Gianni. *After Christianity*. Translated by Luca D'Isanto. New York: Columbia University Press.

Virilio, Paul. *Open Sky*. Translated by Julie Rose. London: Verso, 1997.

Virilio, Paul. *Pure War*. Translated by Sylvère Lotringer. New York: Semiotext(e), 1997.

Virno, Paolo. *A Grammar of the Multitude*. Translated by Isabella Bertoletti, James Cascaito, and Andrea Casson. New York: Semiotext(e), 2004.

Vogel, Steven. *Against Nature*. Albany, NY: SUNY Press, 1996.

Vogel, Steven. "Environmental Philosophy after the End of Nature." *Environmental Ethics* 24 (2002): 23–39.

Ward, Colin. *Anarchy in Action*. London: Freedom Press, 1982.

Westra, Laura. "Let It Be: Heidegger and Future Generations." *Environmental Ethics* 7 (1985): 341–50.

Whiteside, Kerry. *Divided Natures: French Contributions to Political Ecology*. Cambridge, MA: MIT Press, 2004.

Wittgenstein, Ludwig. *Philosophical Investigations*. Translated by G. E. M. Anscombe. Oxford: Blackwell, 1953.

Wittig, Monique. *The Straight Mind and Other Essays*. Boston, MA: Beacon Press, 1992.

Wolf, Jean-Claude. "Utilitaristische Ethik als Antwort auf die ökologische Krise." *Zeitschrift für philosophische Forschung* 44 (1990): 619–34.

Young, Robert. *Postcolonialism: An Historical Introduction*. Malden, MA: Blackwell, 2001.

Young, Robert. *White Mythologies. Writing History and the West*. New York: Routledge, 1990.

Zimmerman, Michael F. *Contesting Earth's Future: Radical Ecology and Postmodernity*. Berkeley, CA: University of California Press, 1994.

Zimmerman, Michael E. "Implications of Heidegger's Thought for Deep Ecology." *Modern Schoolman* 64 (1986): 19–43.

Zimmerman, Michael E. "Rethinking the Heidegger–Deep Ecology Relationship." *Environmental Ethics* 15 (1993): 195–224.

Zimmerman, Michael E. "What Can Continental Philosophy Contribute to Environmentalism?" In *Rethinking Nature: Essays in Environmental Philosophy*, edited by Bruce V. Foltz and Robert Frodeman, 207–30. Bloomington, IN: Indiana University Press, 2004.

Žižek, Slavoj. *Did Somebody Say Totalitarianism?* London: Verso, 2001.

Žižek, Slavoj. *The Plague of Fantasies*. London: Verso, 1997.

Žižek, Slavoj. *The Sublime Object of Ideology*. London: Verso, 1989.

Žižek, Slavoj. *The Ticklish Subject: The Absent Centre of Political Ontology*. London: Verso, 2000.

Žižek, Slavoj. *Welcome to the Desert of the Real: Five Essays on September 11 and Related Dates*. London: Verso, 2002.

Zourabichvili, François. *Deleuze: Une philosophie de l'événement*. Paris: Presses Universitaires de France, 1996.

INDEX

on materialism   210, 216
on mathematics as science of the real
    216–17, 219
on multiplicity   216–17
on politics and democracy   50, 54n, 55–7,
    66, 76, 78, 81
"The (Re)commencement of Dialectical
    Materialism"   75
and set theory   217
Theory of the Subject   77, 79
Bakunin, Mikhail   207
Balibar, Étienne   8, 32, 135–6, 135n, 146
Barthes, Roland   40
    Writing Degree Zero   40
Baudrillard, Jean   194–8, 200, 208
    Seduction   196
Bauman, Zygmunt   140–41
Beauvoir, Simone de   14–16, 19, 182
    The Second Sex   15
Beckett, Samuel   78
being   74
  and language   80
  and mathematics   71–3
belief   92, 94, 96–7, 99
Bellour, Raymond   31
Benhabib, Seyla   138
Benjamin, Walter   43, 66
Bergson, Henri   76, 117–18
Berlin Wall   1, 206
Bernasconi, Robert   129
Beuys, Joseph   44
    7000 Eichen   44
Bhabha, Homi   9, 150, 152, 163–5
    "The Other Question"   163–4
binaries   18, 20, 128, 134
biopolitics   63–6
biopower   63, 180–81
Birch, Thomas   180
black British subjectivity   144
black studies   3
Blanchot, Maurice   76
body   181
  and art   35–6
  and power   21
borders   51
Bosteels, Bruno   5, 7
botany   110
Bourdieu, Pierre   22, 45
    La Distinction   45

Bradley, F. H.   107
Braidotti, Rosi   8
Brandom, Robert   7, 11, 89, 90n, 94, 103–8
    Making It Explicit   103–4
Brassier, Ray   220
Bush, George   2
Butler, Judith   5, 15–29, 195, 201, 205
    "Against Proper Objects"   20
    Antigone's Claim   27
    Bodies that Matter   21
    Gender Trouble   19, 24–6, 28
    Giving an Account of Oneself   18
    Precarious Life   205
    The Psychic Life of Power   16–17
    Undoing Gender   18, 28
    "Variations on Sex and Gender"   19

Cabral, Amilcar   153
Cacciari, Massimo   132
Canguilhem, Georges   221
Cantor, Georg   71
capitalism   1–3, 201, 207
Carnap, Rudolf   vii
categories   179
causes   99–100
Césaire, Aimé   153, 155
Chakrabarty, Dipesh   153, 170–71
change   119
chaos   117
charity   95–6, 99
Chatterjee, Partha   153
Cheney, Jim   183
Christianity   132, 143
Christianization   168
citizenship   133–4, 145–6
    European   133, 136–8, 145–6
city   61
Cixous, Hélène   132
class struggle   52
climate   188–9
Cohen, Paul   74
Cohn-Bendit, Daniel   130
Cold War   1–2, 131
Collins, Patricia Hill   143
colonialism   128, 142, 144–5, 149–71
commitment   78
communication   2, 194–5
  speed of   197–8
communism   56, 190

history of 149
role of 33
and science 117, 121
photography 43
physics 119
Picasso, Pablo 38
Pizarro, Francisco 167
Platonism 33–4, 42, 44
  naturalized 100–102
poiesis 122
poetry 32–3, 33–6, 84, 84–5n, 175, 180
police 53
political engagement 193n
political paradox 62
politics 83
  and truth 52
  see also democracy
populism 204
Portugal 167
post-Marxism 57, 60–61
postanarchism 207
postcolonialism 3, 128, 143, 149–60, 166,
  170–71, 208
postcontinental philosophy 143
Post-Kantianism, reversal of 213, 220-22
postmodernism 5, 140, 167–8, 170–71, 182,
  209, 222
postoccidentalism 149–52, 169
postorientalism 149–60
poststructuralism x, 32, 42, 131, 139, 209,
  221–2
power 129, 150, 154–5n, 156–8, 207
  coloniality of 152
  and gender 14
  -knowledge 163–4
pragmatism 104–5
Prague Spring 1
praxis 123
Preuss, Ulrich 145
Prigogine, Ilya 8, 114–18
  *Order Our of Chaos, Man's New Dialogue
    with Nature* 114-8
progress 162
Proudhon, Pierre Joseph 207
psychoanalysis 37, 43, 78, 131, 175
psychologism 108

Quijano, Anibal 151–2, 153, 170
Quine, W. V. O. 7, 89–96, 98, 104

"Two Dogmas of Empiricism" 89

race 128, 144–5
racism 129, 133, 142, 165–6, 202
Rama, Angel 153
Rancière, Jacques 5–6, 10, 31, 38–44, 39n,
  193
  on the aesthetic 217
  Badiou on 39–40, 44–5
  criticisms of 46–8
  Disagreement 50
  Hatred of Democracy 51
  "The Janus-Face of Politicized Art" 47n
  on materiality 217
  and Nancy 217–18
  on politics and democracy 50–57, 218
  on the sensible 217–18
  On the Shores of Politics 51
  "Who is the Subject of the Rights of Man?"
    56
reading, politics of 160–61
real, the 209–22
reason 128, 150
  and history 149
reference 104
regularism 105
relativism, moral 140
Renaissance 1, 152
representation 42, 72
responsibility 177
Retamar, Roberto Fernández 153
revolutionary politics 176
rights 56, 63–5, 135, 187–8
Riley, Denise 14
  Am I That Name? 14
riots 202
Robinet, André 41–2
Rockhill, Gabriel 5
Rorty, Richard 79, 167, 183
Rousseau, Jean-Jacques 80
Rubin, Gayle 14, 19
  "Thinking Sex" 15
  "The Traffic in Women" 14, 19
Ruby, Christian 31
Russell, Bertrand 107

Said, Edward 8–9, 150, 153–60, 162–4,
  166–71
  Bhabha's critique of 163–4